The Streatham Sketchbook

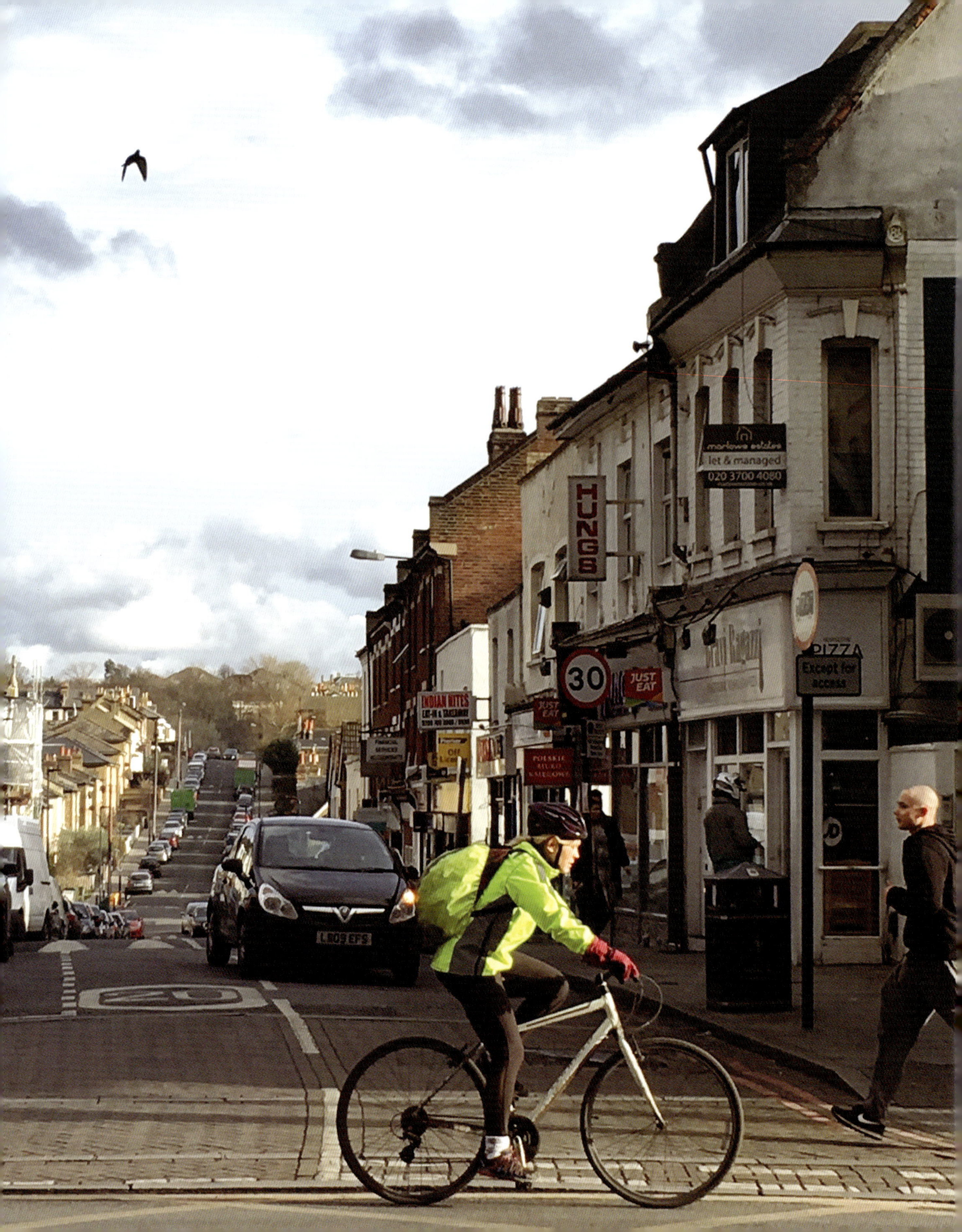
let & managed
020 3700 4080
HUNGS
30
JUST EAT
JUST EAT
PIZZA
Except for access

Jiro Osuga and
Mireille Galinou

The Streatham Sketchbook

Photography by Torla Evans

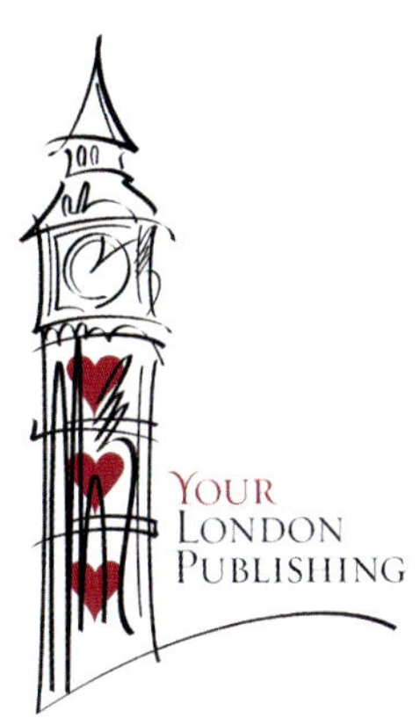

First published 2017

Published by Your London Publishing in 2017

ISBN 978-0-9933610-1-2

Sub-editor: Valerie Cumming
Designer: Mick Keates
Printed and bound in Italy by L.E.G.O.S.p.A.

This book is dedicated to the memory of Christiane Galinou without whose final generosity the work could not have been published.
Mireille Galinou

For my parents. Jiro Osuga

Front cover:
Jiro Osuga, painter and co-author of this book, was photographed at work in his Streatham studio in December 2016 (also see p. 47). Looking out of the window, we substituted the actual view with a more recognisable landscape which includes the two church steeples at the junction of Tooting Bec Gardens with the High Road (see p. 59 for the full photograph).

Back cover:
Jiro Osuga, 'Under a Tree', 2003, oil on canvas, 97 x 33 cm. Flowers Gallery.

Frontispiece:
This photograph of Sunnyhill Road gives a glimpse of the topographical profile of Streatham. The village started close to where this photograph was taken; it grew along the valley of the High Road and up the slope leading to Crown Point (see p. 126 for the reverse viewpoint).

CONTENTS

PREFACE – TWO VOICES

There are those individuals who connect to their environment like fish to water. The association of the Thrale family and their interesting guests with Streatham is one such powerful connection. They may have thrived in this part of London for a mere twenty years, but their former roots are still visible: Thrale Road, Dr Johnson Avenue, the Thrale Almshouses and family tombs and monuments at St Leonard's church.

Which begs the question: should we all stick to the well-trodden path of history, venerate the old gods at their usual altars or should we seek to interact with new, unknown histories?

This book tries to do both: it will give you a taste of traditional Streatham histories but also chase new ones – little known suffragettes, exciting Japanese adventures or a wonderful, forgotten female painter who flourished in the first half of the twentieth century.

The Streatham Sketchbook has two voices. The volume seeks to evoke Streatham's history but also focus on its creativity in past and present times; so a dialogue has been set up between a London historian and an artist. Mireille Galinou and Jiro Osuga became friends when Mireille, a former Curator of Paintings, Prints and Drawings at the Museum of London purchased one of Jiro's London paintings for the Museum's collection. This was in 1998.

The Streatham Sketchbook is the first volume in a new series concentrating on the theme of 'The Artist in the City'. The city is London and the artists are long-term residents of the capital. One of the most significant trends of the late-twentieth century has been the opening of artists' studios to the public in London's residential neighbourhoods. It was pioneered by SPACE Studios back in 1975, and it emphasised the fact that artists are linked to specific parts of London such as Gilbert & George with Spitalfields, Frank Auerbach with north west London, David Hepher with Camberwell and Timothy Hyman with his beloved Islington.

But this trend has not received the attention it deserves; Art with a capital A continues to dominate, seemingly divorced from the places with which it is associated. As a result, the interaction between artists and their neighbourhoods remains little explored. *The Streatham Sketchbook* seeks to redress this state of affairs. We want to highlight both the sense of place we should all experience and the attractive asset a creative suburb represents.

Double take: Jiro Osuga was photographed sipping a drink on the terrace of Café Barcelona next to his painting. Without being prompted, he naturally adopted the same hand and arm gesture depicted in his self-portrait. This work was part of the 'The Man of The Crowd' series of works scattered around the shops of the High Road for Art23 in the 2016 Streatham Festival (see pp. 168 and 192).

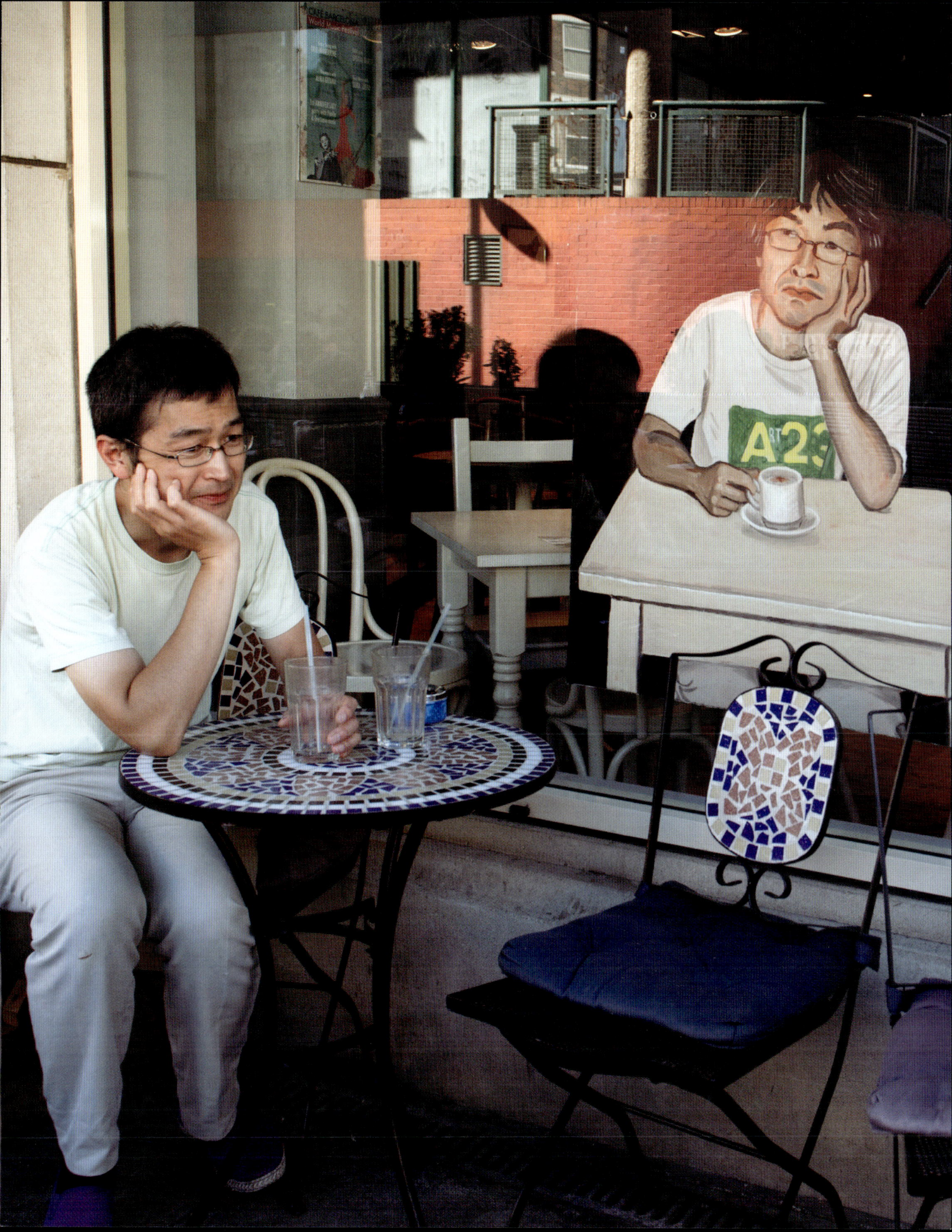
ART 23

This navigational map for Streatham and immediate surroundings has been prepared by Mireille Galinou and drawn by the illustrator Stephen Conlin. © Stephen Conlin.

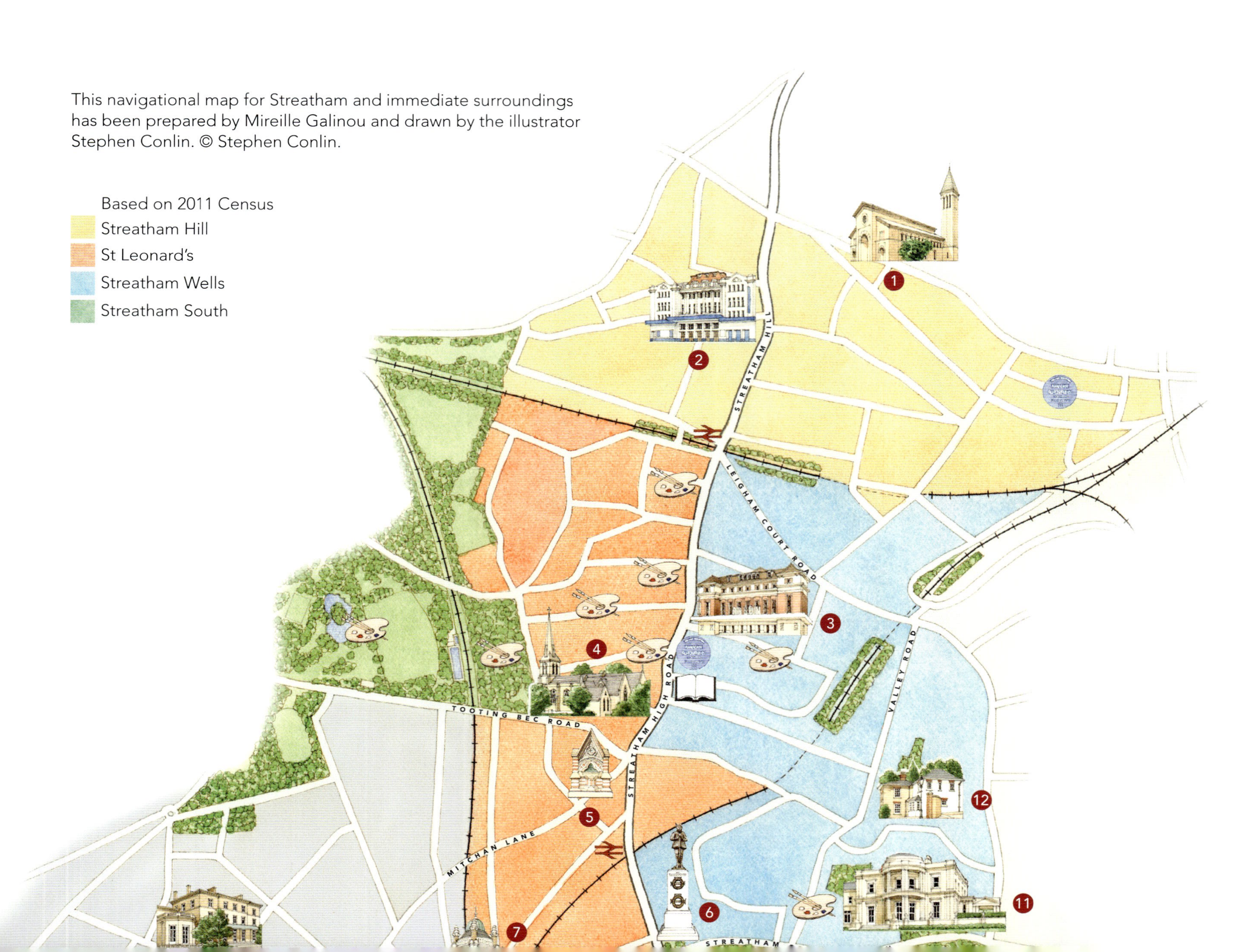

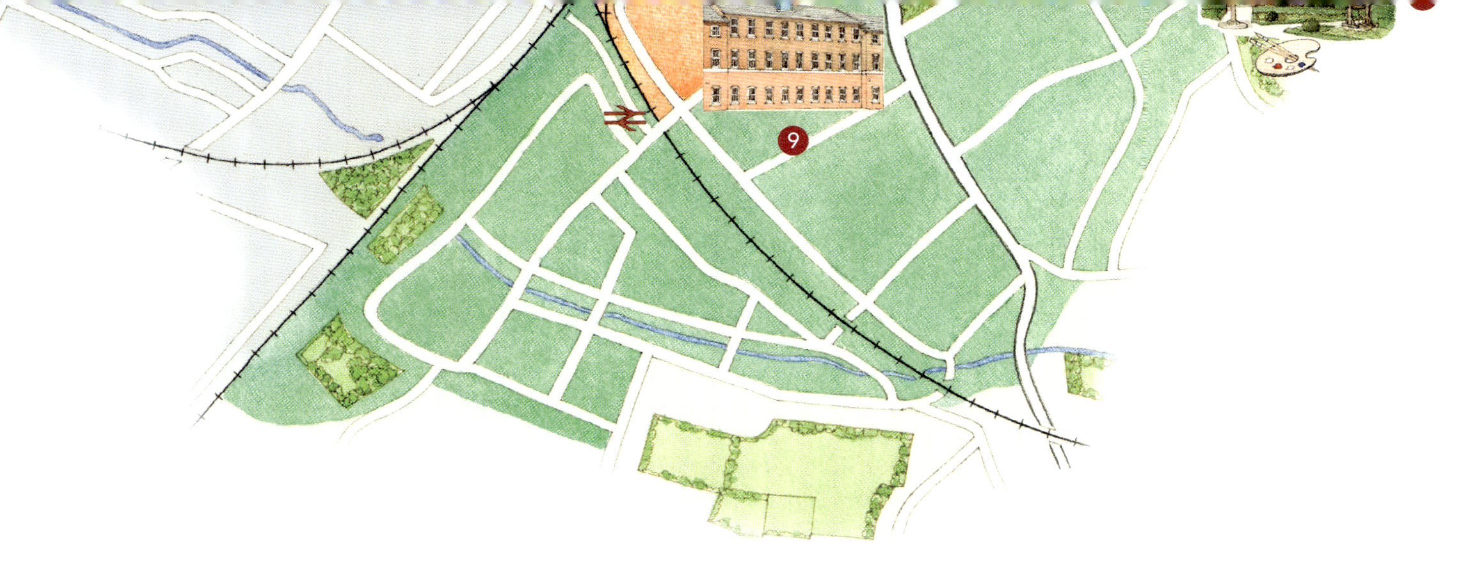

1 Christ Church
2 Streatham Hill Theatre
3 Odeon Cinema – formerly the Astoria
4 St Leonard's church
5 Dyce Fountain
6 First World War Memorial by Albert Toft
7 Water Pumping Station, Conyers Road
8 Furzedown House, now part of Graveney School
9 Former Silk Mill (now Sainsbury's)
10 The Rookery Gardens on Streatham Common
11 Park Hill House
12 The Well House, off Valley Road

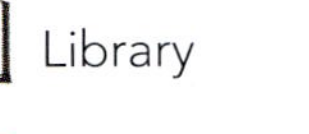 Library

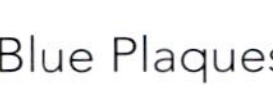 Stations

 Blue Plaques

Sites connected to the Streatham paintings by Jiro Osuga reproduced in this book.

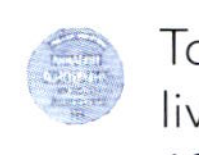 Top right: Arthur Mee (1875–1943) lived at 27 Lanercost Road between 1899 and 1902. Journalist, author, topographer and editor of the *Evening News* aged 20.

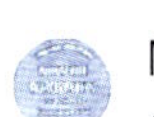 Middle: Sir Arnold Bax (1883–1953), composer and poet, was born at 13 Pendennis Road, moved next door a year later and lived at other Streatham addresses until 1896. Best known for 'Tintagel' (1917–19) and his music for David Lean's 'Oliver Twist' (1948).

1.
TO STAND AND STARE

Jiro Osuga

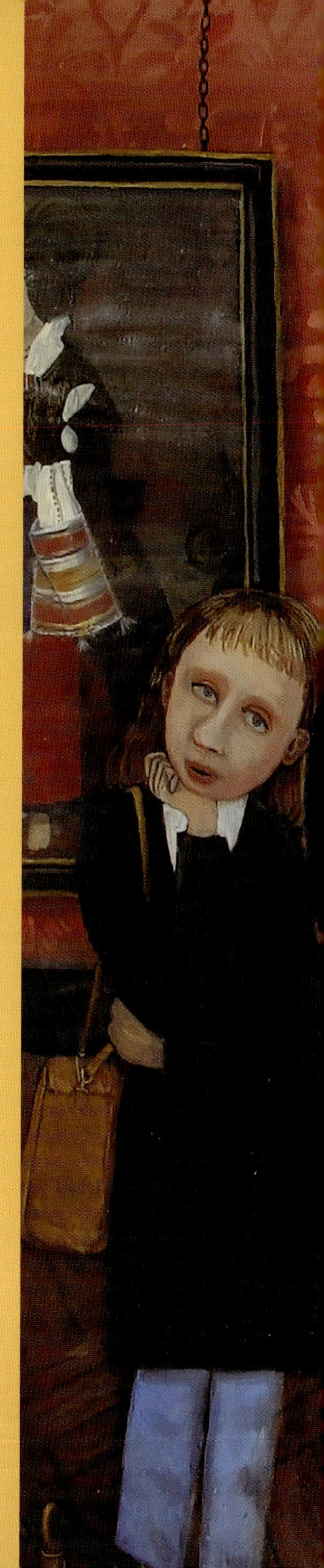

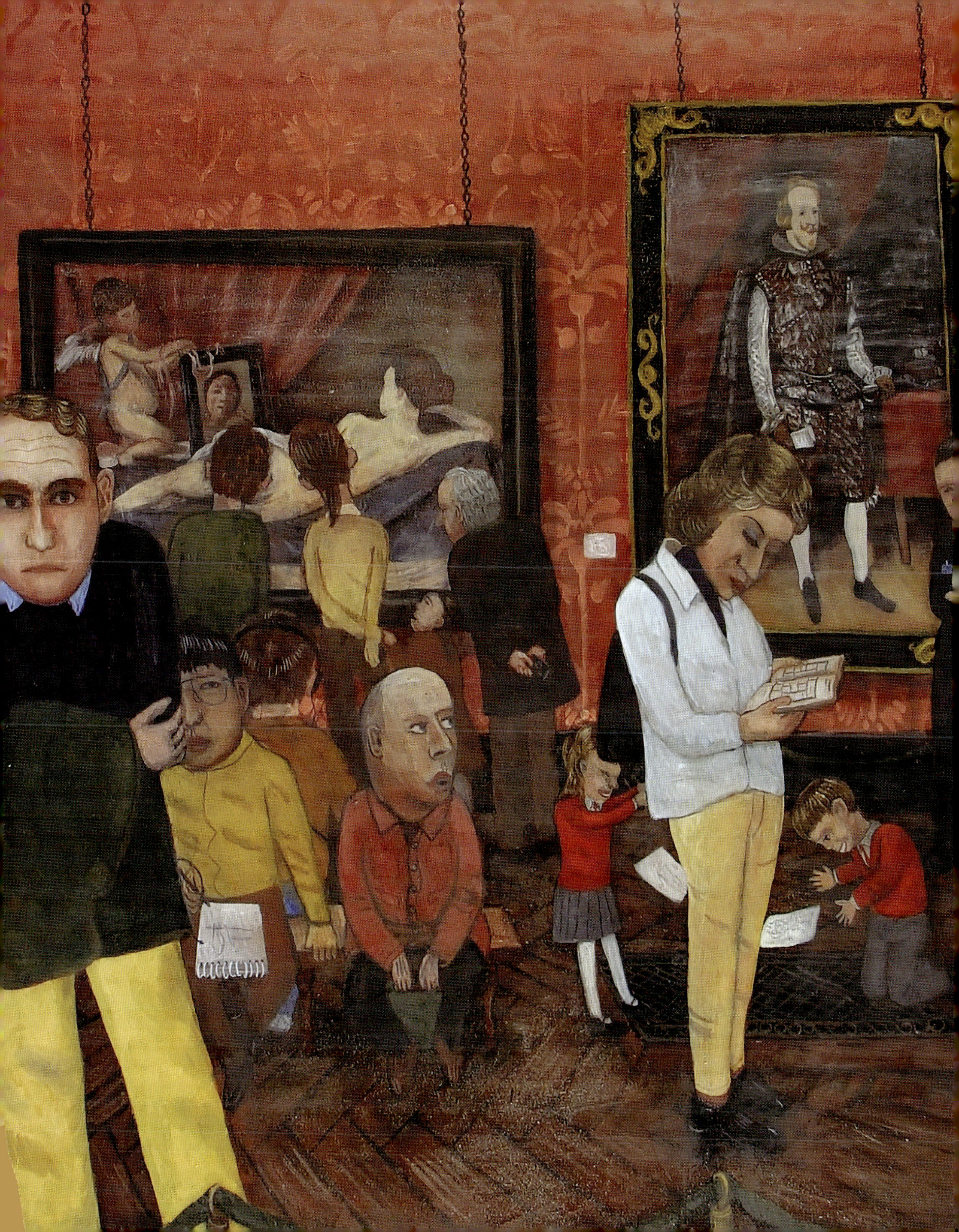

What is this life if, full of care,
We have no time to stand and stare?—

W H Davies 'Leisure' from *Songs of Joy and Others*, 1911

I like to think that what unites all my paintings – Streatham paintings as well as others not included in this book – is the enjoyment I derive from observing the world around me. Observation is the cornerstone of my work. Close scrutiny of my surroundings leads me to one discovery, and then another, setting me off on an endless trail that very occasionally lets me glimpse something much larger than myself.

It is unfortunate that in our time-poor, information-saturated age, close observation is not in common practice. When I am out in the streets or a park looking at things, standing still and staring at an object of interest, people often give me a wide berth. Some would cross over to the other side of the street to avoid the weirdo with the fixed stare, though some kindlier people might ask me if I am looking for something. Occasionally, in the park, I do see people standing stock-still, eyes fixed on a particular spot. Great, a kindred spirit, I think for a moment, until I hear the person cry out 'Come here Charlie!', and realise that they are dog-walkers waiting for their pets to emerge from a bush where they had dived chasing after a squirrel. Sadly, the only places where people do stand and stare for long periods of time unprompted are at the sites of fires or traffic accidents. Here people do gather in their multitudes and gawp at the gruesome spectacle, even though they should know better than to take delight in the misfortune of others. Even at art galleries, where people are positively encouraged to stand and stare, the attention span of an average gallery-goer in front of a painting appears to be only a few seconds.

I invite people to stare at Streatham. I invite people to stand and stare, not at fires and road accidents, but at the maddeningly rich and complex 'ordinary' reality around them. Even the smallest, most mundane detail in a south London street corner, on close inspection can reveal wonders and send you off on an endless imaginary journey. To see the extraordinary in the ordinary is to be on a road to transcendence. As another poet, William Blake wrote in his poem *Auguries of Innocence* (1803):

To see a World in a Grain of Sand,
And a Heaven in a Wild Flower,
Hold Infinity in the palm of your hand,
And Eternity in an hour.

And Blake is known to have roamed what was then countryside around Streatham in his youth!

Previous pages:
'National Gallery', 2001, acrylic and oil on canvas, 189 x 162.5 cm. Set in the Spanish room of the National Gallery in London, this painting explores the implications of the act of looking. *Private collection. Photo: Flowers Gallery.*

'Shadow', 2013, oil on canvas, 165 x 110 cm. The setting of this painting is the embankment of the viaduct that carries Bedford Hill over the railway line to Streatham Common station. In early summer it is overrun by cow parsley. When I set off on my daily walks or cycle-rides first thing in the morning, the sun is low in the sky and casts long shadows. Shadows lack substance, fated to disappear should a wisp of a cloud obscure the sun. But then so do flowers, once summer is over, and so will I.

It is fitting that one of the few survivors from Streatham's medieval past are its Commons, humble patches of open space for the peasantry, when all the man-made edifices, from the original medieval church to the gorgeous villas of the gentry and opulent picture palaces have long disappeared. *Flowers Gallery.*

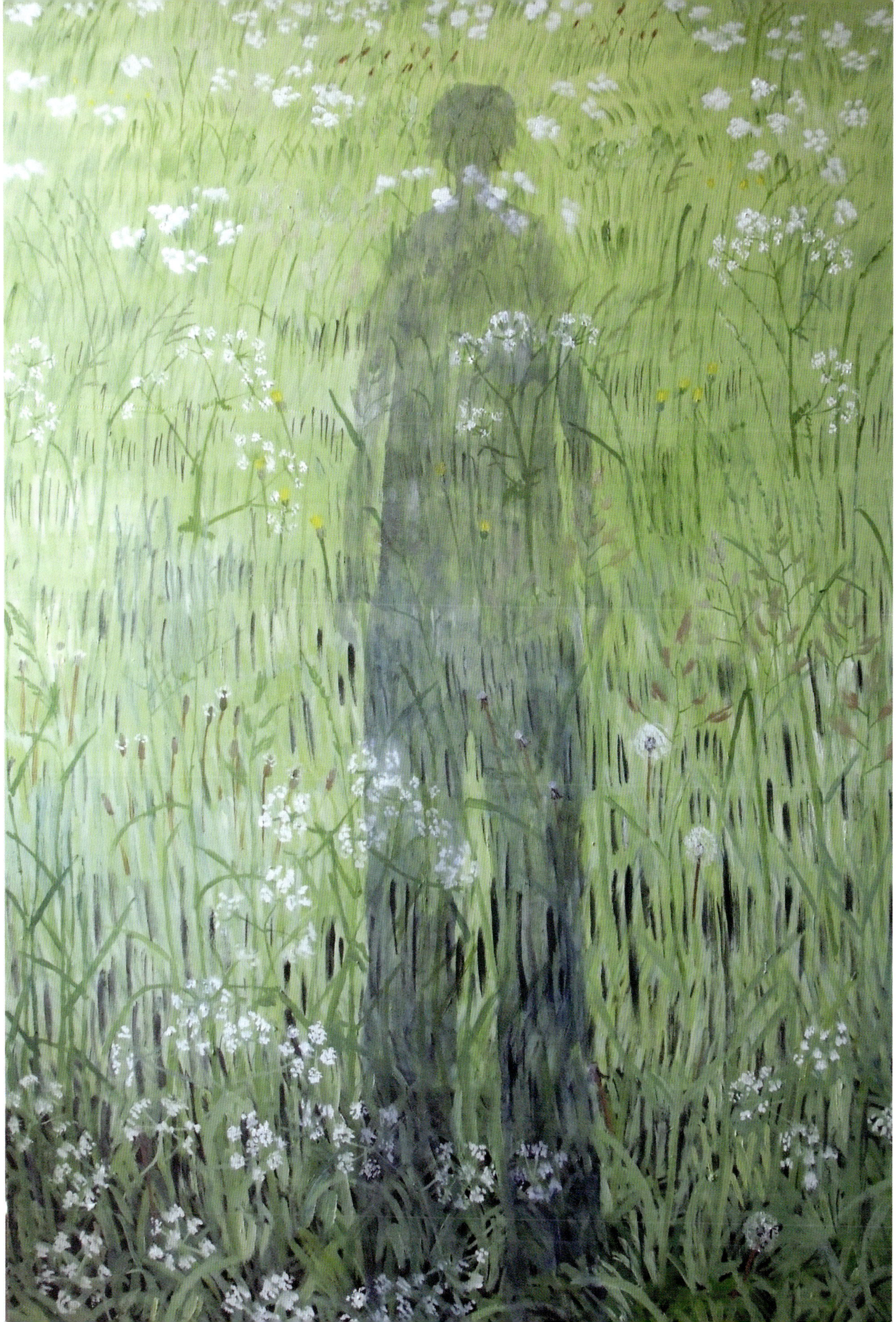

2.

LIFE IN STREATHAM – An Artist's Perspective

Jiro Osuga

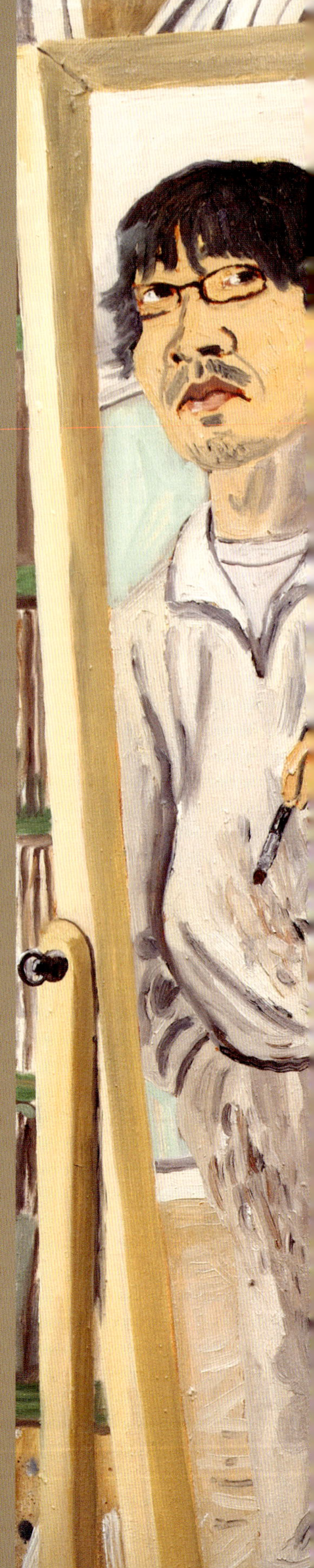

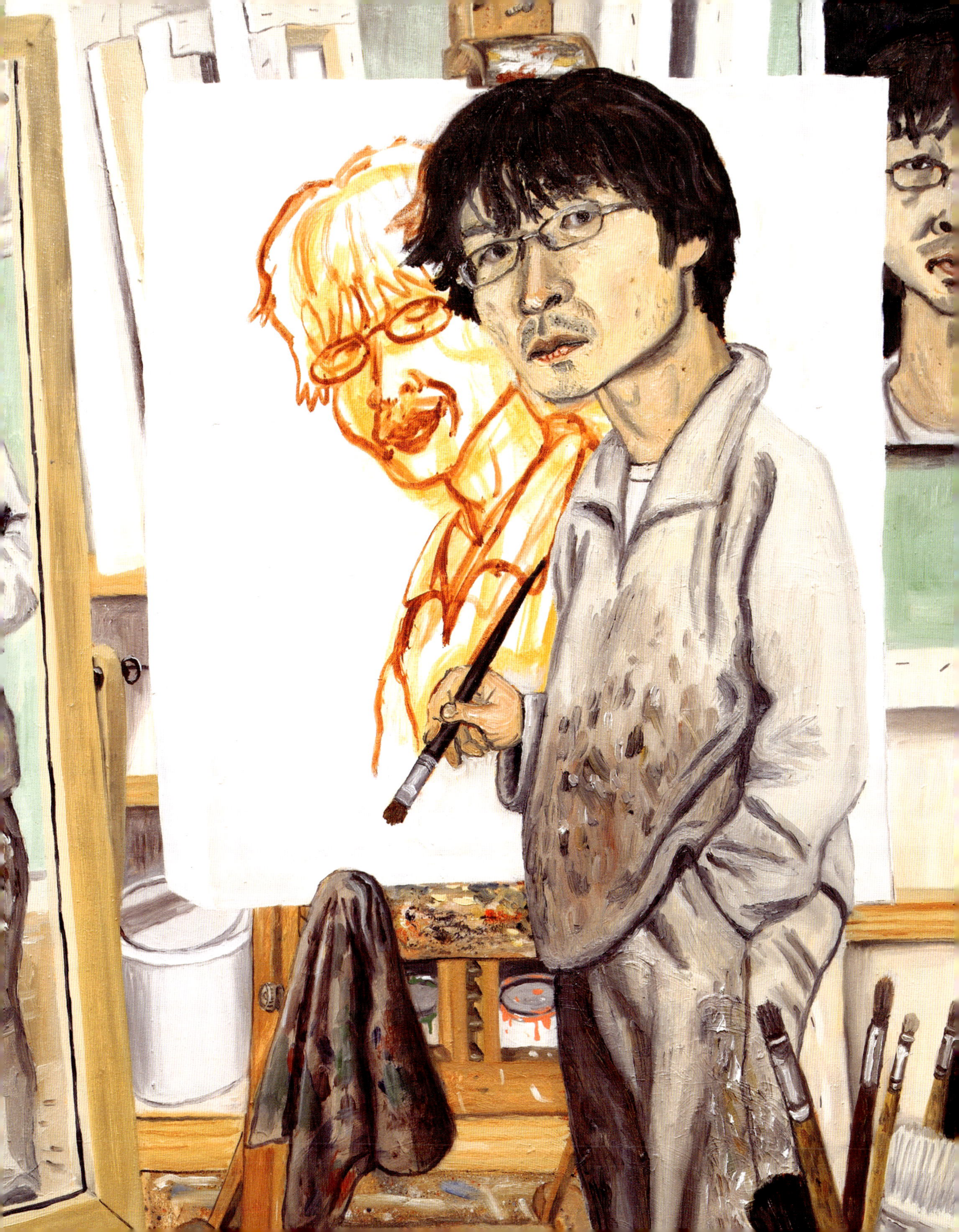

Musings on history

Streatham is an extraordinarily aptly named town. Once you understand that 'strete' means street, and 'ham' dwelling, etymologically related to home or homestead rather than to salted pork, nothing could be more appropriate, as Streatham started life as a Saxon village on a Roman road – today's High Road, connecting London and the south coast. What's more, the name is still spot-on a thousand years after it is first documented, as the High Road still dominates the suburb. This is quite unlike say Peckham (peak-ham, hill dwellings), where if you stand in the middle of Rye Lane, buildings obscure the hills after which the original settlement was named, or Croydon (crocus hill) where there is no trace of crocus fields today.

The linearity of Streatham strung along the High Road always calls to my mind history. Along this road, Roman soldiers with plumed helmets must have passed, as did ruff-wearing Elizabethans and Victorian omnibuses. The thought has inspired me to make a number of paintings musing on the linear progression of history, such as 'Memory Lane', illustrated here. In this painting, you go back in time the further you look down the street. There is a modern figure in the foreground – me. In the middle-ground a horse-drawn omnibus rattles by in front of nineteenth-century shops. Further back, there is a medieval dwelling, a Roman temple with a passing chariot, an iron-age hut, and in the far distance, what looks like Neolithic megaliths.

Once I almost witnessed the fantasy depicted in this painting in real life. On a freezing cold day a few years ago, I happened to be on the High Road when the annual London to Brighton vintage car race was passing through town. Hundreds of open-topped vintage vehicles of all types, with passengers inadequately wrapped against the chill winds in Edwardian motoring outfits streamed down the street. There was even a penny-farthing rider, dressed from head to toe in tweeds. For a split second, when the cars passed in front of façades on the High Road dating from around the same period as the cars, I experienced a queer sensation of going back in time, of time collapsing in on itself – an intimation that what we perceive as linear time and history is in fact illusory.

My own history in Streatham goes back to 1987 when I lived in the ILEA Uplands Halls of Residence on Leigham Court Road during my first year at Chelsea School of Art (ILEA: the Inner London Education Authority). I do not have very fond memories of this time. I was a morose youth who always ate alone in my room, too shy to mix with fellow students in the common rooms. I remember trudging down Wellfield Walk to Safeways on the High Road on Saturdays to stock up on groceries for the week, stepping over a host of snails crawling out of the grassy verges. Later on in the day I might go on a melancholic walk to nearby open spaces of Streatham Common and Norwood Grove, sketchbook and pencils in my pocket. The unlovely 1960s halls have since been demolished. A care home and a housing development rendered in a mock vernacular style now stand on the site.

Previous pages:
'Portrait Painting' (detail), 2013, oil on canvas, 104 x 90 cm.
In this scene set in my Streatham studio, the four recurring self-portraits each appear to have a life of their own. The title indulges in wordplay – the word 'Painting' could be a verb or a noun.
Flowers Gallery.

Right: 'Memory Lane', 2014, oil on canvas, 43 x 50 cm.
In this painting, inspired by the twists and turns of the High Road in Streatham, you go back in time the further you look down the street.
Flowers Gallery.

Return to Streatham

I returned to live in Streatham sixteen years later in 2003, this time to Woodbourne Avenue, between the High Road and Tooting Common. By then I was a fledgling artist in my early thirties with several solo exhibitions under my belt. In the intervening years I had moved

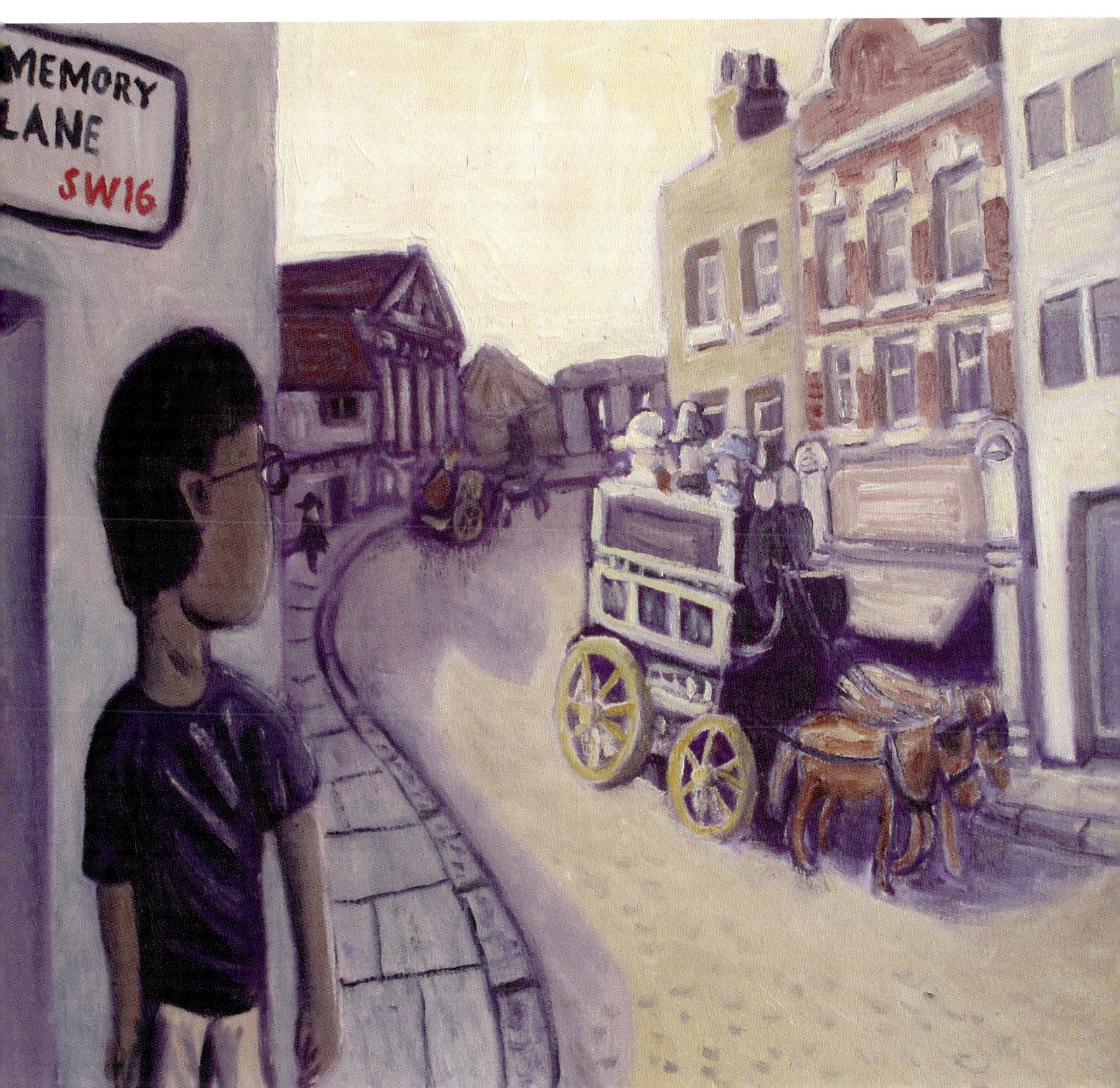
MEMORY
LANE
SW16

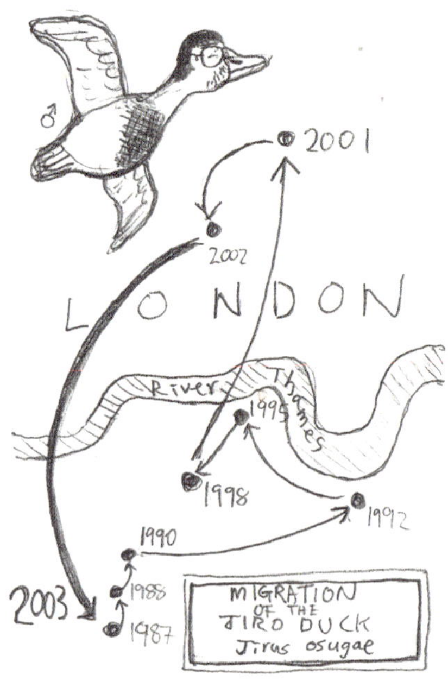

around different parts of London, following a roughly anti-clockwise trajectory: Balham, Clapham, Blackheath, Rotherhithe, Camberwell, Tottenham and Highbury, until I found myself back in Streatham where I had started off. My return to Streatham after a sixteen-year circumnavigation of London impressed me enough to commemorate the occasion with an 'I have Moved' card I photocopied for all my friends, jokingly entitled: 'Migration of the Jiro Duck *Jirus osugae*'.

Little did I imagine then that the Jiro duck would stay put in SW16 for almost fifteen years. I have now lived in Streatham longer than in any other place in my entire life, and made hundreds of paintings in my Streatham studio. Has the neighbourhood had any significant bearing on my work as an artist?

My instinctive response to that question would be a vehement 'No'. As an artist, I hate to be hidebound by agenda of any kind – geographical, political, or stylistic. I do not consider myself a topographical artist – I never set up my easel in the streets of Streatham. Neither am I a social realist dedicated to documenting the everyday life of the local community. I can't even say that I am particularly fond of Streatham – I am just comfortable here, and grateful that it has not yet succumbed to gentrification, remaining an unpretentious town for normal people.

But observation of my surroundings is important to me, and my work is always based on the lived experience of my own life, the last fifteen years of which has been lived in Streatham. As a result, the neighbourhood does crop up in my paintings with noticeable frequency. As you will see in chapter 3, the High Road, different parts of Tooting Common, the Rookery gardens and other places in the area all feature in my paintings. Sometimes the local references are direct, as in the painting 'Holding Streatham Library', or the number 159 bus that appears in 'Bus'. At other times, Streatham is used as the setting for the action, rather like the way painters of the Northern Renaissance might use a contemporary Flemish town to stand in for Jerusalem in Biblical scenes. Clearly, without any conscious intention on my part, Streatham had become part of my DNA as an artist.

Do my Streatham paintings merely reflect the fact that I have lived in Streatham for a long time? Or do they shed interesting new light on the neighbourhood? That is for the reader to decide in the pages to follow.

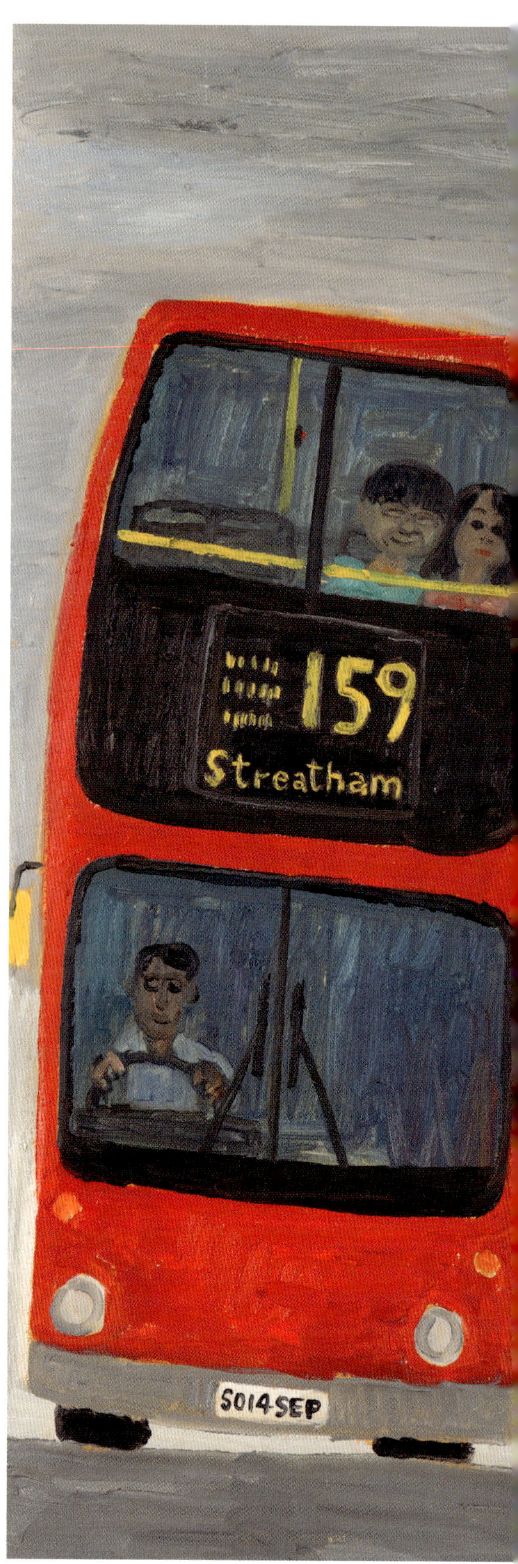

Far left: 'Migration of the Jiro Duck *Jirus osugae*', 2003, photocopy, 15 x 10.5 cm. *Collection of the artist.*

Left: 'Bus' 2014, oil on canvas, 80 x 31cm. Route 159 runs between Streatham Station and Marble Arch. *© Jiro Osuga, collection of the artist. Photo: Flowers Gallery.*

Right: 'Holding Streatham Library', 2016, oil on canvas, 100 x 50 cm. I am seen here holding Streatham's Tate Library in my arms in the manner of medieval religious painting. Exactly what this signifies is unclear, even to me. The gables just visible at the bottom of the painting belong to shops that line Streatham High Road. *© Jiro Osuga, collection of the artist. Photo: Flowers Gallery.*

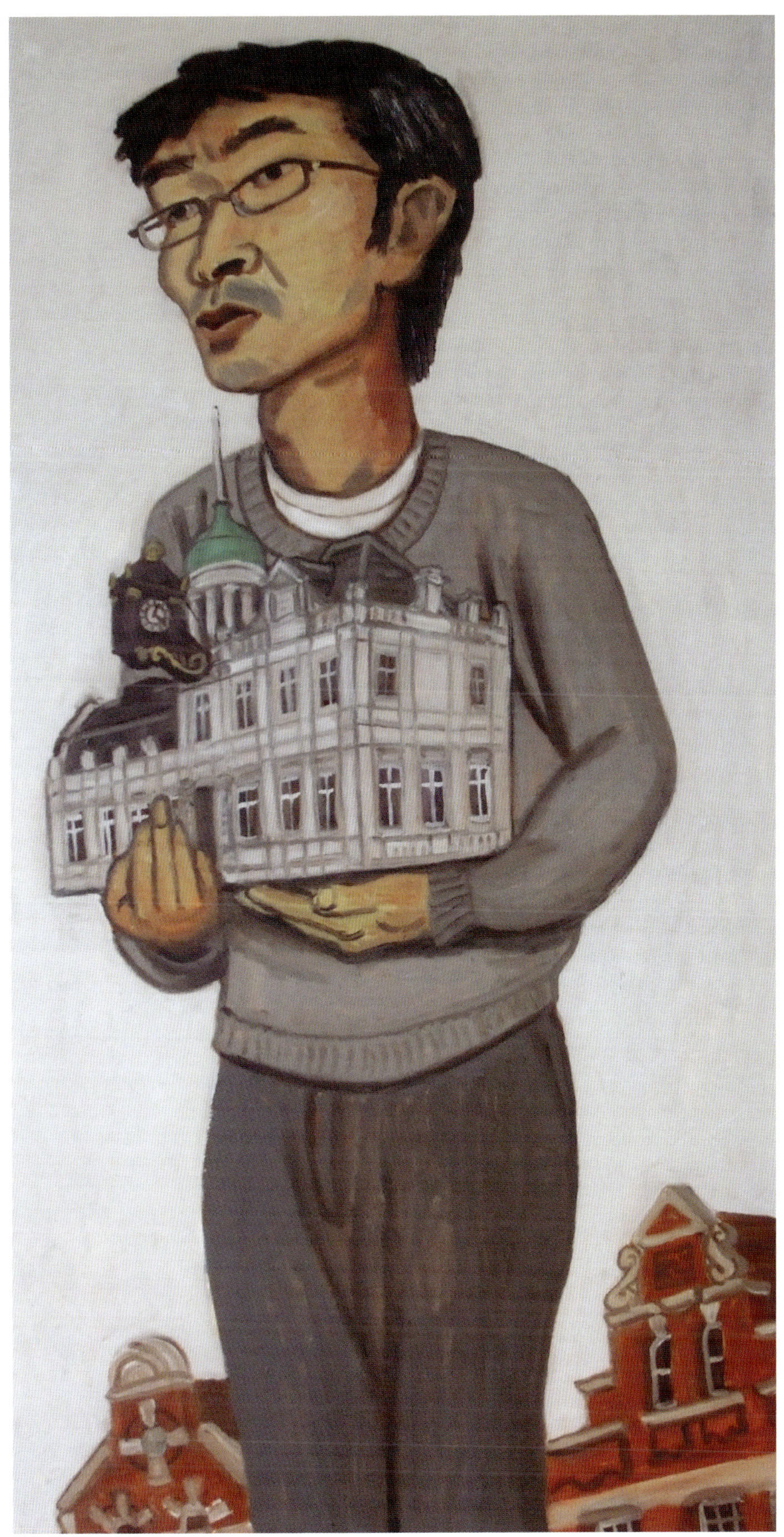

3.

A TOUR OF STREATHAM IN TEN LANDMARKS

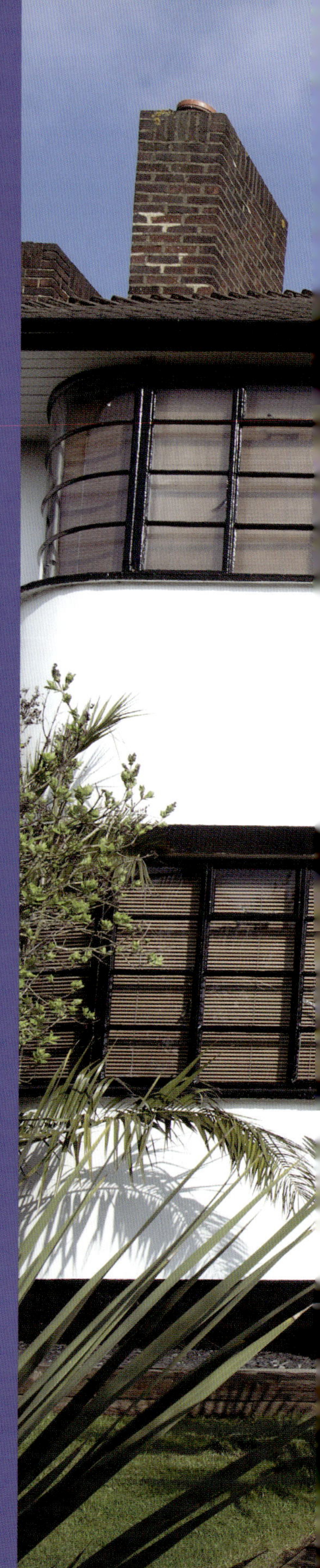

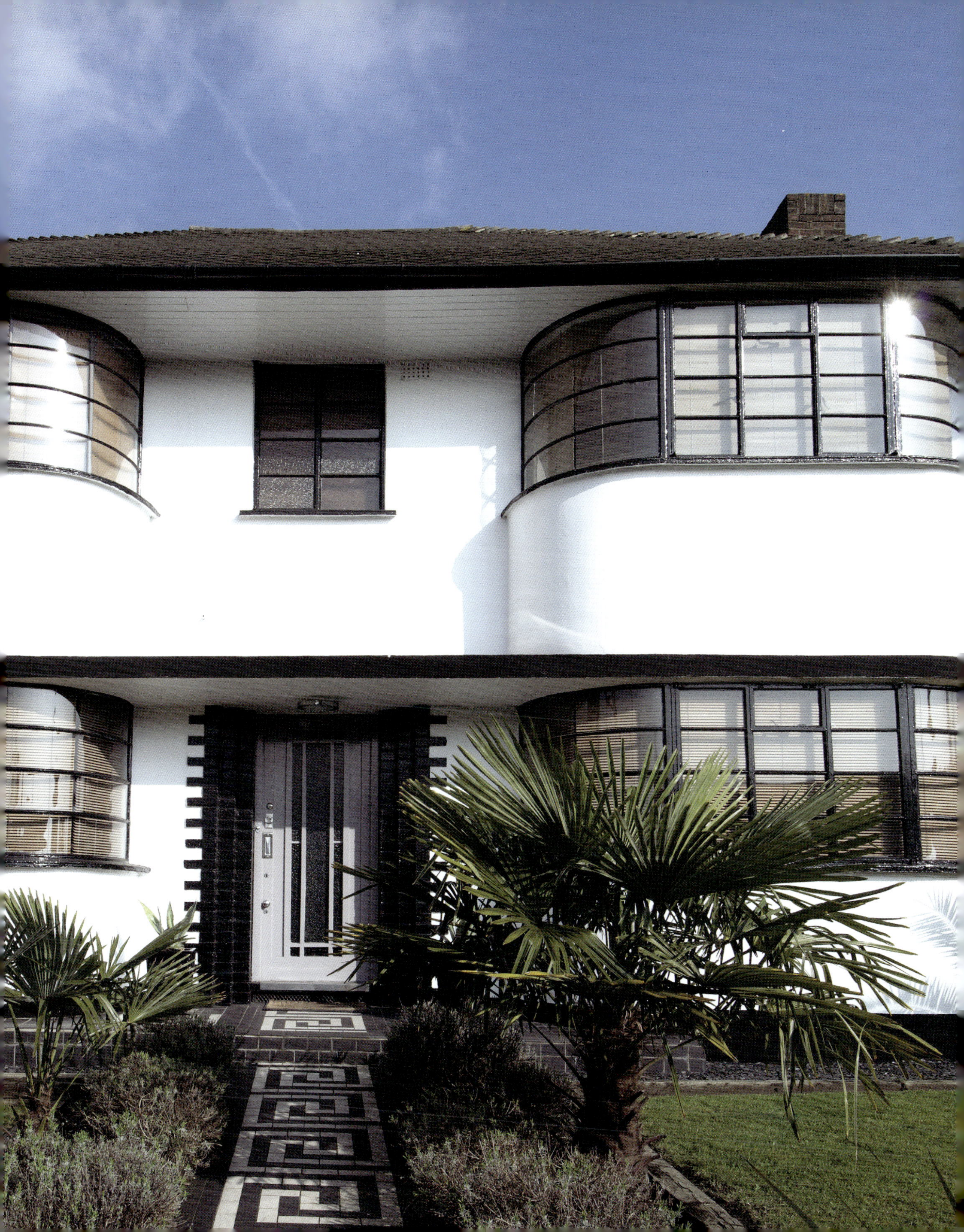

How this chapter works …

This chapter has been structured to echo each of the themes selected by artist Jiro Osuga in his 'Tour of Streatham in Ten Paintings' (p. 78). What follows is a brief historical survey which offers an informative overview of Streatham in the past. Those same themes are also partially examined in recent times in this chapter, and from the point of view of the artist in the next chapter.

Streatham residents are fortunate that John W Brown lives in their midst; he is a local historian who has been a pillar of the Streatham Society for over thirty-five years. John Brown has a real flair for communication (he gives excellent talks and guided tours) and he is an indefatigable archivist; he has accumulated the most extraordinary collection of printed ephemera relating to Streatham that I have found and it is making his house burst at the seams, so he has annexed the garden as well. This book has drawn important information from this collection and other related publications by John W Brown.

Boundaries

Although, in the words of local historian Graham Gower, the origins of Streatham are 'uncertain and clouded by the mist of time', Streatham was first a recognisable neighbourhood in the Middle Ages, when it became a parish, the village church of St Leonard being first mentioned in 1291 (an earlier chapel was recorded in the 1086 Domesday Survey without revealing its site). The parish of Streatham was large, bringing together the villages of Streatham, South Streatham, Tooting Bec and Balham. The map we present at the opening of this book shows the length of the former parish, running from Brixton Hill to Hermitage Bridge over the Graveney river, by Lahore Kebab House. The inclusion of Furzedown shows how far west the parish used to stretch into Tooting, but we have not included Balham. The two former Roman roads which now make up the A22 (through Balham) and the A23 (through Streatham) were originally both in the parish of Streatham, giving added vitality to an area which was already well connected.

Previous pages: This attractive Art Deco house in Leigham Court Road was built by Wates in 1937. This popular building firm, founded by Edward Wates in 1897 was active in Streatham through their Norbury branch.

Right: This garden shed room forms part of the comprehensive archive of local historian John W Brown. It is open to researchers by appointment.

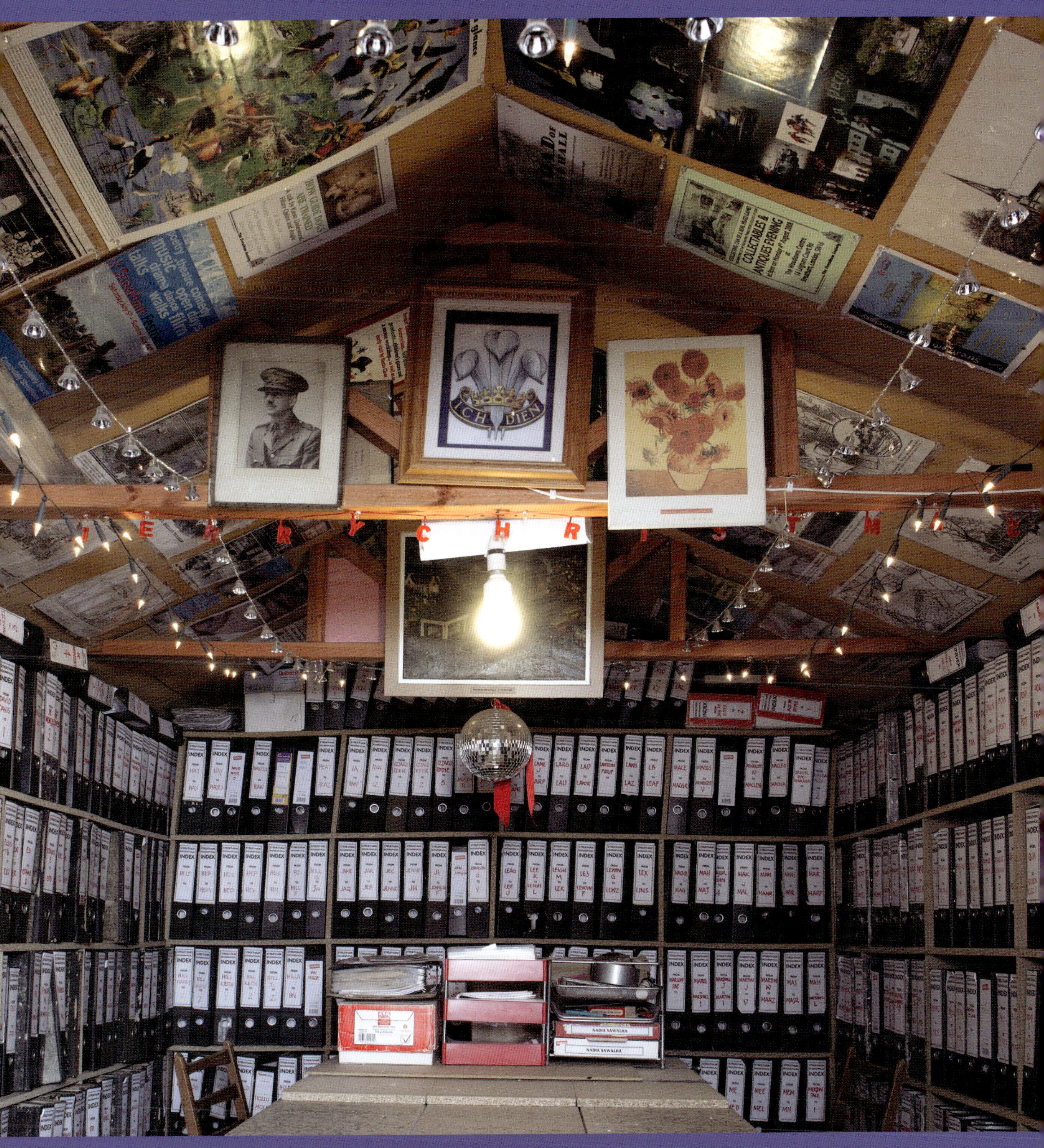
ICH DIEN
COLLECTABLES & ANTIQUES EVENING
music drama dance film
talks walks

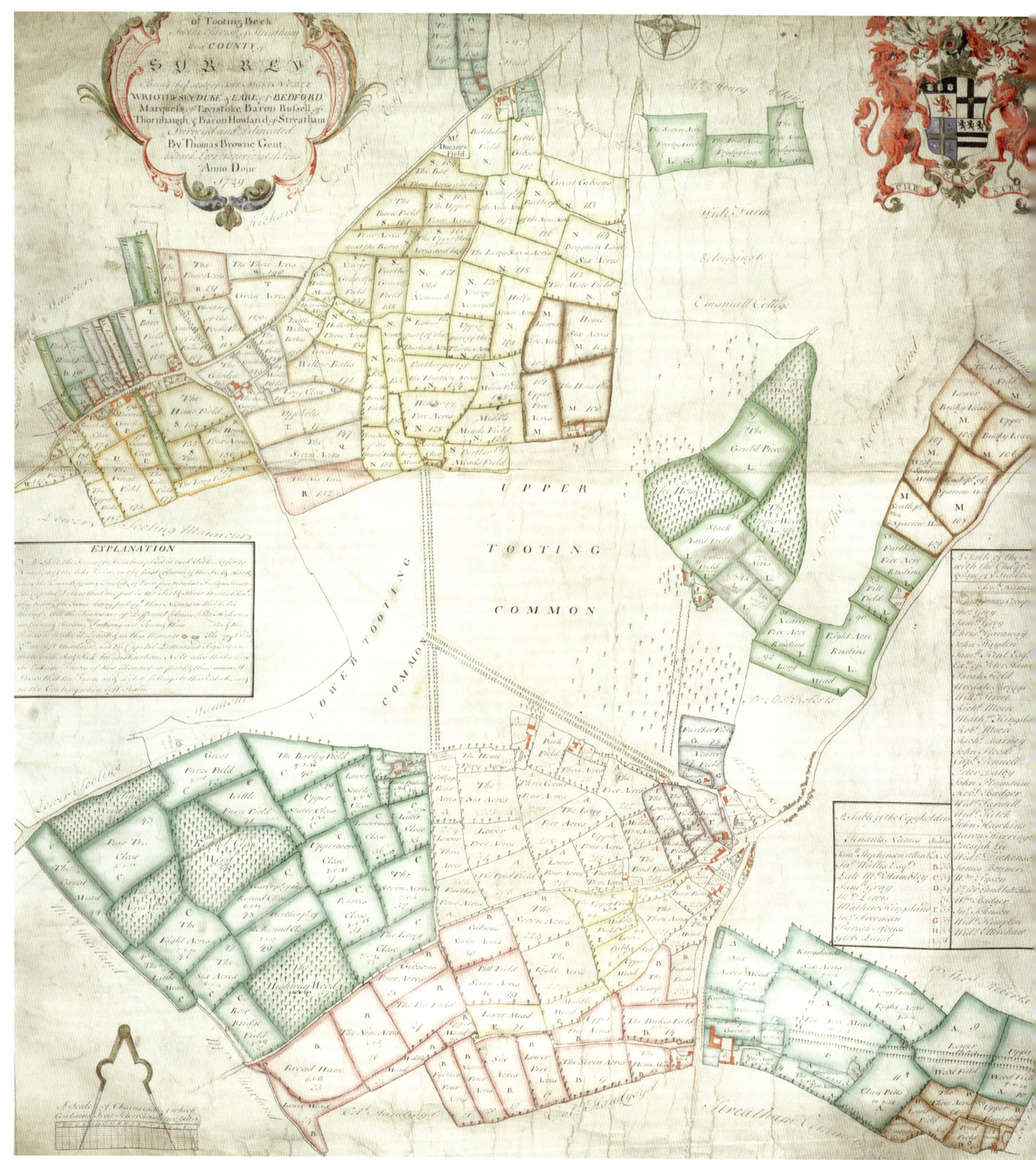
of Tooting Beck
COUNTY
SURREY
WRIOTHESLY DUKE & EARL of BEDFORD
Marquess of Tavistoke Baron Russell of
Thornhaugh & Baron Howland of Streatham
By Thomas Browne Gent.
Anno Dom:
1749
UPPER
TOOTING
COMMON

These two very early estate maps, on parchment, cover most of the area which we now regard as Streatham.

Left: The Bedford Estate, surveyed by Thomas Browne, encompasses the old village, Tooting Common, sections of the High Road and the Bedford House estate east of the main road, 1729. *Woburn Abbey Collection © His Grace, The Duke of Bedford and the Trustees of The Bedford Estates. Photo: London Metropolitan Archives, City of London.*

Right: This 1780 map of Streatham, surveyed by John Willock, shows the land which was in the hands of John Crosse Cooke, Henry Bates and Thomas Ellison. This is the southern section of Streatham, west of Streatham Common and down to the Hermitage Bridge – including Streatham Vale. *Lambeth Archives Department.*

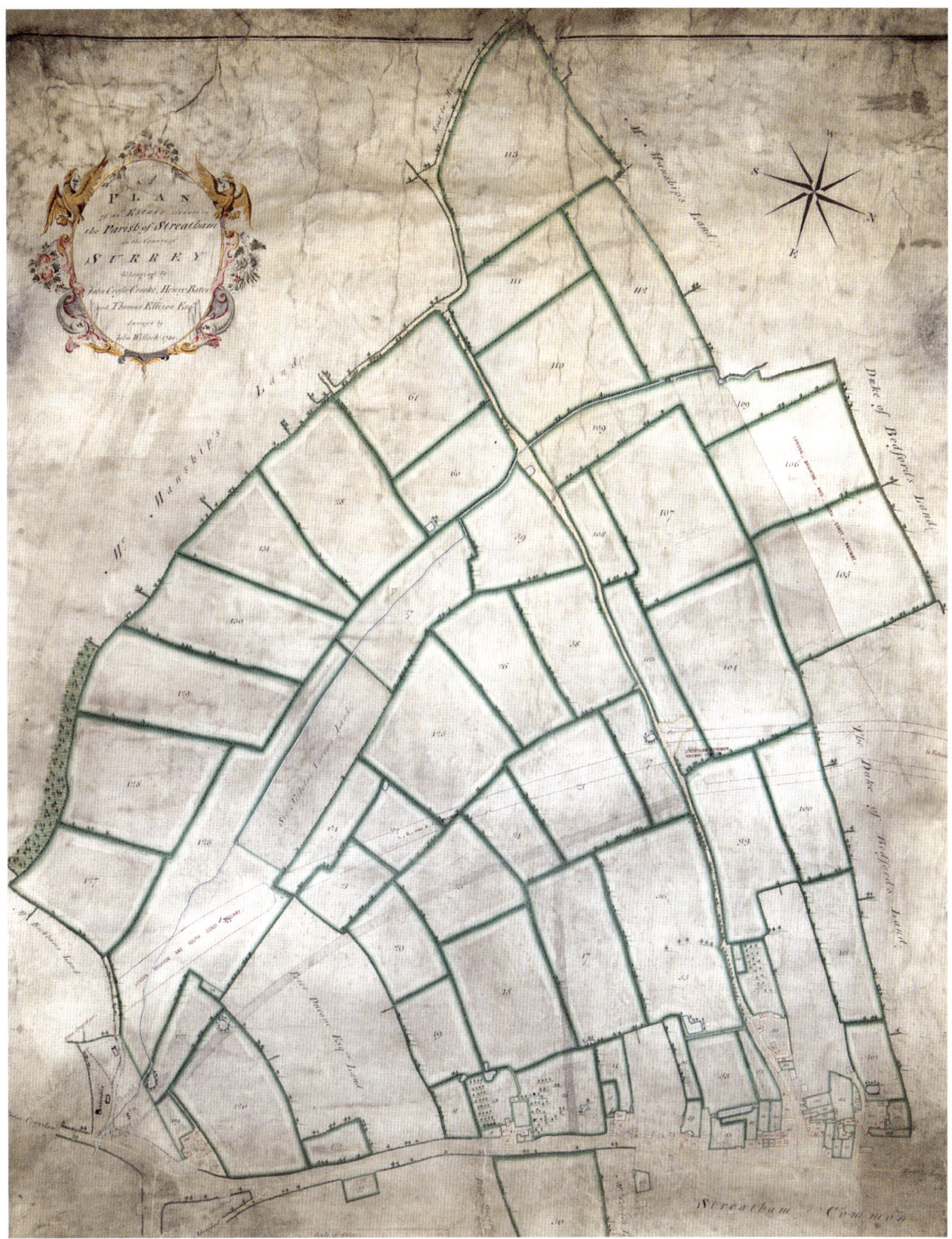

The other invisible boundaries relate to the three manors which came under church rule in the Middle Ages before falling into secular hands after the Reformation (1536): Tooting Bec, South Streatham and Leigham Court Manor. In the seventeenth century, the manors of Streatham and Leigham Court were purchased by the Howland family, merchants by trade, who owned the land in Rotherhithe where Howland Great Dock, London's largest dock, was built in 1696. Through the 1695 marriage of Elizabeth Howland to Wriothesley, second Duke of Bedford, the Howland estate passed onto the dukes of Bedford (see map on previous pages).

In more recent history, the constant expansion of London and the occasional re-organisation of its administrative divisions was confusing. Between 1900 and 1965 Streatham was part of the Borough of Wandsworth but since that date it has been in the Borough of Lambeth. This is bound to have affected the neighbourhood's sense of identity. The 1956 official guide to the Borough of Wandsworth described it as 'essentially an area of residential development … [which] has long been regarded as a 'dormitory' to the metropolis'. While the Lambeth guide for the same date describes the Borough as 'a slice of the London Cake – the only metropolitan borough extending from the centre to the county boundary'. In short: the traditional battle of city v country.

The area which is now unquestionably 'Streatham' is shown in colour on our introductory map (p. 8): four different colours for the four areas which have been used for the last Census (2011) – useful in connection with the final chapter, 'Streatham Connections' which attempts to describe the nature of multi-cultural Streatham by using some of the Census results.

Top right: The earliest pictorial representation of Streatham Village, a detail from the 1729 map of the Bedford Estate reproduced on the previous page: the church of St Leonard at this important crossroads predates the present building while the High Road has a string of early houses – none of them have survived.

Far right: This picture of a bleak and snowy winter's day on Streatham Common was drawn by Clough Bromley for an article on 'London Commons' published in *The Illustrated Magazine* in November 1885. The artist was a regular exhibitor at the Royal Academy between 1872 and 1891. He was a local since he appears to have resided mostly in South London and in Clapham from around 1878.

Bottom right: Kite Day, 2010, see overleaf © *Roy Reed.*

1. Open Spaces

(paired with 'In the Woods' on p. 80)

The 1729 map of Streatham reproduced on p. 24 records the presence of several avenue of trees across Tooting Common, a fashionable feature which marked the entrance to properties of some standing. Graham Gower draws our attention to one which has survived to this very day: 'this ancient feature containing some oaks of great age, runs almost parallel to Garrad's Road [the eastern edge of Tooting Common], beginning at Tooting Bec Road and reaching to Bedford Hill'. Perhaps Jiro was inspired by some of these very old trees when he painted 'In the Woods'?

More recently, we read in *The Illustrated Magazine* of October 1885:

> In the fortunate SW district every parish has its common – Clapham, Wandsworth, Putney, Barnes, Wimbledon, Mitcham, Tooting, Streatham.

The Illustrated Magazine published a two-part article on London's commons (1 October 1885 and 2 November 1885); the illustrations by Clough Bromley are well composed and provide an attractive record of once familiar landmarks (see opposite and p. 48). The text, by Robert Hunter, fails to point out that the parish of Streatham did not have one but two commons, each overlooked by grand properties such as Park Hill (for Streatham) and Streatham Park (for Tooting). But the text also provides a useful reminder of the role played by commons in history:

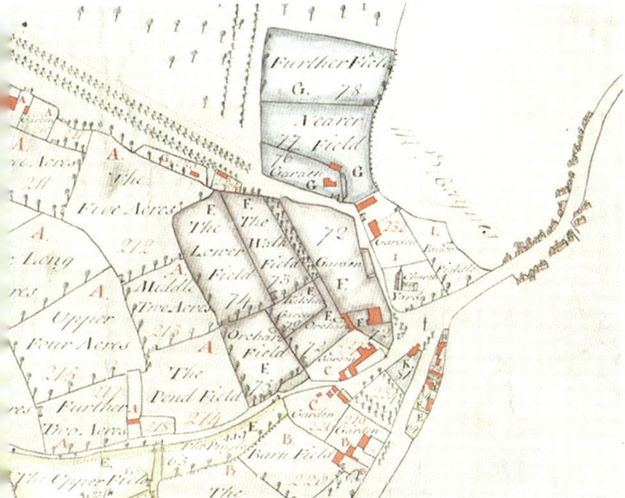

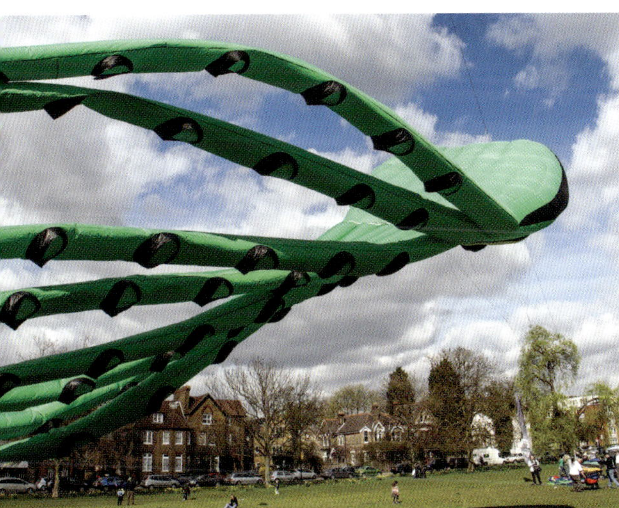

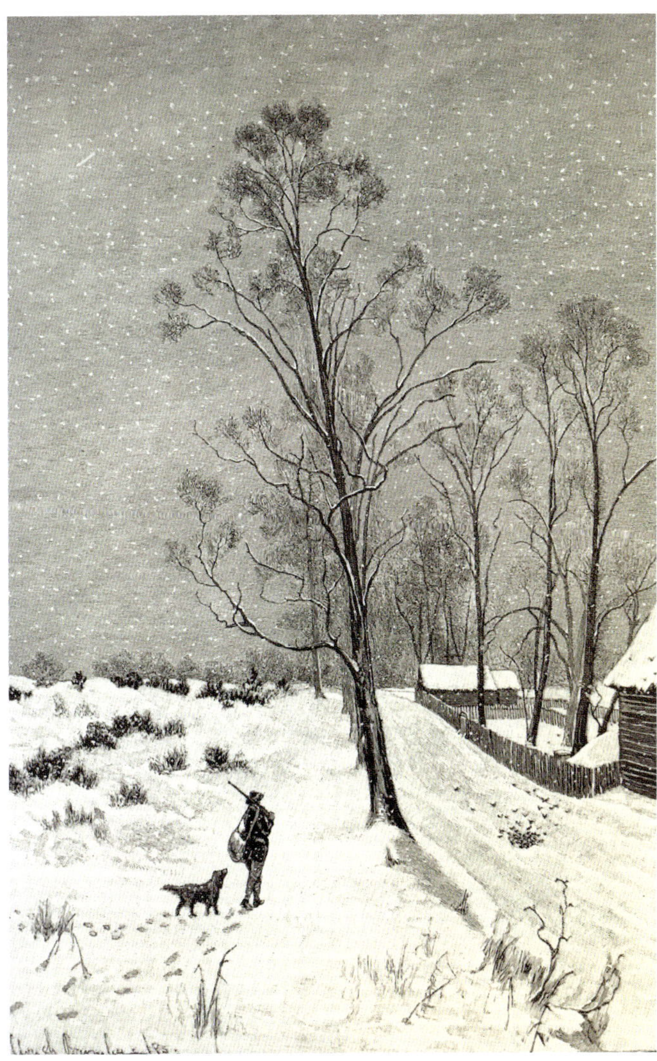

> A common … is a bit of history, for it is not only the most palpable relic of the manorial system, but it carries us back to the time when England was tilled in common, and private ownership of land in the modern sense was unknown.

Not surprisingly, the man who wrote these words, Sir Robert Hunter (1834–1913), a solicitor who later co-founded the National Trust, was one of the committee members who had set up the Commons Preservation Society twenty years earlier, in 1865. He was in good company as other members included such important figures as Octavia Hill (1838–1912), the social reformer, Professor Thomas Henry Huxley (1825–1895) and the MPs Sir Charles Dilke and James Bryce. Most of the society's members initially came from England's south east, so their interests focused on London.

Despite the urbanisation of Streatham, the neighbourhood has retained a strong rural element. In 1920 painter Winifred Knights (see p. 132) was delighted with the presence of 'pockets of rurality'. Even back then, people laughed at the idea of rural Streatham and her friend Allan Gwynne-Jones wrote to Winifred: 'I want to hear about your lanes, "lanes" really? In Streatham? With wild plums? I am sure no one else at Streatham finds them and that really they sprout out of the lamp posts' (see Llewellyn in bibliography).

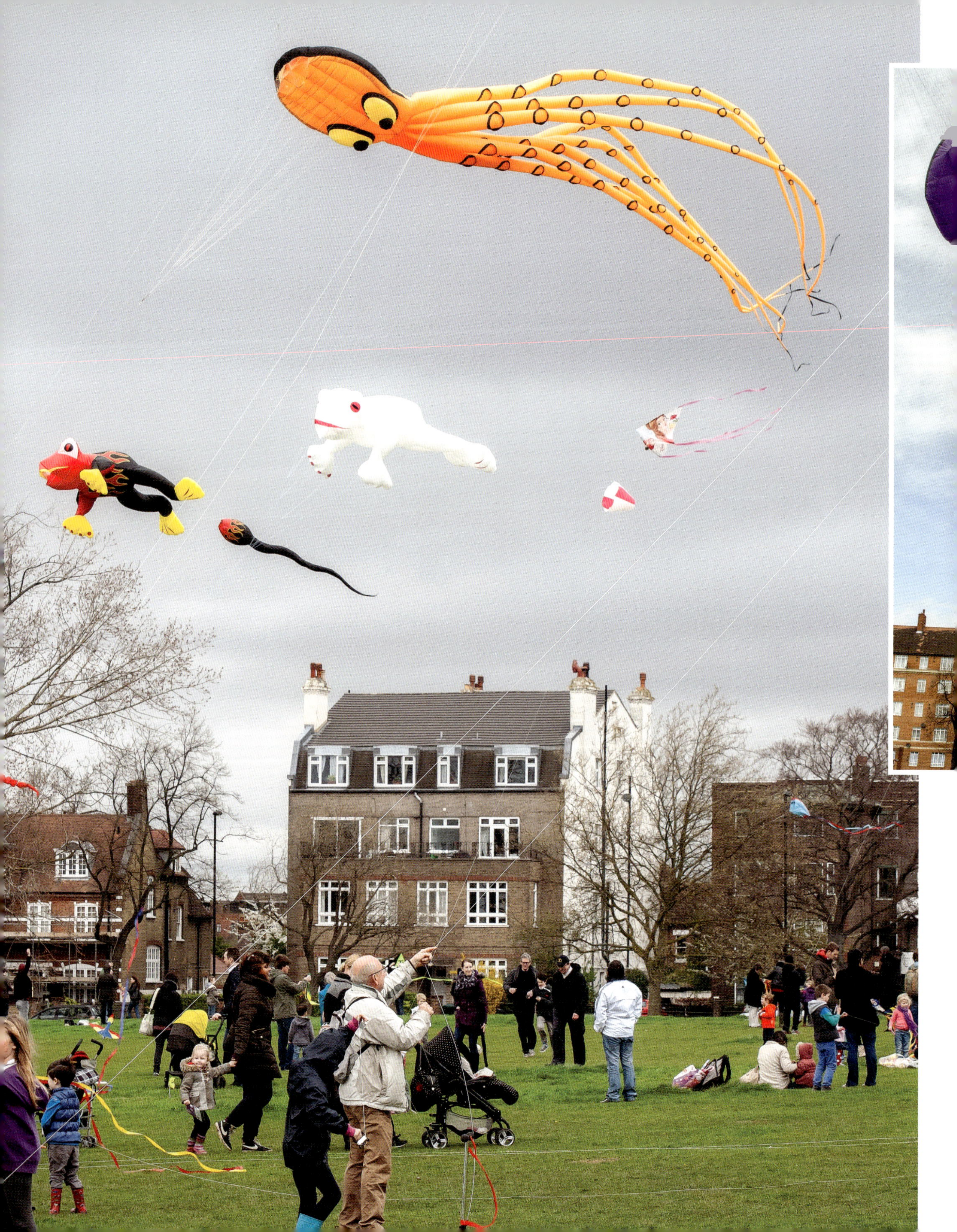

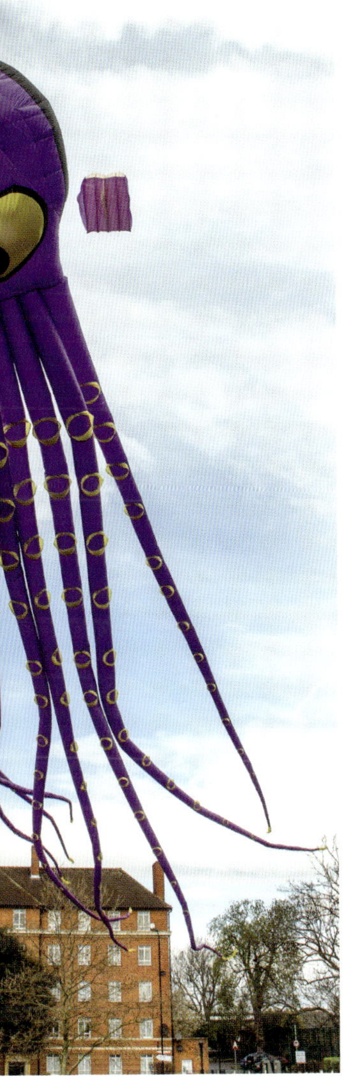

The very first kite event on Streatham Common was held in 1998. It was founded by Roy Reed and Bob Colover. Since that time, the annual event has grown in size to become a crowded and spectacular attraction. Roy Reed who was on the organising committee for the first thirteen years, has documented the event every year (see streathamkiteday.org.uk). The purple octopus was shot in 2008, the green kite on the previous page in 2010 and the photograph on the left dates from 2014. © *Roy Reed.*

But Graham Gower has discovered and written about all the lanes and rural heritage of Streatham. Anyone interested should get hold of a copy of his delightful *Streatham Heights, Footpaths and Woods*, published by the Streatham Society alongside guides on both Tooting and Streatham Commons.

In our own time both commons have received a new lease of life – with lottery money for the ongoing Tooting Common Heritage Project (in the borough of Wandsworth) and more lottery money for the Friends of Streatham Common (e.g. the restoration of the White Garden, see p. 70) accompanied by some dedicated volunteering work. Peter Newmark has been editing the Newsletter of the Friends of Streatham Common for over ten years and is very informative about the organisation's history and goals. The Friends sprang up after the Council cut its arts funding in 1997 and withdrew from organising events on the common. The Friends' first event was held in March 1998 'Wind Day' – thereafter 'Kite Day'. It has grown to become a major event in the common's calendar.

Peter Newmark, who regularly leads bird-spotting walks, is justly proud of the Friends' achievements at 'keeping the common a common'. He contrasts Streatham Common with the adjacent Norwood Grove which is kept mown, pruned and generally manicured by Croydon Council, like a park would be. On parts of Streatham Common, the grass is only cut once a year, the woods are deliberately a little scruffy and a large part of the common has received the status of 'Local Nature Reserve'. This is promoted through the 'Streatham Common Nature Trail'. Peter also draws comfort from the success of the Friends' intervention in campaigning against the erection of a temporary ice rink on Streatham Common. The Council had made a promise to keep ice skating going while the Tesco site was being redeveloped (2002-2013): the temporary ice-rink was built in Brixton instead.

2. Streatham High Road

(paired with 'The Multitude' on p. 82)

Streatham High Road's pedigree is both distinguished and problematic – it started life as a vital Roman road linking London and the south coast. It continued to play a strategic role in medieval times and throughout the modern period, and eventually the section between Westminster and Purley was re-classified as the A23 in 1935. It found a new lease of life in the twentieth century when the Streatham Hill Theatre was being marketed as 'West End shows at Provincial prices' (see Cresswell in bibliography) and a large number of recreational venues sprouted on both sides of this road – dance hall, theatres and cinemas (see p. 72).

For this chapter we have treated the two sections of this major axis Streatham High Road and Streatham Hill as one, in order to comment on shops and architectural landmarks. On the ground there really is little distinction between the shops and buildings situated north and south of Streatham Hill station. The total length of the road is 2.3 miles (the High Road: 1.8 miles and Streatham Hill: 0.5 mile).

The worst street in Britain

In our own times Streatham High Road was first declared to be the longest high street in Britain/Europe (accounts vary) before it was voted, rather arbitrarily, the worst high street in Britain in September 2002. This last survey was organised through the joint efforts of the BBC and CABE (the Commission for Architecture and the Built Environment), the

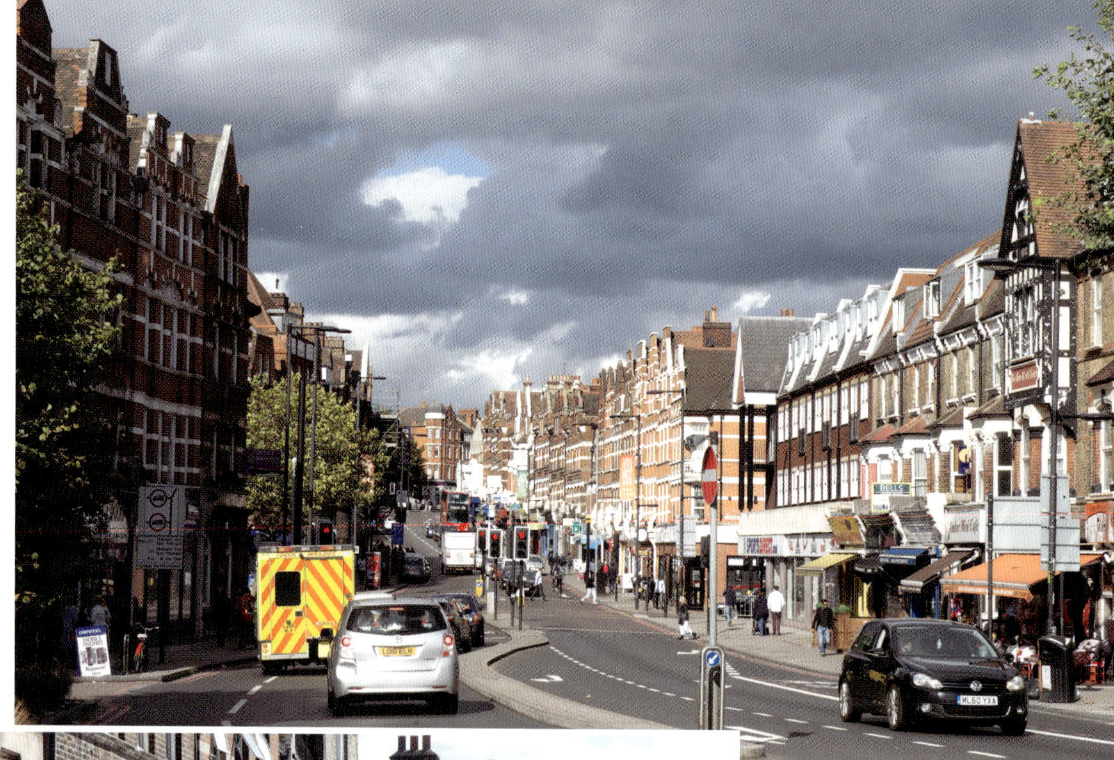

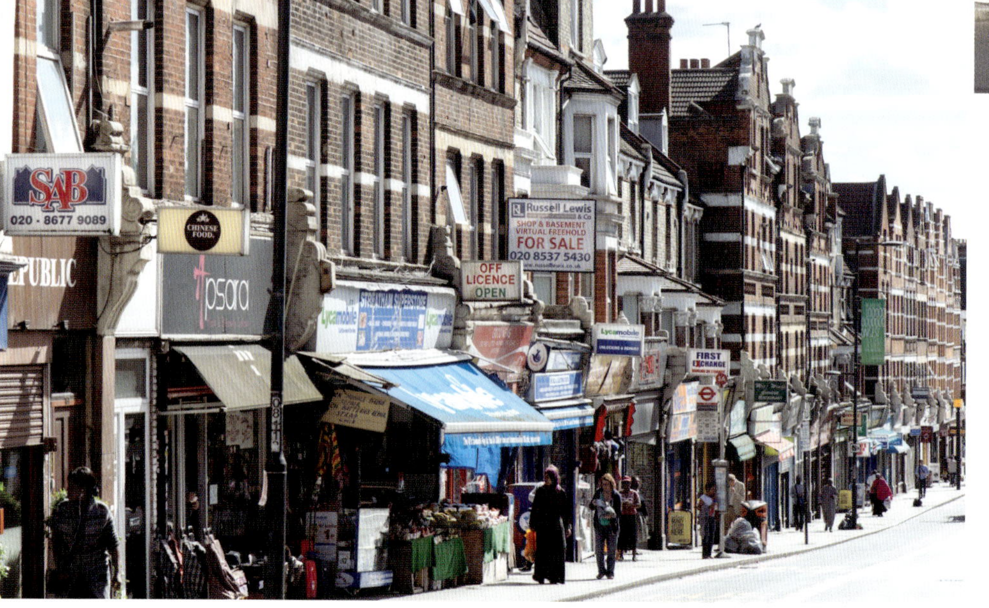

These photographs of the High Road were taken in 2016 and show the dense fabric of Victorian buildings on the east side of the A23, at a place known as the Dip – between Gleneldon and Stanhope Roads with the (former) Bedford Park Hotel on the extreme right (above). By the 1880s 'the fully fledged shopping parade, with capacious upper-floor accommodation had arrived' explained Kathryn Morrison (*Shopping Parades*). The brightly coloured shops at the foot of the tall buildings contrast with the upper floors but are neatly contained within the overall pattern created by regular cornices marking each shop as a unit.

former encouraging people to send nominations, the latter assessing them. Grey Street in Newcastle was the happy winner and Streatham the sad loser. CABE's Chief Executive, John Rouse, justified the outcome by insisting that:

> Streets are places not just routes, they're where we congregate, they're where we meet, they're where ideas are born … They're part of our civic structure and we ought to respect them.

The High Road is indeed a critical element of the Streatham landscape and this nasty blow gave the impetus required to embark on a much needed regeneration programme. By February 2009 Lambeth Council had prepared a draft 'Masterplan' which set out on the first page 'A Vision for Streatham': it promised that 'Streatham will become an increasingly attractive place to live', also emphasising that 'the High Road will remain at Streatham's heart and will be an asset to the whole area'. By 2013 Streatham had its own Business Initiative District (BID, see below) soon followed by its 'Streatham Street Manual', prepared by We Made That and funded by the Mayor's Outer London Fund with the London Borough of Lambeth.

The BID is now playing a critical role in the implementation of the 'Vision for Streatham'. It was set up by a collective of local business owners, community members and the town centre manager Angelina Purcell MBE. Its first chair was Lee Alley (Lee, a Streatham resident, also joined forces with Jane Wroe Wright to create *Heart Streatham*, the much loved magazine and associated website). How the BID works: local businesses agree to pay a little more council tax in order to channel the extra money into improvement schemes to benefit the area's traders. BIDs first appeared in Toronto, Canada in 1970 but in England and Wales they emerged as a result of the Local Government Act of 2003. At first five were set up in London. Now there are six BIDs operating in Lambeth alone – the first one to be set up was Waterloo.

Architectural Heritage

But we should also survey Streatham's existing assets – both the High Road's landmarks and the nature of its commerce.

A street's shopping facilities can make the upper storeys of its buildings almost invisible: it takes a deliberate effort to become aware of the architecture of a busy shopping area. But this was made relatively easy with the help of Graham Gower's essential guide *The High Road in Streatham* (see bibliography). Our own summary on pp. 32–37 is a condensed version which seeks to highlight Streatham's abundant Art Deco heritage without omitting other important architectural or visual landmarks.

We should also draw attention to two architects (locally-based for a time) who, as well as a general involvement with the architectural scene of their time, also contributed to the Streatham scene in particular. Sir Ernest George (1839–1922) is best known for his work on the Rousdon estate in Devon and for designing Southwark Bridge, while Frederick Wheeler (1853–1931) is remembered for his St Paul's [artists'] Studios on Talgarth Road (1890). In Streatham Sir Ernest designed, with Harold Peto, Hambley Mansions and the Old Beehive Coffee House (see p. 34 (24)). Sir Ernest was also a distinguished artist (etchings but also watercolours) who became a Royal Academician. He exhibited there on his own between 1860 and 1886 and with his business partner Harold Peto between 1876 and 1895 – notably 'Coffee House, Streatham Common' (1879) and 'House on Streatham Common' (1888).

Frederick Wheeler, who lived at 7 Rydal Road, designed many buildings on the Woodlands estate and Streatham Park estate, including Sussex School House, now Sussex House, at the junction of Tooting Bec Gardens and Ambleside Avenue. He also designed the electricity sub-station in Tooting Bec Gardens as a neo-Gothic building blending in with the adjoining Catholic church. On the High Road he designed the Broadway and the Triangle (see p. 37).

Streatham High Road boasts many examples of 'heritage' buildings; it also has thriving shops which are surveyed on p. 55. But this book is always keen to home in on examples of lovely creativity, so we should introduce Beep Studio to the reader.

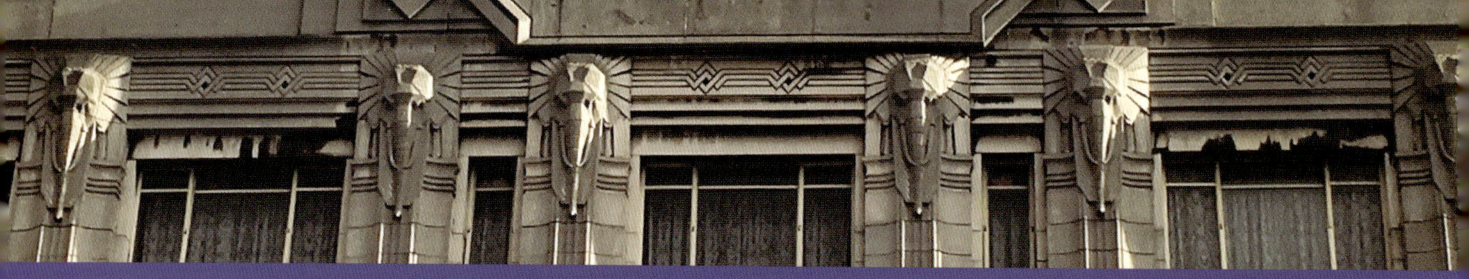

ART DECO STREATHAM on the A23 – with other landmarks too!

A23 NORTH

Numbers 1–14 and A–M. See pages 36–37.

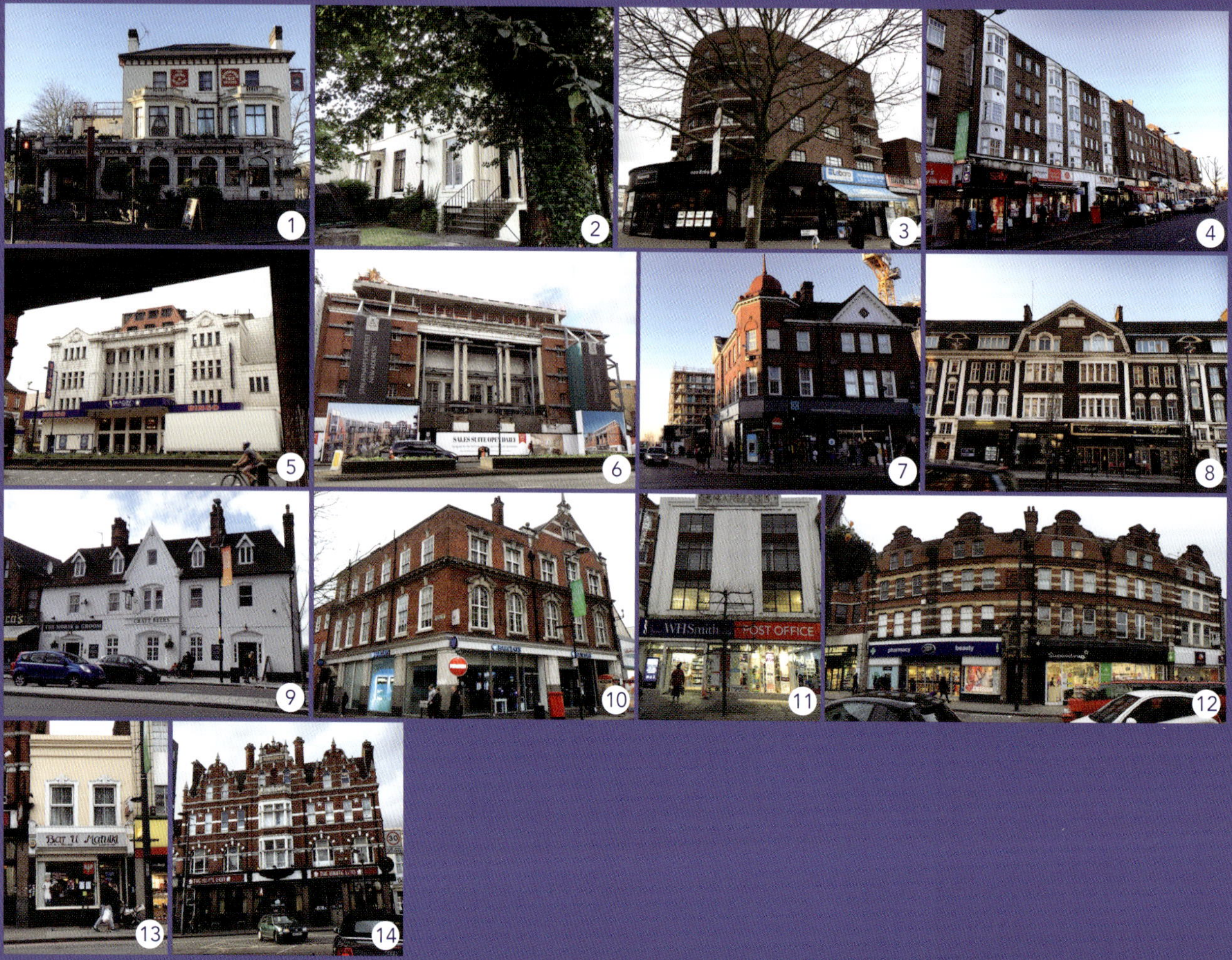

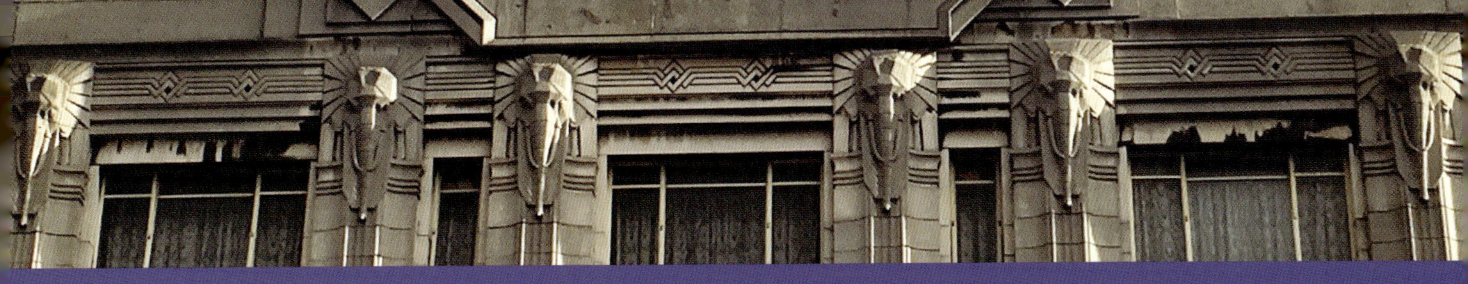

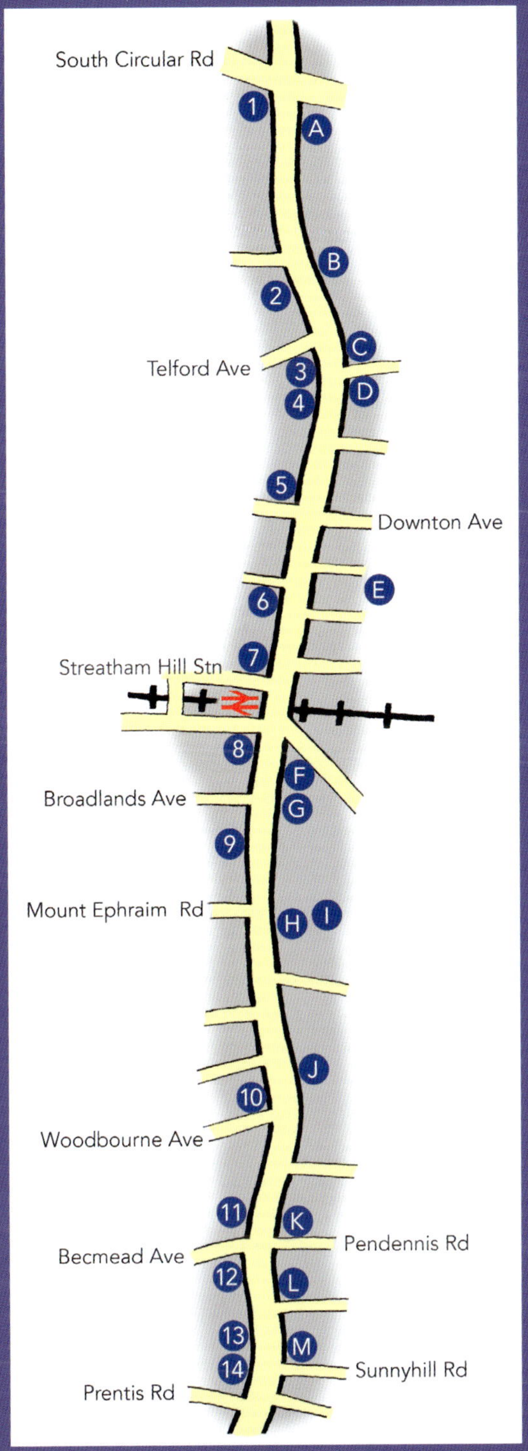
South Circular Rd
1
A
B
2
Telford Ave
C
3
D
4
5
Downton Ave
E
6
Streatham Hill Stn
7
8
F
Broadlands Ave
G
9
Mount Ephraim Rd
H
I
J
10
Woodbourne Ave
11
K
Becmead Ave
Pendennis Rd
12
L
13
M
14
Sunnyhill Rd
Prentis Rd

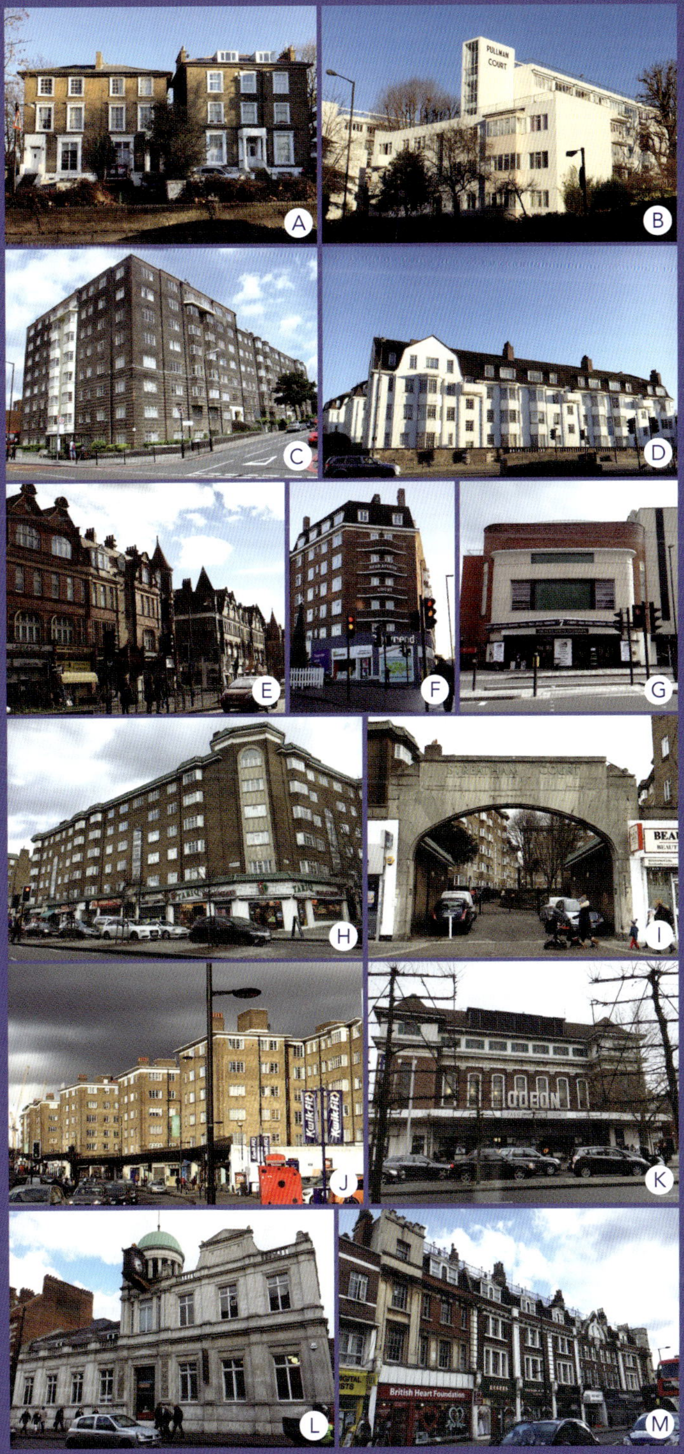

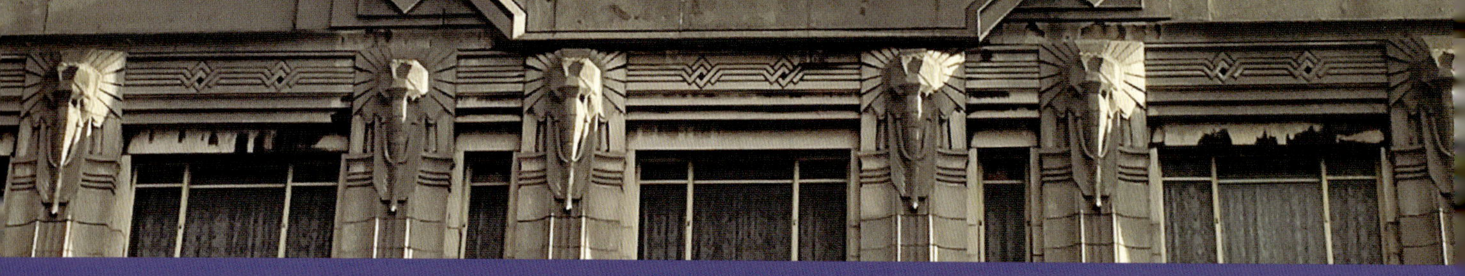

ART DECO STREATHAM on the A23 – with other landmarks too!

A23 SOUTH

Numbers 15–26 and N–S. See pages 36–37.

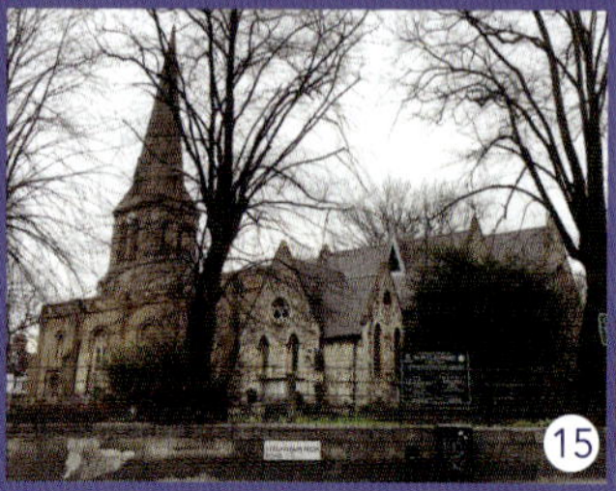

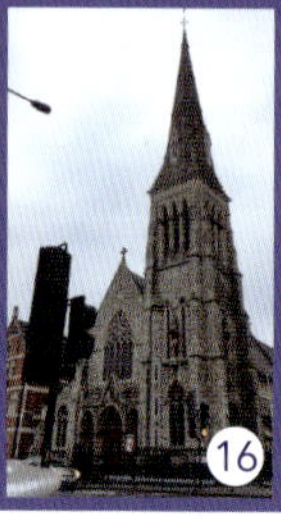

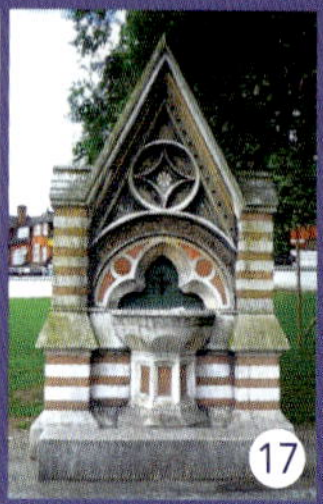

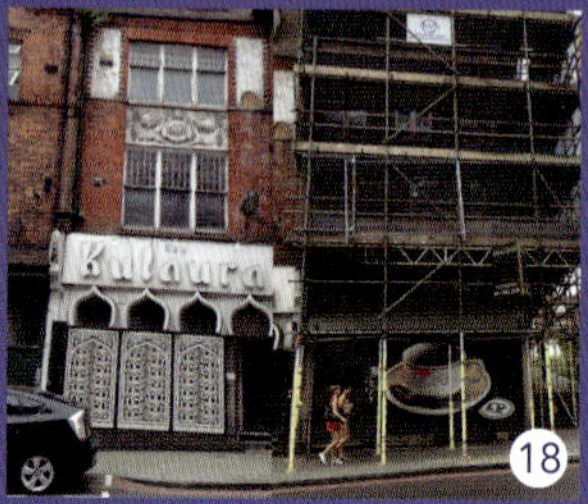

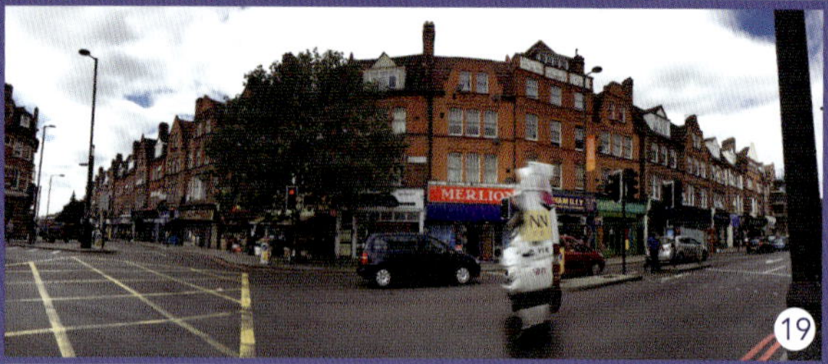

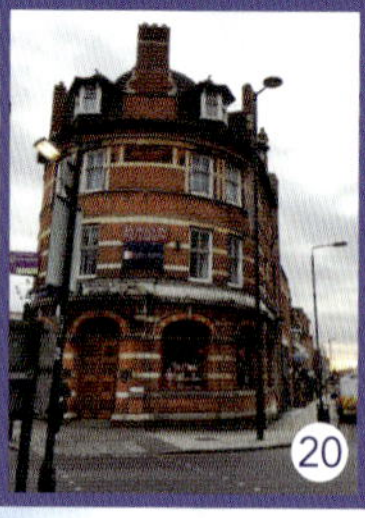

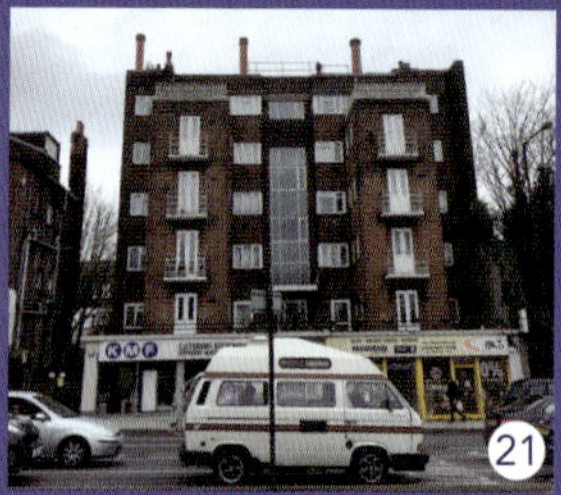

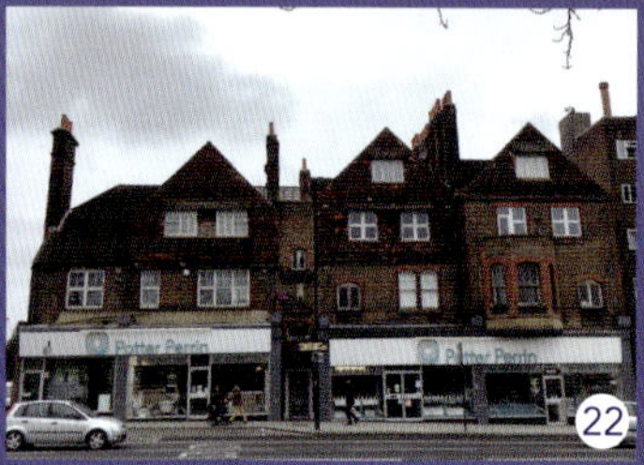

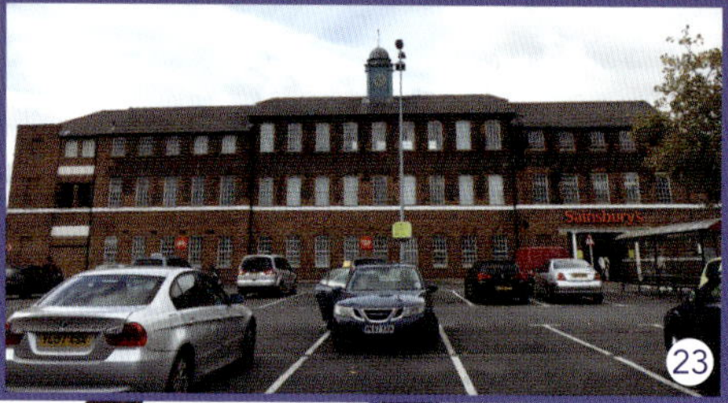

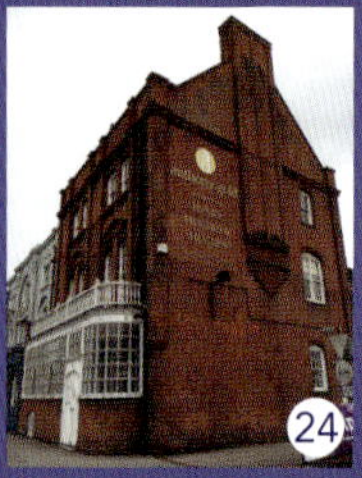

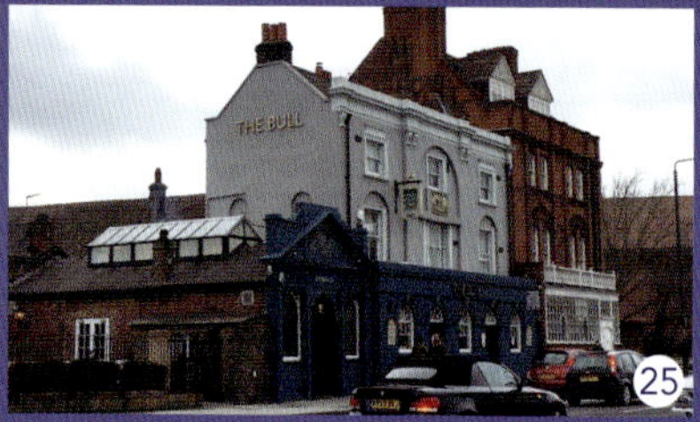

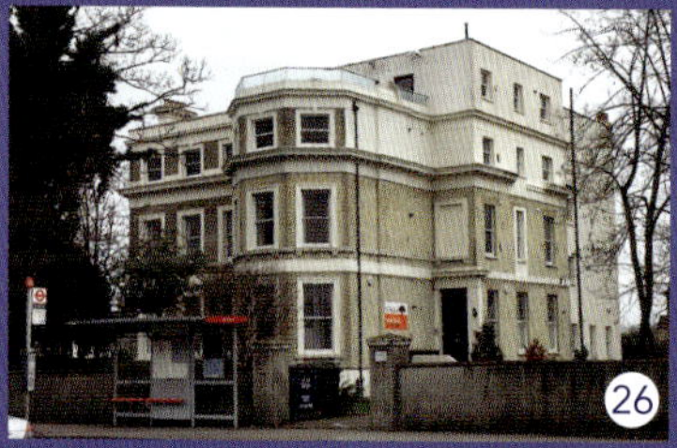

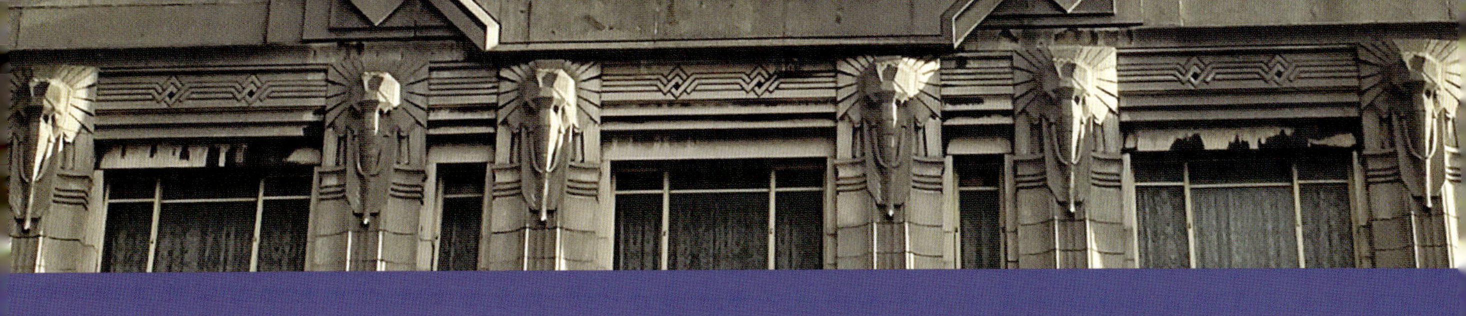

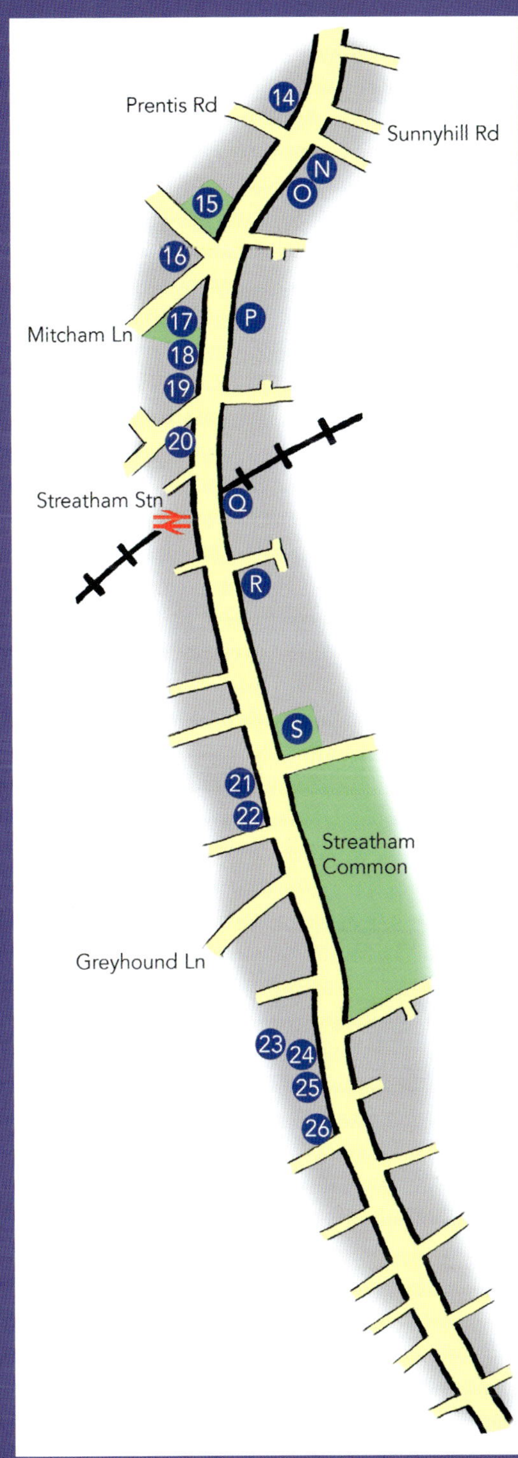

Prentis Rd
Sunnyhill Rd
Mitcham Ln
Streatham Stn
Streatham Common
Greyhound Ln
14
N
O
15
16
17
P
18
19
20
Q
R
S
21
22
23
24
25
26

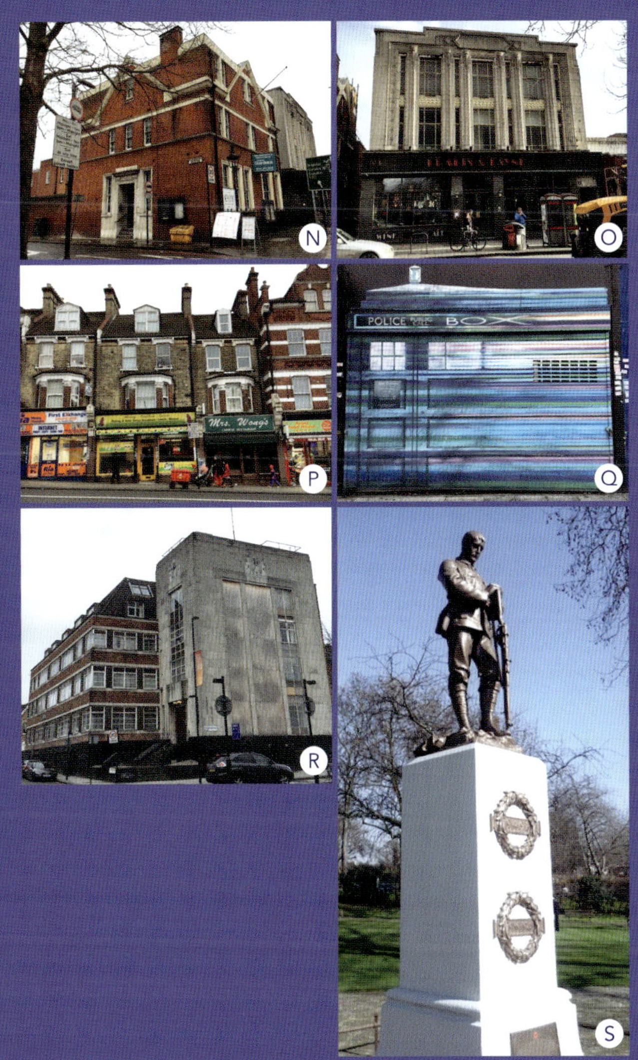

N
O
P
Q
R
S
POLICE BOX
Mrs. Wongs

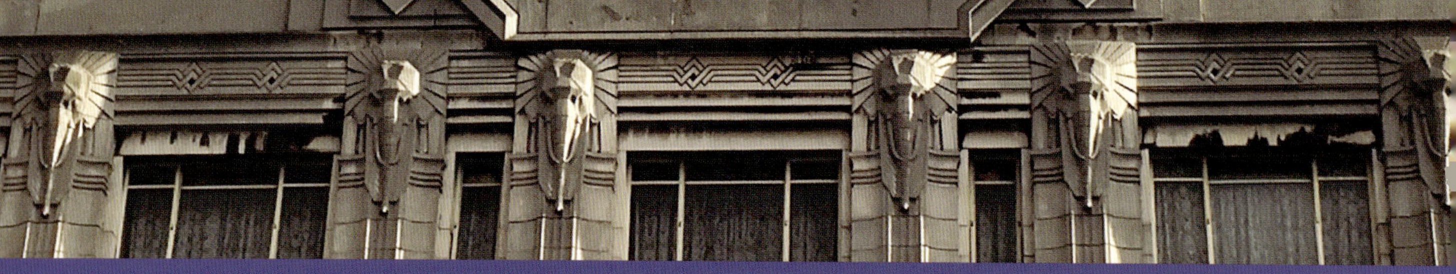

NORTH

1. **Crown and Sceptre pub**, see p. 56.

2. **The Paragon**: a Regency development of some twenty houses once lined the west side of Streatham Hill roughly between the present South Circular and Telford Avenue. Of these only three survive: Nos 40, 42, 44, bearing witness to the time when suburban villas started being built en masse, in the footsteps of what had happened in St John's Wood.

3. **Telford Parade Mansions** (on the High Road) **& Telford Avenue Mansions** (round the corner in Telford Avenue), were both designed by **Frank Verity and Beverley and Horner**, 1935. Frank Verity (1864–1937), son of Thomas (of Criterion Theatre fame) is best known for his cinema and theatre architecture such as the Carlton and the Plaza in Lower Regent Street. Son in law Sam Beverley joined the practice in the 1920s and the practice is still in existence as Verity & Beverley.

4. **Wyatt Park Mansions** – the white vertical bands highlighting the bay windows are the main decoration. Built in 1937 by H J S Abrams & Sons architects based at 19 Buckingham Street.

5. **Streatham Hill Theatre**, formerly the Streatham Hill Playhouse, then a Bingo Hall which closed in 2017, now with an uncertain future. Designed by **William George Robert Sprague** (1863–1933) with William Henry Barton, it was built in 1929. See p. 72.

6. **Gaumont Palace**: a bowling alley, Megabowl, between 1962 and 2008, was built in 1932 by **Charles Nicholas and J E Dixon-Spain** and rebuilt to designs by T P Bennett in 1955. It seated around 2380 people, down to 1873 seats by 1955 and when the weather was good, tea was served on the balcony above the entrance. The site is being completely re-developed but the Streatham Society was successful in saving the main façade, now incorporated into the new London Square residential development.

7. **Arborfield House** on the corner of Sternhold Avenue was built by an unknown architect in an Edwardian style though it is closer in date to the Art Deco period. It is one of a number of buildings on that stretch of the High Road to boast an elegant corner turret (also on both sides of Kingscourt Road). It replaced the original Arborfield House destroyed in a Zeppelin bombing raid in 1916. Also see p. 52.

8. **Stonehill Mansions**, one of the High Road's most intricate facades. The design, Dutch-influenced, is by Meech and Goodall, and dates from 1905.

9. **Horse and Groom pub**, see p. 56.

10. **Former Post Office and Telephone Exchange**: on the corner of Woodbourne Avenue which dates from the Edwardian period. The Museum of London has two photographs of the interior of the Telephone Exchange being manned by a dozen women (dated 11 February 1910).

11. **W H Smith**, formerly **Sharman's drapers shop**, at Nos 180-182, dates from 1929. The type and proportions of this neat little building echo those of the Burton building further south on the High Road (see 'O' on next page).

12. **North Parade**, at 200-208 Streatham High Road, 1888. This Victorian building also displays a Dutch influence in its design. Date and name are sculpted on plaques above the building's main entrance.

13. This small, unassuming building at **No 230** is one of the oldest buildings along the High Road (see p. 50).

14. **White Lion pub**, 1895. This building by F. Gough & Co was a coaching inn with its coach entrance to the south. Also see p. 56.

A. **5-9 Streatham High Road.** The way things were: these are the only grand Victorian houses to have survived along this stretch of the High Road (see the 1894 O/S map for the full contingent of houses between Streatham Hill Station and Streatham Place – now the South Circular Road).

B. **Pullman Court**, designed by **Frederick Gibberd** in 1935, Grade II listed (also see p. 138).

C. **Corner Fielde**, designed by **Toms and Partners** and advertised as 'Mayfair in Streatham', 1937. © John W Brown.

D. **Wavertree Court**, with its distinctive Dutch looking gables and attractive gardens. Built in 1933 to designs by **Frank Harrington**.

E. **Leigham Court Estate**. Also known as the ABCD estate – it runs between Amesbury and Downton Avenues; from above, the road pattern is Roman-grid style, contrasting with local street patterns. The houses themselves are anything but regular, the architects having introduced much variety in their elevations. Mostly built between 1894 and 1905 by the Artisans' Labourers' & General Dwellings Company and finally finished in 1928. The Artisans' Company was formed in 1867 to build decent housing for the working classes and they already had a good track record in London, with their now famous Shaftesbury Park Estate in Battersea (1873) followed by the Queen's Park Estate in West London (1879). This development was designed by **Rowland Plumbe** and **Harry Bell Measures**.

F. **Streatleigh Court**, designed by **Frank Harrington** and completed in 1937.

G. 'The Picture House', built as The Regal Cinema in 1938. See p. 74.

H. Leigham Hall, c. 1936, designed by R Toms & Partners.

I. Streatham Court, at the back of Leigham Hall, was also designed by R Toms for the Bell Property Trust, ready by 1936.

J. The High: a long continuous building set back from the High Road and connected to five projectings 'towers' with shops sited in between, designed by R Toms & Partners for the Bell Property Trust, and completed by 1937.

K. Odeon Cinema, the former Astoria which opened on 30 June 1930. See p. 72.

L. Tate Library: Grade II listed building. See p. 44.

M. 73A–89 Streatham High Road. This decorated and decorative Edwardian building is framed by two crenellated towers and dates from 1909. Above the mansard roof windows runs an ironwork balustrade with the date of the building. The architect/developer broke the geometry of the block when he inserted the grand No 83-85, surely the piece de resistance, perhaps for the man who financed the development?

SOUTH

15. St Leonard's Church, see p. 39.

16. The Church of the English Martyrs, Roman Catholic, was designed in the French Gothic style by A E Purdie and built between 1892 and 1894 by local builders – the Hill Brothers and W H Lorden of Tooting; it is Grade II listed. Its steeple forms a striking feature with that of St Leonard's and they may be glimpsed on the cover of this book.

17. The Dyce Fountain on the Green owes its name to the design by Victorian artist William Dyce (see p. 76).

18. Beep Studios' Voids Art project (description on next page): Roger Moore's 'Octopussy' on the left and Cynthia Payne on the right – the latter no longer exists, this may be the last photograph taken (2016) of this once familiar landmark.

19. The Broadway 1883–4 and 1893. This remarkably long and fluid parade runs between the Green and Ambleside Avenue. Built of red brick in 1883-4 and 1893 for the southern section, it includes some Dutch style gables. The builders were the Hill Brothers responsible for the Catholic Church and the architects are believed to have been Frederick Wheeler and Hollands.

20. The Triangle, originally designed as a bank, is attributed to local architect Frederick Wheeler, 1885. See p. 31.

21. Commonside Court, facing Streatham Common, built in a modernist style in the mid-1930s.

22. Hambley Mansions: an English Country style development appropriate for this more rural part of Streatham. Designed by **Sir Ernest George** and **Harold Peto**, it was built by William Mason of Streatham Common in 1877.

23. The remarkable London **Silk Mill** (see p. 46), saved from demolition by the intervention of the Streatham Society, now provides a historic entrance to the large Sainsbury's which has been built alongside it and opened in 1989.

24. The old **Beehive Coffee Hous**e is now an office building occupied by Solicitors Anthony Gold and others. It was also designed by **Sir Ernest George** and **Harold Peto** for the Temperance Movement in 1878 and is Grade II listed (see p. 77).

25. The Bull pub, the oldest pub in Streatham (see p. 56).

26. 508–510 Streatham High Road: the only mid-Victorian houses along the High Road to have survived down to the twenty-first century.

N. Old Police Station (see p. 42).

O. The Burton building, erected in 1932 for Montague Burton of menswear fame on the site of the Regency Thrale Almshouses before they moved to Polworth Road and were rebuilt in 1930. An elegant building, designed by Leeds architect Harry Wilson who became Burton's in-house architect in 1931. He devised the Burton's Art Deco style with its signature decorative features such as the frieze of elephant heads at the top of vertical bands (shown above), and the zig-zags on the upper horizontal line. The original shop has gone, replaced by a popular pub called Pratts & Payne – after George Pratt of Streatham store fame and Cynthia Payne, the notorious brothel keeper.

P. 177 High Road: inside the unprepossessing premises of 'Blessings', a café serving Caribbean cuisine, is a decorative gem, see p. 53.

Q. Beep Studio **police mural** (see p. 43).

R. Century House, 245 Streatham High Road: built in 1938 as the headquarters for James Walker, the silversmiths. The large Art Deco clock was once regarded by the Streatham Society as an icon – it is now barely visible and in need of conservation. After the business closed in 1984, the building was converted into luxury flats, losing much of its character in the process.

S. Streatham **War Memorial** in Albert Carr Gardens, facing the north west corner of Streatham Common. This bronze of a serviceman with rifle reversed is one of a number of First World War Memorials made by Albert Toft (1862–1949). It was unveiled by General Sir Charles Munro in the presence of the Bishop of Southwark on 14 October 1922.

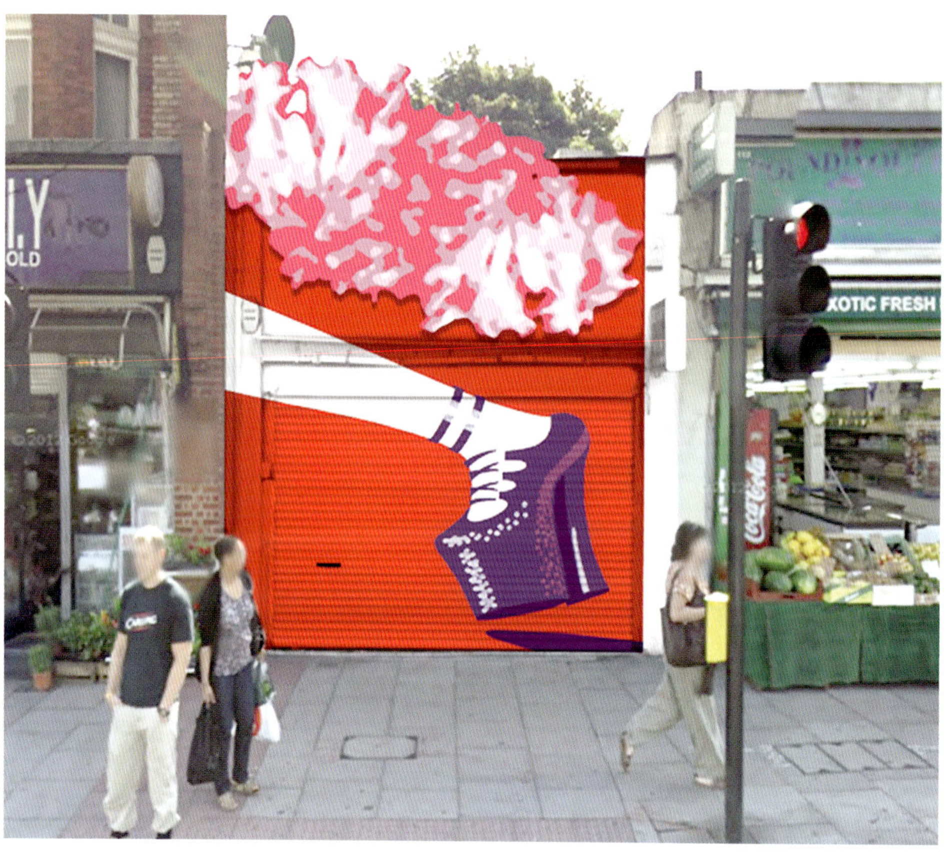

The glamorous supermodel Naomi Campbell, Streatham-born, is one of the 'celebrities' featured in Beep Studio's Voids Art Trail. This image captures a famous incident in Naomi's life: she fell on the catwalk in 1993 wearing platform shoes by Vivienne Westwood. The mural, which no longer exists, was painted on 111 Streatham Hill in 2014 – a shop which has remained empty. *Visual by Beep Studio.*

Two of the stamps found at locations on the Voids Art Trail: Naomi Campbell (born 22 May 1970) and 'hostess' Cynthia Payne (1932-2015) who lived on Ambleside Avenue supplying 'Personal Services' in exchange for Luncheon Vouchers (also see p. 49). *Stamp designs by Beep Studio with Camberwell Press.*

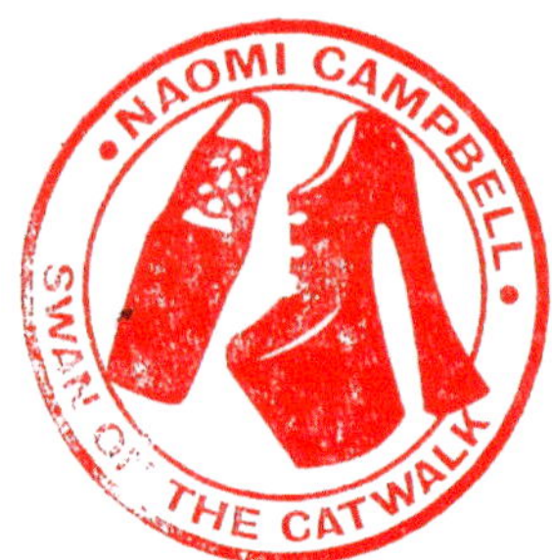

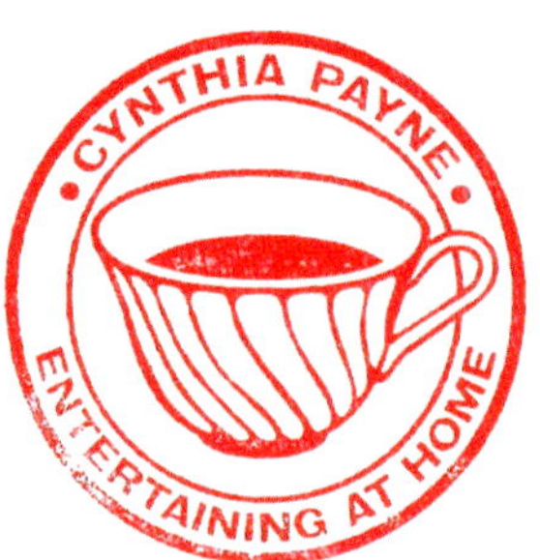

Beep Studio

This is a small, enterprising architectural and design consultancy firm based in Forest Hill. They became involved with three projects which aimed to improve the High Road in 2013–14 – two of them – shop front improvements and a project to illuminate the High Street – were spearheaded by Lambeth Council and a third was initiated by InStreatham, the BID (see p. 31).

The first shop to receive a 'facelift' from Beep Studio was Jane's Organic at 54 Streatham Hill (closed at the time of writing), followed by Kara, a ladies clothes shop (at No 128); the charming Boyce da Roca Café (at No 74) came next – the latter was the winner of *Time Out* 'Love London' award in 2014. Other shops were given a facelift with the help of another firm called 'Designed by Good People'.

What was to be done about the neglected look of empty premises – many south of St Leonard's church? The BID appointed Beep Studio to develop their proposed 'Voids Art Trail'. 'Voids' as in empty shops, and 'Art' as a way of capitalising on those gaps along the High Road by introducing artwork related to Streatham's famous sons and daughters. But this was carried out in a subtle and slightly enigmatic way. Described as a 'trail', it encouraged local residents to find the artworks with the help of a map which would be stamped at the correct locations. The ephemeral artworks which have survived to this day have been inserted in the High Road map at p. 35 (18), also see the police station mural on p. 43.

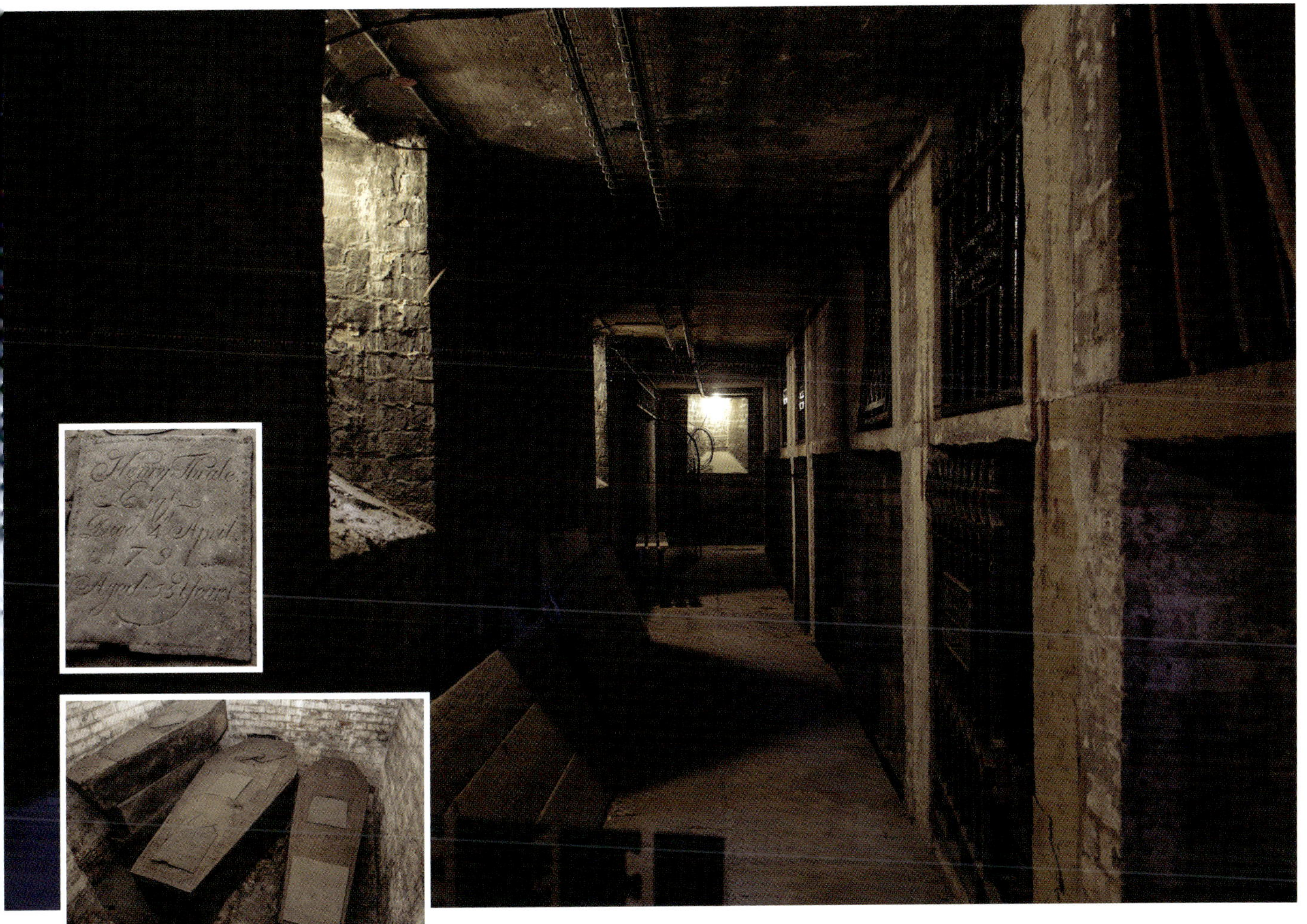

The crypt of St Leonard's is not for the faint-hearted, as it is the last home of thousands of local residents – many to be found in charnel pits underneath the floor of the crypt, others placed in coffins lining the cells of the crypt's three dark alleyways. One of the cells contains the remains of the eighteenth-century Thrale family (their coffins, relocated to the crypt, were found under the floor of the old church). The enormous coffin of Mr Thrale (inscription above) is framed by that of his mother-in-law and three of his children.

Churches

The acquisition of a parish church generally ensured that a neighbourhood featured in records: this, literally and metaphorically, put the place on the map. It is easy to see on p. 27 how Streatham congregated around its church, judiciously placed at a crossroads. However, if you Google churches in Streatham you may be surprised to discover that in the main they are not distributed along the High Road but along the diagonal axis of Mitcham Lane which continues roughly in the same direction east of the High Road. Even the prominent churches of St Leonard (Anglican) and of the English Martyrs (Catholic) are placed along this axis.

St Leonard's is the original parish church, rebuilt several times, the last time after the disastrous fire of 5 May 1975. The main body of the church dates from 1831, the chancel from the 1860s and the tower, the oldest feature, encased in more recent fabric, dates from the mid-fourteenth century. Much was destroyed in 1975 but a number of precious historic artefacts have survived, very knowledgeably described in John Brown's guide to the church. See p. 129 for an update on William Dyce's memorial.

There are two other churches along the High Road: Streatham Baptist Church (formerly Congregational, opened 1901) and, facing the Common, the Parish Church of Immanuel and St Andrew (original church 1854, rebuilt 1988). However, for much of the nineteenth century St Leonard's was connected to another Streatham church – Christ Church, for an Anglo-Catholic congregation (1841, designed by James William Wild in a neo-Byzantine style). It was built to save the souls living on the Roupell Estate in North Streatham, with money raised by the Rector of St Leonard's. Christ Church is the only Grade I listed building in Streatham and the decoration of the apse, by the celebrated Owen Jones (1809–1874) achieves considerable impact, as does the prominent location of the church.

What Christ Church and St Leonard's have in common is the stained-glass designed by John Hayward (1929–2007). Tooting born, he was a local man who in 1955, as a Christ Church parishioner, presented his church with a stained-glass window (St Michael), the first he designed and made. His first large-scale commission was for the church of St Mary-le-Bow in the City with stained glass windows, rood and etched glass screen for the crypt. By 1961 he had set up a professional workshop in Bletchingley and when St Leonard's went up in flames in 1975, his name, by now well-established, was a natural choice. The Streatham window which tells the story of Streatham is particularly fine with a level of detail and harmonious design which is exquisite.

Right: The Streatham window in the church of St Leonard is by stained-glass artist John Hayward (1930–2007). It is beautifully composed using a palette of colours designed not to darken the church. It was installed in 1980. The detail below depicts the 1975 fire.

Below left: The signed, but otherwise undocumented, pair of stained glass windows by Walter Crane (1845–1915) are one of Christ Church's highlights. They are dated 1891 and bear the artist's mark. This detail from 'Weep Not' shows Jesus speaking to the women of Jerusalem, the other window depicts Jesus exhorting Peter to 'Feed my Sheep'.

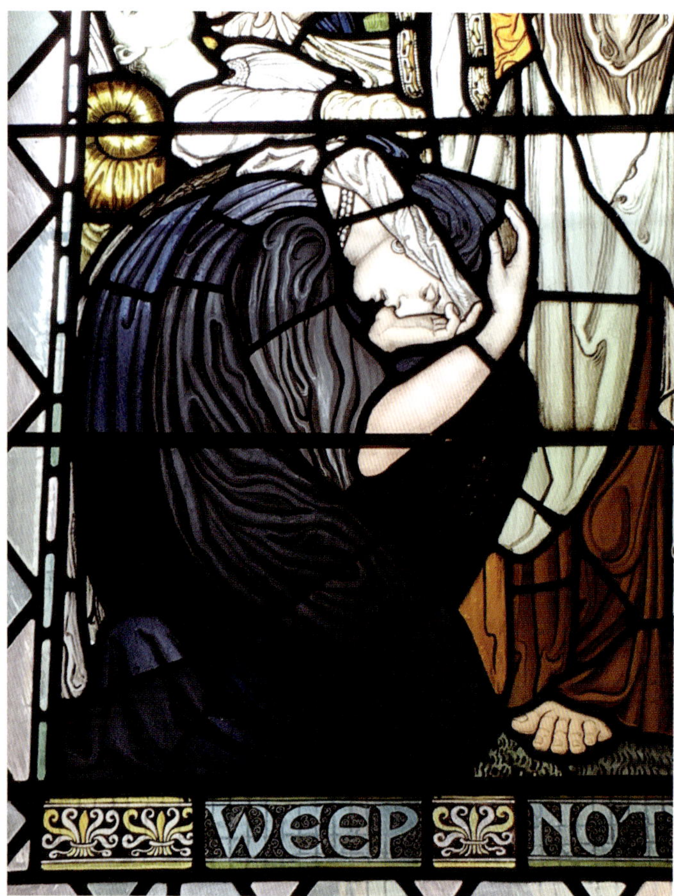

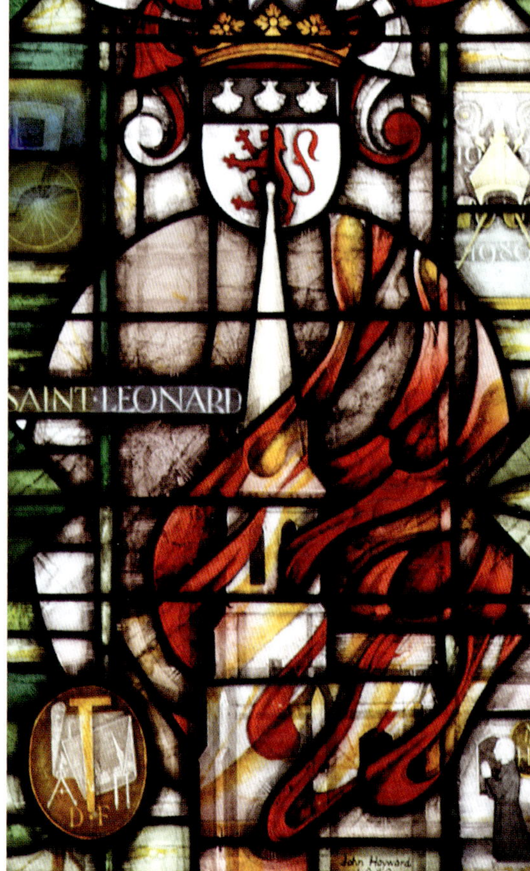

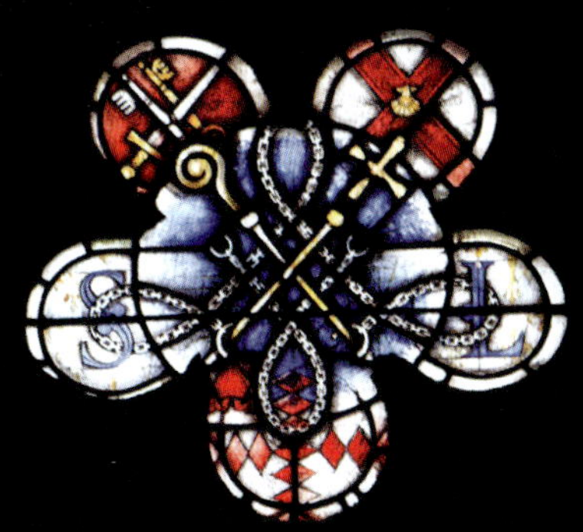

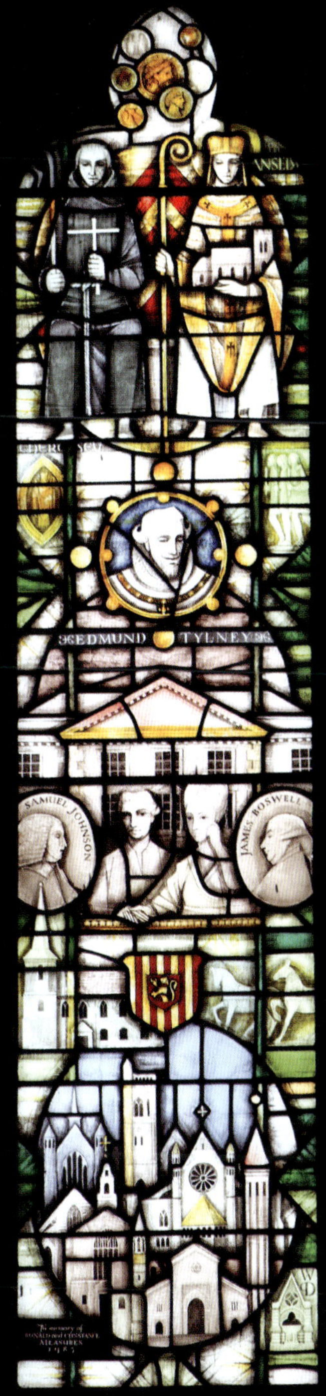
EDMUND TYLNEY
SAMUEL JOHNSON
JAMES BOSWELL

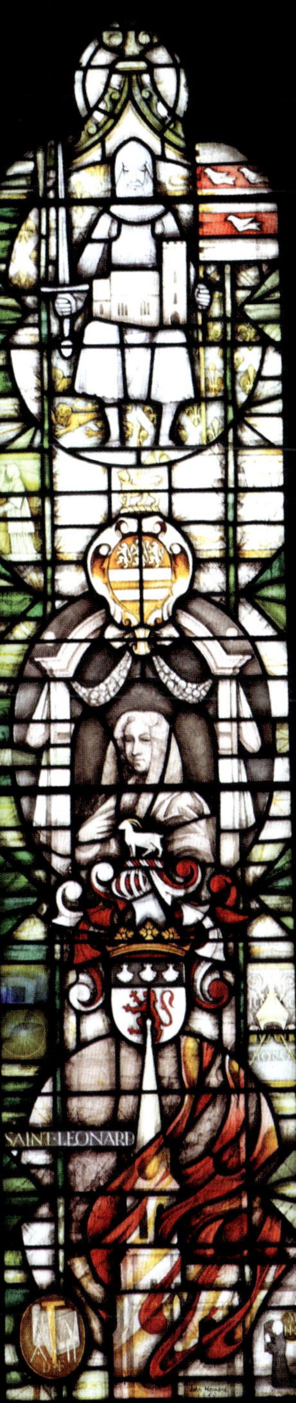
SAINT·LEONARD

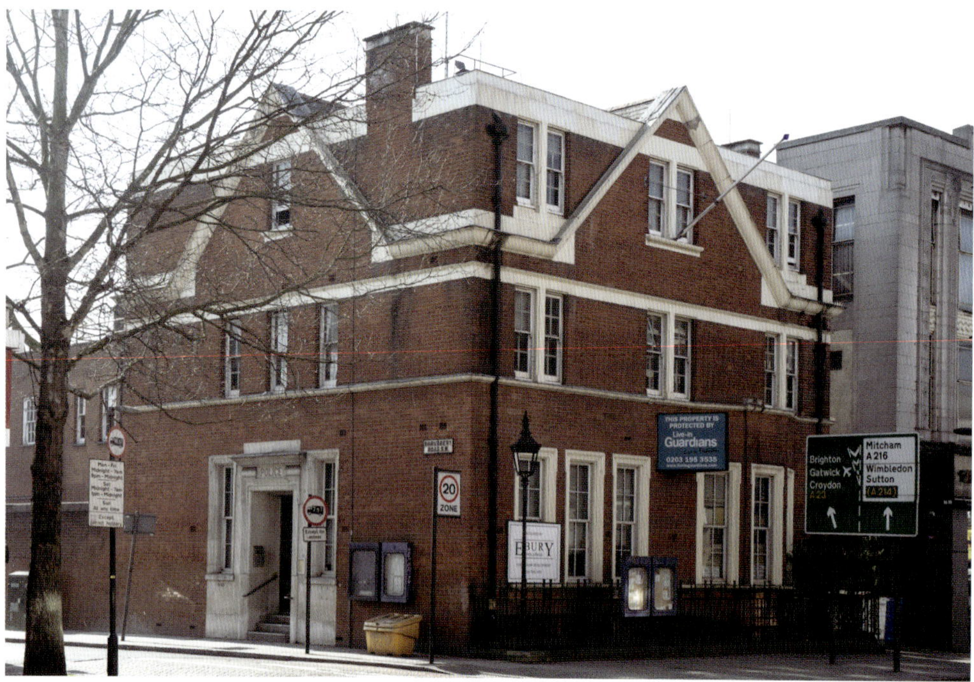

Streatham Old Police Station at 101 Streatham High Road. It was built in 1912 to replace an earlier building dated 1865. The Edwardian premises were designed by John Dixon Butler (1861–1920) who had been appointed architect to the Metropolitan Police in 1895. He designed the police stations of Hackney (1904), Muswell Hill (1904), Highbury (1910), Tottenham (1913) and Hornsey (1915).

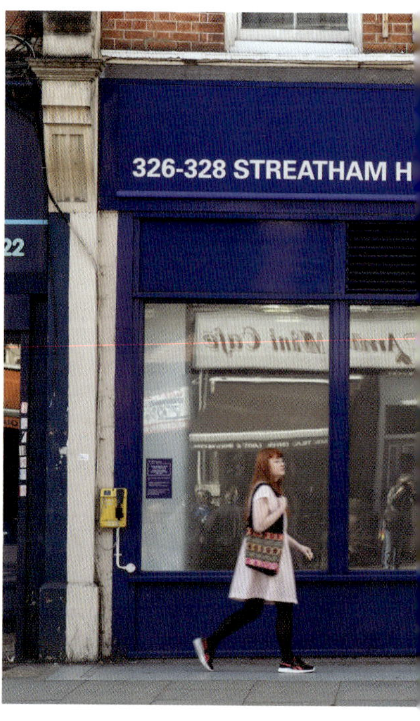

In 2015 the red brick police station was abandoned in favour of 326–328 Streatham High Road. It is apparently not as modestly-sized as it looks because there is a great deal of office accommodation in the basement. In 2000 there were three 'response teams' to 999 calls in Lambeth: Kennington, Brixton and Streatham. This subsequently dropped to two (Brixton and Streatham) and since 2013 it is down to one, Brixton, the only station to remain open all night.

Police Station – downsizing … with a smile!

The earliest Old Bailey record for Streatham appears to date from 21 January 1747. Most of the misdemeanours for the eighteenth and early nineteenth centuries in these records concerned theft – of animals or other goods.

But on 26 October 1868, a certain John Lee was found guilty of 'feloniously cutting and wounding Edward Glossop' and was given an eighteen months prison sentence. The incident was the outcome of an altercation at the Greyhound pub in Streatham where a group of friends from Wells Lane were enjoying a drink. The assault took place when they left the pub and the local policeman, James Ottway, declared at the trial: 'I heard cries of "Police," and apprehended the prisoner—I saw Glossop, with blood on him—the prisoner

Jiro Osuga and
Mireille Galinou

The Streatham Sketchbook

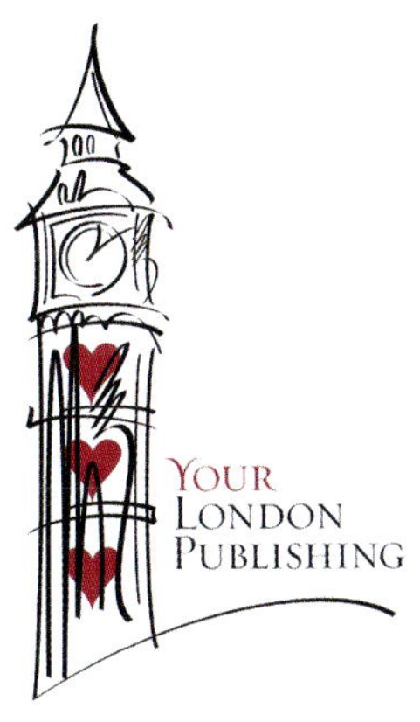

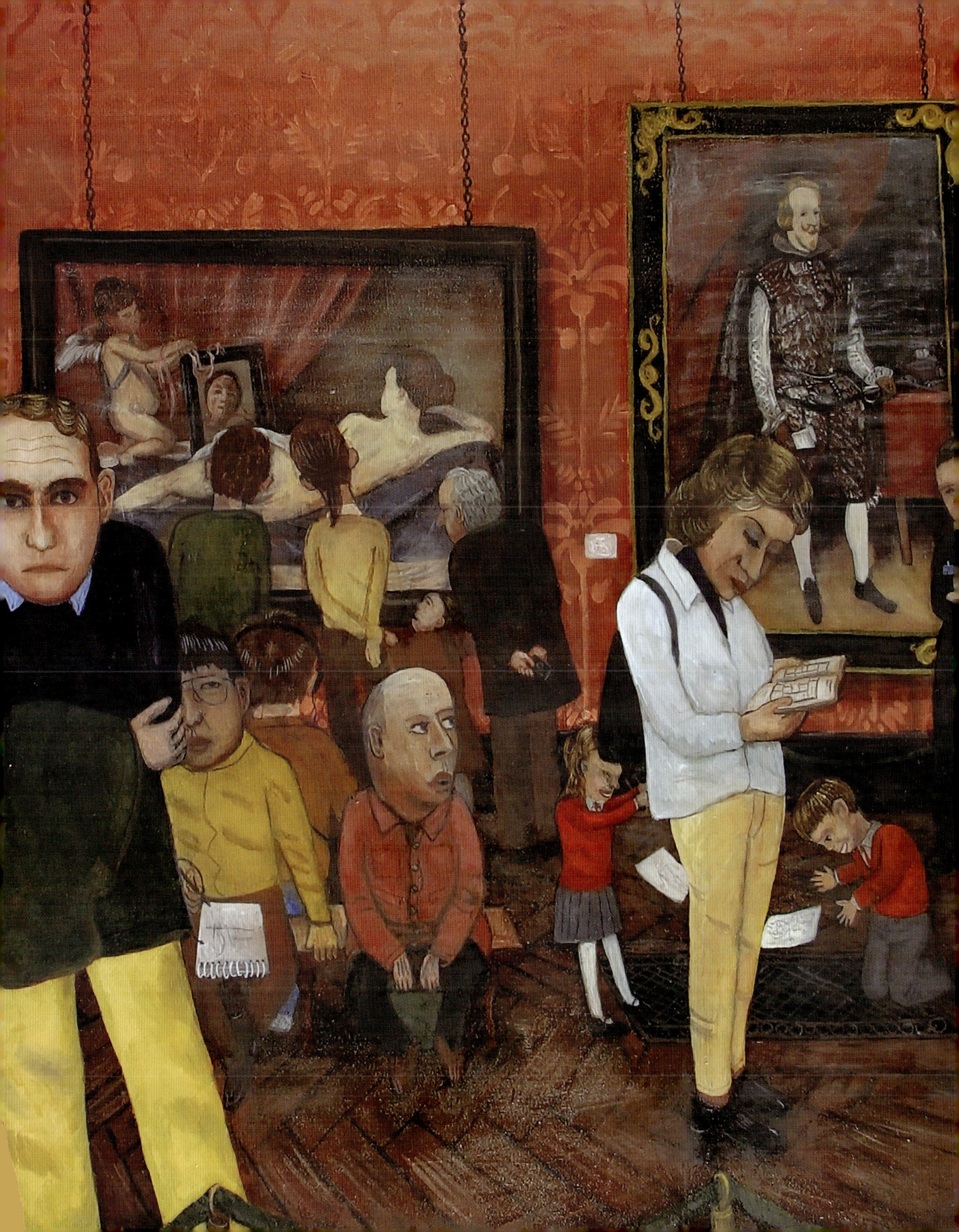

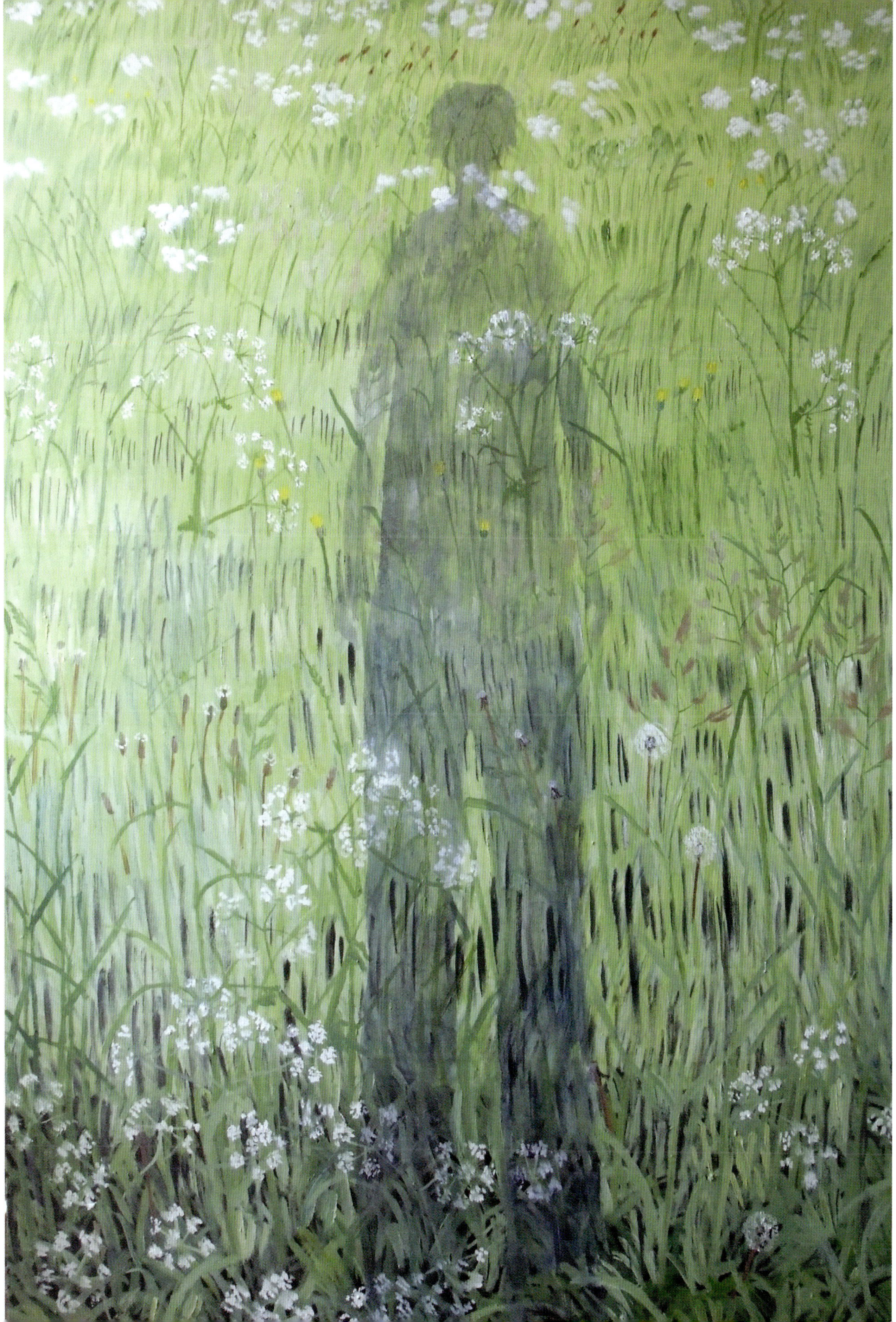

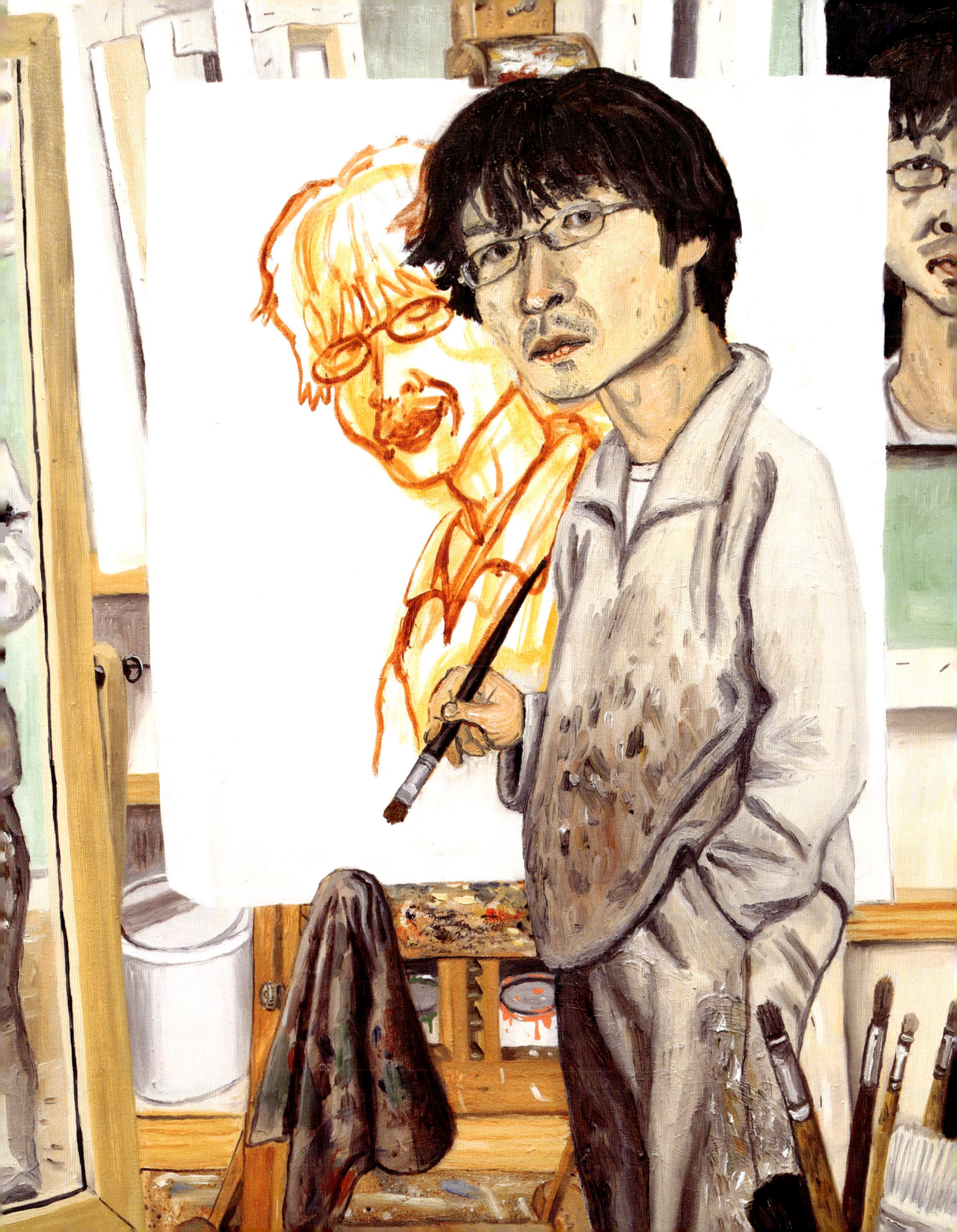

Previous pages:
'Portrait Painting' (detail), 2013, oil on canvas, 104 x 90 cm.
In this scene set in my Streatham studio, the four recurring self-portraits each appear to have a life of their own. The title indulges in wordplay – the word 'Painting' could be a verb or a noun.
Flowers Gallery.

Right: 'Memory Lane', 2014, oil on canvas, 43 x 50 cm.
In this painting, inspired by the twists and turns of the High Road in Streatham, you go back in time the further you look down the street.
Flowers Gallery.

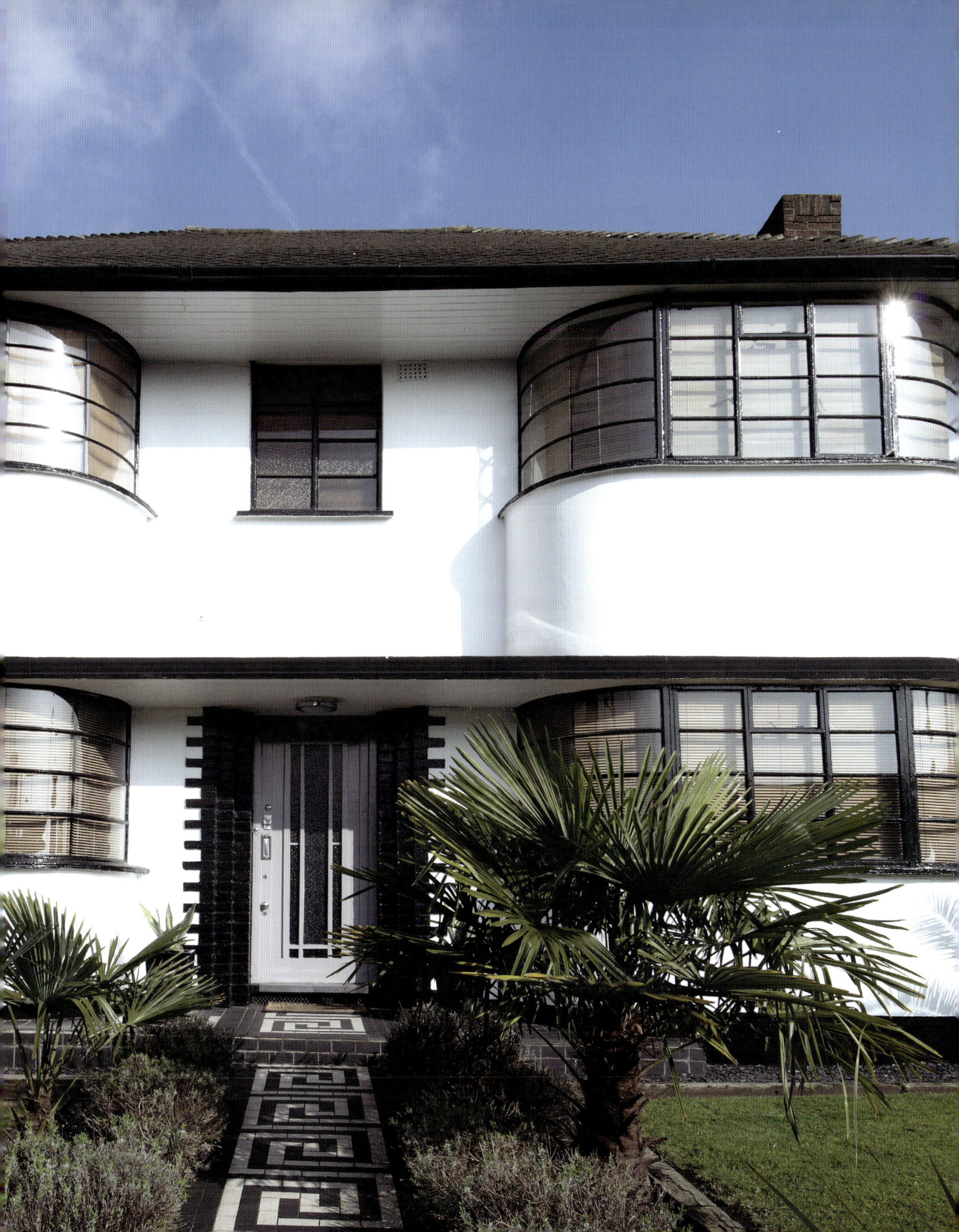

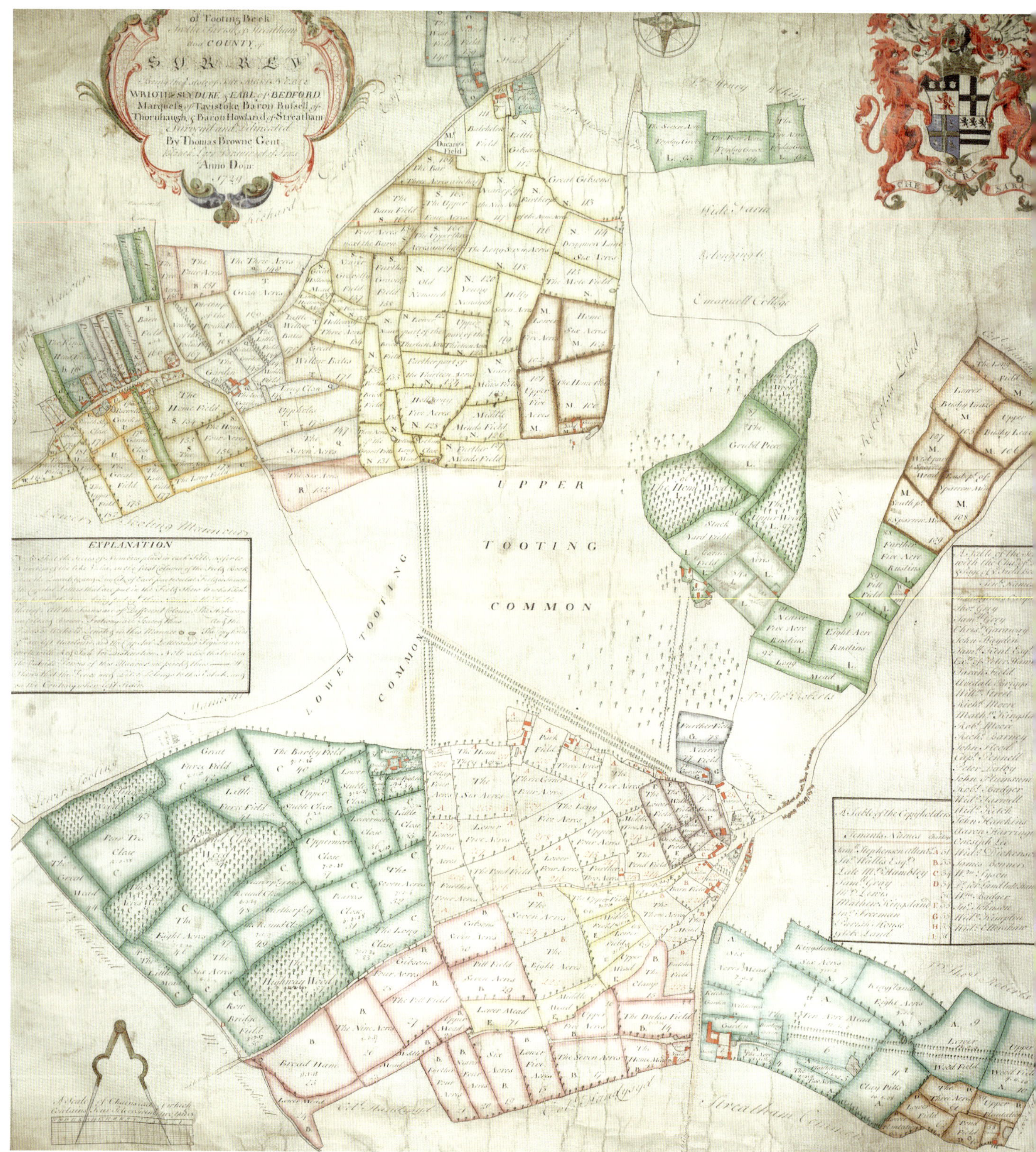
of Tooting Beck
and COUNTY of
SURREY
WRIOTHESLY DUKE & EARL of BEDFORD
Marquess of Tavistoke Baron Russell of
Thornhaugh & Baron Howland of Streatham
By Thomas Browne Gent.
Anno Dom:
1729
UPPER
TOOTING
COMMON
LOWER TOOTING
COMMON
EXPLANATION
Emanuell College
Streatham Common

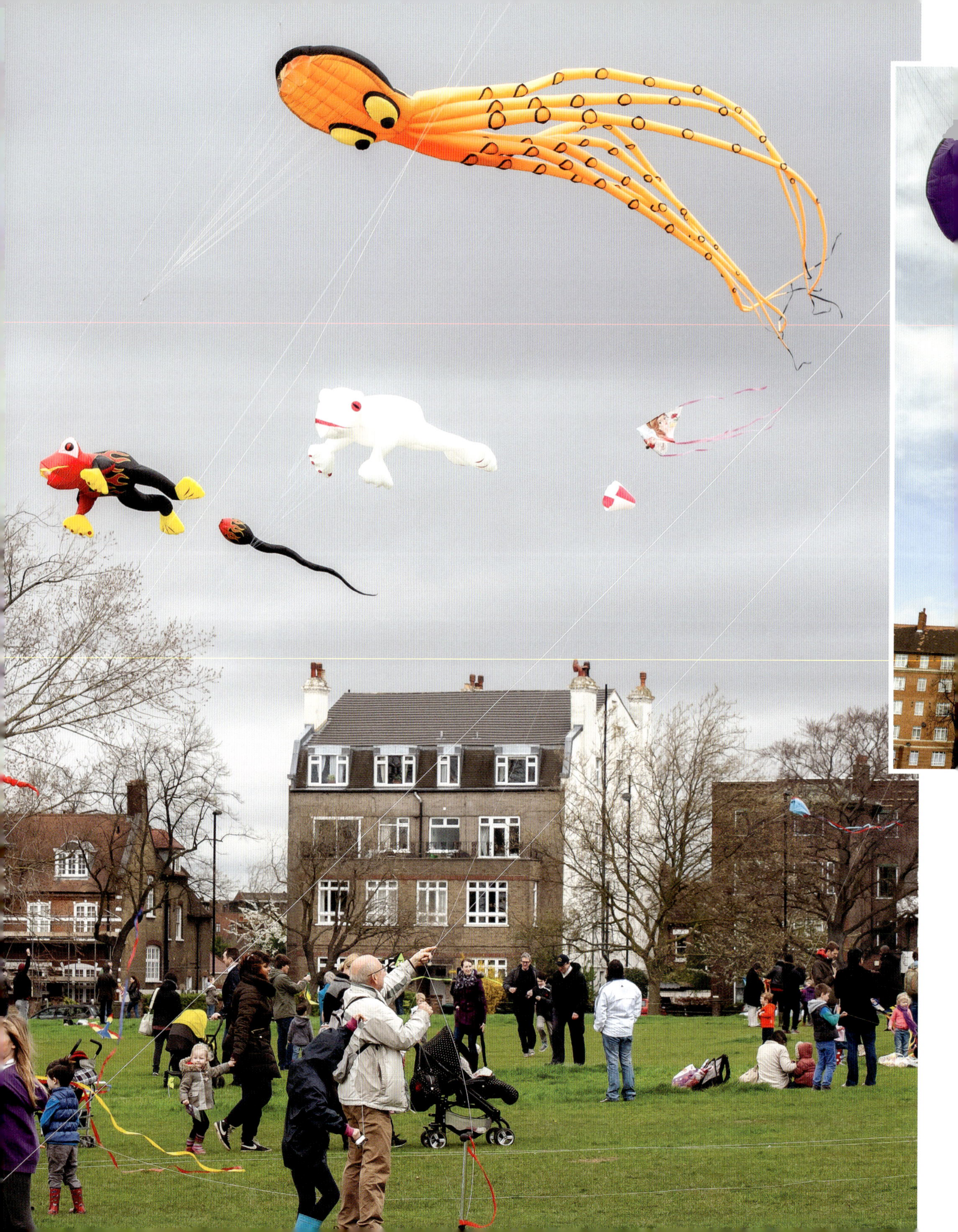

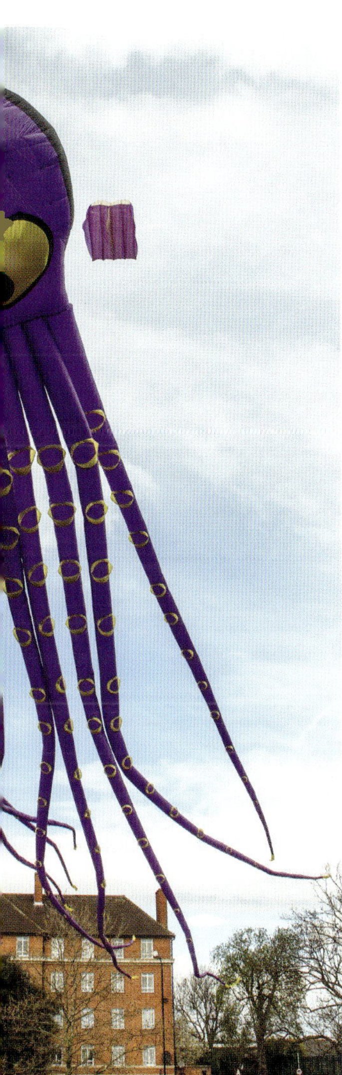

The very first kite event on Streatham Common was held in 1998. It was founded by Roy Reed and Bob Colover. Since that time, the annual event has grown in size to become a crowded and spectacular attraction. Roy Reed who was on the organising committee for the first thirteen years, has documented the event every year (see streathamkiteday.org.uk). The purple octopus was shot in 2008, the green kite on the previous page in 2010 and the photograph on the left dates from 2014. © *Roy Reed.*

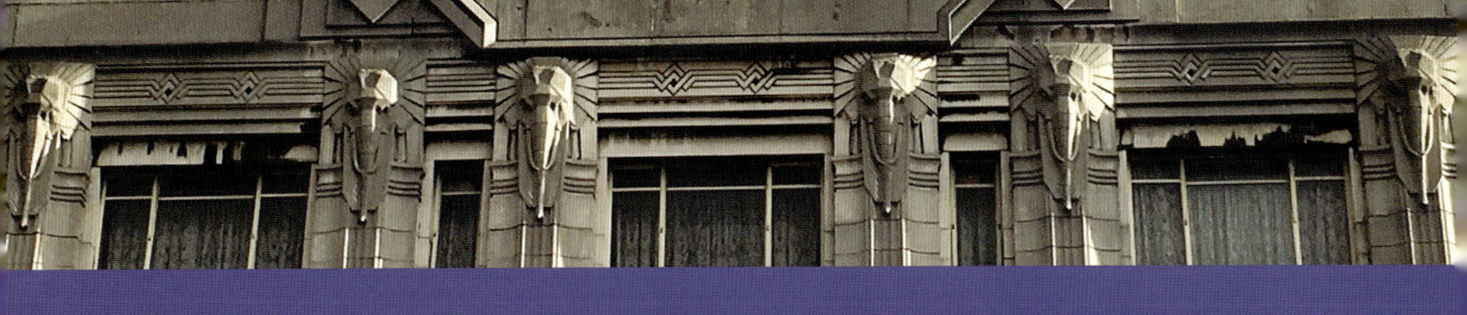

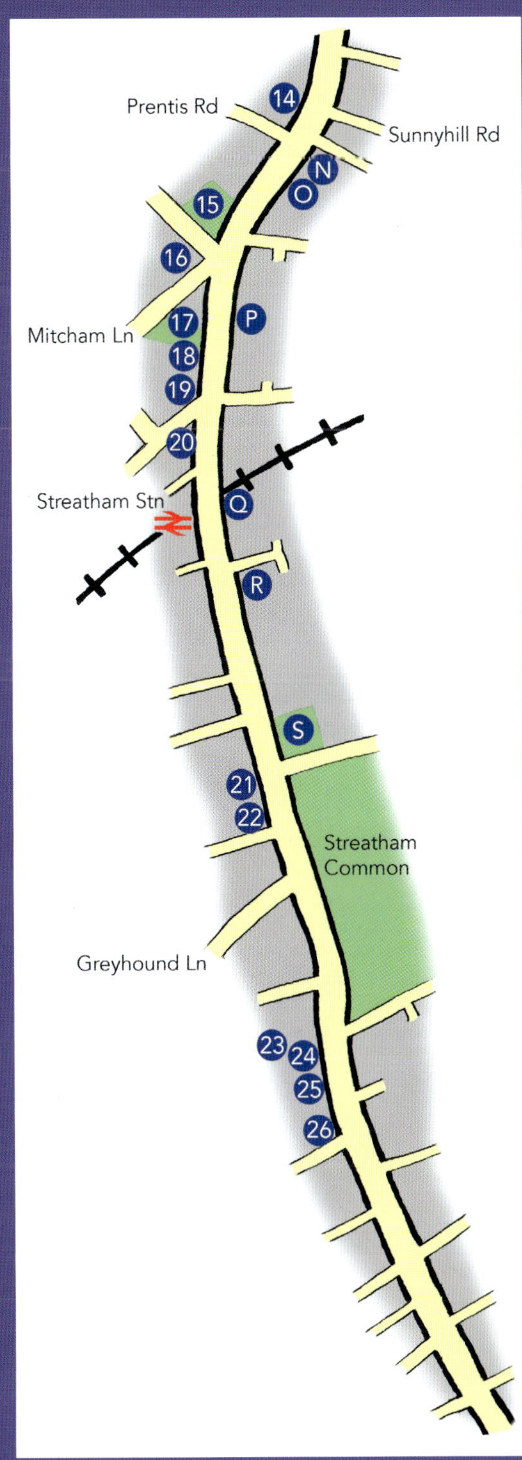
Prentis Rd
14
Sunnyhill Rd
N
O
15
16
P
Mitcham Ln
17
18
19
20
Streatham Stn
Q
R
S
21
22
Streatham Common
Greyhound Ln
23
24
25
26

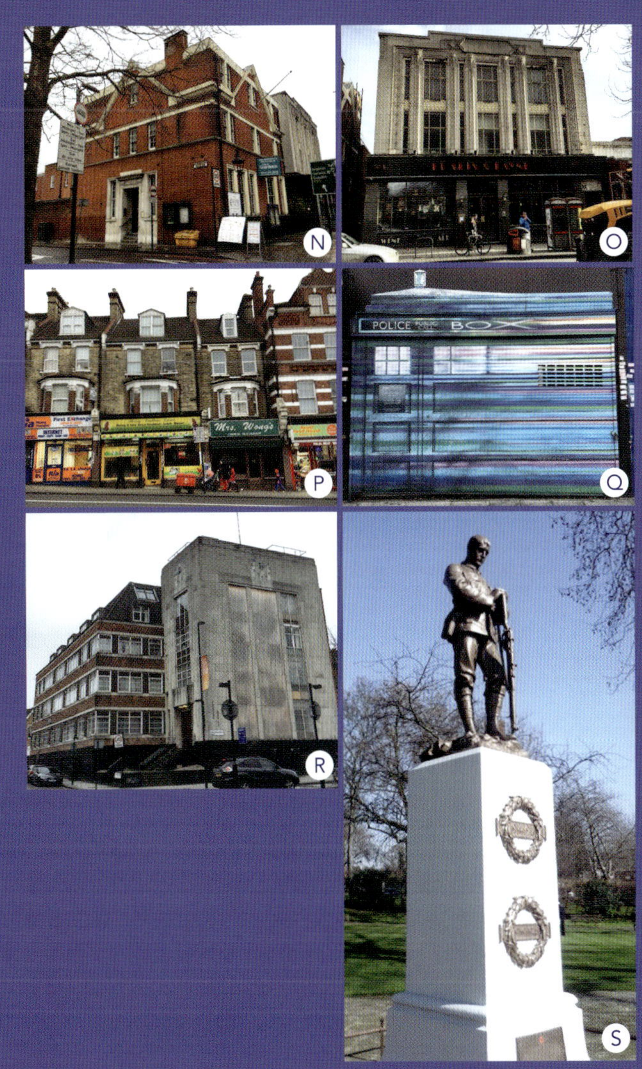
N
O
P
Mrs. Wongs
POLICE BOX
Q
R
S

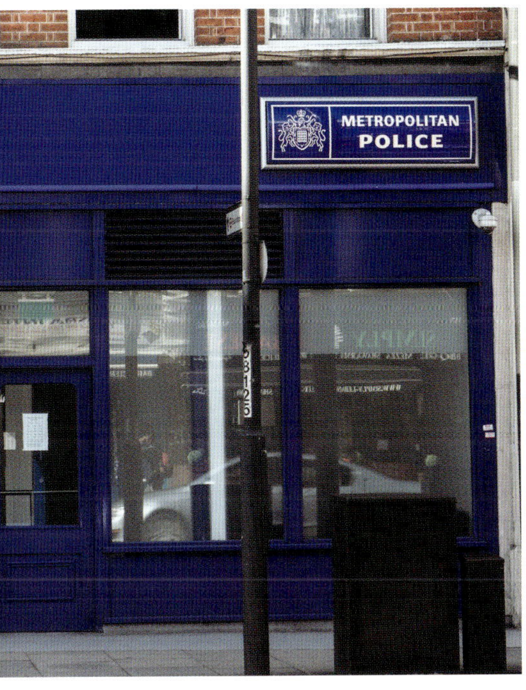

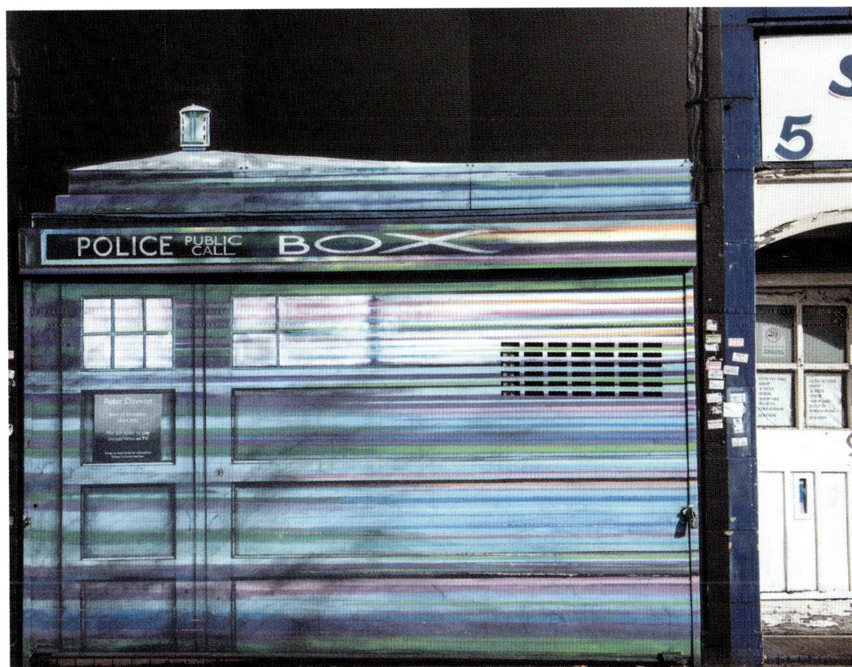

We could not resist the irony of Emma Harrison's mural of a blue police box sited a little further south, at 5 Bridge Parade, opposite Streatham Station: the final stage in the downsizing theme? It is one of Beep Studio's murals (see p. 38), originally designed (in 2014) for hoardings outside the 1912 police station: an allusion to BBC cult series *Doctor Who* when the Doctor was played by Peter Davison, born in Streatham on 15 April 1951 – the fifth actor to play Dr Who.

said, "I did not do it"—he had marks of fresh blood on his shoulders where he had placed his hands.' The full account may be read online in the Records of the Old Bailey. But by that date Streatham had had a proper police station for about three years, on the site of the Shrubbery Road building. No doubt the violent John Lee would have been taken there in the first instance.

After the establishment of the 'Bow Street Runners' in London in 1747, the nineteenth century seemed a time of new beginnings – the Metropolitan Police force was founded in 1829, followed by regular expansion. By comparison, the early decades of the twenty-first century when budgetary concerns are looming large, have led to a 'rationalisation' of resources and a steady decline in buildings and manpower.

Tate Library

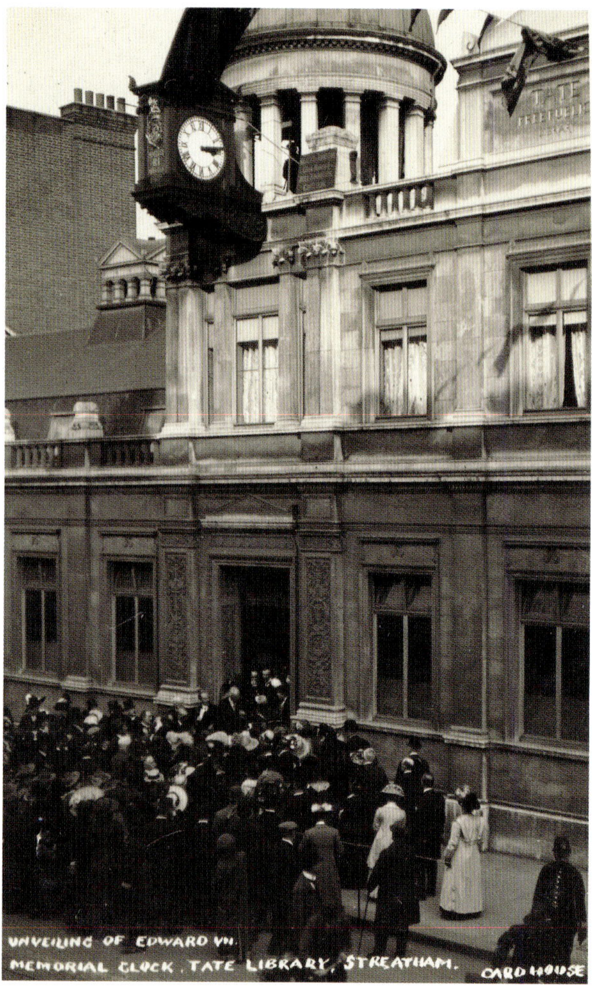

Postcard: the unveiling of the memorial clock to King Edward VII (1841–1910) at Tate Library on 5 October 1912. The clock cost £440 and was made by Gillett & Johnston of Croydon who were responsible for building the freestanding 'Little Ben' in Brockwell Park. The Streatham organising committee had been keen on a clock tower but the funds raised were insufficient. *© John W Brown, Local History Publications.*

Ken Severn's account of the history of Lambeth libraries is very detailed but one thing is clear: these institutions, now widely regarded as essential houses of culture despite council closures, were difficult to introduce. They were originally created for the working classes, their rules enshrined in several Acts of Parliament (1850, 1855 and 1892), the last two enabling boroughs or parishes to levy money to set up and maintain libraries. But a journalist eloquently summed up the effect of the Acts in the early years:

> The promoters seem as determined to thrust their schemes down the popular throat as the popular throat seems determined to reject them.

The historian of the Public Library movement, Thomas Greenwood, rejoiced at the thought that his native city, Manchester, was the first to adopt the Act in 1852 but he expressed dismay about London: 'the capital was apparently content to be left far behind', over thirty years behind for South London! Greenwood, emphasising the point, added: 'Up to the end of 1886 only two parishes within the metropolitan area had adopted the Acts': the parish of St Margaret and St John, Westminster in 1856 and Wandsworth in 1883.

It was in fact the philanthropists who ensured the birth and spread of libraries, and the celebrations for Queen Victoria's Jubilee Year in 1887 also galvanised patriotic energies and at last the library movement gathered momentum. Greenwood would later praise 'the noble role of Lambeth' where a cluster of libraries were ready by the late 1880s: the first library to open was West Norwood Library in 1888, then Durning and South Lambeth Libraries followed, all with philanthropist backing.

> The struggle to secure the adoption of the Acts was exceedingly arduous, and nothing but the indomitable energy and determination of the promoters was to carry the question through … The promoters, however, were brave men'.

Streatham at that time was not in the borough of Lambeth (see p. 26). But its library and adjoining hall were ready next, opening in 1891, once again the outcome of a philanthropic gesture, that of Henry Tate (see p. 130) who along with Andrew Carnegie (1835–1919) and John Passmore Edwards (1823–1911) invigorated the library movement in Britain in decisive ways.

The architect of all four libraries (Norwood, Durning, South Lambeth and Streatham) was 'the' library architect par excellence: Sidney R J Smith (1858–1913). He was also responsible for Brixton and Balham Libraries. And he was Henry Tate's favourite architect: he redesigned Park Hill House for him (see p. 122) and also masterminded the Tate Gallery (p. 126). He seemed to have attracted critical comments, at times dragging down Henry Tate with him: 'one rather less worthy act of (Henry) Tate was his insistence that a Mr Sidney Smith be employed for the Streatham and Lambeth Central Libraries when there are far better architects available'. This seems rather unfair and perhaps we should give Ken Severn the last word:

> One interesting and rather melancholy fact is that it is the newer Lambeth libraries, rather than these old, mostly Victorian buildings, which have gone to the wall. The Streatham Vale (1938), the Clapham Park (1854), the Jeffreys (1960), the St Martin's (1962), and the South Island Place (1962) libraries have all gone. There is a lesson here somewhere'.

Memento Mori

Demolition is too often presented as the first resort rather than the last. Let's pause briefly to consider some of Streatham's losses – deliberate or otherwise:

- A row of mature elms along the High Road at Streatham Green were cut down in 1904 to widen the road: they were 300 years old.
- The old sixteenth-century Bedford House, was purchased by George Pratt, transformed into Pratt's repository (of furniture and other goods), and burnt down on 1 August 1936 (the year of the Crystal Palace fire).
- Streatham Park, the home of the Thrale family and one of Dr Johnson's adopted homes was demolished in 1863. Colson Way housing estate was built on the site, with a Streatham Society plaque on the exact site of the house's famous library (see p. 111).
- The early Empire cinema which opened in 1910 was a Second World War casualty.
- The Gaumont Palace Cinema (1932) became the Streatham Bowl but the building was lost to the London Square Development at Streatham Hill. Campaigning by the Streatham Society saved the façade which was incorporated into the new development scheduled to open in phases, starting in July 2017.
- Pratt's Department Store – lots of nooks and crannies, with the charm of a Victorian time capsule (1867) but there is none whatsoever in the buildings which replaced it: Lidl and Argos (1996). Pratt's was demolished in 1995.
- The Locarno Dance Hall, 1929: all seem to agree that the building was unremarkable (see p. 73) but it was one of the large halls which made Streatham famous, all are disappearing one by one.
- The ice rink, opened in 1931, designed by cinema specialist Robert Cromie was demolished in 2011. Some will miss the elongated and stylish Art Deco exterior.
- Streatham Town Hall, built in 1887, represented solid Victorian worthiness: demolished in 1988 and replaced by a housing block.
- Streatham Baths, 1928: 'one of six historic baths to have been lost in the capital since 2000', writes sport historian Simon Inglis.
- The hall of the United Reform Church (former Sunday School building) was a victim of the Streatham Hub and demolished in 2008.

3. Work

(paired with 'Studio' on p. 84)

On 5 December 2016, photographer Torla Evans and I spent most of the day in the studio of Jiro Osuga, photographing some of his work and capturing his studio from different angles, with and without the artist, talking and partaking in a rustic Korean meal which his painter friend Sinn prepared. The outcome was some wonderful photographs, including this book's cover and the image opposite: they capture the memories of that day, a way of life, a way of working and thinking, and they are now a permanent record for others to enjoy.

By contrast, there is precious little bearing witness to the peasants, labourers and servants who were Streatham's first workers. Medievalist Graham Gower has patiently reconstructed aspects of their lives in his informative *Streatham – Origins and Early History*.

> We know what food they were growing and selling on the open markets of London or Croydon. Richard Haywood grew peas and vetches, Robert Crafte toiled on his three acres of oats, one acre of wheat and one of beans. Richard Bradwater was proud of his herd of sixty beasts. Others tended their fields and strips and worked the normal rotation of ploughing, sowing and reaping, along with keeping their livestock and pursuing other profitable activities.

Industry

Industry is recorded from the sixteenth century onwards: brick and tile making as well as gravel digging. Tile making in particular was sufficiently developed to cope with an order of 1000 tiles for the roofing of the Old Mint in Southwark (1526) and 84,000 tiles for the building of Nonsuch Palace near Cheam in the 1530s. For the latter, Streatham's two major sites joined forces: the Tile House in the High Road (50,000) and Tile Kiln Farm (34,000). Gravel digging was responsible for one of Tooting Common's most romantic features: the pond, remodelled in 1895 into an ornamental lake. Graham Gower points out that until the nineteenth century Tooting Graveney Common was peppered with ponds 'created from centuries of gravel digging'.

Employment on a truly industrial scale also came to rural Streatham in later Georgian times when the Wilson family built a 'silk factory' on the site they had owned since 1810 – on the west side of the High Road opposite Streatham Common. The mill was ready in 1820, when rates were paid by Stephen Wilson. Local historian Brian Bloice established that the Wilson family, originally from Derbyshire, had been silk weavers for two generations. He also identified at least five apprentices and twenty one workers at the mill between 1825 and 1831, thirteen of them described as silk weavers and the workforce lived locally.

Stephen Wilson had been apprenticed to a silk weaver based in Old Jewry (City of London), whose daughter he married, consolidating the family's connections with this trade. Brian Bloice also demonstrated that Wilson was probably responsible for introducing the Jacquard loom into this country – a French invention which revolutionised the weaving industry. Bloice concluded:

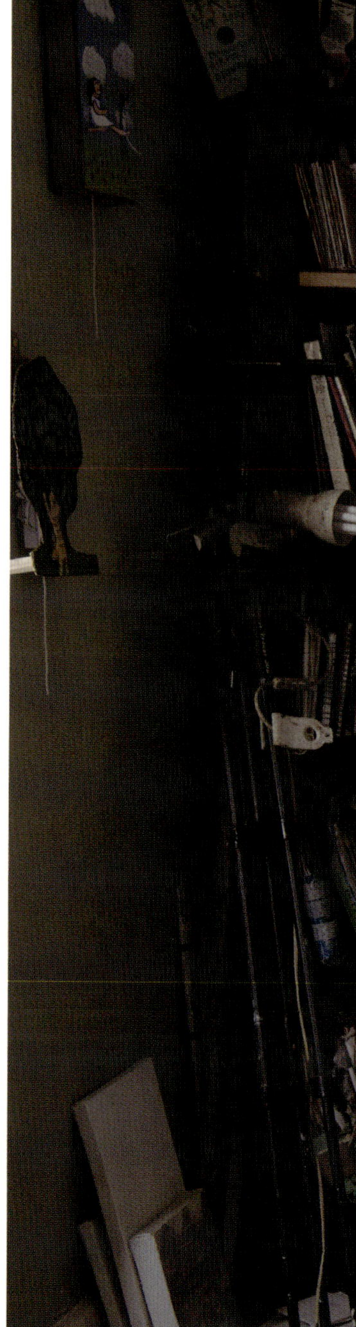

Jiro Osuga photographed in his Streatham studio in December 2016.

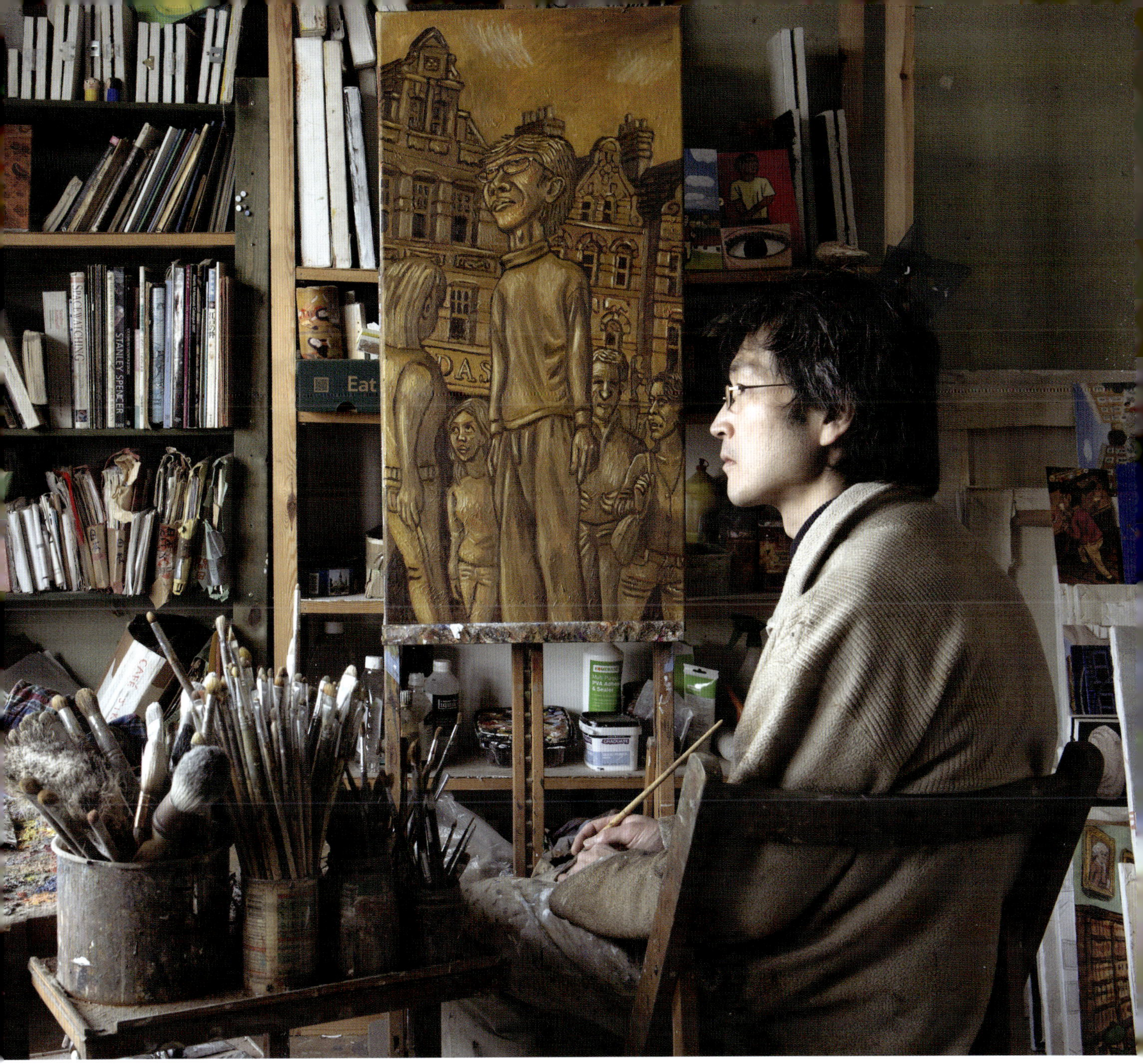

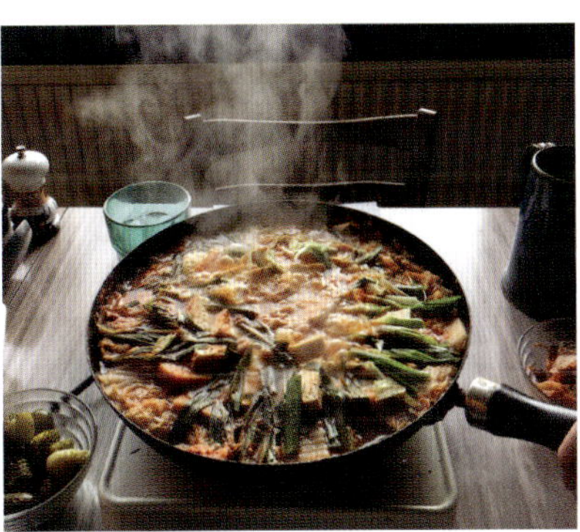

> Streatham is the site of the first attempt to industrialise the silk weaving industry of Great Britain and … the site where the innovative Jacquard loom was first used successfully'

However, this brave experiment was ultimately not successful and after eighteen years the factory was leased to Thomas Forster who adapted it to produce India Rubber – or the art of waterproofing fabric (1838). A second factory was built in 1847 and by 1851 Forster was employing forty people, though the land itself was still in the hands of Stephen Wilson – until 1860 when it was acquired by Peter Brussey Cow I, son of John, boat builder at Woolwich Dockyard. Forster managed the factory for the new owners and it continued to expand. By 1881 the work force stood at 175.

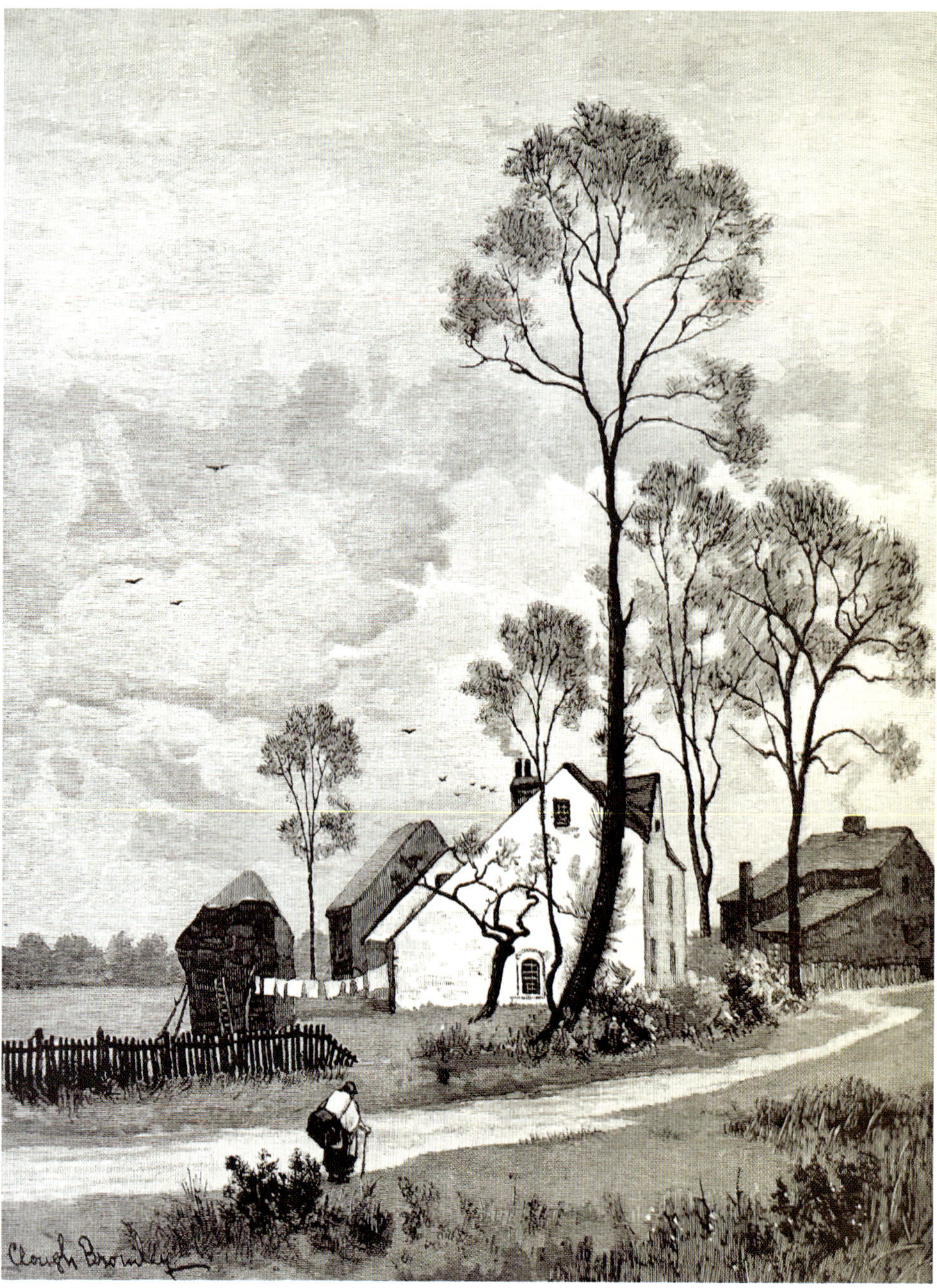

Hyde Farm in Bleak Hall Lane sat on the edge of Tooting Bec Common (named on the Bedford Estate map of 1729, see p. XX). It started in the seventeenth century when the land was in the hands of Emmanuel College in Cambridge. It survived long enough to be depicted by the illustrator Clough Bromley in *The Illustrated Magazine* in 1885 (November, Part 2 of an article on 'London Commons'). It was a pig farm in the 1880s.

Eventually, the Streatham mill ceased to be a profitable concern in the 1980s and the company decided to relocate in 1986. This historic mill was very nearly demolished when Sainsbury's purchased the site in 1987 but the efforts of English Heritage and the Streatham Society saved the remarkable structure for later generations as a service block for the new superstore.

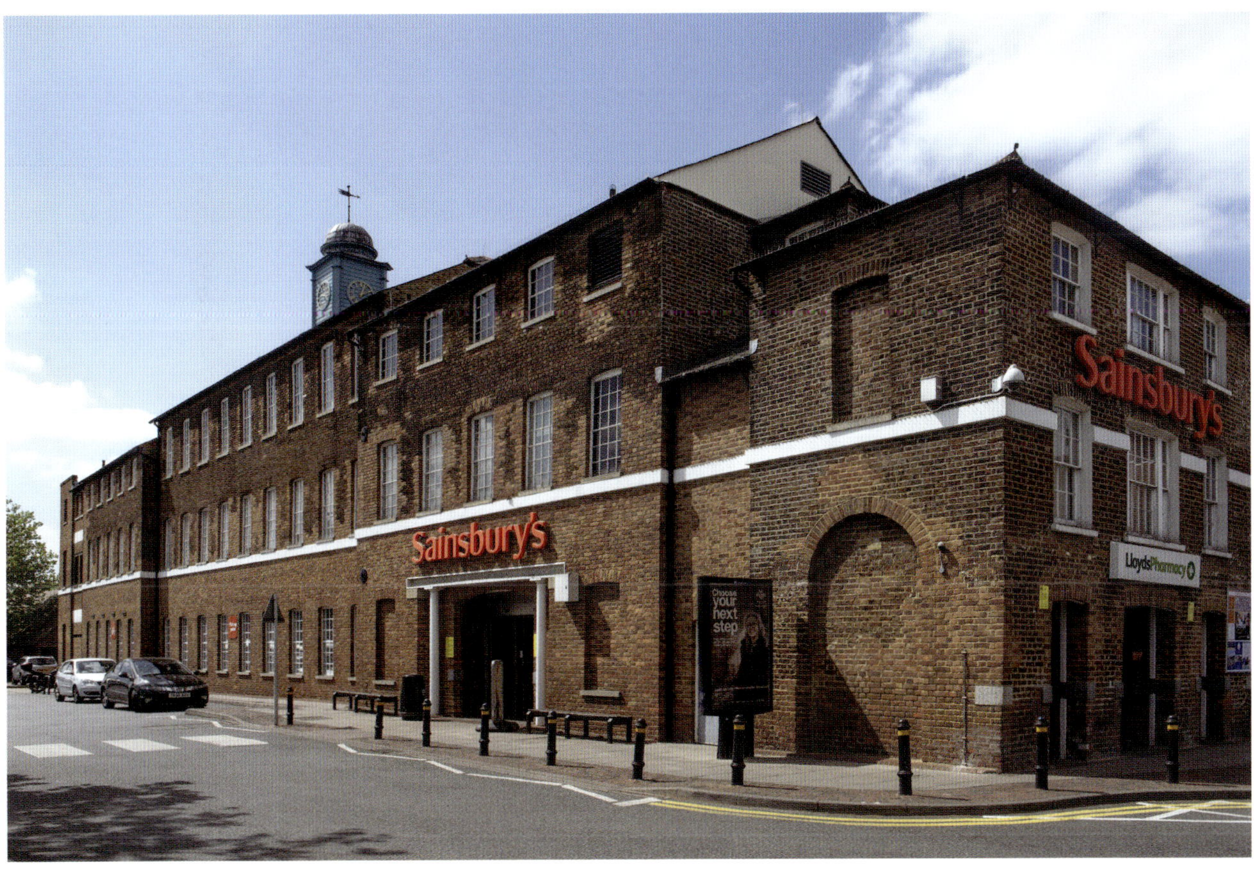

Streatham's original Silk Mill, later a manufacture of India Rubber, was saved from demolition by the Streatham Society joining forces with the Greater London Industrial Archaeology Society (GLIAS) and English Heritage. Its local champion, Brian Bloice said: 'we have also an extremely rare building of its type, in a unique location, representing the first and only silk factory in the London area'.

Service industries

The diagram on p. 55 shows clearly that the dominant source of employment in the High Road now is what we call 'service industries'; defined as 'hairdressers, cafés, restaurants, takeaways, tattoo parlours, tanning salons and nail bars' (full quote on p. 55).

There are some interesting testimonies of the nature of the new service industry as it emerged between the wars, in Michael and Janet Fitzgerald's book *The Making of Modern Streatham*. Margaret Hodge's account of life as a film musician accompanying silent films first at Streatham's Golden Domes then at the Empire is really interesting: it was in the late 1920s, she was well paid but worked very long hours. But perhaps the most famous example of 'services' rendered must be those so cleverly marketed by the notorious Cynthia Payne (1932–2015): her brothels in Edencourt Road and at 32 Ambleside Avenue catered for an older but keen clientele. Known as 'Madame Cyn' she was finally arrested in 1978 during a police raid when they 'found 53 men huddled in the hall. Most were queuing on the stairs leading up to the bedrooms, and were clutching vouchers to be redeemed for sex; some appeared to have come straight from the office. Of the 13 women on the premises, some were completely naked' (*The Telegraph* Obituary of 16 November 2015). This entrepreneurial woman so captivated society for a while that her life inspired the film *Personal Services* by Terry Jones (1987, with Julie Walters). What better way to commemorate the 'service industries'?

4. Shopping then

(paired with 'Corner Shop' on pp. 86–89)

The owner or employee of the corner shop opposite, looking charming but territorial, reminds us of Charles Dickens' description in *A Tale of two Cities* (1859): 'The wine-shop was a corner shop, better than most others in its appearance and degree, and the master of the wine-shop had stood outside it, in a yellow waistcoat and green breeches …'. This great chronicler of life in the nineteenth century knew the significance of corner shops – their commandeering presence on two rather than one street.

Shopping parades

Historic England recently published a most useful summary of purpose-built shopping parades (see bibliography). In this brief nationwide survey Streatham is mentioned no less than five times. The author, Kathryn Morrison, starts by pointing out that parades of shops existed long before they were named parades, going back to the Middle Ages. 'Terraces' of shops with accommodation above for the traders was the norm by mid-Victorian London – and 230 Streatham High Road (next to The White Lion pub) is a rare survival, likely to have been part of a terrace, and dating from the early years of the nineteenth century as does its shop front. It is the only building to have survived from the old Streatham Village, local historian Graham Gower tells us. We could also mention the purpose-built 'Commerce Place' in Dulwich Village (1860s), though it was not yet called a 'parade'. The parade appears more frequently in the 1870s and 1880s and in Streatham we could cite Queens Parade (1882–1900), on the east side of the High Road close to the former Bedford Park Hotel, North Parade (1888) on the west side, opposite the Library and Bank Parade (1890) opposite Streatham Common.

At first, shops with accommodation above were conceived as one unit and leased/sold together but by the time of the First World War the ground floor was a separate and self-contained unit which necessitated separate entrances for shops and flats above. From the late nineteenth century the height of buildings grew (see Queens Parade on p. 30) and mansion flats developed with shops on the ground floor. Kathryn Morrison describes the gradual integration of the two with shared entrances on the main façade: she picks Stonehills Mansions near Streatham Hill Station (see p. 32 (B)) as a particularly good example. Rear access which meant a lower rental was adopted at 73A–89 Streatham High Road (see p. 33 (M)).

The inter-war period is often considered the 'heyday of the shopping parade'. We have come to expect Art Deco to be *moderne* but the range of styles adopted in the 1920s and 30s was truly eclectic: with popular neo-Georgian, but also neo-classicism (for instance De Montfort Parade close to The Horse and Groom pub), 'stockbroker Tudor', baronial style, Tudor or modern Gothic style (for instance Dorchester Parade in Leigham Court Road, or the first floor of No 250 close to Prentis Road). In Streatham, however, there is clearly an abundance of *moderne* Art Deco buildings and this is illustrated in 'Art Deco Streatham' on pp. 32–37. Morrison homes in on Leigham Hall Mansions and The High, as examples of 'great scale, with the shops effectively forming the base to monumental blocks of flats'.

Kathryn Morrison points out that in the interwar period, a parade 'should include a

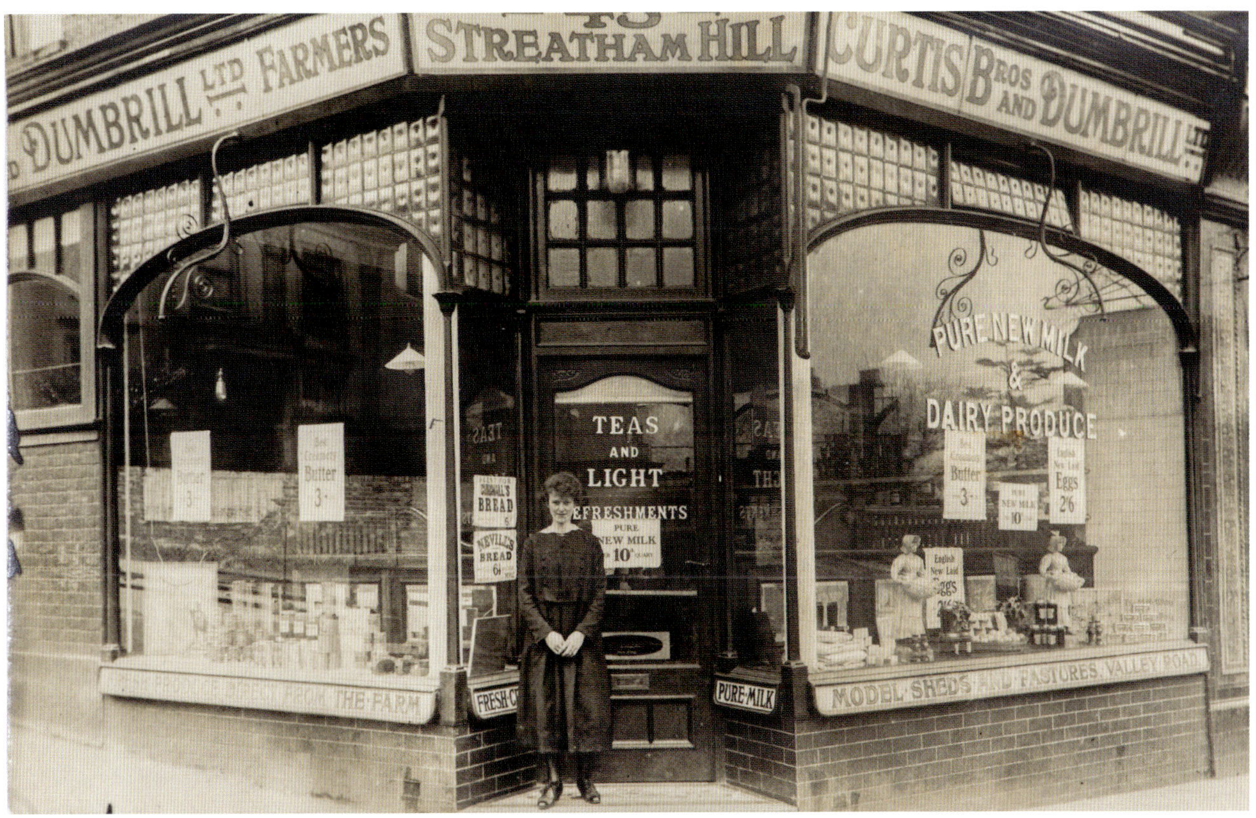

Curtis Bros and Dumbrill Ltd at 45 Streatham Hill, postcard, c.1916. Rather cunningly, Thomas Curtis acquired the (second) site of the Streatham Wells, off Valley Road in 1875. There he set up a dairy farm, marketing milk and water from a single site. His sons took over the business (1883) and built a model dairy in Valley Road in 1910. It merged with Dumbrill's dairy in 1916, then with the United Dairies. At that time Curtis had only one shop on the High Road (at No 69). Between 1916 and 1920 Curtis and Dumbrill had taken over an additional six premises on the future A23, including this one. *Collection of the author.*

butcher, baker, grocer, greengrocer, dairyman, newsagent/confectioner and dispensing chemist'. This is confirmed by inspecting Kelly's Directory for 1934. The most popular trades are confectionary/newsagents/tobacconists (47), grocers (26), butchers (21), greengrocers (19), bakers (15), chemists, (13), dairy (8). But to that list we should also add clothes shops (27), hairdressers (23), shoes (17), cleaners (including dyers 17), tailors (13), and café/tea rooms (11) – a trade distribution which brings us closer to the diagram for our own times on p. 55.

The rise of the Supermarket

There is one other notable shopping development which may be identified in the High Road: the gradual ascent of the national multiple retailers – Sainsbury's (1869), Woolworths (1909 in England) and Tesco (1919) who started building their own parades. In the case of Sainsbury's, Historic England believes that one of its earliest developments may have been in Streatham Hill at the turreted Arborfield House, beside the station: 'a block of four shops, with upper floor accommodation arranged around light wells'. Sainsbury's operated through their development company – Cheyne Investments and the shop at No 176 was none other than J. Sainsbury Ltd (in 1934). Some eighty years later, in November 2013, the ambitious 'Hub' development near Streatham Station delivered a massive Tesco supermarket, alongside housing and a new leisure centre with an ice rink. The very first planning application had been submitted in 2001, it was later withdrawn – the project took twelve years to complete.

Special shops

But there is one shop in Streatham which many remember with nostalgia: Pratt's Department Store. It closed in 1990 after uninterrupted trading of 125 years. From modest beginnings as a small draper's shop in Bedford Row opposite Streatham Green, George Pratt built Eldon House in 1867 from where his expanded business thrived. He then divided his estate between his three sons in 1885 which led to his department store being purchased by the John Lewis partnership. The building was demolished in 1995 and the utilitarian Lidl built on the vacant site.

One remarkable shop is Streatham's best kept secret: No 177 on the High Road is Grade II listed and we hope that this will keep its lovely interior decoration safe. It was formerly one of David Greig's grocers' shops – the first shop opened in Brixton in 1870 and its success led to a proliferation of shops which later turned into supermarkets. The early rivalry between Sainsbury's and Greig's was notorious. By the 1960s Greig's operation was thriving but, crippled by death duties at the end of that decade, the popular chain soon disappeared into supermarket mergers – bought by Key Markets, then Gateway, rebranded Somerfield, taken over by Asda and then bought by the Co-Op group. The interior decoration of No 177 has been dated to around 1900.

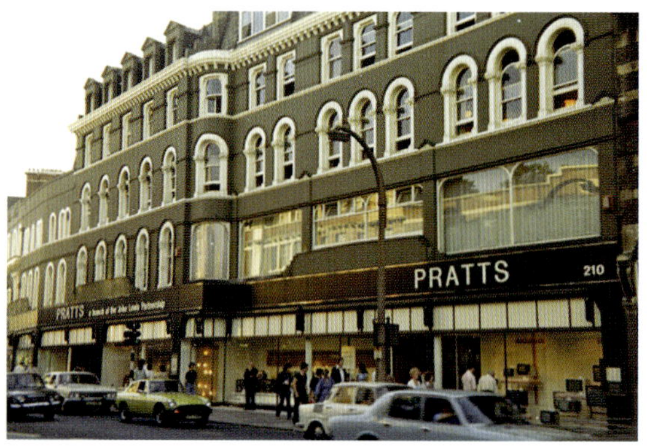

Above: This is Pratt's Department Store in Streatham High Road as many people still remember it. It was photographed in 1978. *© Brian Whittle. Photo: Wikimedia Commons.*

Below: The shops on the ground floor of the turreted Arborfield House (corner of Sternhold Avenue by Streatham Hill station) are likely to have been one of J. Sainsbury's shop parade developments. *© John W Brown, Local History Publications.*

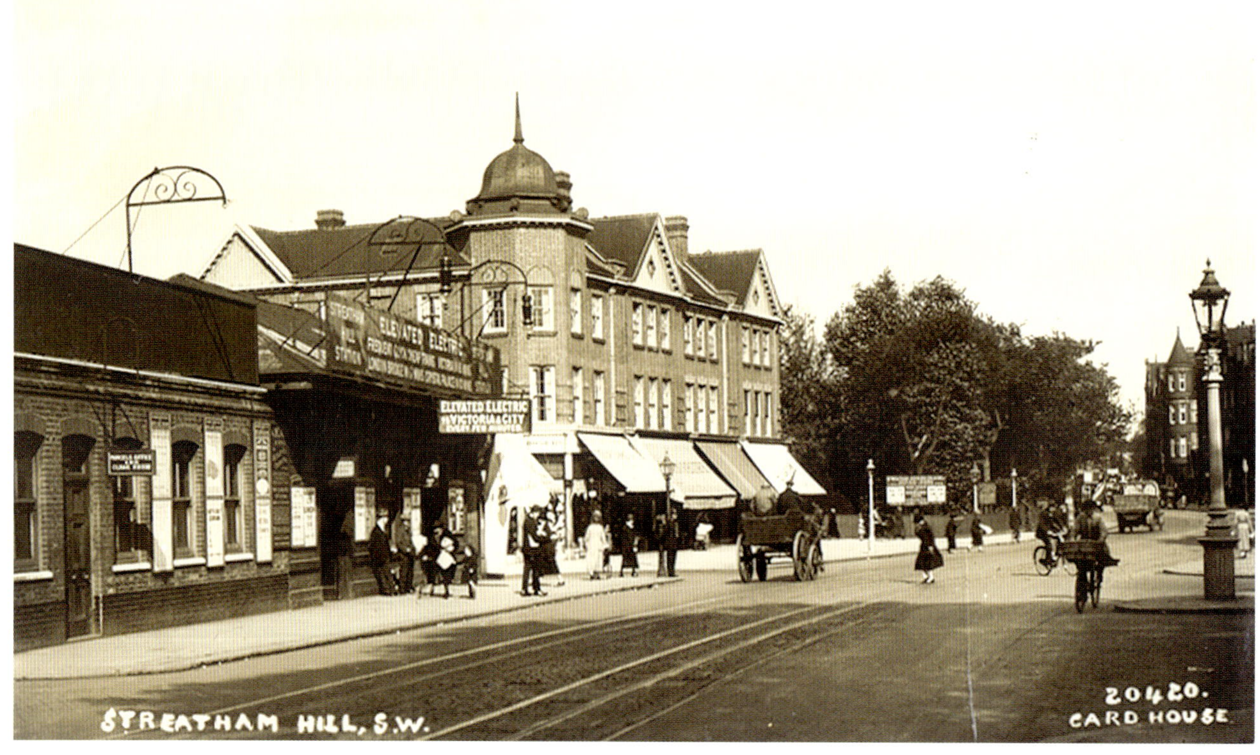

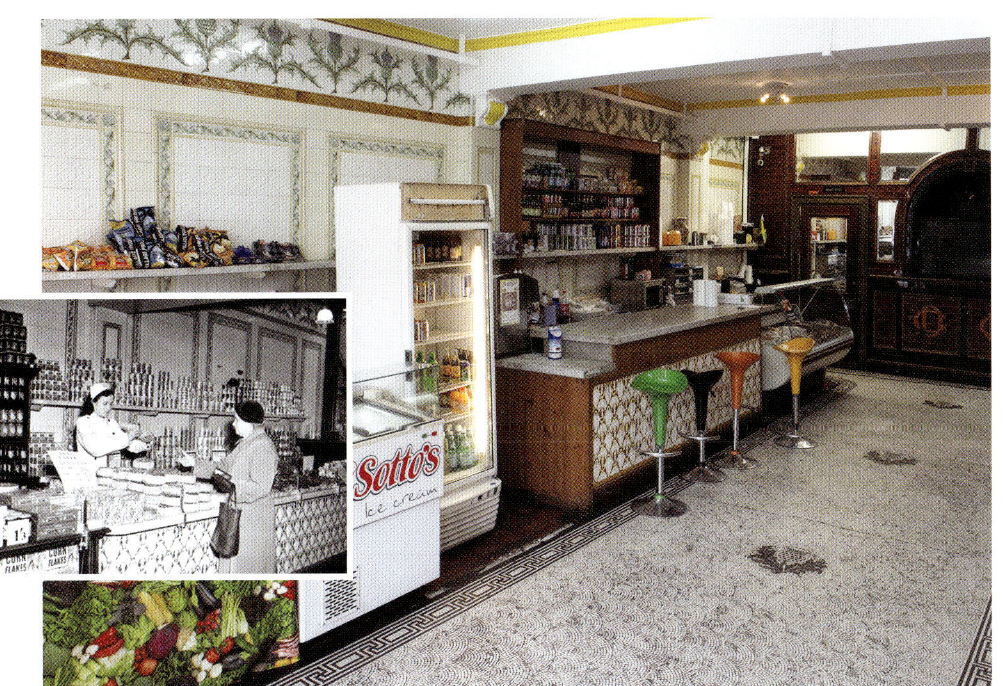

No 177 Streatham High Road, opposite Streatham Green, used to be David Greig, the grocery stores and Sainsbury's competitors. Graham Gower photographed the outside in 1971 (middle left) and the interior of a Greig shop found on the internet (source unknown) perhaps shows the interior of No 177. The other photographs show the shop as it is now.

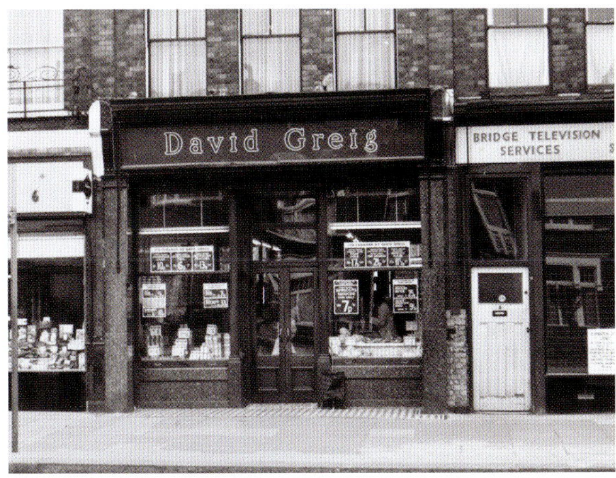

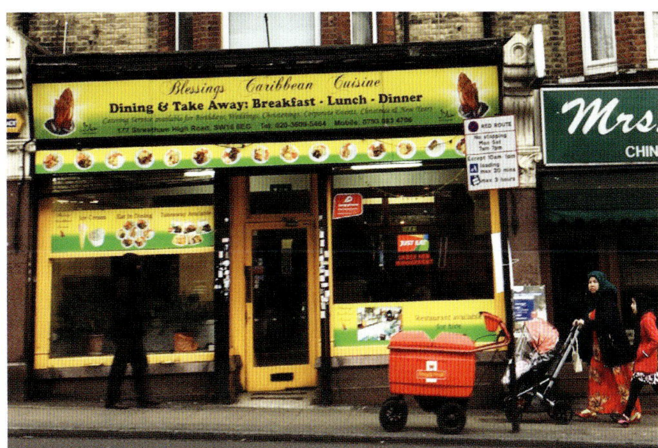

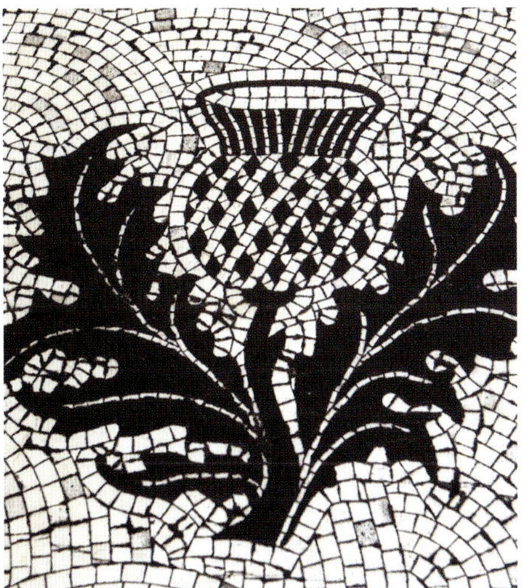

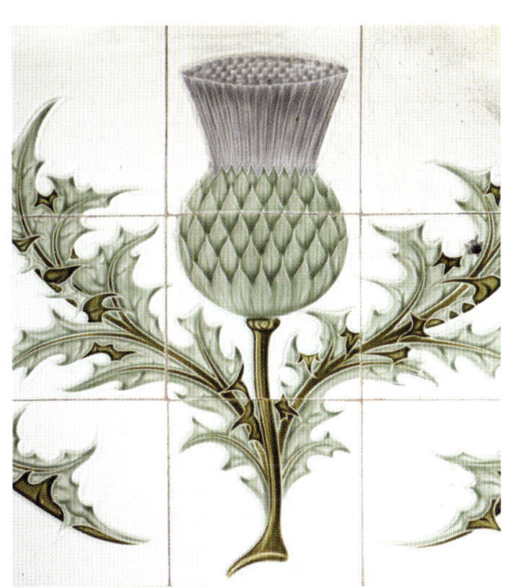

5. Shopping now

(paired with 'Own Brand' on p. 90)

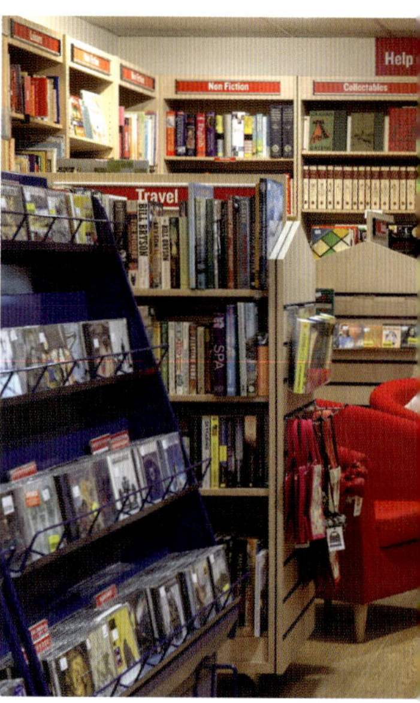

This author has systematically walked the length of the Streatham section of the A23 (Streatham Hill and High Road) – both sides – on numerous occasions and an attempt has been made to survey the shops along this axis (see below). It is an imprecise guide – first because it was compiled 'on the go' and only cross-referenced with Google; secondly, we are dealing with a moveable feast – when I started working on this book, the large Oxfam Furniture shop held a prominent place but a few months later it was gone and when I started the shops survey, Streatham Hill Theatre was a Bingo Hall and Beyrouth's a restaurant – both had closed by the time I completed the survey.

This brief survey has led to some interesting observations on the nature of shopping along Streatham's busiest axis; some useful insight about the distribution of shops on the east versus the west side of the High Road was gained in the process.

I counted **435** 'shops' – including those closed and empty – some of them sheltering more than one business. There are a greater number of shops on the west side of the A23: 239 against 196 on the east side.

Overall, the largest number of outlets are **restaurants and cafés** which number **56**. The number of cafés is roughly the same on both sides of the road (around fifteen per side) but the east side has the edge over the west side in terms of restaurants: 17 against 12.

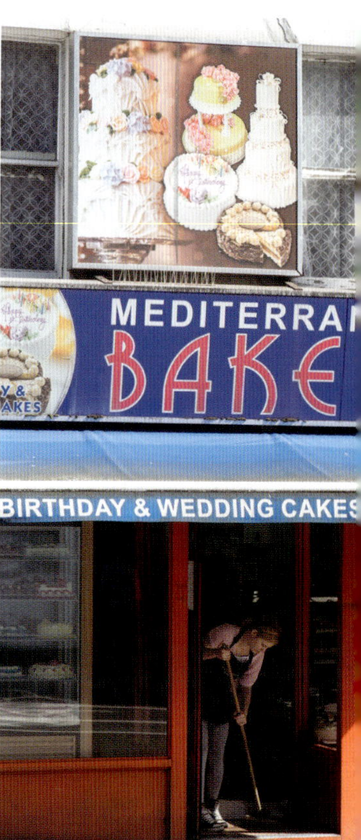

The next largest number of outlets cater for shoppers' physical appearance: **51** shops selling their services in **hairdressing** (including barbers), **beauty salon**, **nails** and **tanning**. The east side is a clear winner in this category with an extra 11 shops.

Food and drink is the next largest category, this time the west side wins by a small margin. Altogether there are **39** food outlets but we should bear in mind that this numerical approach does not differentiate between the massive Tesco near Streatham Station and Swarnya Mini Market or between Tariq Halal's specialised meat shop and the large Sainsbury's selling a vast range of products.

There are **25 takeaway** shops which include the usual suspects (Morley's, KFC, Chicken Cottage, Domino's, Subway, Pizza Gogo, Topps Pizza) as well as many other independent shops. Perhaps surprisingly there is no MacDonald's or Burger King in Streatham – the former to be found on the Brixton side of the South Circular Road and Burger King in Clapham.

The number of **estate agents** on the west side is almost double that on the east side, but altogether I counted **25**.

There are many more outlets dealing with **financial services** on the west side than on the east side – this is not simply banks (they are also more numerous on the west side) but also establishments such as pawnbrokers, accountants, insurance companies and money lenders. The figure of **22** is to be used with caution, as it only includes establishments with 'shop' premises.

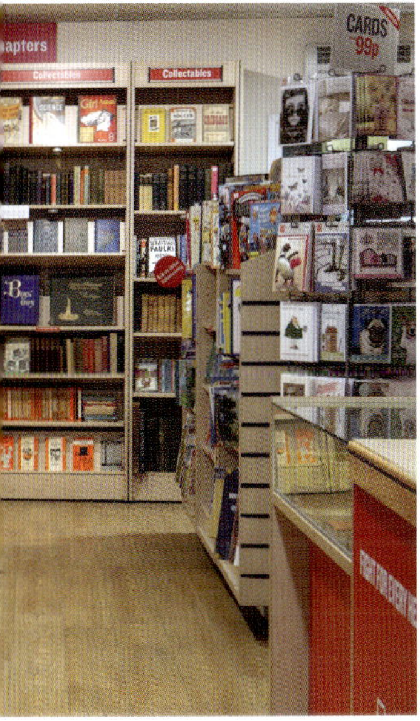

Above: This is the interior of 'Books and Music', one of the British Heart Foundation's charity shops on Streatham High Road (at No 94). Unusually for a second hand bookshop, it succeeds in looking attractive and being organised in a clear and rational manner.

Left: The Mediterranean Bakery was fairly recently acquired by a Turkish shopkeeper. It appears to cater for British taste at the front of the shop but their interesting exotic pastries – sweet and savoury – are at the back of the shop which is where you will find the advertised 'Mediterranean' connection.

Betting too is well catered for: **13** outlets in all, dominated by William Hill (4) and Ladbrokes (2).

Streatham is rich in **charity shops** and many are represented in the **14** shops I counted at the beginning of 2017: Cancer Research, Oxfam (despite its large furniture store closing in 2016), British Heart Foundation, Royal Trinity Hospice, Shelter and a few others.

Empty shops, a problem which has plagued Streatham for many years and one that the BID was anxious to alleviate when they were first set up in 2013 (see p. 38). This problem remains despite the general improvement of the High Road. I counted **25** in all (15 on the west side and 10 on the east side), including substantial premises such as the former Morrison's, soon to be tenanted, and Oxfam Furniture Shop).

THE SHOPPING SCENE ALONG THE A23 – from the South Circular to Hermitage Bridge

Clockwise from top right corner:

BODY: hairdressers, barbers, beauty salons, nails, chemists, clothes shops (including sport), launderettes, and funeral parlours **GOING OUT:** restaurants, betting shops, pubs, cafés **FOOD AND DRINK:** food and drink shops including supermarkets, off licence and takeaways **OTHER:** newsagents, solicitors, charity shops **HOME:** home goods, DIY, antiques, flowers **EMPTY** shops **MONEY:** banks, insurance, money lending **PHONES AND COMPUTERS** **TRANSPORT:** minicabs, garages, tyres, cycling shops

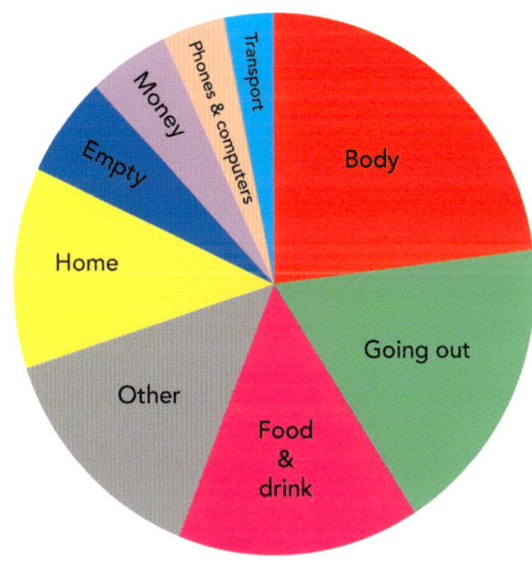

These results tally with Historic England's conclusion in their survey of Shopping Parades (see p. 49 and bibliography):

Over the last 30 years the content of local parades has swung away from the traditional retailing (greengrocers, butchers, small supermarkets, and so on) in favour of service industries (such as hairdressers, cafés, restaurants, takeaways, tattoo parlours, tanning salons and nail bars). By and large, parades are surviving this shift, but with such a high turnover of occupants they are increasingly unlikely to retain original shop interiors and frontages.

6. Pubs and Cafés

(paired with 'Drinker' on p. 92)

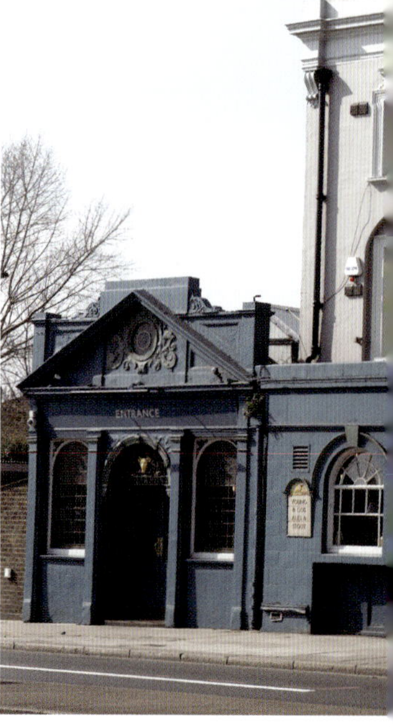

Local historian Graham Gower thinks the earliest surviving record of a named pub in Streatham is likely to be around 1690 for the Green Man Inn near Hermitage Bridge – close to the site of the Lahore Kebab House which we feature on p. 174. There is a noticeable paradox about this unlicensed Halal Pakistani restaurant turning up on a site with a heavy drinking past: the building they occupy used to be another pub – The Sussex. The building dates from 1937 and was briefly called Brass Farthing in the 1990s, before its old name was restored. The pub closed in 2002: the upstairs was converted into flats and the downstairs into a restaurant.

Despite the current infectious closures of pubs up and down the country, the Streatham section of the A23 has retained many of its drinking establishments – seven on the west side between the South Circular and Hermitage bridge: the Crown & Sceptre, the Horse & Groom, the Five Bells, the Standard, the White Lion, the Greyhound and the Bull. All the pubs on the east side are recent arrivals such as Brighton Way, Pratts & Payne and the Holland Tringham, named after a little known Streatham-based artist and illustrator (1861–1908). This Wetherspoon pub really ought to be called the 'William Dyce' as it is situated in front of the painter's last abode at 107/109 Streatham High Road.

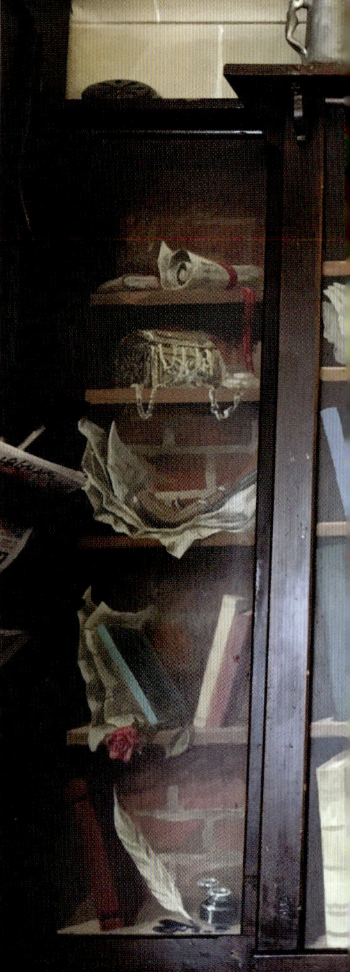

It might be useful to divide all pubs into two categories: those which predate the Victorian period (even if the present buildings are later reincarnations of their ancestors) and the rest. Those which are on sites connected to very ancient pubs are:

- The Greyhound (1920): its 'Tudoresque' style is perhaps in keeping with the existence of a pub on this site going back to the seventeenth or eighteenth centuries.
- The Horse & Groom (1865): this may look like a Victorian pub but its previous incarnation was a coaching inn named The Halfway House going back to 1717.
- The Crown & Sceptre (1822) at the junction with the South Circular Road: a late Georgian pub in its own right but with later alterations, and the second oldest pub in Streatham. It has been a Wetherspoon pub since 2002.
- The White Lion (1895) was preceded by earlier buildings going back to 1547 when the site is described as 'a tenement now called the Lyon with orchard and garden'. An old inn was rebuilt in 1812. The striking later building which has come down to us was designed by F Gough & Co.
- The Bull, formerly The Pied Bull: the origin of this pub goes back to the seventeenth century when it catered for the crowds drawn to the popular Streatham Wells (see p. 69) up on the Common. This is the oldest pub in Streatham, some of its fabric dating back to the eighteenth century.

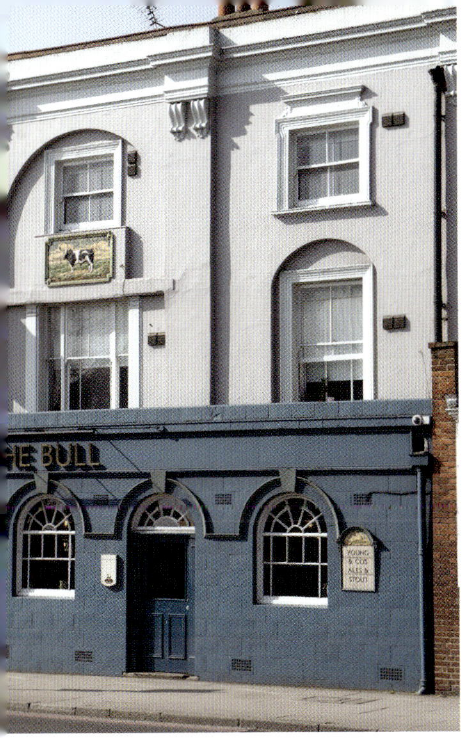

Left: The Bull, facing Streatham Common, is the oldest pub in Streatham.

Below and right:The Leigham Arms dates from 1865 and stands in a neighbourhood developed for people of modest means. Away from the busy High Road, it has the charm of a true 'local'. The pub has recently changed hands and its painted decoration is likely to disappear. *Photographed by the author in 2016.*

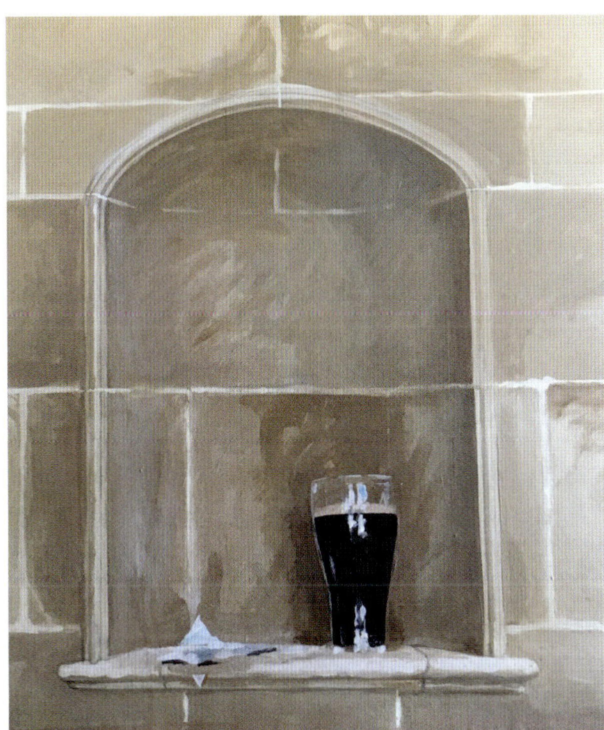

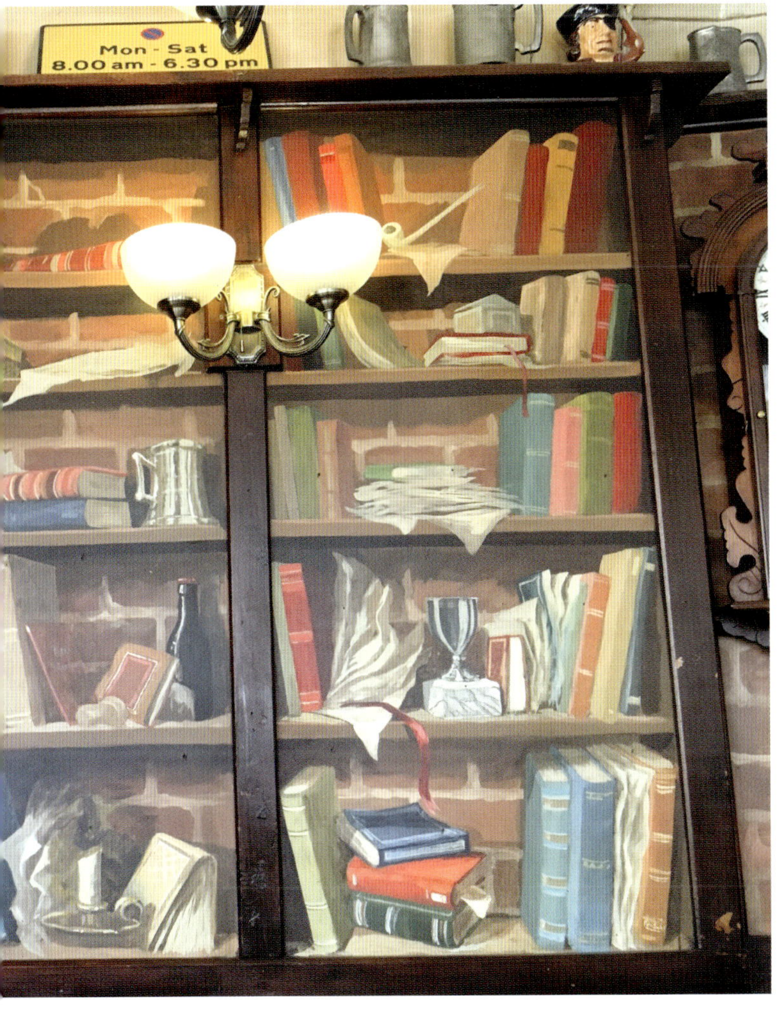

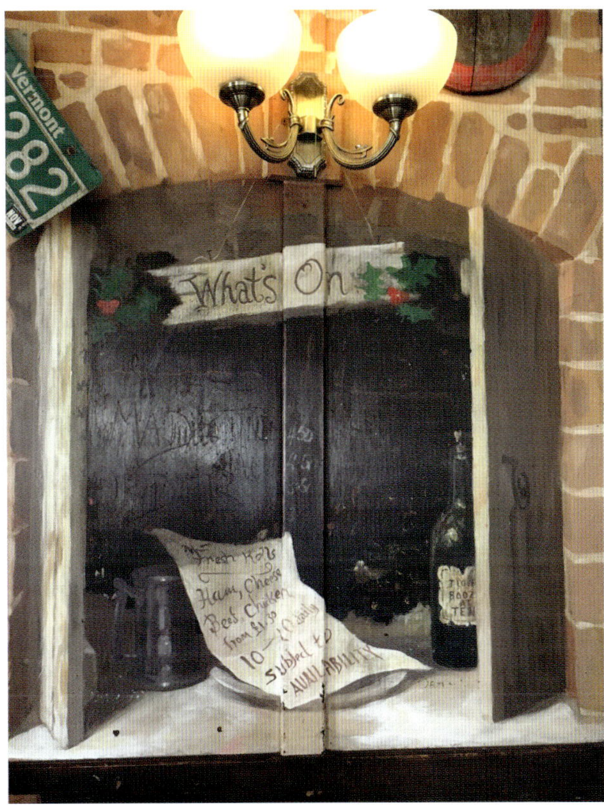

7. Suburban Street

(paired with 'Hill' on p. 95)

In his 'Hill' painting Jiro looks on Streatham as a residential suburb, away from the busy High Road: this is quiet and picturesque Streatham. The ground rises east of the High Road to reach Crown Point in Norwood, yielding some breathtaking panoramic views in the process. One of the best viewpoints for observing this phenomenon from the High Road is at the junction with Gleneldon Road (see frontispiece). The nearby Gleneldon Mews, described in 1902 as an 'evil-smelling, narrow passage in a wretched condition' with people protesting 'against the farm-yard reminiscences that reached them when they left their windows open' – those Gleneldon Mews are now regarded as quite an extraordinary time capsule.

But perhaps the best way to try and understand the transformation of a piece of open landscape into suburban cityscape is to feature one well documented case study. Local historian Marion Gower has charted in graphic and fascinating detail such a transformation in her book *Guildersfield – The History of a Streatham Country House*: she discusses the estate of John Crosse Crooke, Henry Bates and Thomas Ellison (see p. 25). Part of this rural estate will gradually be turned into a single wealthy residence with generous grounds, before it is finally overrun by rows of houses and shops. It is a Streatham case study but also a piece of generic research which could stand for many a London suburb.

The site, on the west side of Streatham High Road, is just south of The Bull pub. The farm which stood there once and the pub are documented from the early eighteenth century. Around 1830 and in the words of Marion Gower, a 'desirable, modern residence', was built which would become Springfield Lodge. At that time the property is 'consolidated', excluding the pub.

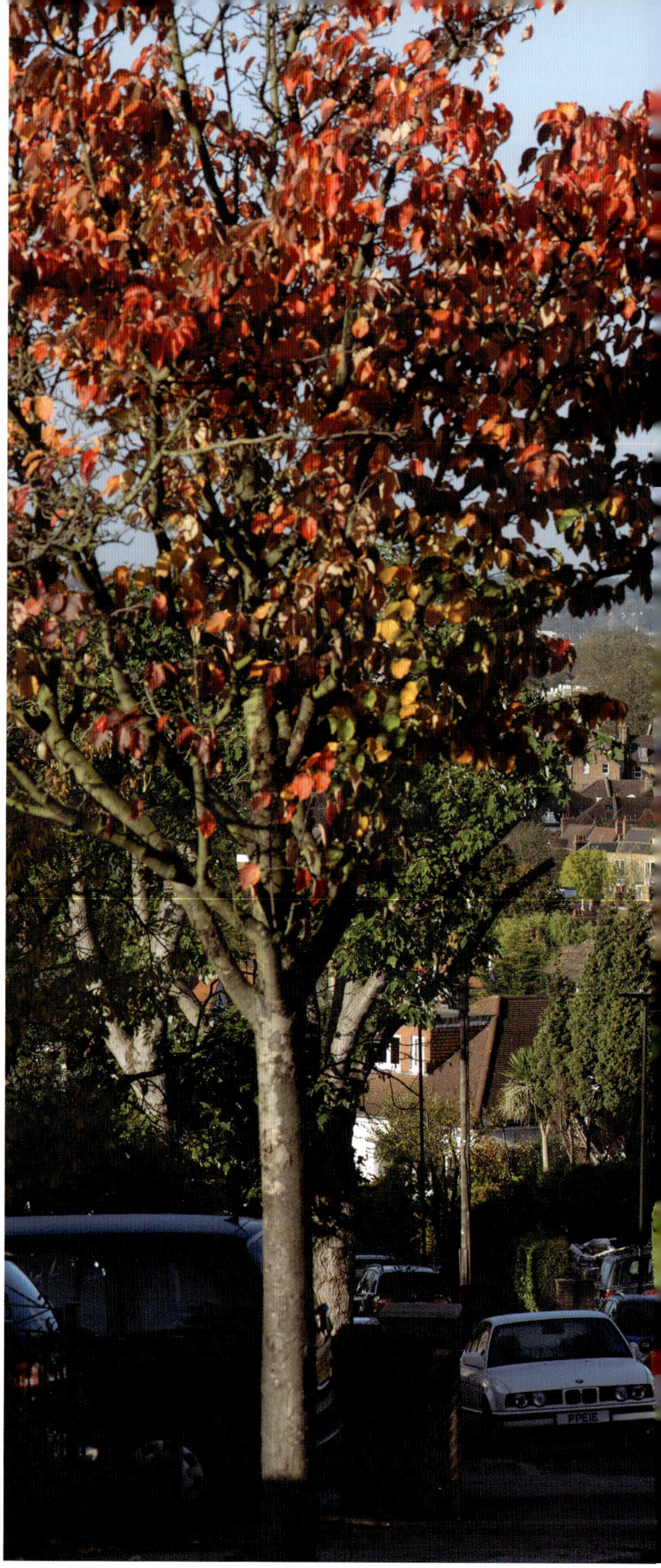

Perched at the top of Hill House Road, our photographer Torla Evans has captured the view looking west, 2016

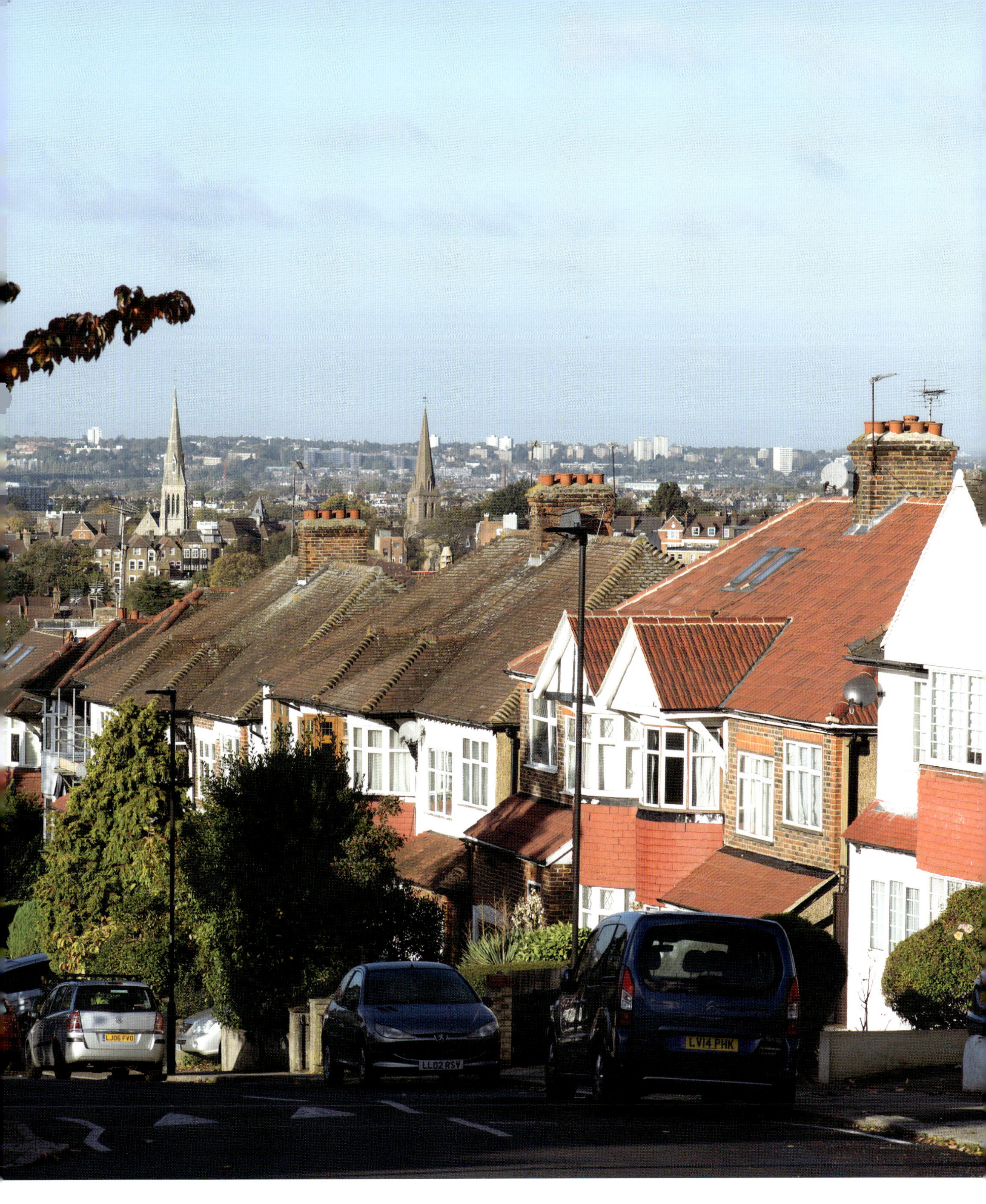
LJ06 FVO
LL02 RSV
LV14 PHK

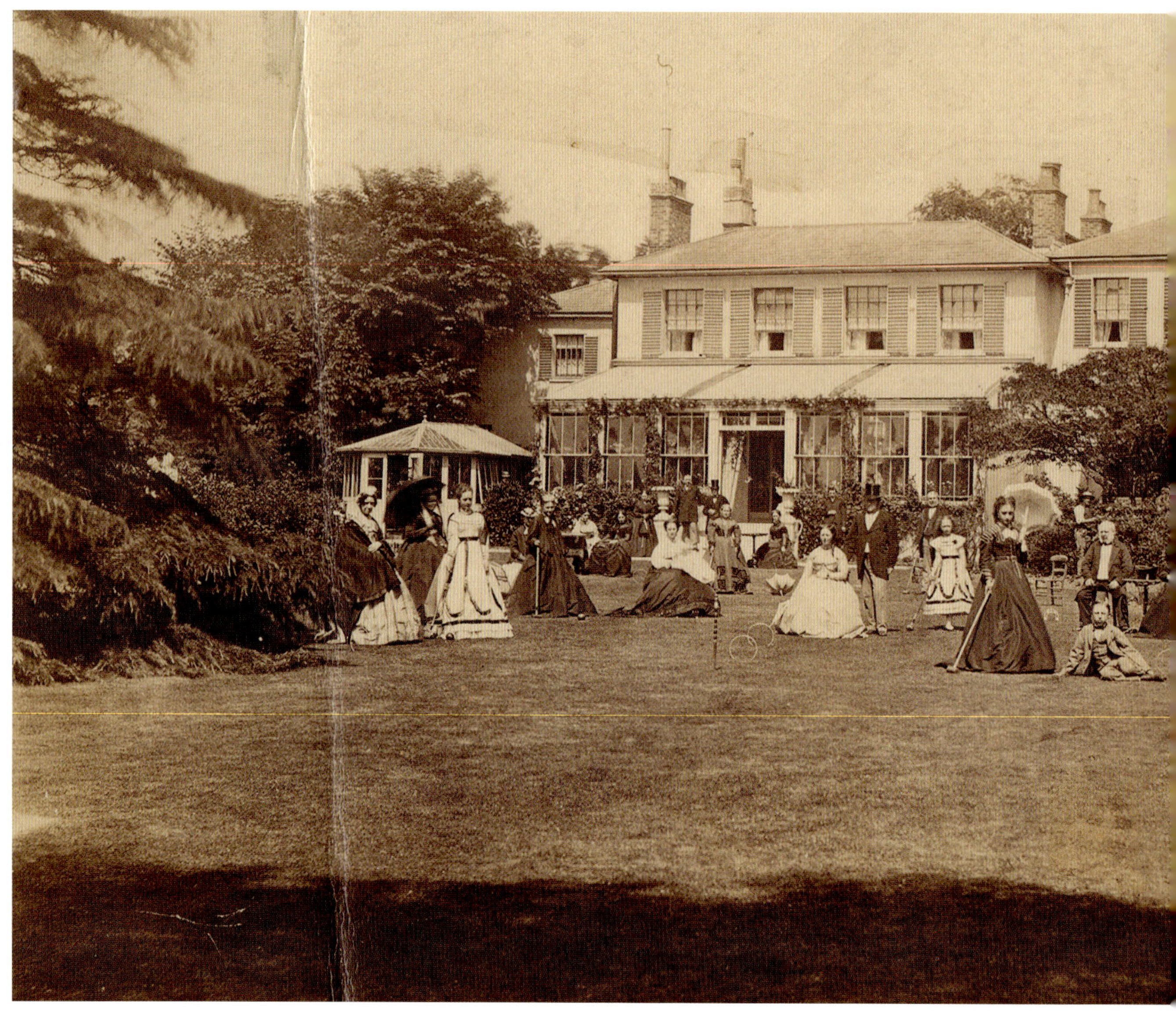

The merchant Francis Nalder changed the property's name to Guildersfield when he settled there in 1837. It was the home of various wealthy tradesmen and merchants throughout the Victorian period, the Murleys leaving a memorable visual record of their house and family. The last residents, the Dowsons, settled there between 1890 and 1906. House building in Streatham had started in the 1870s but development gathered momentum during the following decades, with the appearance of Buckleigh Road from 1879, then Tankerville Road from 1882, and Guildersfield Road in the early 1880s. But most houses arrived much later, in the first decades of the twentieth century. Guildersfield House itself was finally demolished to make room for a parade of shops, an essential Victorian tool of suburban development.

Guildersfield House in South Streatham was built as Springfield Lodge around 1830. It was the home of many respectable Victorian families including the Murleys who lived there between 1866 and 1871. The head of the household, Mary Ann Murley is sitting on the right of the photograph taken in 1868. Photo: courtesy of Marion Gower.

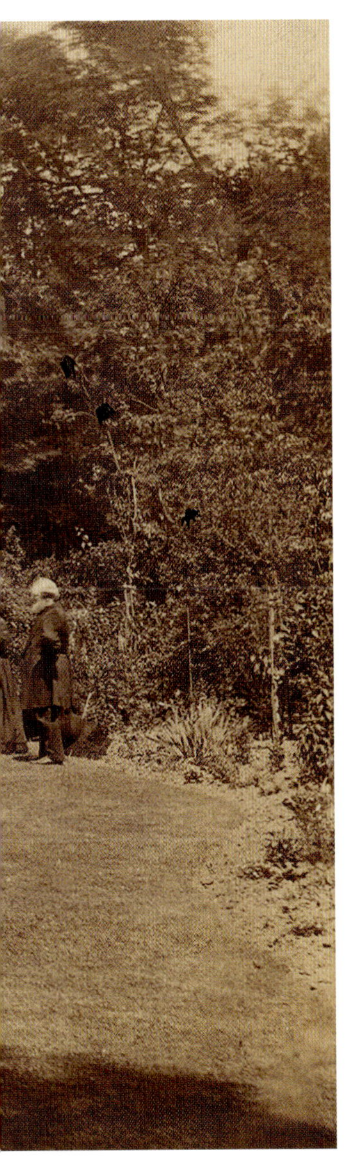

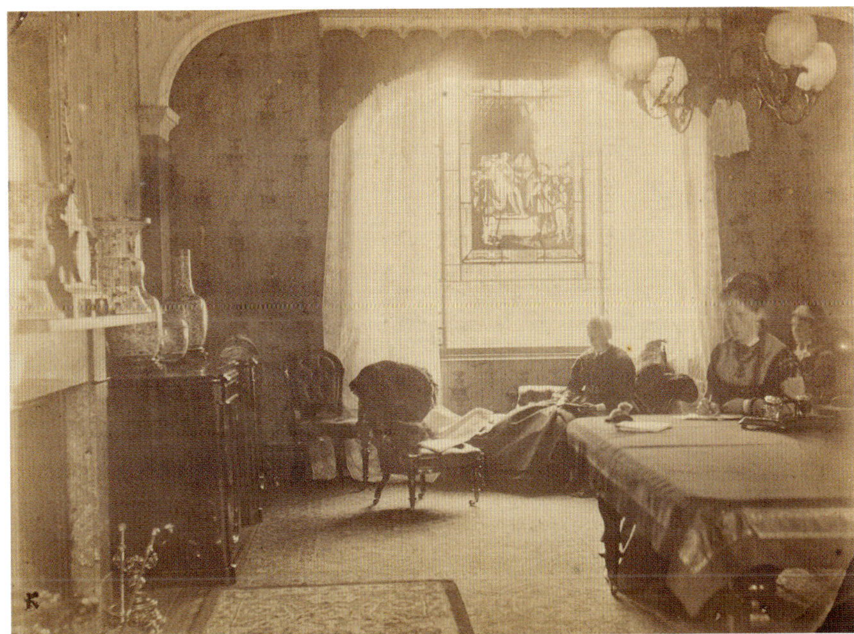

Guildersfield House: this rare 1868 photograph of the Murleys' dining room features the unusual stained glass window decoration of that room. Marion Gower established that the glass depicting 'King John signing the Magna Carta' after the 1776 painting by John Hamilton Mortimer, cost £100 and originally came from London's Guildhall. The subject, the date of the photograph and the provenance of the glass appear to point to the time when the Mansion House was extensively refurbished in the 1860s. The Corporation commissioned two stained-glass windows for the Egyptian Hall; one of these, the 'royal window' was decorated with 'King John signing the Magna Carta' (a different composition). Did one of the four glassmakers approached by the City prepare a miniature version to sway the committee in his favour? The full size window was 28 x 13 ft as opposed to 8 x 6 ft for the Murley window. *Photo: courtesy of Marion Gower.*

However, the earliest area to be suburbanised was not in South but North Streatham. Roupell Park, immediately south of the South Circular Road was created between the 1840s and 1880s – a prestigious development centred on Christchurch and Palace Roads. It was soon followed by Thomas Cubitt's Clapham Park development on the west side of Streatham Hill. From the 1880s the pace of development quickened with the sale of large country houses in Telford Park and then the estates of Coventry Park, Manor Park, Bedford Park, Norfolk House and Streatham Lodge. In Furzedown the estate's manor house miraculously escaped demolition (now part of Graveney School) unlike Streatham Park House, Leigham Court Manor, Norfolk House, Bedford House and Manor House. The density of Streatham increased considerably – also spurred on by the arrival of the railways: Streatham Hill in 1856, Streatham station in 1868 and Norbury in 1878.

What happened to the Guildersfield House site also occurred in areas devoid of historic grand houses. Wyatt Park Road, for instance, since its development is also well documented: it was built over land where lofty, comfortable Victorian houses with spacious gardens had been erected. It was redeveloped in 1908 when it was in the hands of Robert

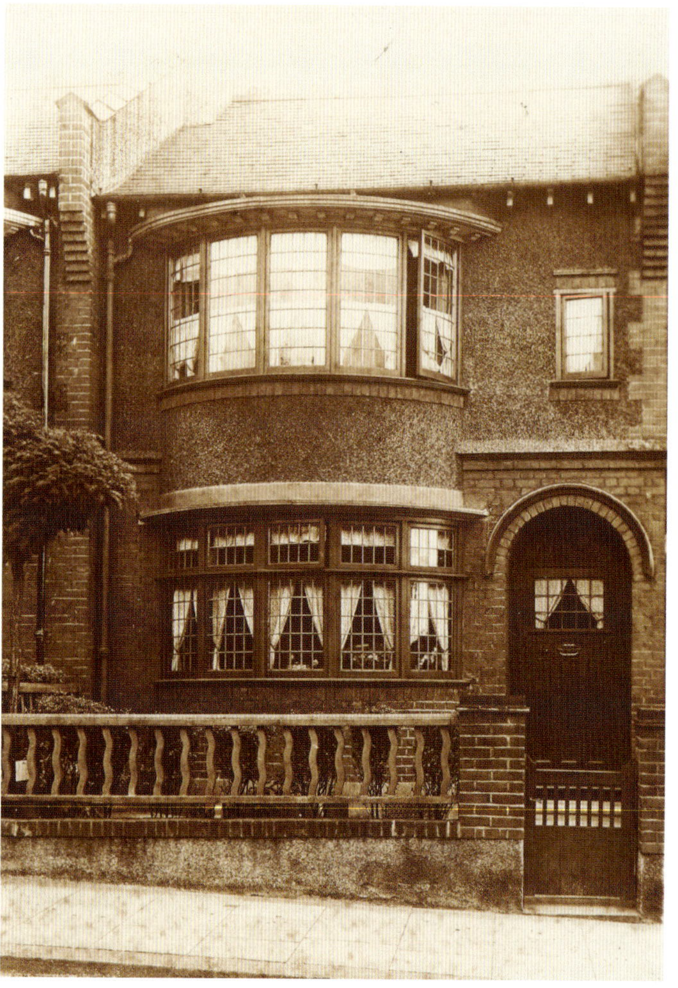

Right: This group of images were collected by Mr Alan Rolfe who lived for ninety three years at No 10 Wyatt Park Road. All pictures bar one (the front of the house, pictured left) come from the original estate prospectus dating from around 1908 when the development was ready. The picture on the right shows the back of the house. The Dining Room, at the front of the house and close to the kitchen, is a bright room shown with period furniture and captioned 'This illustration is to show how readily the Dining Room yields itself to the proper disposition of the Furniture'. © John W Brown, Local History Publications and © Museum of London for the front of the house.

H Miller. At no 10 lived the actor Alan Rolfe who moved into the new development in 1912 and stayed there until his death in 2005. He kept the Wyatt Park Road Estate prospectus which described the new homes as 'moderate size House[s], designed, built and fitted in a manner equal to that of the more pretentious and costly residences, but at a price within the range of the average city clerk or professional man'. In other words: glamour on a shoestring budget. But the 'situation' was the first selling point: 'Owing to its altitude the air is at all seasons fresh and invigorating, the roads are exceedingly well kept, and the whole district evinces the healthy, pleasant, prosperous residential suburb'.

Alan Rolfe has left a diary, now in Lambeth Archives (see p. 74), but he was also interviewed by the Museum of London on 15 April 2003. The interview transcript is quite evocative of the atmosphere of the emerging suburb:

> 'He remembers the empty streets. There were no cars. If you had a car, you could not leave it on the street overnight. You had to rent a lock up. The police were not keen on people leaving their cars out on the road. Busy traffic did not develop until after the Second World War.'

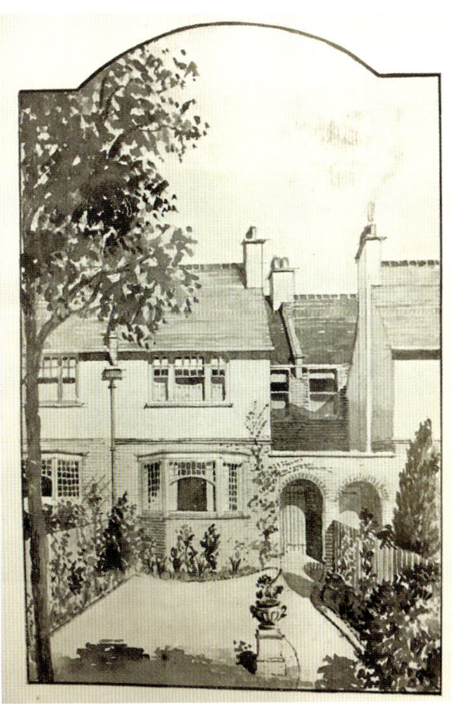

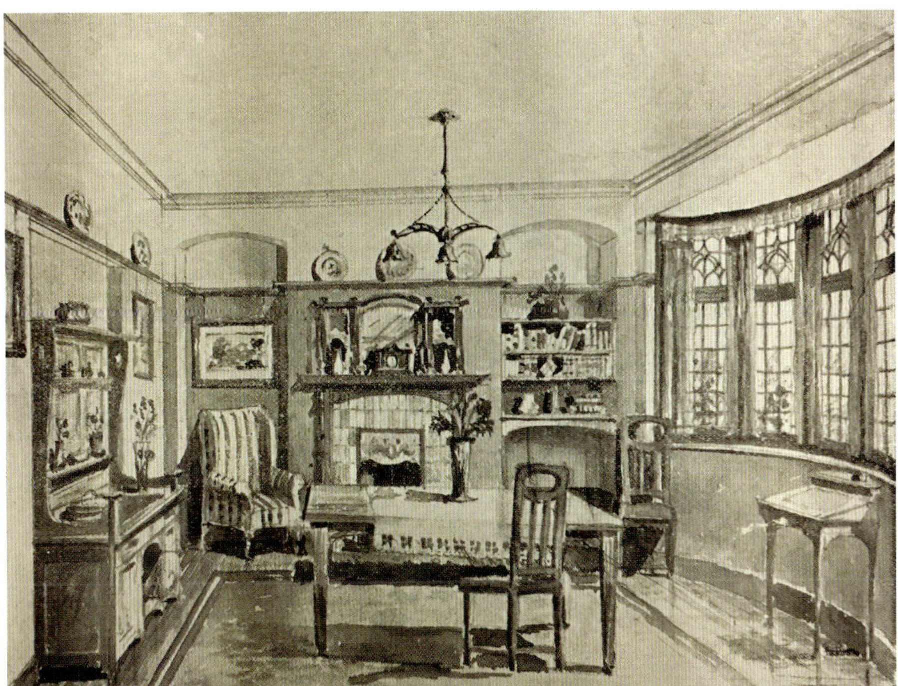

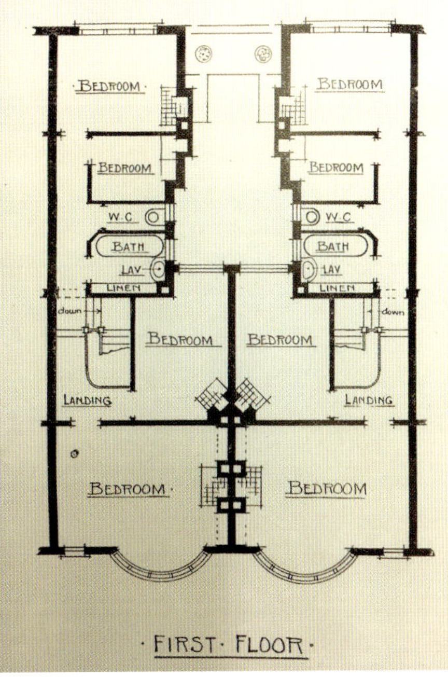
BEDROOM
BEDROOM
BEDROOM
BEDROOM
W.C
W.C
BATH
BATH
LAV
LAV
LINEN
LINEN
down
down
BEDROOM
BEDROOM
LANDING
LANDING
BEDROOM
BEDROOM
·FIRST· FLOOR·

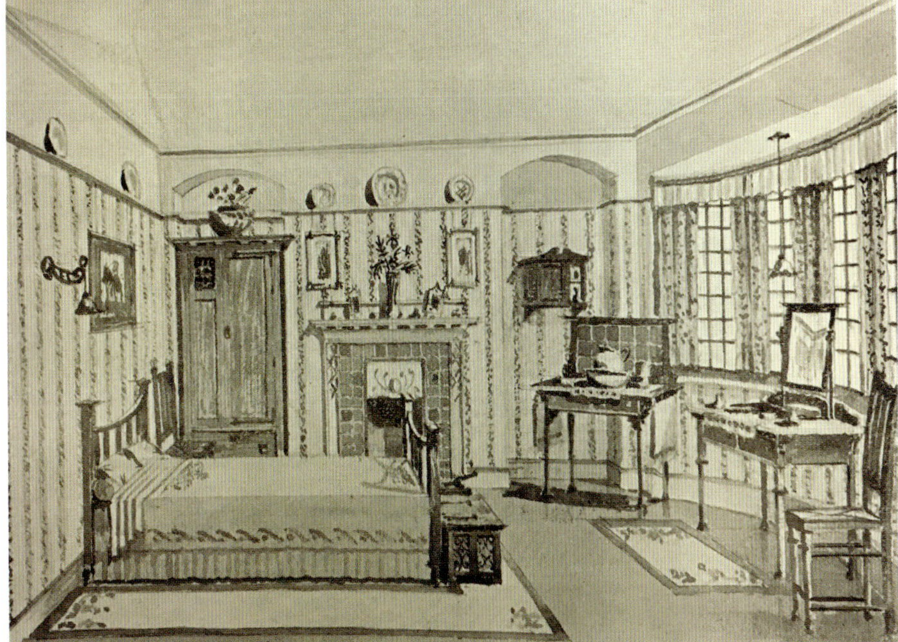

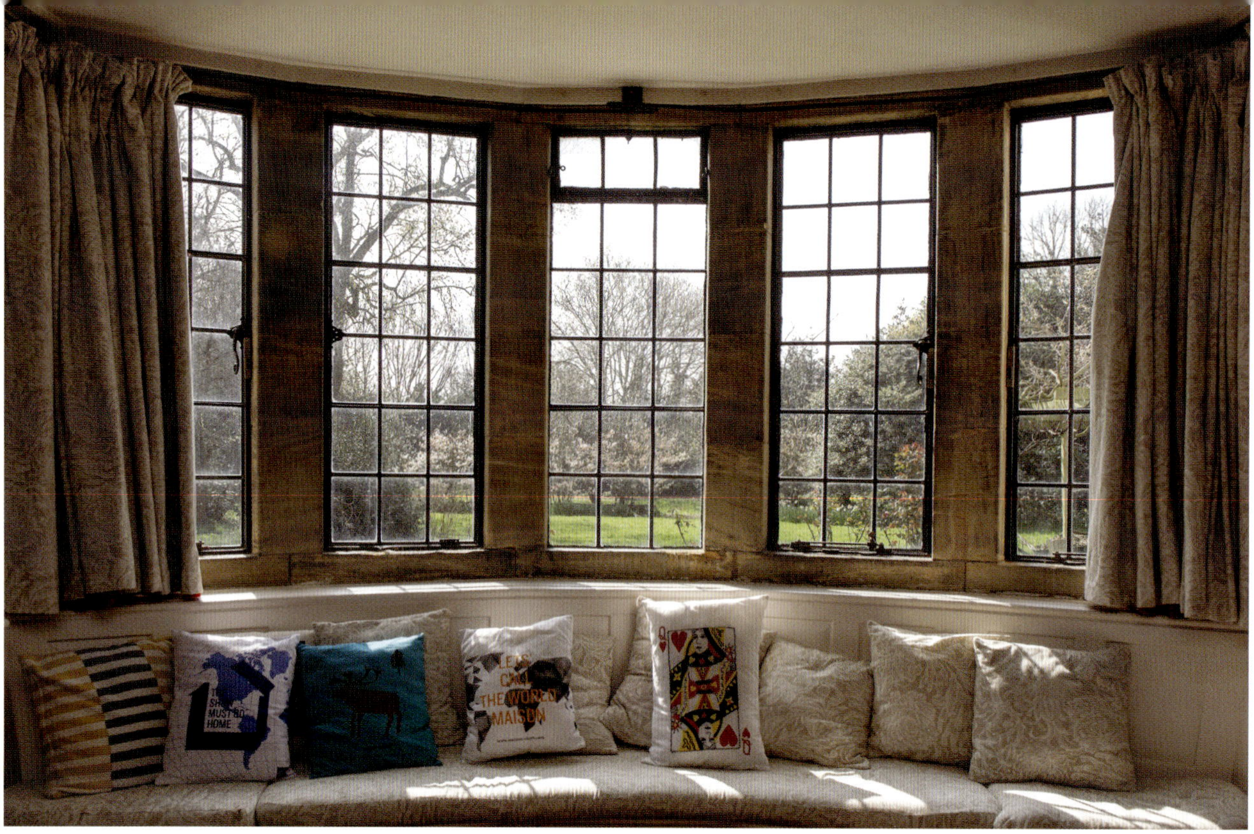

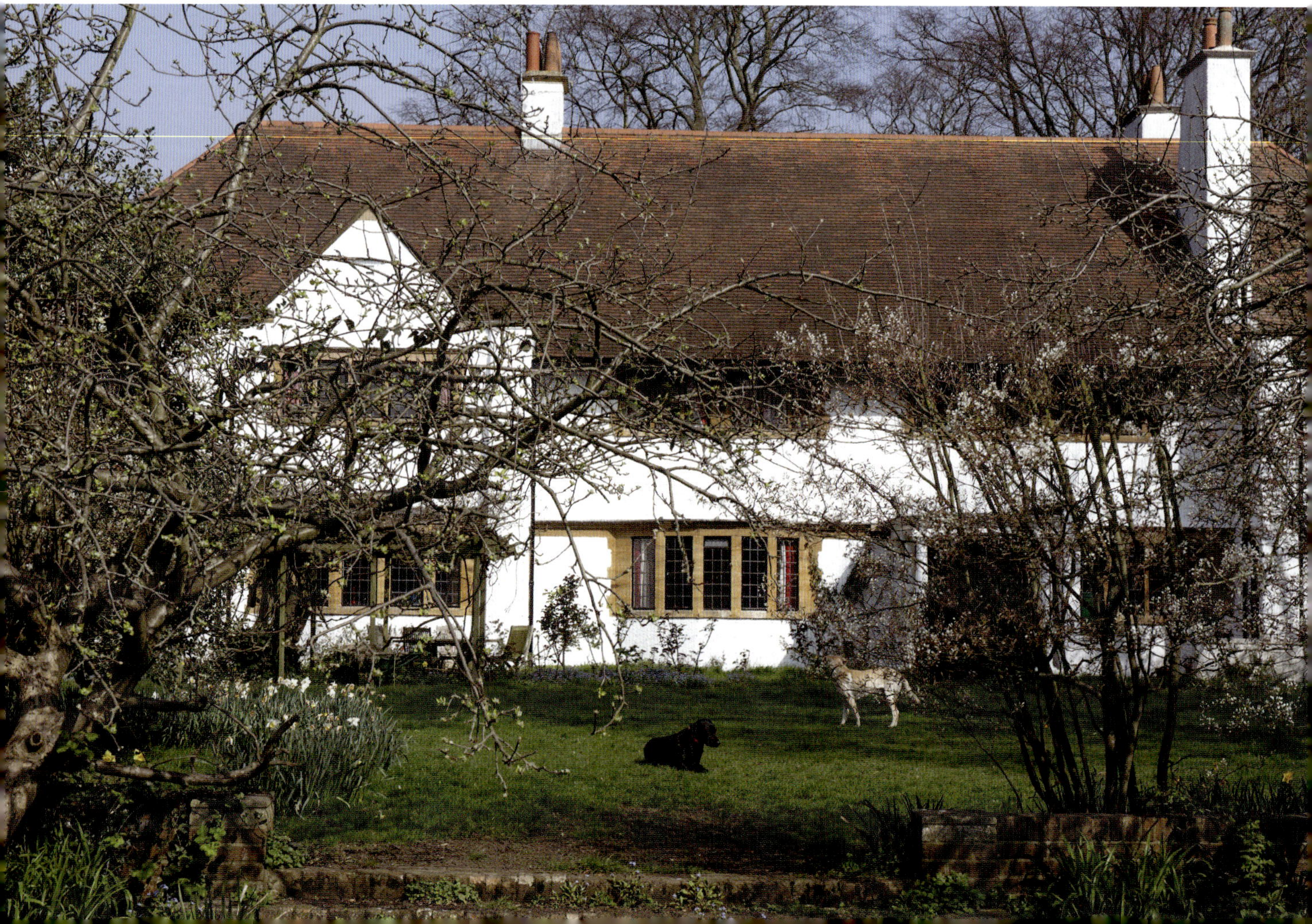

Dixcot overlooks Tooting Common in North Drive, standing on the former Streatham Park Estate (see p. 110). On this extensive plot sits the largest London house designed by one of Britain's most famous Arts and Crafts architects – C F A Voysey (1857–1941). Voysey designed the house in 1897, but the commission was executed by Walter Cave, with some alterations, perhaps as a result of a conflict between Voysey and his clients. This architect's 'rare outbursts of temper' were documented in his own lifetime in an April 1899 article published in *The Studio* (quoted by Duncan Simpson in his book on Voysey). The architect ranted 'against those inconsiderate clients who endeavoured to insist upon his adding a foot or two to the height of a second storey, regardless of the fact that by doing this the entire proportion, that is to say, the main beauty, of their house must be sacrificed'. Voysey believed 'the architect should be supreme touching artistic design and proportion'.

The Dixcot client was R W, later Sir Walter Essex (1857–1940), MP and founder of the wallpaper firm Essex & Co. He was a personal friend of Voysey who designed furniture and wallpaper for Essex before and after the Dixcot commission (it has been suggested the difficulties over this commission were between Voysey and Mrs Essex).

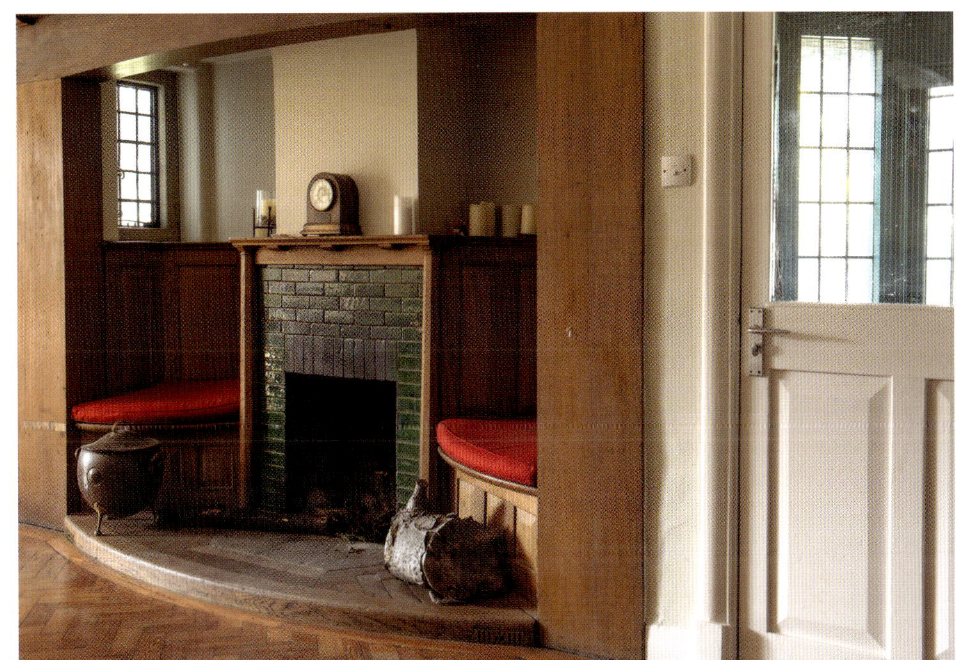

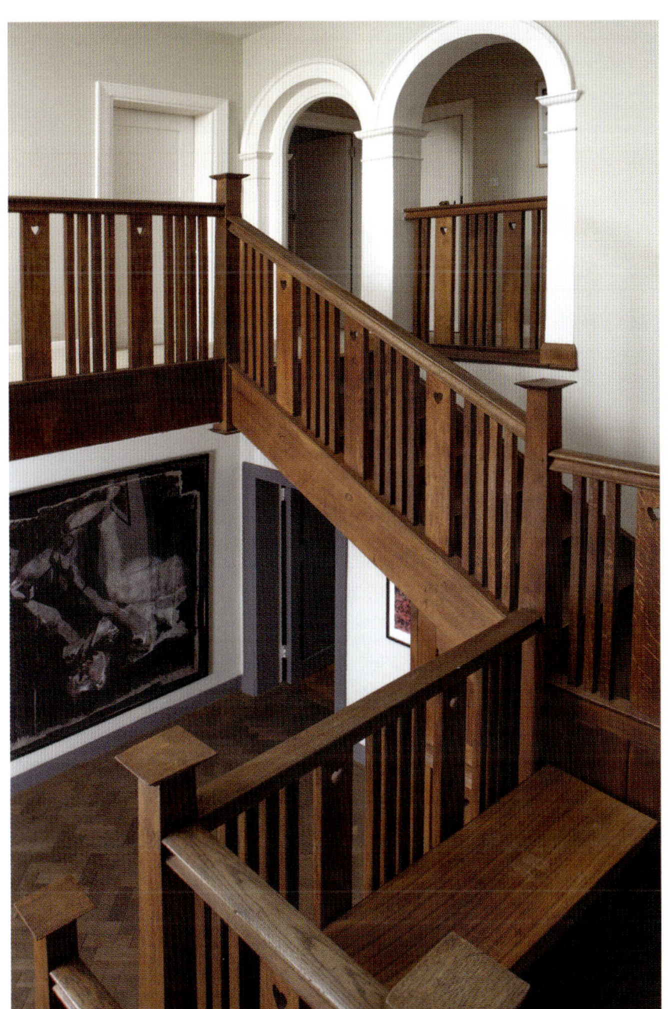

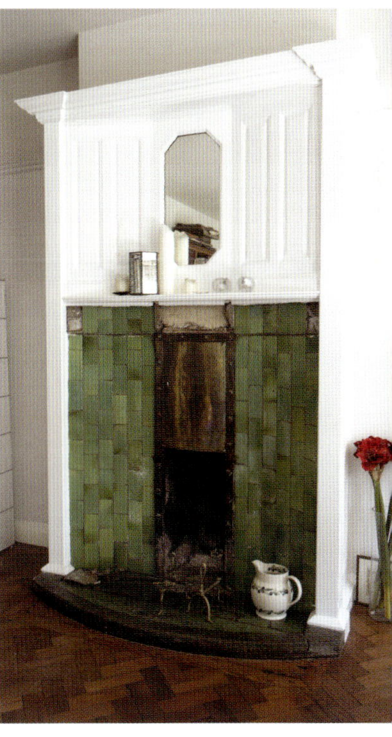

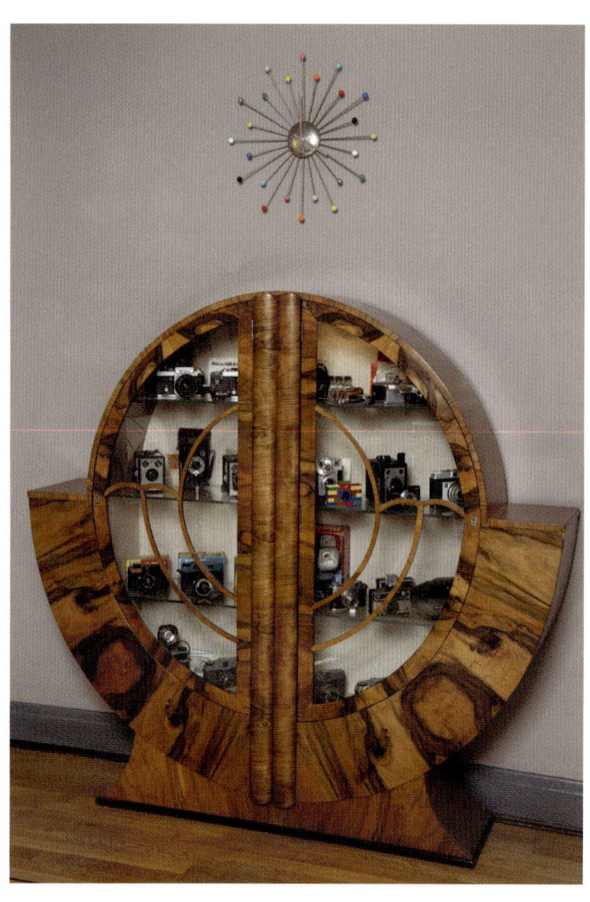

There is a group of six houses at the junction of St Julian's Farm and Leigham Court Roads which were designed and built in the late 1930s by Wates (Streatham) then based at 1258–1260 London Road, Norbury. In a prominent position on the large corner plot, stands a house which looks more Art Deco than any of the others, largely because its current owner, Sean Queenan, has embraced and then enhanced the 1930s design repertoire. Period details such as the Crittall windows have been preserved and the spiky, exotic planting in the garden brings out, by contrast, the smooth geometry of the architecture. The curving windows dominate the façade – an excellent example of the 'suntrap' house calculated to let in as much light as possible into the rooms. This attractive house has been restored and furnished with a real attention to the original design and period detail.

The first resident of this house was a 'commercial traveller' and a local man, Douglas Frederick Turpin. Two further owners are listed in Post Office directories during and after the Second World War before the directories fall silent from 1955 onwards. The owner Sean has been based at this address for the last twenty two years.

Bottom right: © *Sean Queenan*

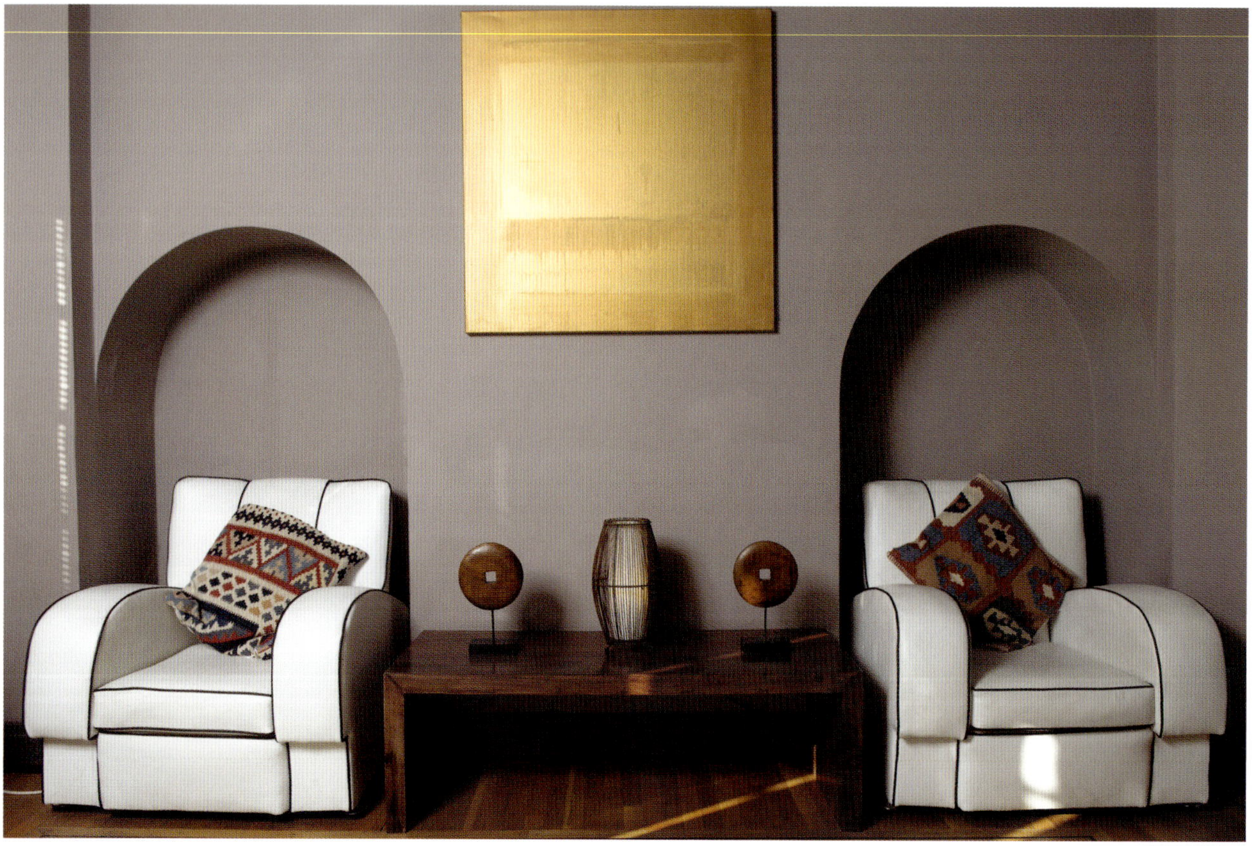

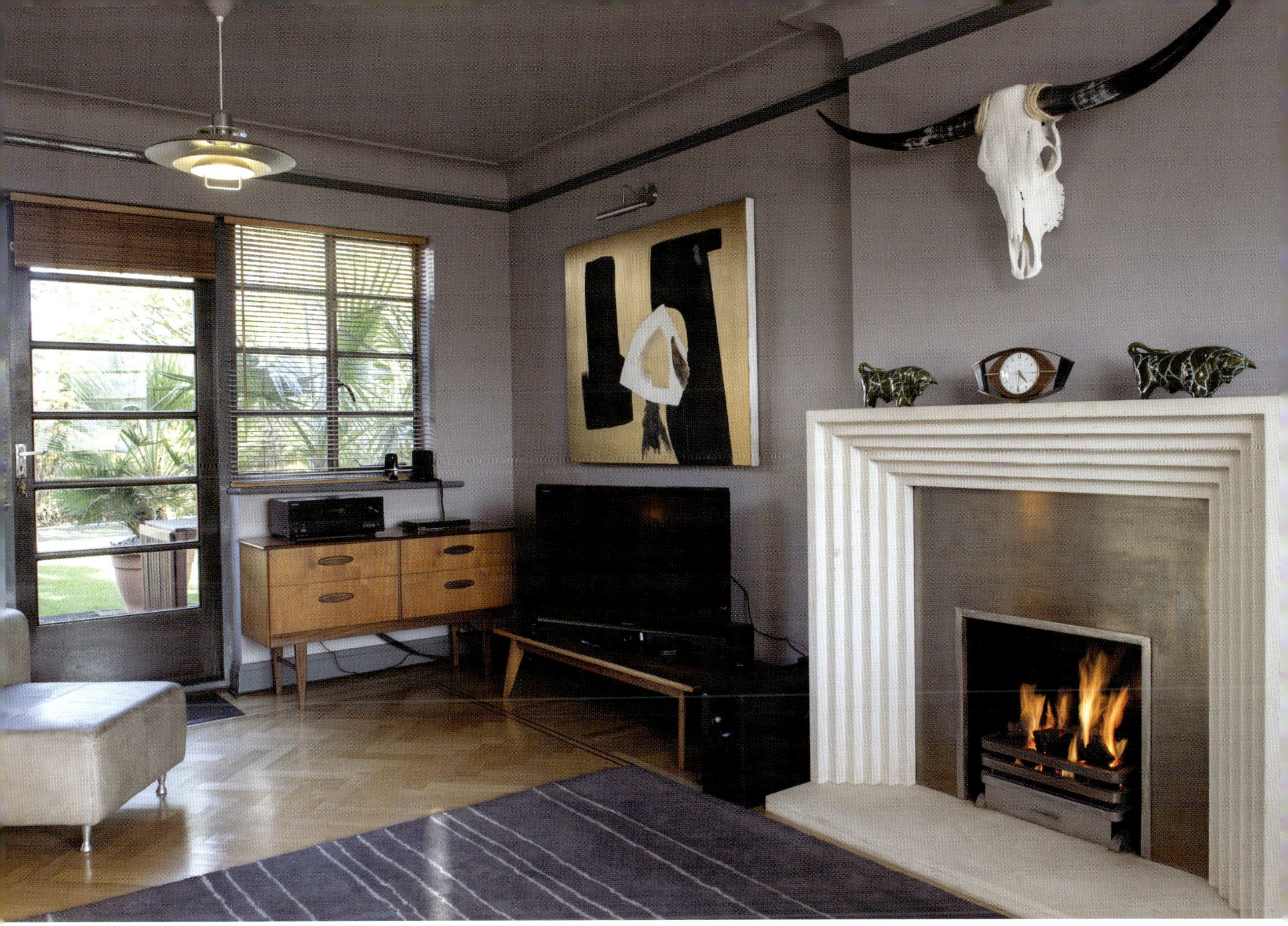

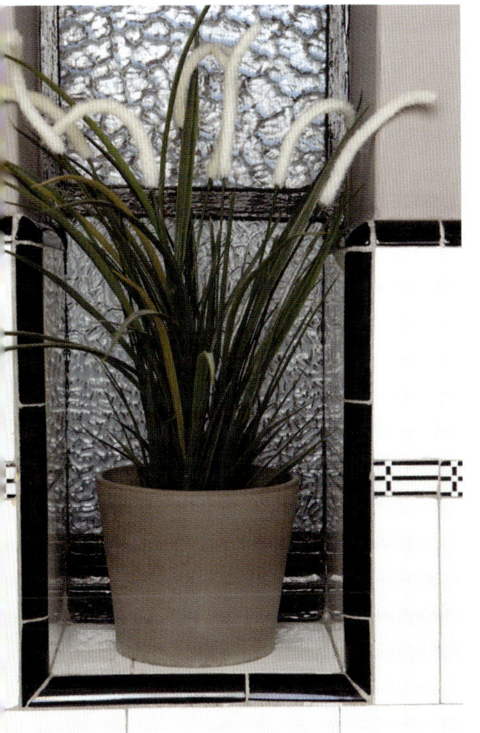

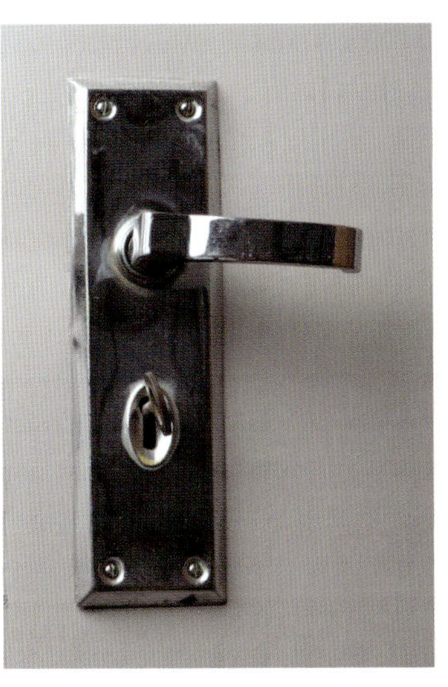

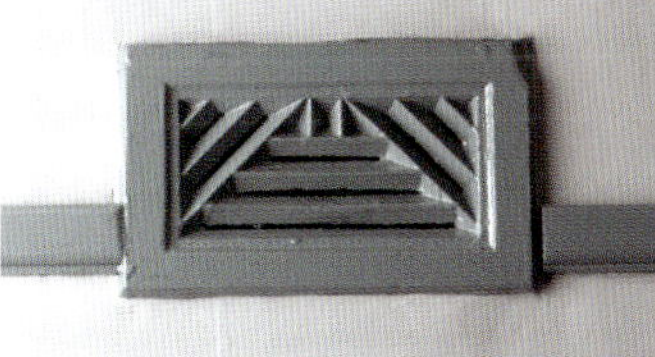

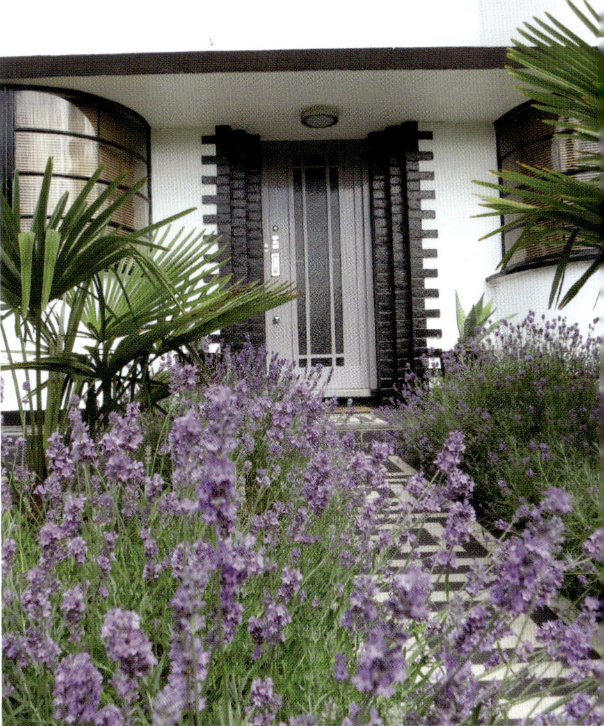

8. The discreet charm of Streatham Gardens

(paired with 'The Walled Garden' on pp. 96–99)

If you look closely at Streatham's earliest map (1729) reproduced on pp. 24 and 27, you may be able to see a proliferation of 'gardens'. They are found close to where people lived – in the village by the church of St Leonard and further south around Bedford House with the occasional 'garden' on the High Road to London. Some of these gardens are visually fleshed out when John Rocque published his 'Exact Survey of the City of London, Westminster ye Borough of Sout'wark and the Country near ten miles round' in 1746.

In the early nineteenth century the large Tooting nurseries of William Rollisson made history by being the earliest firm to employ their own plant collectors. They were also noted for their hybridisation of Cape heaths and had an enviable stock of New Zealand plants. An (unsubstantiated) story also credits them with introducing by mistake the first specimen of *Begonia rex* in this country!

Streatham continued to hold a prominent place in the nursery trade throughout the nineteenth and twentieth centuries with the extraordinary empire of John Peed and Sons – three generations running nurseries in Roupell Park, Mitcham Lane, Norbury and Kingston. In May 1880, John Peed of Roupell Park nurseries (living at 80 Mitcham Lane) with his son Benjamin of Norbury nurseries were the recipients of prizes for greenhouse plants at the Crystal Palace Flower show. They specialized in caladiums and would be the last of the specialist foliage plant nurseries in London.

Local historian Judy Harris documented in detail Lambeth's thriving horticultural societies. The successful Royal South London Floricultural Society, started in 1834, met at Kennington's Horns Tavern and attracted Streatham gardeners (for instance William Leaf,

Local historian Graham Gower wrote movingly about growing up in the 1940s and 50s in his 'other garden' – Streatham Common; how he would play 'cricket or football there to my heart's content, climb the trees in the woods, run in and out of the allotments, charge around the Rookery, and at times challenge the good nature of the park keepers' (from the Friends of Streatham Common *Newsletter*, August 2016). This contrasts with the well-behaved children of the Edwardian postcard reproduced on the left. *© John W Brown Local History Publications.*

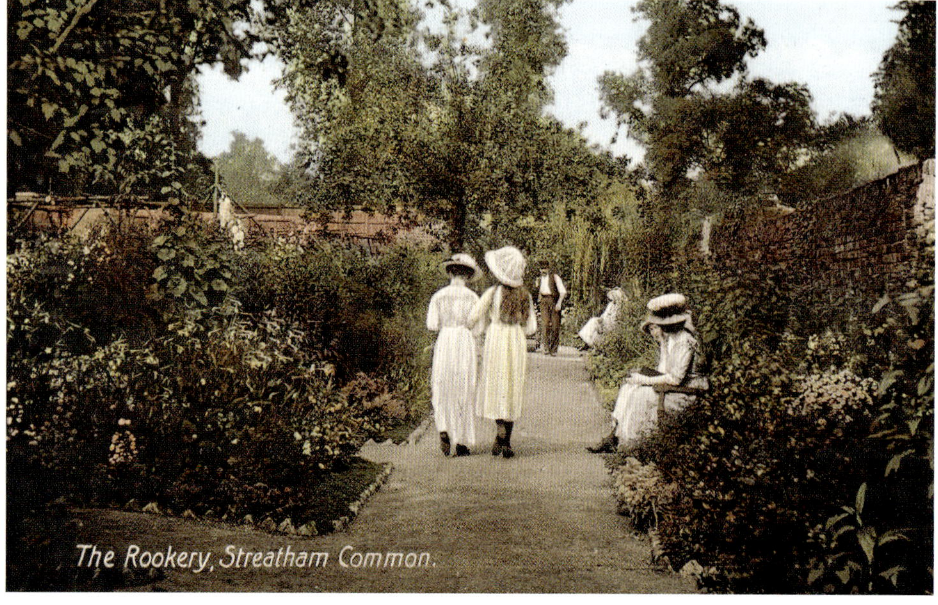

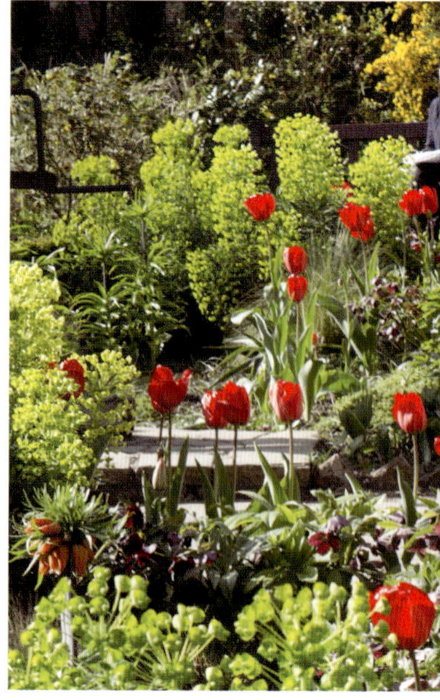

see p. 116) but the most directly relevant organisations would have been the Streatham Gardeners Association established in 1840 and twenty years later the Brixton, Streatham and Clapham Horticultural Society (BSCHS, established in 1860). The latter's first patron was William Roupell (1931–1909), Liberal MP for Lambeth between 1857 and 1862, illegitimate son of lead merchant Richard Palmer Roupell who developed Waterloo's Roupell Street and Roupell Park at Streatham Hill. William is sometimes regarded as the black sheep of the family for frittering away his father's considerable fortune and for being imprisoned fourteen years for forgery. But gardening was his redemption and he wrote movingly about it: 'I am never happier than when I am in the company of gardeners, and I have been associated with them all my life'.

When William Roupell was released from Portland prison, he lived in poverty in a small cottage in Garden Lane (a stone's throw from his former grand home on Brixton Hill) but he was able to cultivate a nearby nursery – clearly shown on the 1894 O/S map abutting the Lambeth Water Works Reservoir and St Pancras Workhouse (close to the Pullman Court estate). In 1890 he became the secretary of BSCHS and remained in the post for ten years seemingly 'injecting a new enthusiasm into the society' (Harris) and winning prizes at the Society's new exhibiting venue – Streatham Town Hall by Streatham Station. He is buried in the family vault at West Norwood cemetery.

The Rookery Gardens, Streatham Common

These gardens were created to adorn a substantial mansion house, Wells House, designed by architect Michael Searles (1751–1813) for William Wilkinson. The house was ready by 1786 and demolished in 1912. It was built on the same site as the first early eighteenth-century building to which crowds had flocked sometime after the wells were discovered there in 1659. After the water was found to be contaminated (in the 1760s) the wells moved to a different site off Valley Road. Little has been published about the appearance of the Georgian and Victorian Rookery gardens, but the garden is well documented and

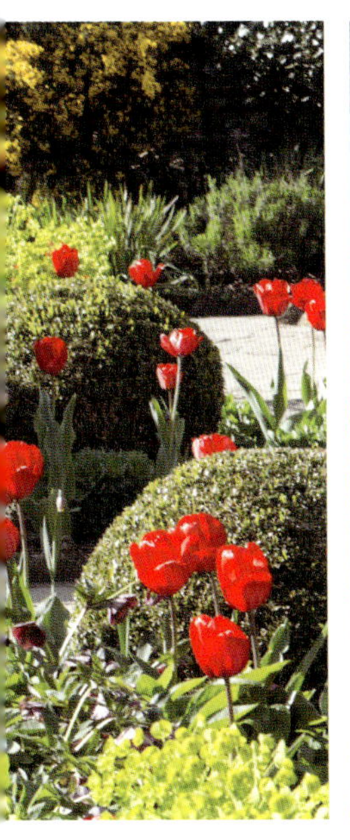

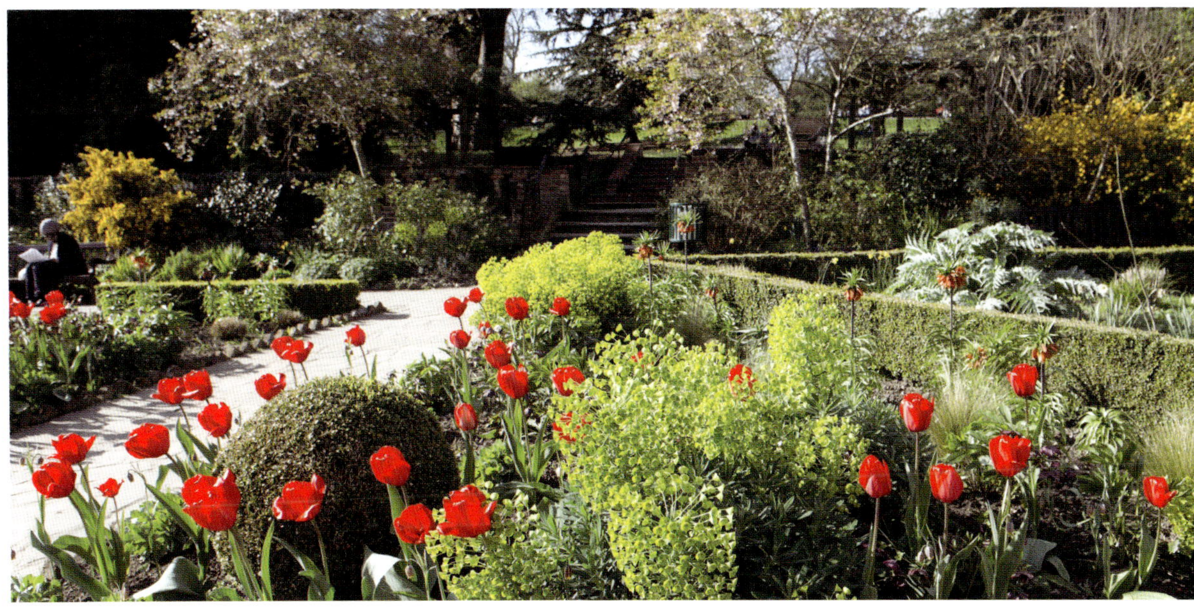

illustrated from the time it opened to the public in 1913. This was achieved with the help of Stenton Covington: he set up a subscribers scheme and convened meetings with the Metropolitan Gardens Association under the auspices of the London County Council (LCC) who purchased the land and continued to increase its acreage over ensuing decades. The land was finally transferred to the Borough of Lambeth in 1971.

In *The Dulwich Notebook* I described how Brockwell Park broke new ground by introducing the first 'Shakespeare garden' in its walled garden: it proved such a popular feature that it was soon replicated elsewhere. At the Rookery, garden volunteer Terka Acton pointed out that the White Garden is also a ground-breaking piece of garden design: it is 'still the only white garden in any of London's public parks' and 'pre-dates Vita Sackville-West's famous "grey, green and white garden" at Sissinghurst by at least 30 years' (in the 2015 spring issue of *London Landscapes*). The White Garden was originally designed by Major Philip Maud of the LCC but in recent times had fallen into disrepair. For the 2013 centenary the Friends of Streatham Common organised its restoration with the help of a Heritage Lottery Fund grant. In 2016, it won a Bronze gilt award in the London Gardens Society's category 'Best Garden in a Public Place'. It is now the sole responsibility of SCOOP – Streatham Common Co-Operative, the organisation appointed by Lambeth Council in 2015 to help it run Streatham Common (also see p. 29).

Below: The pioneering White Garden was lovingly restored by a group of volunteers and was the recipient of the 2016 London Gardens Society award.

Right: residents of the Telford Park estate celebrate the royal wedding of Prince William and Catherine Middleton on 29 April 2011. The cake competition was judged by celebrity chef John Torode!

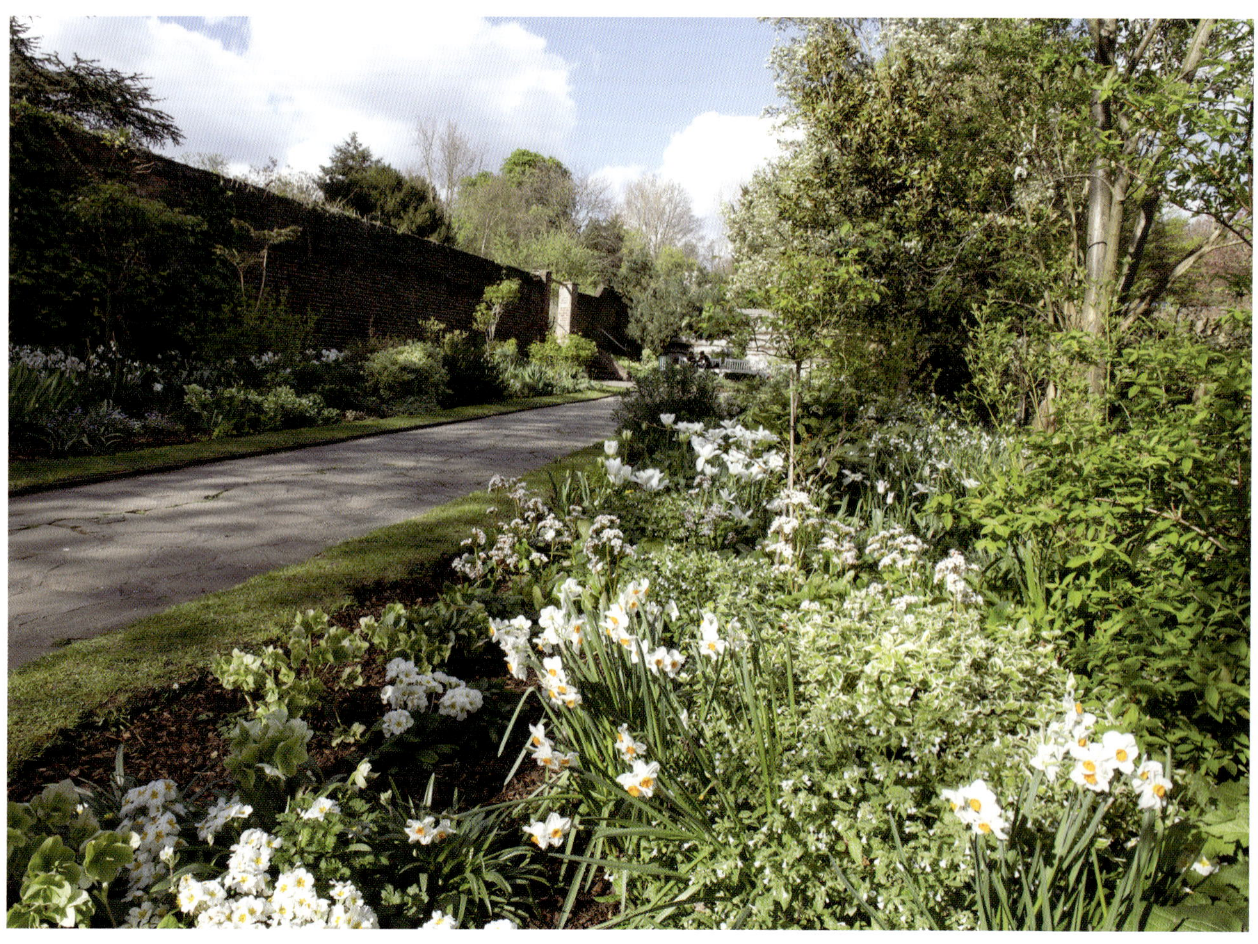

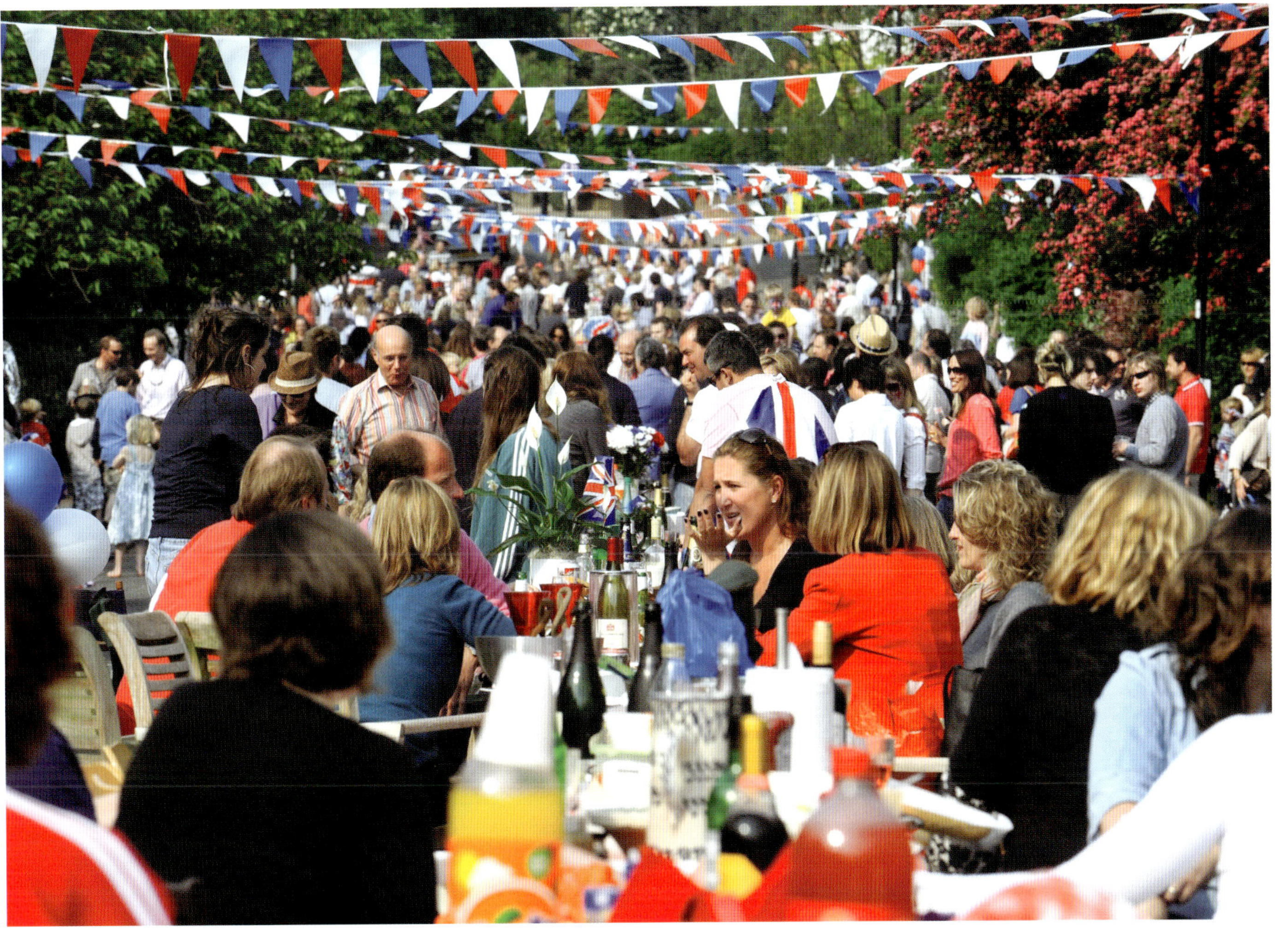

The Telford Park estate

Manicured gardens and crowds do not normally sit happily together, but our photographer Torla Evans was moved to record a garden and street party taking place on the Telford Park Estate on 29 April 2011. It was part of the country's celebrations for the royal wedding of Prince William and Catherine Middleton. Traffic was halted in Killieser Avenue and all the residents and their friends joined the party. Perhaps we should point out that its success was in part due to the way the Telford Park Estate was developed between 1877 and 1882. The owners, the Scottish Kymer/Stewart family, employed developers who appointed the architect E J Tarver and a large building firm, Sutton and Dudley. The architect, a champion of the Queen Anne Revival style (along with C F A Voysey), was influenced by what was happening on the Bedford Park estate in West London. Tarver spared no effort in designing large and beautiful houses sitting in large gardens. There is plenty of space on the Telford Park estate for street and garden parties, particularly if you compare it to the ABCD estate on the other side of the road (check Google satellite views).

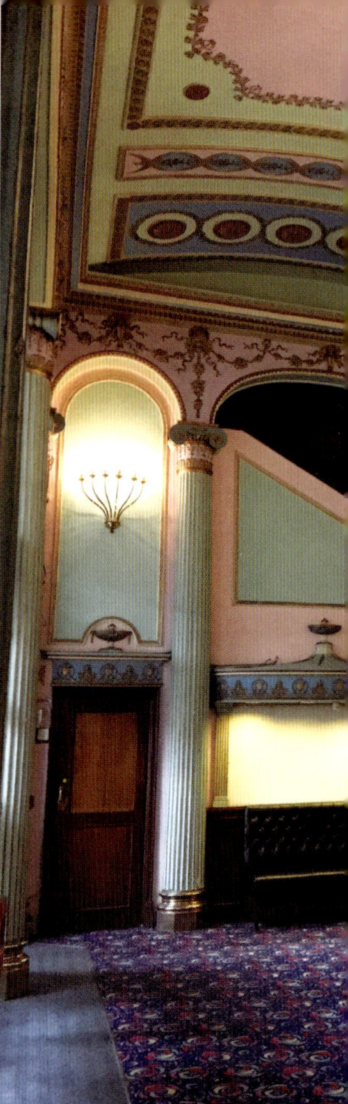

9. Recreational Streatham

(paired with 'Me, a Film by Me' on p. 100)

The sheer number of amenities built in Streatham in the first decades of the twentieth century seems quite unusual. John Cresswell in is excellent history *The Streatham Hill Theatre* succeeds in conjuring a most vivid picture of the men who engineered the performing arts scene in Streatham: buying/leasing the land, negotiating deals and delivering … but not without the occasional bloody battle; for instance between Hugh Sewell Kingdon who was attempting to mastermind the dance hall (the future Locarno) and the Streatham Hill Theatre when he discovered that the architect Edward Albert Stone had just bought the site of the future Astoria and was also proposing to build a theatre. 'Both agreed the foolishness of having two large theatres so close pursuing the same policy but neither would yield'. The battle was won by a third party, the determined Joseph Clavering of Golders Green Hippodrome fame.

'During its heydays of the 1930s and 1950s, the Streatham Hill Theatre was to be a veritable microcosm of the West End' wrote John Cresswell who also acknowledged Clavering's genius at securing the most popular shows for his theatres adding 'the Streatham Hill was alone … in securing those all important Number One touring stars'.

CHRONOLOGY

1910 Empire Picture Palace opens, destroyed in 1944, not rebuilt.

1912 Streatham Picture Theatre, 130–145 High Road opens. Renamed Golden Domes in 1915. First place of entertainment to open on Sunday (1913) which caused a furore. It was enlarged and rewired in 1929 for talkies. It closed in 1938. The building is now unrecognisable but the auditorium has apparently been recycled as a show room for Carpet Right at 130–132 Streatham High Road.

1927 ABC Cinemas is established by Warner Brothers: they acquired the Streatham Picture Theatre above in 1935 (also see 1938 and 1969, overleaf).

1928 Streatham Baths opens

1929 Streatham Hill Theatre opens, designed by William G R Sprague with William Henry Barton. Badly damaged by a V1 on 3 July 1944. Restored and reopened in 1950; Grade II listed, also see 2017 overleaf.

1929 1 October, The Locarno Dance Hall opens: around 1500 people came to the opening night. It closed in the 1960s and was demolished in 2015.

1930 30 June, Astoria Cinema, by Edward A Stone who designed the interior as an 'atmospheric' theatre, Egyptian style, most of it sadly gone. The Astoria was one of four London Astorias (Brixton, Old Kent Road and Finsbury Park) and it is the only one which is still a cinema, now as an Odeon.

1931 Ice Arena opens, near Streatham Station, demolished.

continued overleaf

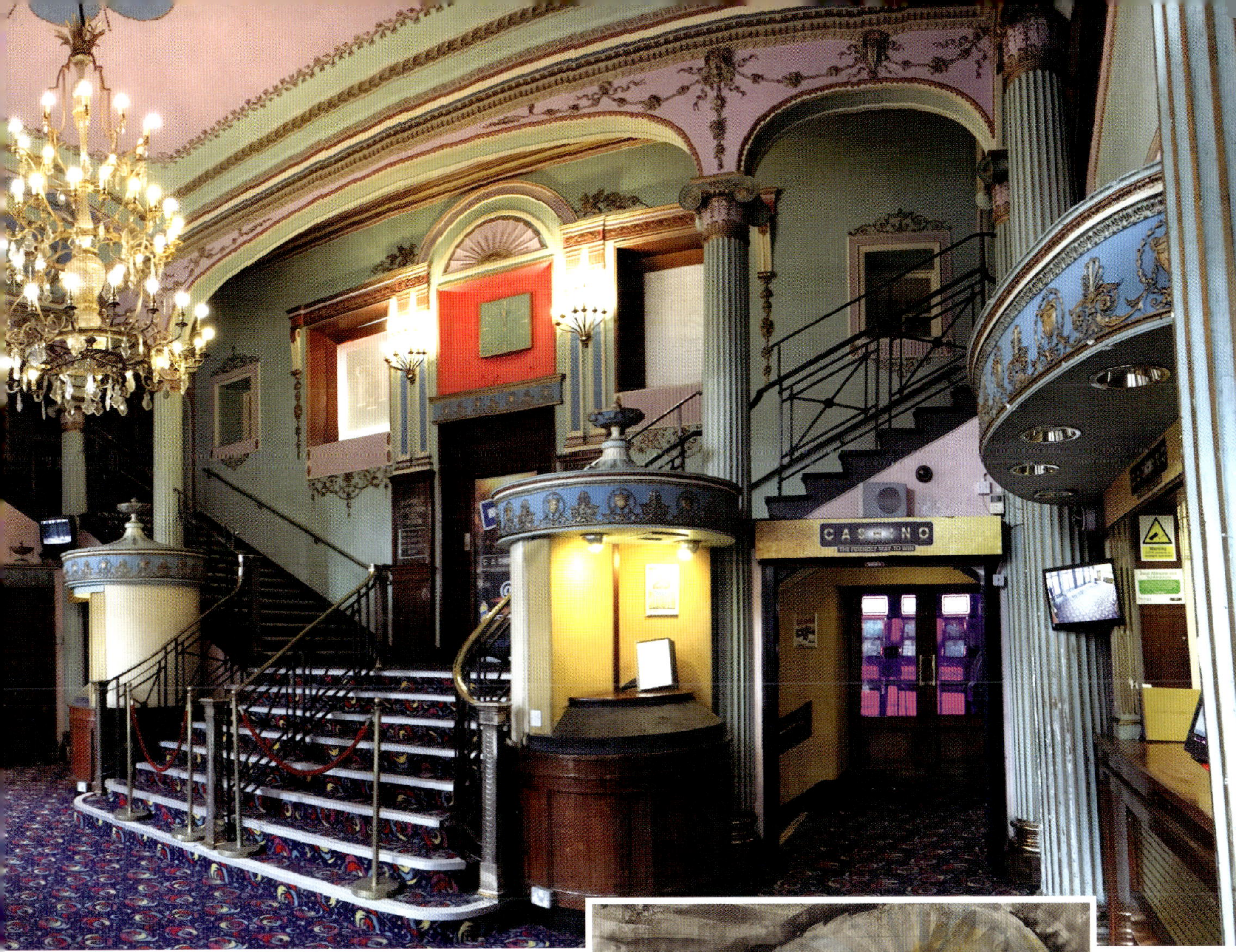

Streatham Hill Theatre's entrance lobby; the theatre was designed by William G R Sprague, a prolific theatre architect who was active in the West End – where thirteen of his theatres survive, says arthurlloyd.co.uk. He was also active in suburbia, most memorably with his Kilburn's Empire and the Notting Hill Coronet. Streatham was Sprague's final project 'possibly his largest and one of the best-equipped in London, outside the West End' (Theatres Trust database).

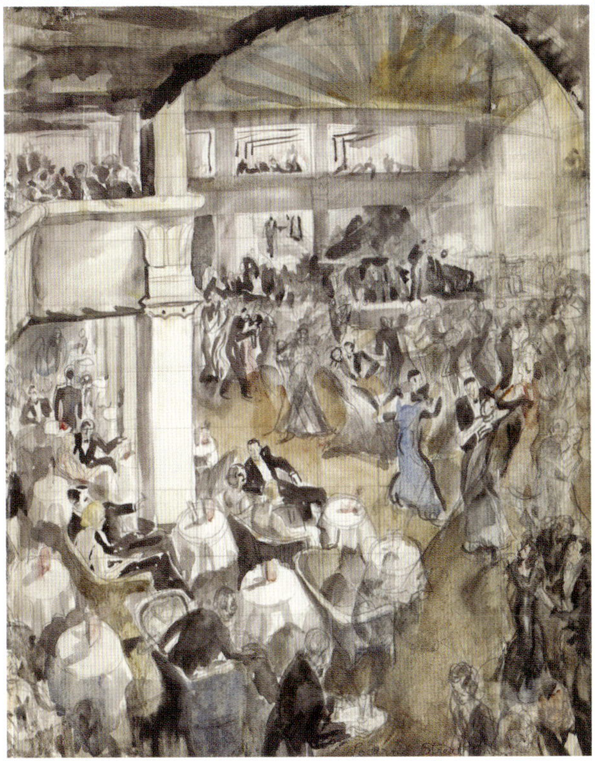

Right: *The Locarno Dance Hall*, undated pencil and watercolour drawing by Grace Golden (1904–1993) The Locarno Dance Hall opened in 1929 'where dancing is the poetry of motion' claimed a 1932 advertisement! By the time it was demolished in 2015 it had become Caesar's Nightclub (from 1995). Grace Golden (1904–1993) captured the glamour of the original establishment in its early days. *Photo: The Museum of London © The Estate of Grace Golden.*

1932 14 March, Gaumont Palace cinema, Streatham Hill. Hit by flying bomb in 1942. A scaled down Gaumont Palace was rebuilt which re-opened in 1955. The last screening was in March 1961. It then became the largest bowling rink in Britain (see 1962).
1938 ABC Cinemas opens the Regal Cinema, 35 High Road to replace the Golden Domes. Designed by William Reddell Glen and later renamed the ABC (1960). Triple ABC cinema in 1977 subsequently renamed the Cannon. It was converted into residential flats with shop on the ground floor in 2007 and is now called the Picture House (see p. 33 (G)); it is Grade II listed.
1962 The Streatham Bowl opens in the same year as the Streatham Hill Theatre opened as a Mecca Bingo Hall.
1969 EMI acquires the ABC Cinemas chain.
1972 From this date EMI converts its cinemas into triples. It was Streatham's turn in 1977.
1985 EMI sells ABC cinemas to Australian businessman Alan Bond who resold them to the Cannon group.
1986/7 All ABC cinemas are renamed Cannon.
1995 Caesar's Night Club opened in the old Locarno Dance Hall, after various incarnations as the Cat's Whiskers (1969), the Studio (1984) and the Ritzy (1990).
1997 Brian Fraser purchased the Mecca Bingo Hall (see 1962), renamed 'Mayfair Bingo'.
2013 A 26 million pounds leisure centre opens on the site of the old baths. Uniquely in Britain it has an Olympic size ice rink on its upper floor, the new home of the local ice hockey team, the Streatham Redskins. The new development incorporates two stained-glass windows of the old baths and three of the 'snowcrete' panels which decorated the Art Deco ice rink.
2017 January, the Bingo Hall in the old Streatham Hill Theatre closes down. For now, the Cashino (slot machines) is kept going. Nick Harding, CEO at Praesepe, the owners of the Bingo club, is hoping to find partners to revive the theatre and bring back to life the cocktail bar upstairs.
2017 The London Square development by Streatham Hill station will incorporate a 'community' theatre along Sternhold Avenue, to be ready by 2018.

This chronology indicates that there is considerable commercial creativity in Streatham, matched by receptivity from a local audience. In his diary, actor and Streatham resident Alan Rolfe describes his activities on returning home from touring *Jane Eyre* for four months. Between mid-December 1937 and the end of January 1938, he saw ten plays – two of them in Streatham – and also two films – one of them in Streatham. Basically he saw all that Streatham had to offer during that time: 'Jack and the Beanstalk' and a matinee ice show 'Switzerland' at the Streatham Hill Theatre and 'Victoria the Great' at the Astoria.

The archive of the lesser known music hall artiste George French survives (uncatalogued). He was Streatham-based and the documents and some objects which survive would undoubtedly throw fascinating new light on the performing arts scene. Equally the diary and archive connected with the actor Alan Rolfe should also reveal grassroots history to complement the study of large institutions such as the Streatham Hill Theatre (see p. 62).

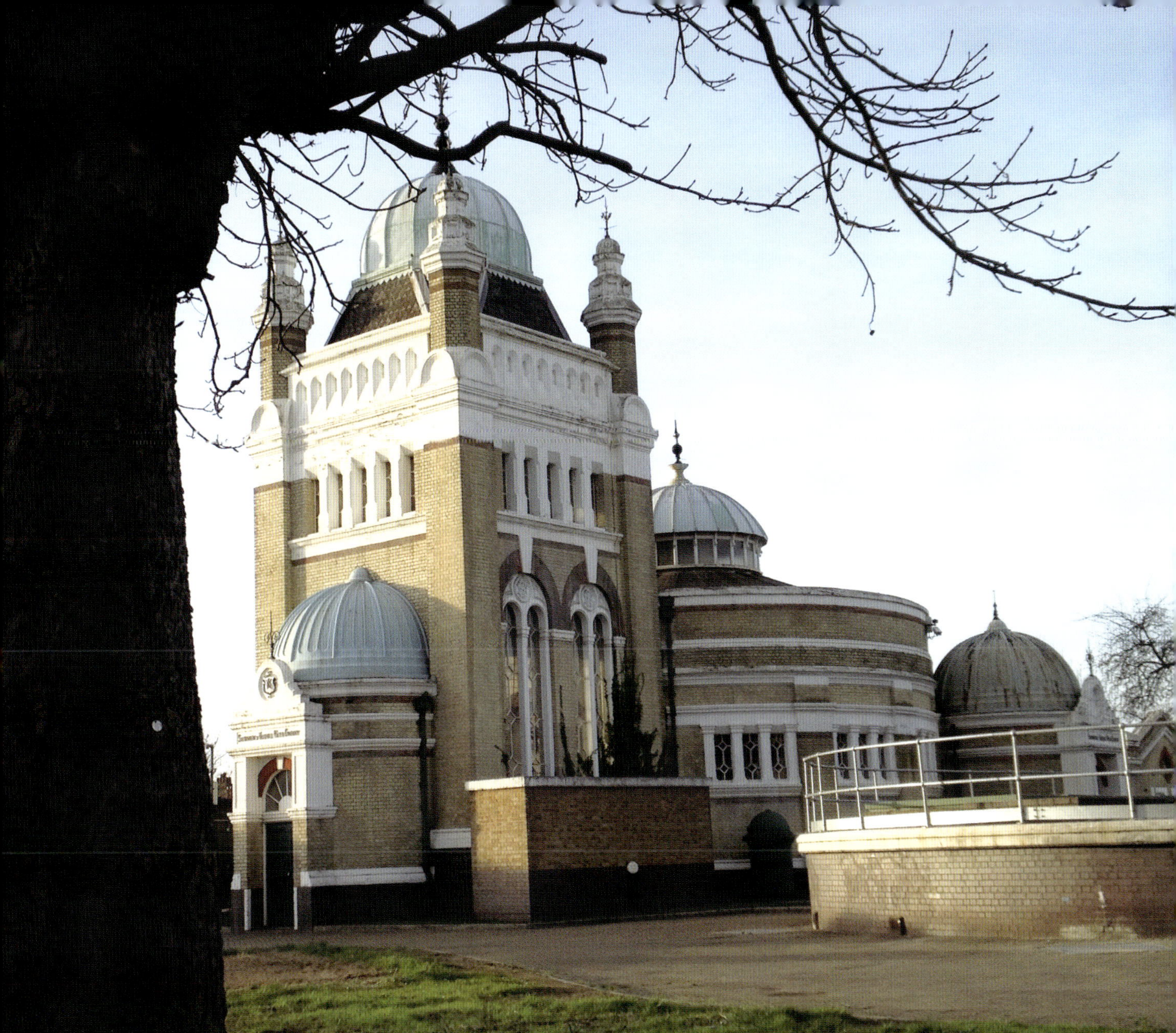

The Pumping Station in Conyers Road: John W Brown has noted that the freeholder of the land, Mr Thompson, agreed to the erection of a pumping station provided it was of an ornamental character and that he should approve the design before building went ahead. This wonderful structure obviously met with his approval.

10. Water

(paired with 'Pond' on p. 102)

'The preponderance of surface water across the parish was a perennial problem to villagers' wrote Graham Gower in his book *Streatham – Origins and Early History*. Keeping the water from flooding the main roads was a major concern and there were numerous examples of villagers being fined for not clearing their ditches properly. In nineteenth-century London, the great age for water management, they tamed the water but have left many signs of its presence throughout the neighbourhood ranging from 'nature sites' such as Hermitage Bridge, at the southern tip of Streatham High Road, to large infrastructure sites as at Conyers Road (pump engine) and Streatham Hill (reservoir).

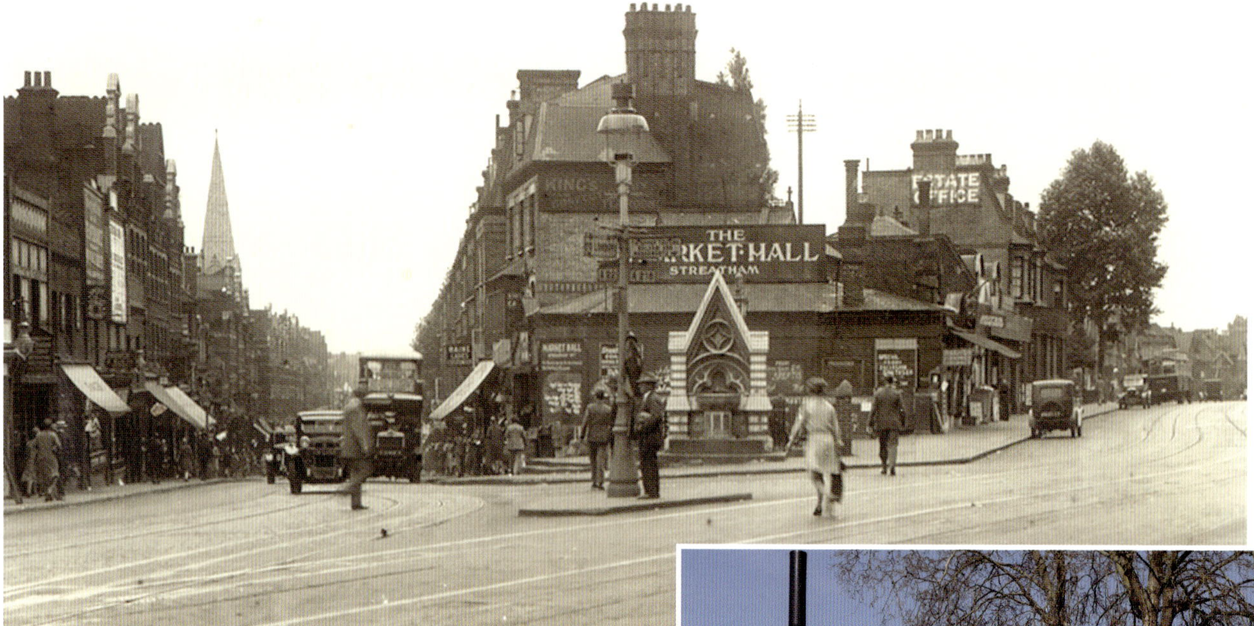

The Dyce Fountain, then – at the junction of Mitcham Lane and the High Road – and now – on Streatham Green. *© John W Brown, Local History Publications for the postcard.*

To replace the late eighteenth-century pump house in Streatham High Road, the Lambeth Water Company, established in 1785, brought piped water to Streatham in 1832 after building a large reservoir at Streatham Hill. This covered facility still exists, at the back of Pullman Court: it provides a green opening for residents on the east side of Pullman Court – for their eyes only as public access is prohibited. The gradual suburbanisation of Streatham, slow at first, became so relentless that this led to the building of the beautiful pumping station in Conyers Road in 1888, sometimes described as a 'Moorish temple' or mistaken for a mosque. It was built for the Southwark and Vauxhall water company in 1894. Water companies disappeared with the creation of the Metropolitan Water Board in 1903.

In Streatham there is a vast array of sites linked to water and they come in all shapes and sizes:

- **River Graveney** flowing at the southern end of Streatham under Hermitage bridge
- **Wells**: those found on Streatham Common represented a great draw to Streatham; they were later replaced by the wells off Valley Road
- **Fountain**: Dyce Fountain is featured in the artistic chapter but is mentioned here as an example of the London Fountain movement which began in 1859 (see below).
- **Holy well**: Graham Gower has established, through patient examination of archival records, that there was a holy well or spring at the site where Ritherdon Road and Balham High Road meet – formerly in the parish of Streatham. It was first mentioned in 1312.
- **Ponds**: they were dotted around the whole area, on commons but also on private estates such as Park Hill or Bedford House, often the result of digging for gravel. See p. 46 for the pond on Tooting Common.

- **Swimming pools**: the magnificent Lido on Tooting Common will be familiar. Built in 1906 it is the oldest and largest outdoor pool in London. Simon Inglis points out that 'of the ten built [in London] from 1875–1913, just one survives, at Tooting Bec'. But less well known, now that they have all been filled in or covered up, are the private swimming pools to be found on the ambitious Art Deco estates such as Pullman Court and the High.

A fountain movement in a city awash with water deserves an explanation. This organisation started in 1859 with a first fountain erected outside the church of St Sepulchre in the City of London: they called themselves The Metropolitan Free Drinking Fountain Association soon revised, in 1867, to The Metropolitan Drinking Fountain and Cattle Trough Association, one of their troughs survives outside the Rookery Café on Streatham Common. Three years later, in 1862, Streatham would acquire its own fountain, designed by William Dyce, the grand Victorian artist who was closely involved with his local church – St Leonard's. His fountain, across the road from the church, was one of eighty five erected in the first six years of the London fountain movement. Historians frequently cite sanitation and the fear of cholera – but despite early breakthroughs in the 1840s and 1850s, scientists failed to persuade the authorities before the mid-1860s that this disease was water- rather than air-borne.

What everyone knew however, was that the quality of water coming from the water companies could be unreliable. An early and vivid example from north west London could be cited here. Acting on behalf of the landlord of the St John's Wood estate, Walpole Eyre writes to the Grand Junction Water Works in 1814:

> 'I send a Jug of Water that you may see the State it came into my house yesterday … I have now submitted to use the Grand Junction Water for above six months in the most filthy and dirty state & I am constantly under the necessity of sending for other Water to boil Fish and other things in'.

Forty years later during the cholera epidemic of 1854, the physician John Snow (1813–1858) established that the cause of the outbreak in Soho was the public pump and also that the Southwark and Vauxhall waterworks company was drawing water from sewage-polluted sections of the Thames. But no further action was taken until 1866, by which time public fountains had been appearing all over London for seven years, with the basic tenet 'That no fountain be erected or promoted by the Association which shall not be so constructed as to ensure by filters, or other suitable means, the perfect purity and coldness of the water.'

Both the fountain and temperance movements (the latter had developed in the first half of the nineteenth century) quickly realised that each reinforced the other's cause. And the temperance movement had a powerful Streatham advocate in Sir Kingsmill Grove Key, Bart. and his wife. In 1877 he married the widow of James Hill, the tobacco manufacturer, who lived at the Rookery on Streatham Common between 1851 and 1871. He may have helped finance the building of the Beehive Coffee House designed by Ernest George and George Peto for the Immanuel Church Temperance Association, concerned that the mill workers were spending too much time and money at the nearby Pied Bull pub. The Keys held an annual Christmas dinner for the poor at the Beehive Coffee House.

4.

A TOUR OF STREATHAM IN TEN PAINTINGS

Jiro Osuga

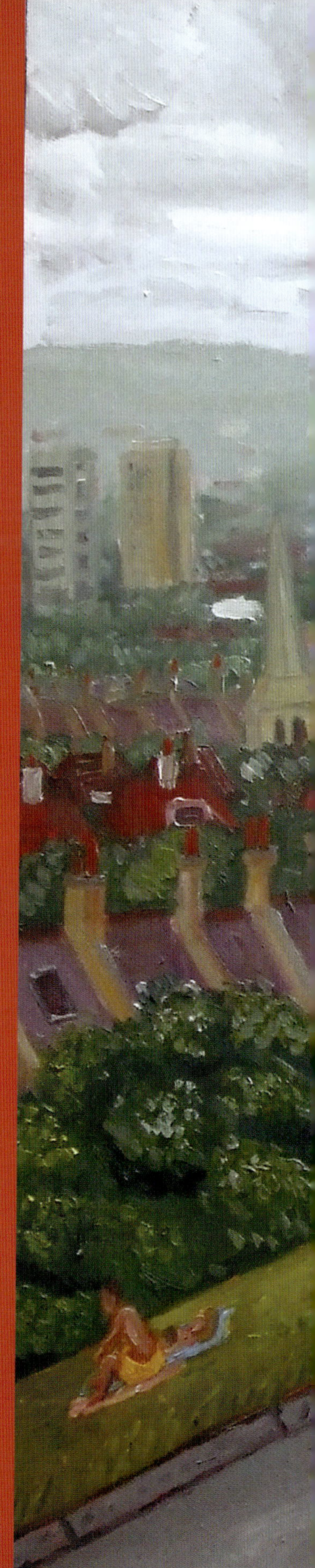

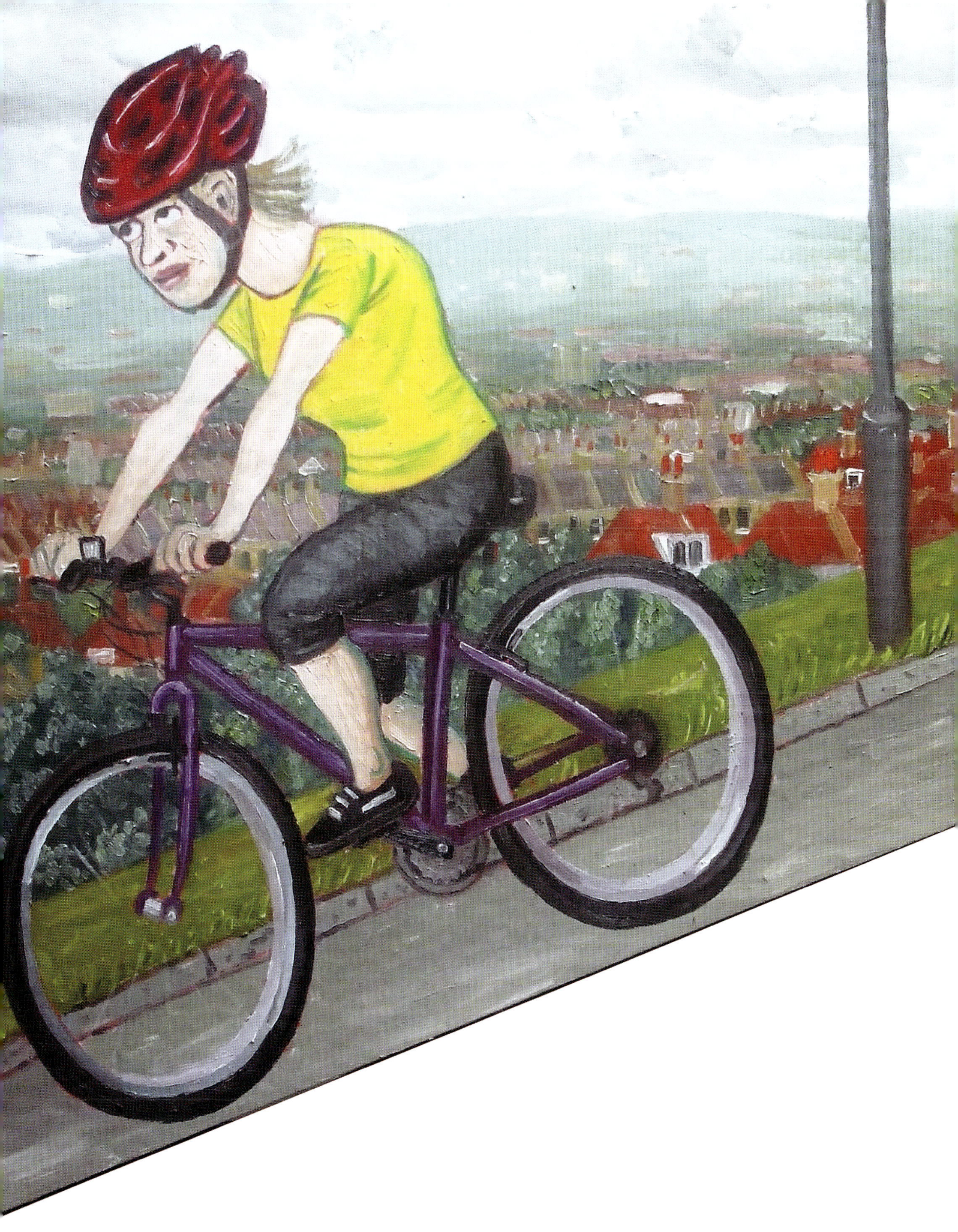

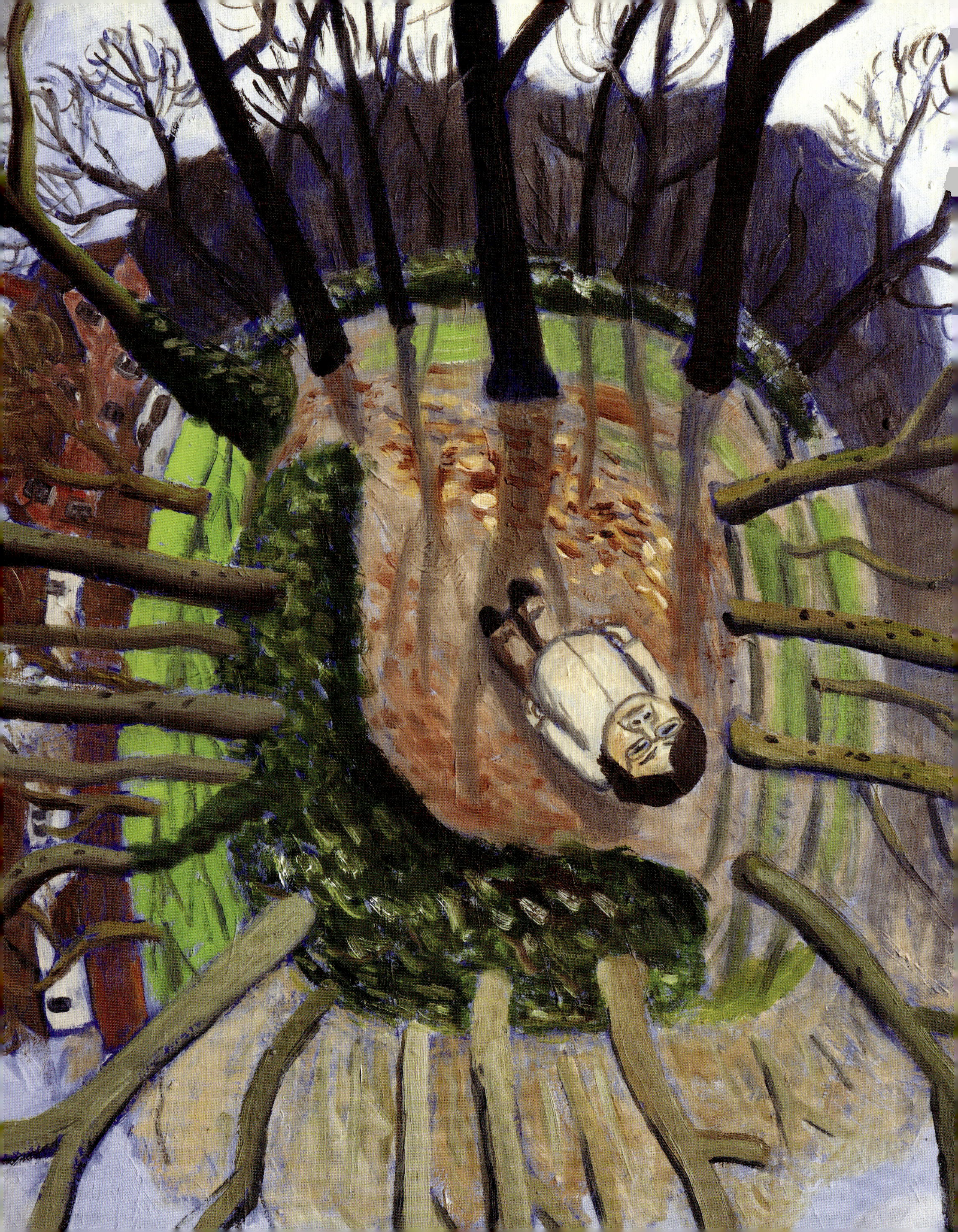

In this chapter I would like to take the reader on a tour of Streatham by looking at ten of my paintings in which the neighbourhood is prominently represented. These paintings interpret Streatham themes which are discussed in the preceding chapter – A Tour of Streatham in Ten Landmarks (p. 20). For instance 'In the Woods' is paired with Open Spaces and 'Pond' with Water.

1. 'In the Woods'

2012, oil on canvas, 56 x 50 cm, Flowers Gallery.

Previous pages:

'Downhill'

from the painting 'Uphill Downhill', 2014, oil on canvas, 120 x 120cm. This was painted for Art23 (see p. 95 and 165) when Balfe's Bikes on Streatham Hill hosted my paintings during the 2014 Streatham Festival. The cityscape in the background is loosely based on views from Streatham Common. *Flowers Gallery.*

Tooting Bec Common is my local park, within sight from my studio window. It is my daily routine to go for a cycle-ride or a walk in the morning before breakfast, during the course of which I almost always pass through the Common.

There are many spots in the Common where I like to stop to take in the scenery: on the viaduct on Bedford Hill where I study the effects of the atmosphere on distant trees; the pond in the middle of the Common with its waterfowl and ever-changing reflections on water (see p. 102); the clump of tall Italian poplars by the railway line towards Balham with their shimmering traceries of overlapping branches.

This painting celebrates one of my other regular haunts, the woods between the railway line and Garrad's Road. I love to stand in the middle of the woods in sunny winter or early spring days before the trees have come into leaf, and look at the effect of sunlight on the trunk and branches: silhouetted *contre-jour* against the light, etched with dark shadows, or ablaze in the face of sunlight. The painting attempts to capture the effect of light in all direction by adopting a 360-degrees panoramic composition.

The way the railway lines cut off this and other parts of the Common from the rest is unfortunate. It is a brutal act of Victorian engineering vandalism the likes of which would not nowadays be tolerated – the equivalent of carving out a spaghetti junction inside a park. But the viaducts do make nice vantage points from which to survey the surrounding scenery.

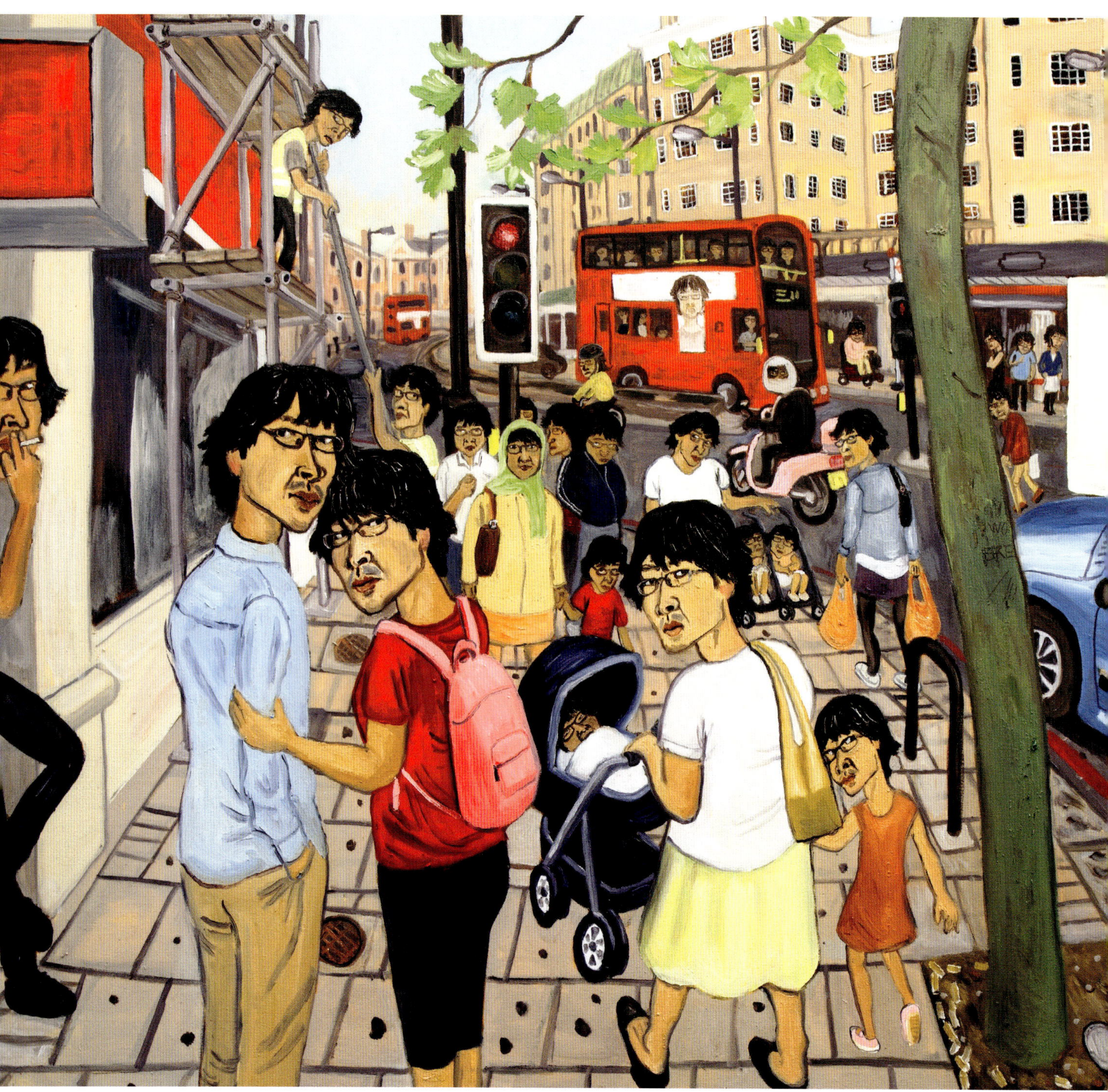

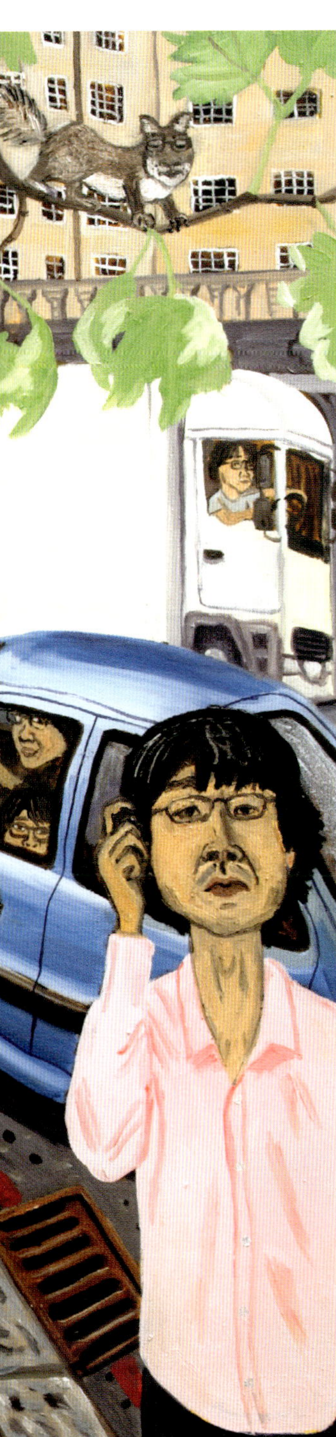

2. 'The Multitude'

2013, oil on canvas, 90 x 131cm, private collection.

This is one of the very few paintings in which the setting is quite closely based on a recognisable street in Streatham – namely the High Road, looking north, opposite The High apartments. I never paint directly from nature, but in this case, I made sketches in situ which were then transposed to canvas.

But the people in the painting are anything but realistic. Every man, woman and child in the painting, even the squirrel and the pigeon have my face! Why this is so, I do not know myself, even though I painted the picture – you have to understand, painting at its best is a semi-conscious activity. It may be that I was thinking about compassion – how, if you could put yourself in other people's shoes – if you could *become* other people – all the fear, hatred and aggravation that bedevil our world will cease. But on the other hand, if that were so, wouldn't you be very lonely – the equivalent of being the only person left alive on the planet? I also remember wondering if I should call the painting *For Whom the Bell Tolls*, referencing John Donne's famous poem:

> *No man is an I[s]land, intire of it selfe; every man is a piece of the Continent, a part of the Maine; if a Clo[u]d bee washed away by the Sea, Europe is the lesse, as well as if a Premontory were, as well as if a Manner of thy Friends, or of thine own were; Any mans death diminishes mee because I am involved in Mankinde, and therefore never send to know for whom the Bell tolls; It tolls for thee.*

So although in the painting Streatham's culturally diverse population is replaced by an extreme monoculture, its message, if there is one, is a plea for tolerance and inclusivity.

3. 'Studio'

2005, oil on canvas, 50 x 60 cm, private collection.

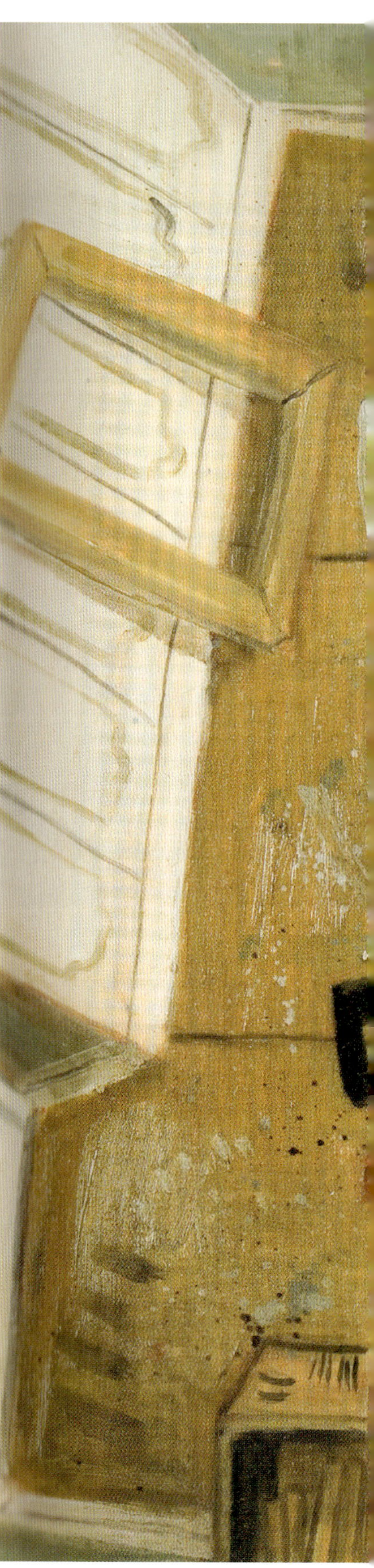

My studio is the front room of a first floor flat in a large early twentieth-century semi on Woodbourne Avenue. The room must have once been the master bedroom. There is a basin in one corner of the room which is handy for cleaning brushes, and the capacious wardrobe serves as storage for smaller paintings. The room faces north, which is traditionally considered to be the optimum aspect for an artist's studio, as light comes from the same direction throughout the day and casts a steady shadow on a posing model. But this is immaterial to me as I never employ models. It would actually make a lot of sense to move the studio to the warmer south-facing room, especially in winter.

In the painting I appear to be having a mid-day nap on the paint-splattered studio floor half-way through the process of making a wooden canvas stretcher. I find sleep is very good for painting. You apprehend things truthfully when you see a painting immediately after waking up. Often, when you have been working for hours and hours, you are wont to develop a misplaced belief in your skills as a painter, or conversely beat yourself up about your inability to get things right. A brief kip instantly clears away these delusions.

Unsurprisingly, the houses on the opposite side of Woodbourne Avenue that I see daily from the studio window make frequent appearances in my paintings. The canvas illustrated below is an example. The inter-war semis are white-washed, and on sunny days, at around midday, they reflect a beautiful light through the studio windows.

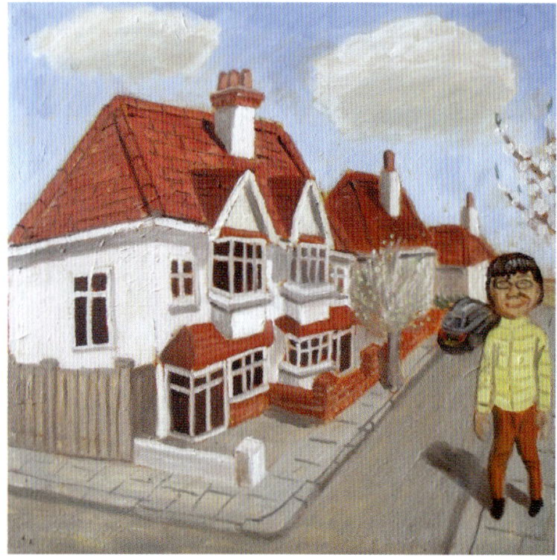

'My Street'

2016, oil on canvas, 46 x 48 cm, *Flowers Gallery*.

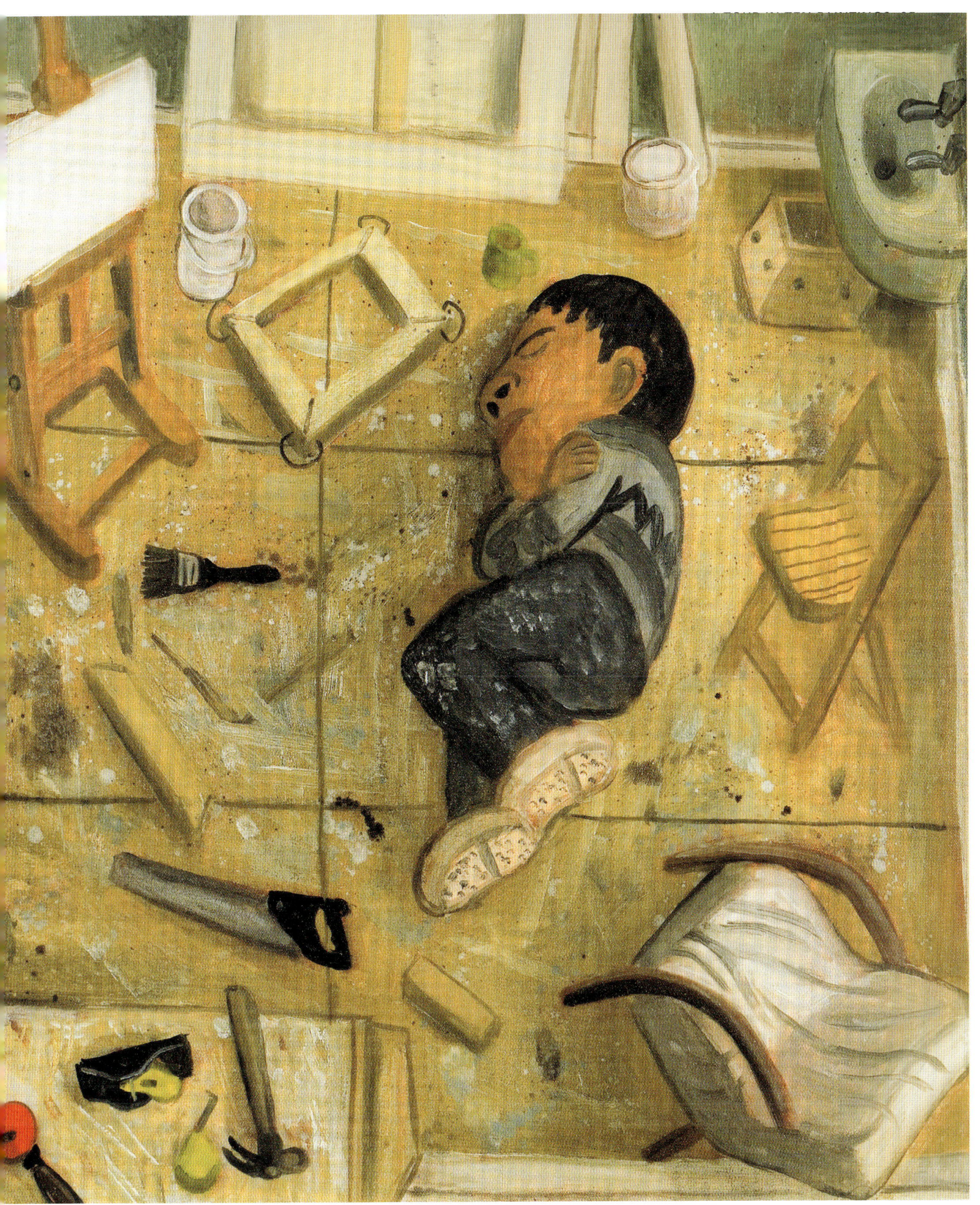

4. 'Corner Shop'

2005, oil on canvas, 180 x 160 cm, Flowers Gallery.

Very often, form comes before subject matter in my painting. 'Corner Shop' is an example. It was the idea of a two panel screen with a corner that inspired me to paint a corner shop, rather than a shop inspiring me to paint it in this format.

As with 'Drinker' (see p. 92), I filled out the details of the painting by carrying out secret research. I can't whip out my pocket sketchbook in a shop. So every morning, when I went to a newsagent's to buy a paper, I would make mental notes of an item or two in the shop, and then draw what I saw back home, slowly building up a complete picture of a corner shop day by day. The structure of the shelves, the shape of the chewing gum rack, the types of ice cream in the fridge... As a point of principle, I avoid painting from my own photographs. In any case this painting was made long before I owned a smart phone.

So the painting is a compendium of various newsagents in and around Streatham where I used to buy my daily paper. Nowadays I rarely buy printed newspapers, opting instead to read my news online like many people. The ritual of morning visits to the newsagents is a thing of the past.

Note some of the names of the items stocked on the shelves. I can't resist wordplay given the opportunity! The very shape of the painting is one big visual pun too.

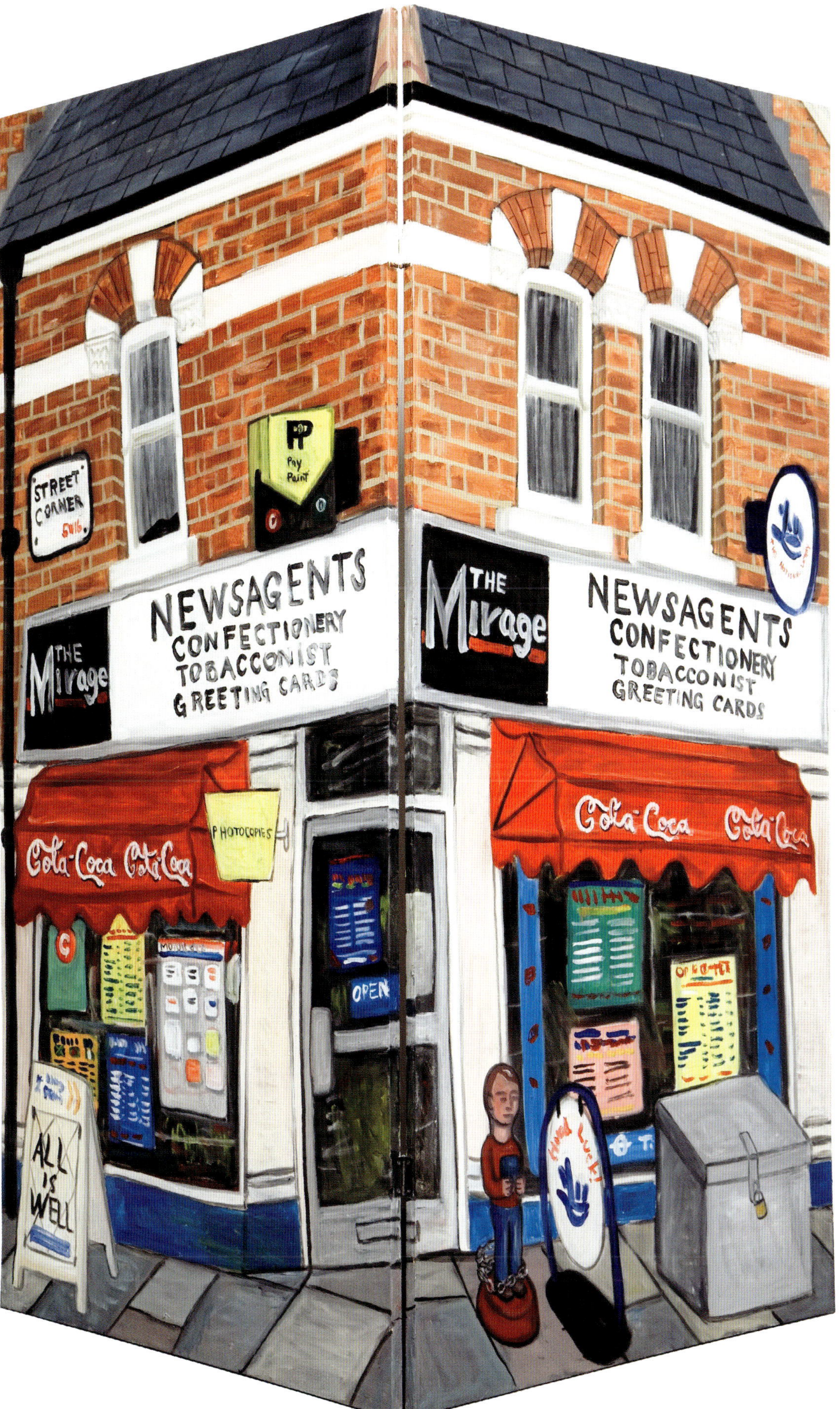
STREET CORNER
Pay Point
THE Mirage
NEWSAGENTS
CONFECTIONERY
TOBACCONIST
GREETING CARDS
THE Mirage
NEWSAGENTS
CONFECTIONERY
TOBACCONIST
GREETING CARDS
PHOTOCOPIES
Cola-Coca Cola-Coca
Cola-Coca Cola-Coca
OPEN
ALL IS WELL

Inside 'Corner Shop'. *Flowers Gallery.*

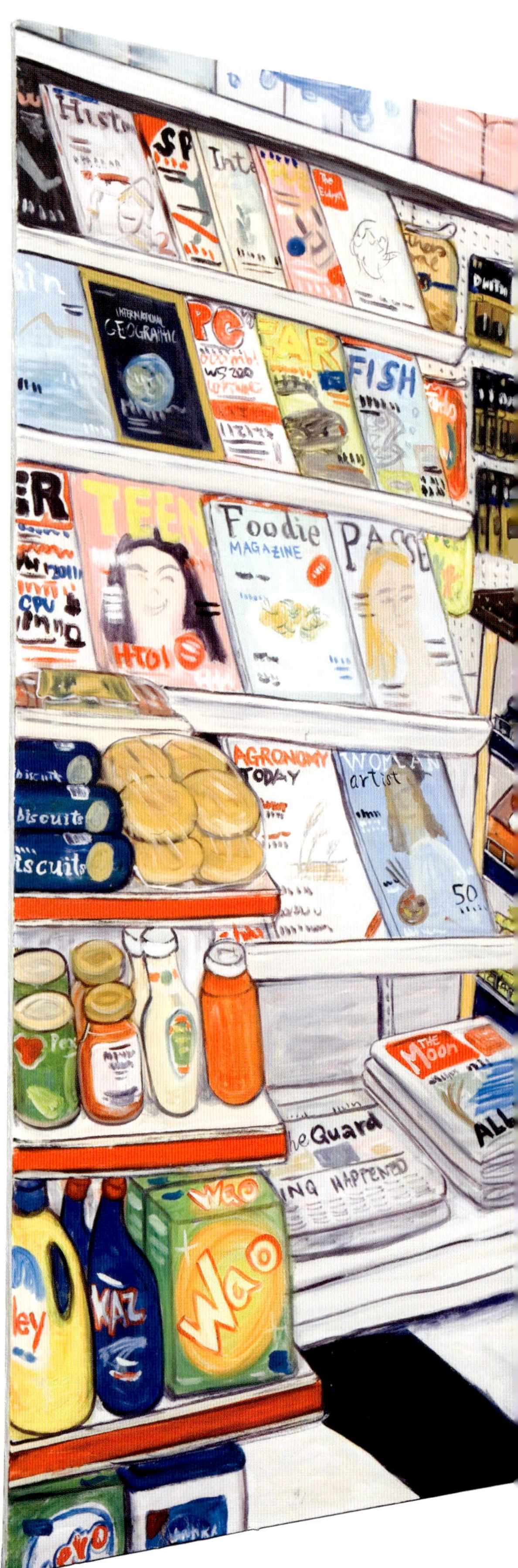

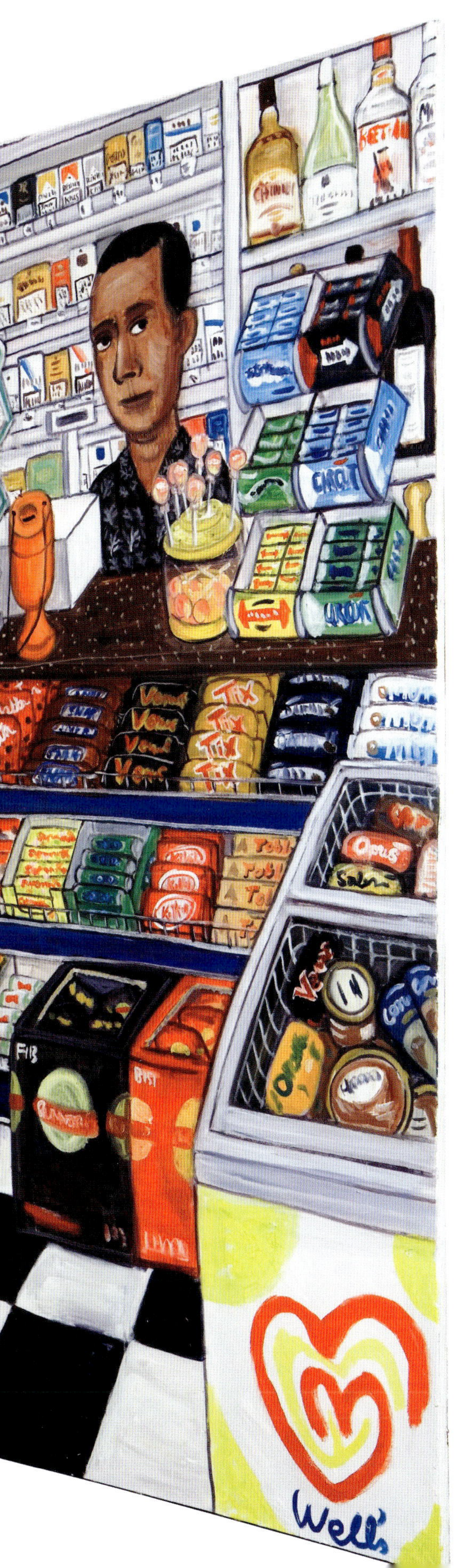
Opus

5. 'Own Brand'

2006, oil on canvas, 80 x 85 cm, Flowers Gallery

On the face of it, it doesn't look as if this contemporary still life has anything to do with Streatham. That is until you read the label on the bottle of red wine to the right of the composition which reads:

Mis en bouteille au château
Chateau Jiro
Streatham
Appellation contrôlée
2006

The 'chateau' pictured on the label is the house in Woodbourne Avenue where my flat is located.

All the other labels in the painting are odd too – they all bear my name or portrait, hence the title of this painting – 'Own Brand'.

I am not a great shopper. As an impecunious artist, I am excluded from modern consumer culture, and I am habituated to seeking out the cheapest price tags for the necessities that I do buy. I pay no heed to fashion, the latest gizmos or food fads. I do not seek out retailers who stock quality products, or quaint establishments known only to the cognoscenti. So those readers who expected an artist's tips on cool places to shop in SW16 will be disappointed. I only ever shop in ordinary places where everybody else goes: WH Smith's, Boots, Sainsbury's, and increasingly, Lidl.

But what does 'Own Brand' mean? Is it a celebration of the sheer variety of modern packaging design – those plastic tubs, tins, boxes and bottles we all discard without as much as a glance? Is it a counter-attack on mass consumerism through the personalisation of mass-produced items? Or is it just another example of my egomania? As is usual with my painting, I don't know!

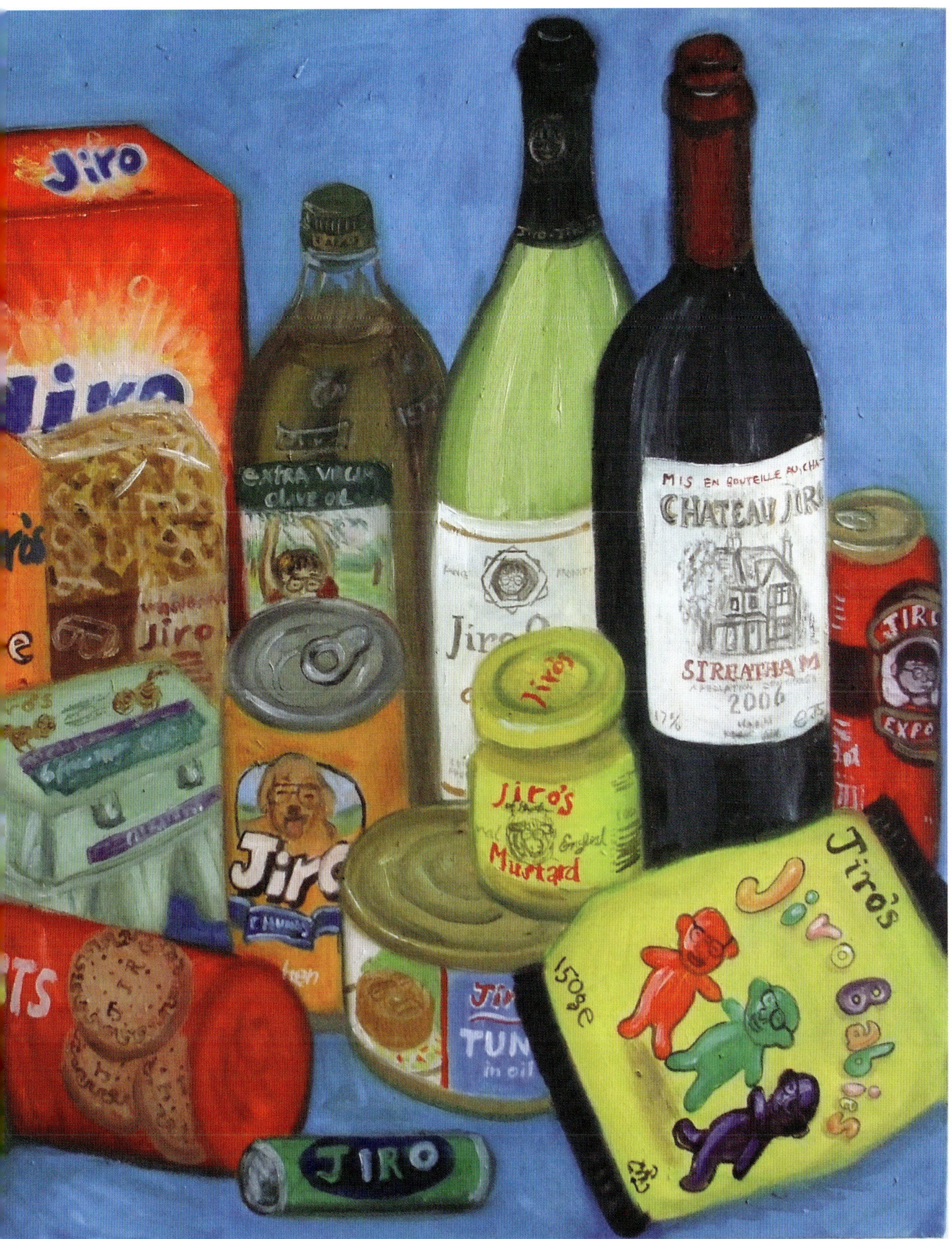

Jiro
Jiro
EXTRA VIRGIN
OLIVE OIL
MIS EN BOUTEILLE AU CHAT
CHATEAU JIR
STREATHAM
2006
Jiro's
Jiro's
Mustard
TUN
in oil
EXPO
Jiro's
Jiro Babies
150ge
JIRO

6. 'Drinker'

2007, oil on canvas, 123 x 91cm, Flowers Gallery.

In the popular imagination, artists are supposed to hang out in disreputable hostelries where they carouse with their bohemian chums, discuss Existentialism over glasses of absinthe, draw up avant-garde manifestoes and flirt with pretty serving wenches. I hardly ever do any of these things, though I am sure some other artists do. In fact, in all my years in Streatham, I have visited a local pub only about five times, and most of those visits were made with the express aim of making sketches for an idea I had for a painting.

One such idea was 'Drinker'. For "research", I went in to the Five Bells on the High Road. Carefully positioning myself on a stool with a good view of the bar, I furtively scribbled away in my pocket sketchbook, pretending to compile a fictitious shopping list while very slowly downing a pint.

The cyclical consumption of alcohol illustrated in the painting is largely fictitious. As far as I am aware, I am not an alcoholic. However, like many people, I do have experience of being trapped in other kinds of vicious circles, and know how hard it is to break free once you are stuck in a rut. The painting was only partly conceived in jest.

Although not a great drinker or a socialite, I do enjoy the atmosphere and decorative details of the British boozer. I like the pumps, the glittering bottles on the racks, and the poses drinkers assume when they prop up the bar.

"Research" is fun too. You can just fire away and draw and draw, not worrying at all if the results are any good or not, because they are only sketches and will never be exhibited. I have heard some writers say much the same about their research.

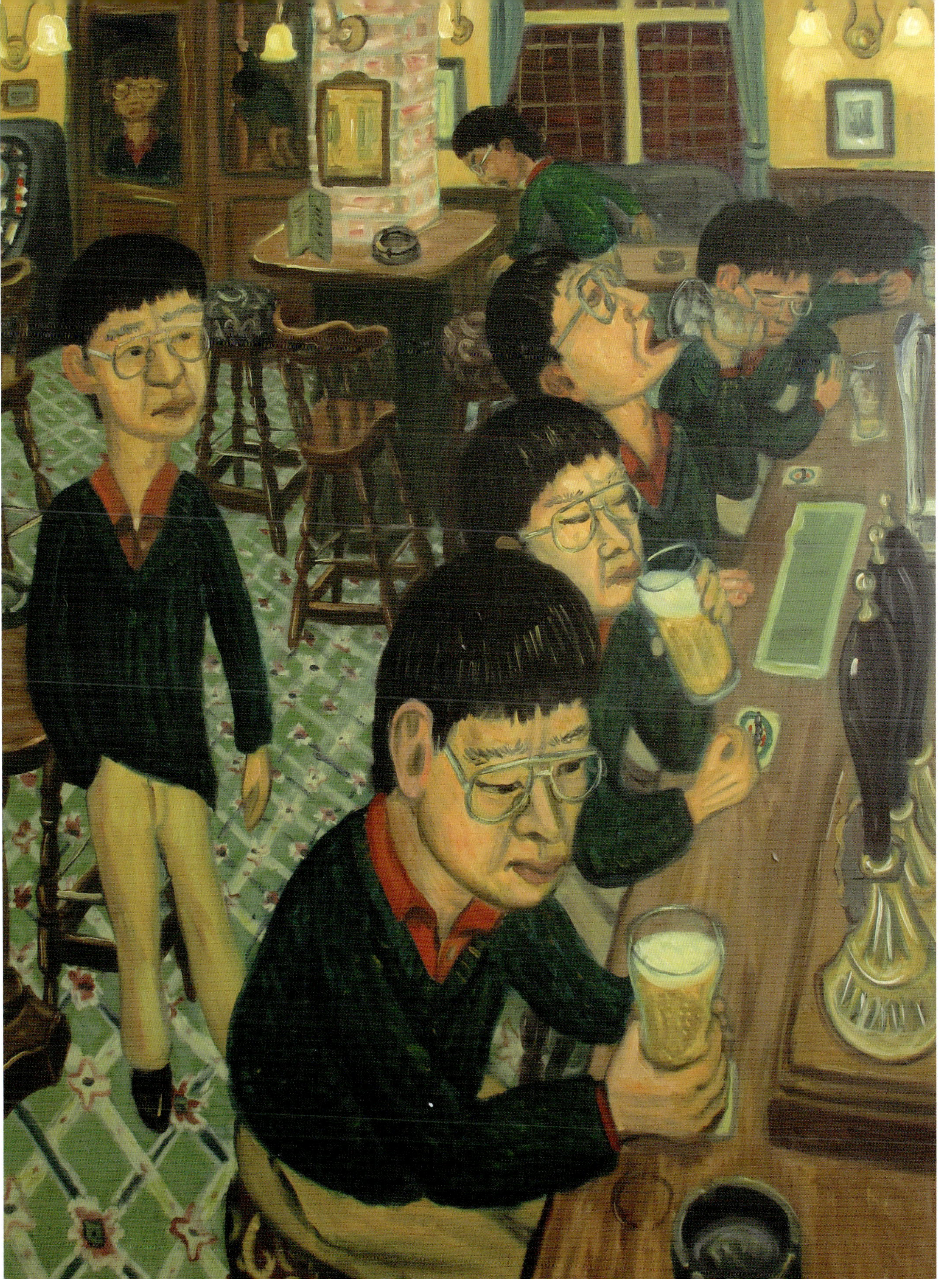

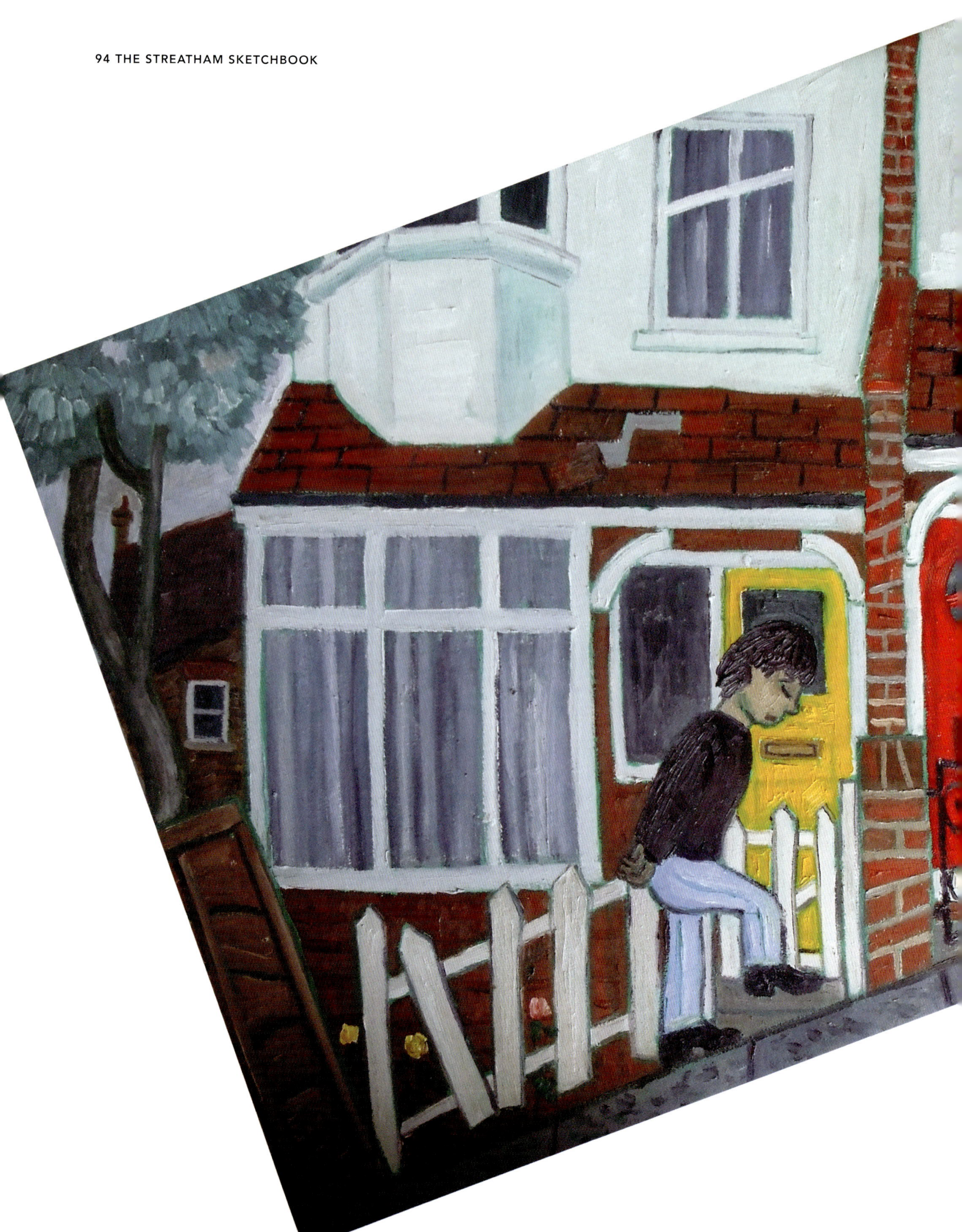

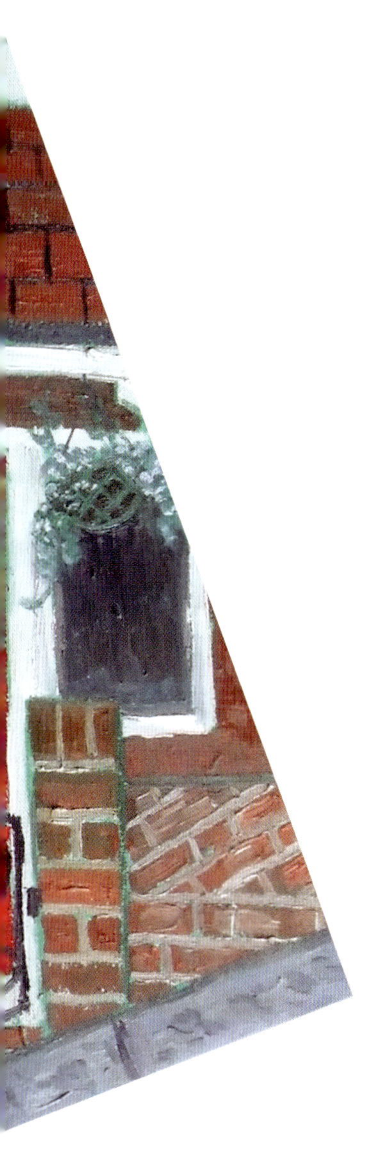

7. 'Hill'

2014, oil on canvas, 63 x 77cm, Flowers Gallery.

I sometimes cycle up Hill House Road, one of the steepest hills in Streatham for a bit of exercise. The slow huffing and puffing ascent gives me ample time to study how the houses and fences of the street cope with the steep incline. I wonder why floors always have to be level. Surely a sloping floor would obviate the need for chairs – all you need is a cushion or two. The Campo, the famous scallop-shaped public square in the heart of Siena slopes gently inwards at an angle very conducive to sitting on the flagstones. Can't we have the equivalent in your lounge if your house happens to be built on a slope? That said, you will have to cut the legs of all your furniture different lengths, rendering them useless should you ever move house...

The painting was based on studies I made on the spot, but exaggerates the steepness of the slope somewhat, and plays with the idea of the perpendicular and angles. There are improbable lozenge-shaped bricks laid parallel to the slope. A building in the background is aligned to the hill, but has a window and a chimney which are perpendicular. The canvas itself is designed to hang at an angle.

The painting was partly inspired by the famous opening lines of *Kusamakura*, a novel by one of the founders of modern Japanese literature, Natsume Soseki (1867–1916):

> *Going up a mountain track, I fell into thinking.*
> *Approach everything rationally, and you become harsh. Pole along in the stream of emotions, and you will be swept away by the current. Give free rein to your desires, and you become uncomfortably confined. It is not a very agreeable place to live, this world of ours.*

Soseki lived in London on a Japanese government scholarship between 1901 and 1903, staying in digs in Clapham and Tooting. I don't know if he ever visited Streatham, but the novel connects to Streatham in a curious way. The novel's protagonist is a painter (as is the case in most novels, not a very convincing portrayal of my profession, if you ask me), who meets a woman who reminds him of Millais's 'Ophelia' in a country inn in deepest Japan. And 'Ophelia' was among Henry Tate's collection which once hung in Park Hill at the top of the hill in my painting! (See p. 122)

'Uphill'

from the painting 'Uphill Downhill', 2014, oil on canvas, 120 x 120 cm. This is the image on the reverse side of one of the pair of canvases that comprise 'Uphill Downhill'. The obverse shows the cyclist cruising downhill (see pp. 79 and 81). *Flowers Gallery.*

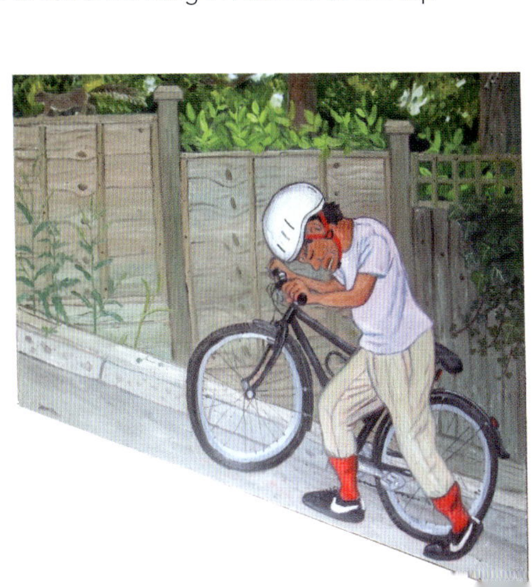

8. 'The Walled Garden'

2003, oil on canvas, 180 x 160 cm, private collection.

Another two-panel screen, this time representing the much-loved Streatham beauty spot, The Rookery in Streatham Common. I first discovered the gardens as a student over twenty years ago, when I lived in a halls of residence on nearby Leigham Court Road. The Gardens have seen its ups and downs in the meantime, but when it is properly cared for, it is as lovely as a Persian miniature. The painting was never meant to be a topographically accurate rendition of the gardens, but was based on drawings made on the spot.

Adjacent Norwood Grove is another favorite haunt of mine. I like to cycle there early in the morning to take in the distant vista of the skyscrapers of Croydon melting in the morning light.

I am fond of painting screens, and have made many over the years. They are half-way between painting and sculpture – a painting you can walk around or surround yourself with, which therefore have a greater sense of immediacy for me.

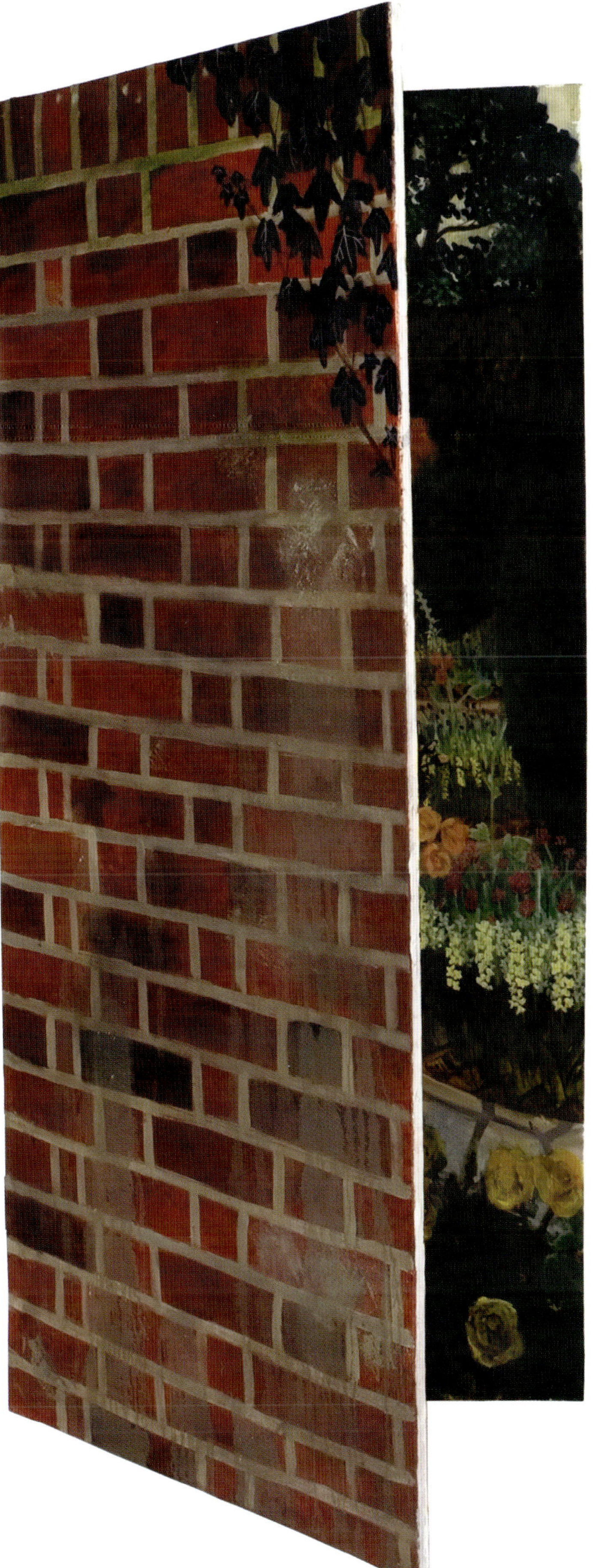

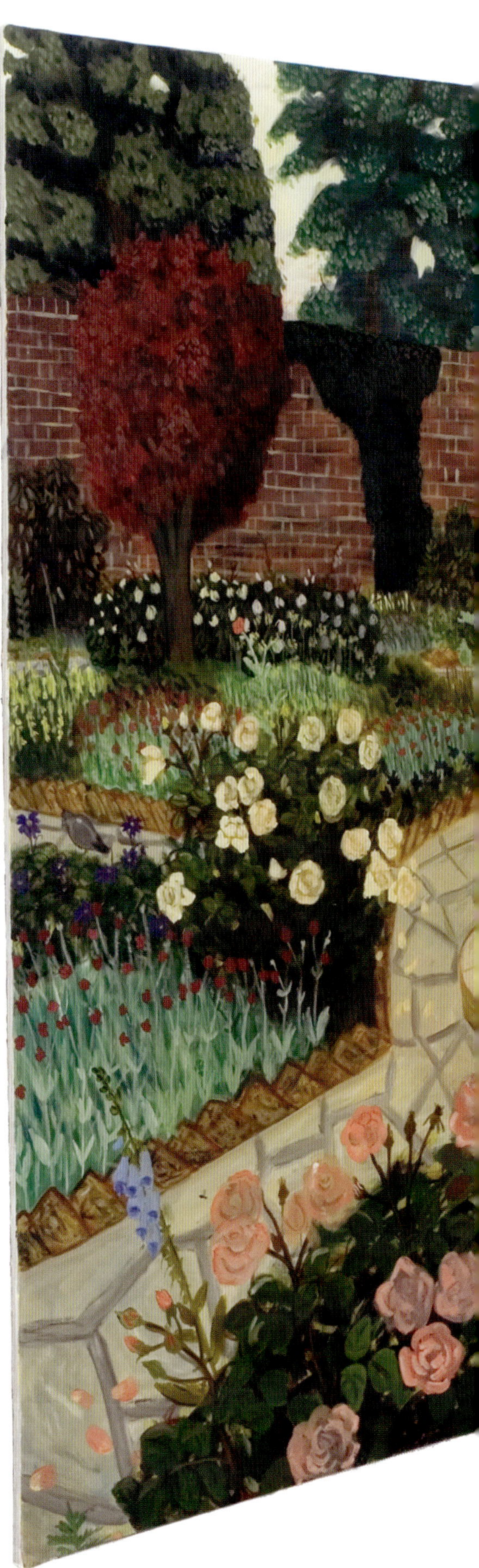

Inside the 'Walled Garden'.
Private Collection. Photo: Flowers Gallery.

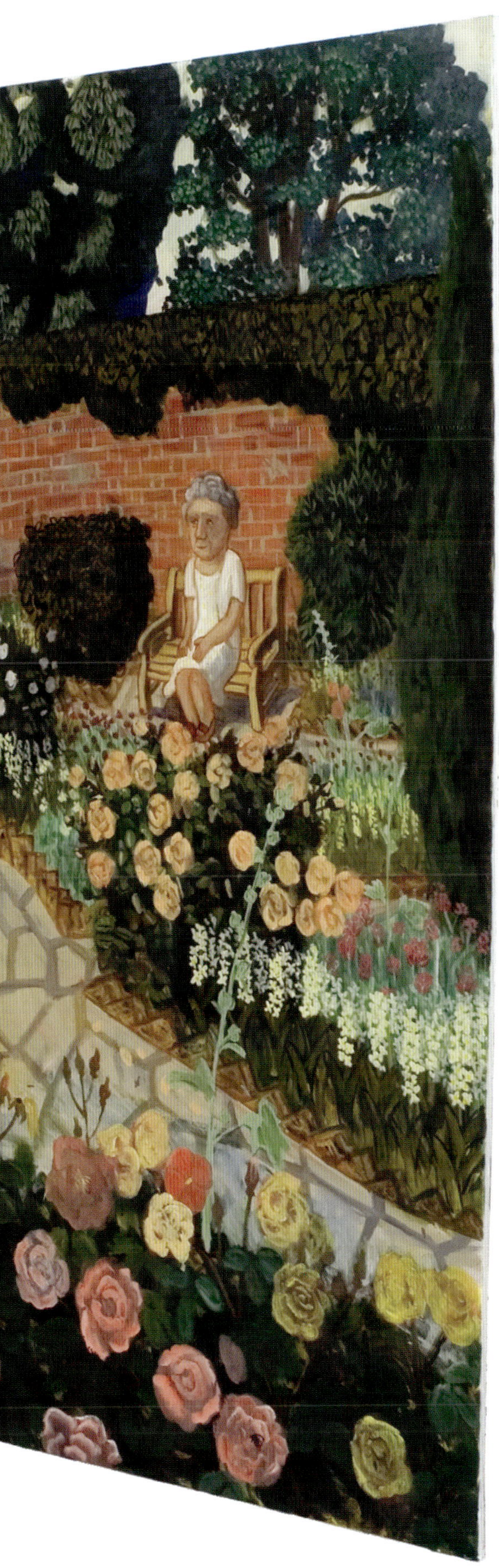

9. 'Me, a Film by Me'

2004, acrylic on paper, 115 x 83 cm, Flowers Gallery.

Unlikely as it may seem, this strange film poster was actually based on an intensive study of real posters, like the ones that line the frontage of the Streatham Odeon. I tried to incorporate every billboard cliché into the design: for example, how posters almost always feature human or anthropomorphic forms as the central focus – you rarely see films advertised by a landscape or a still life! I also noted how they often meld images together using a range of closely related colours – often in a warmish haze as in my mock poster. Another common trope is a city skyline which help add depth to the design – usually that of Manhattan, which I have replaced with the less vertiginous skyline of contemporary London in my version.

The joke in my movie poster of the star, the supporting actor, the cinematographer, the caterer and everyone else being *ME* has its serious side. Whilst it might look like a vanity trip far worse than any film directed and produced by the starring actor, it could be read, as in 'Multitude' (see p. 83), as a cry of desperate loneliness.

Despite making myself look like a one-man Hollywood, and living just a stone's throw from the Streatham Odeon, I have only seen a film there three times in fourteen years. I am no cineaste. I have never owned a TV set, and the entire lifecycle of VHS technology, from its invention to obsolescence went by before I got round to learning how to operate the system. As a child movies scared me. I used to think that people actually died when they were killed on screen. I didn't like that dizzy feeling you got when at the end of the film, you emerge blinking into daylight after immersing yourself in a super-charged, booming world inhabited by giants for the duration of the film.

Neither am I a huge fan of the disproportionate number of huge ex-cinemas that line Streatham High Road. These quaint relics of a by-gone age have their aficionados, but for me cinema-palaces with a veneer of Roman, Baroque or Egyptian styling just look fake.

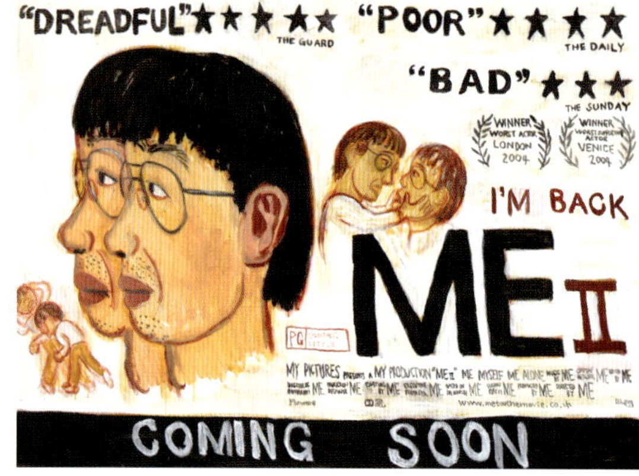

'Me II'

2004, acrylic on paper, 83 x 115 cm.

A sequel to 'Me, a Film by Me'. *Flowers Gallery.*

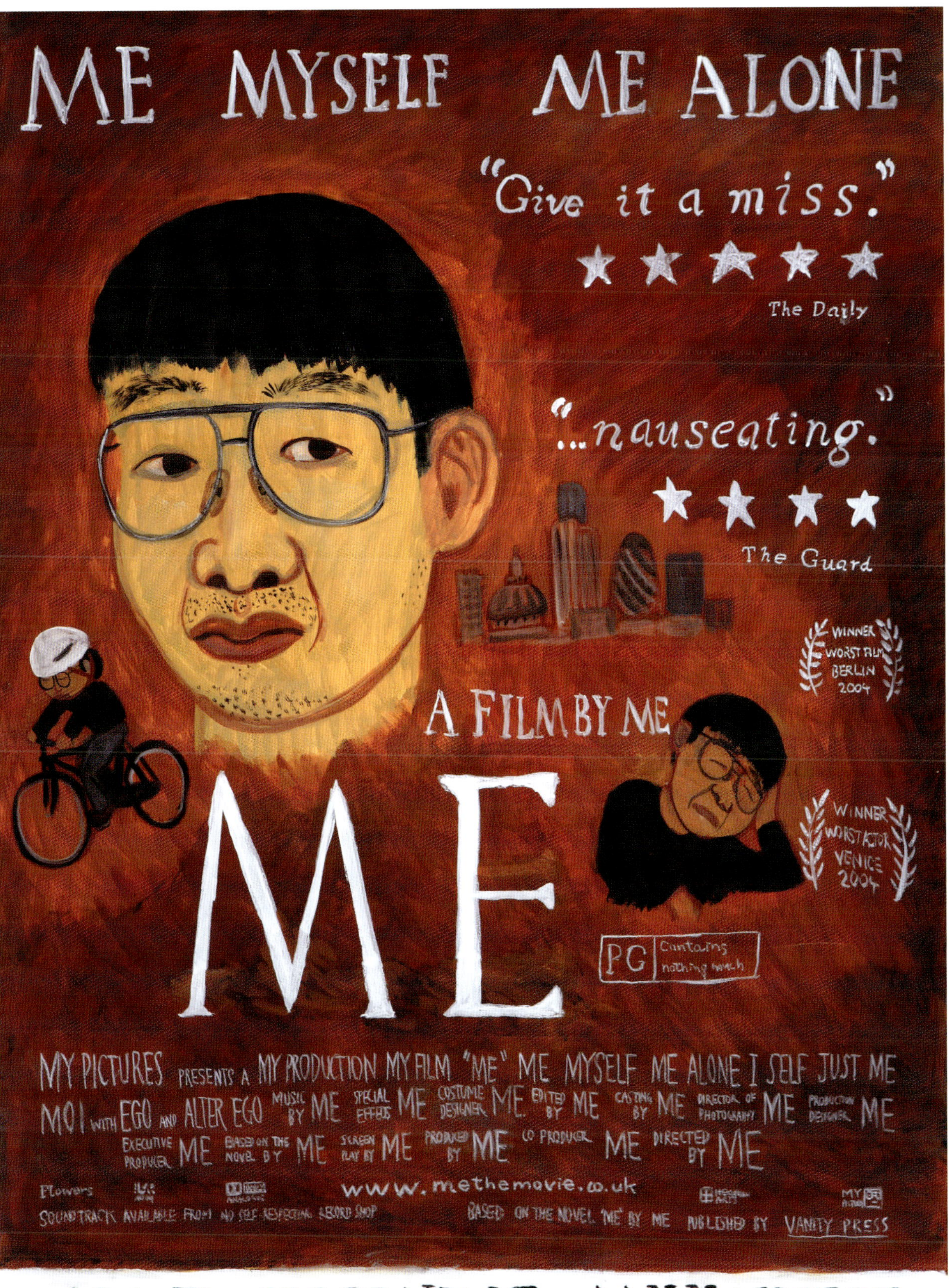

NOT SHOWING ANYWHERE

10. 'Pond'

Page from picture book 'Park', 2003, oil on paper, 40 x 60 cm, Flowers Gallery.

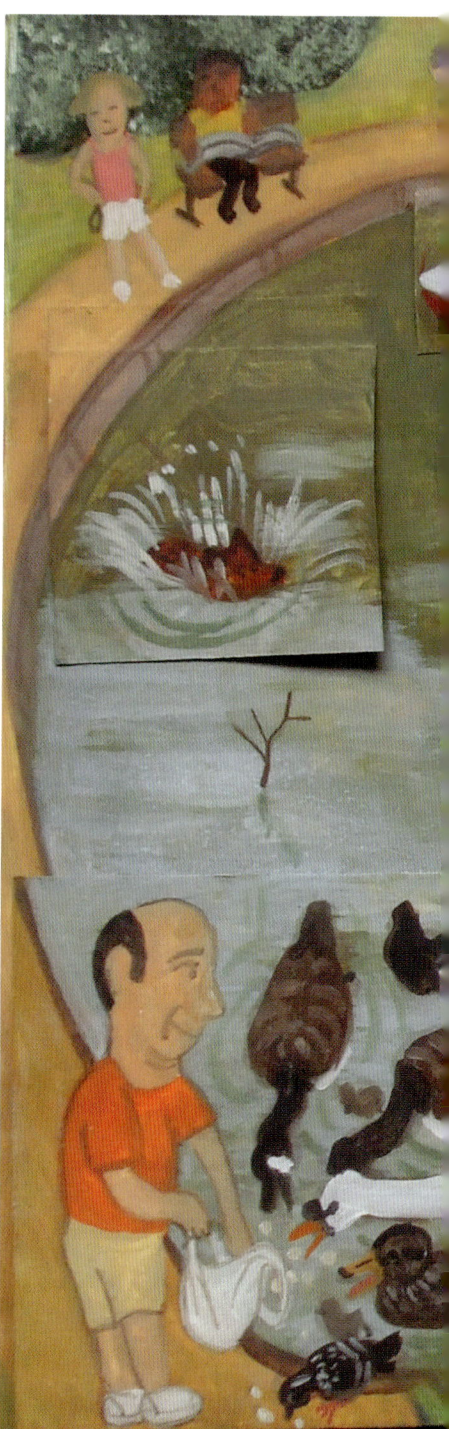

Tooting Common again, this time the lake at its centre. I sometimes halt there during my walks, and study how the rippling water reflects the trees. The ducks that congregate on the water remind me of a flotilla of battleships. The overlapping trees that line its banks are like Monet – not the famous water lilies but those very minimalist paintings of waterside trees fading into the misty distance. I head straight to the lake on bitterly cold mornings in winter when the reflections on the frozen surface have a blurry sheen, while the unfrozen parts of the pond are inky black.

This double-page spread of a pond comes from a large 'flap' book I made exploring all the different activities that goes on in a park. Based largely on Tooting Common, other pages in the book show tennis courts, an avenue of trees and a children's playground among other things. Lifting the flaps initiates all sorts of actions: birds crowd around a man feeding them crumbs, a dog jumps into the water, a heron darts at its prey. For the most part the little vignettes are based on observation, but the periscope which peers out of the water when you lift a flap near the middle of the pond is an exception!

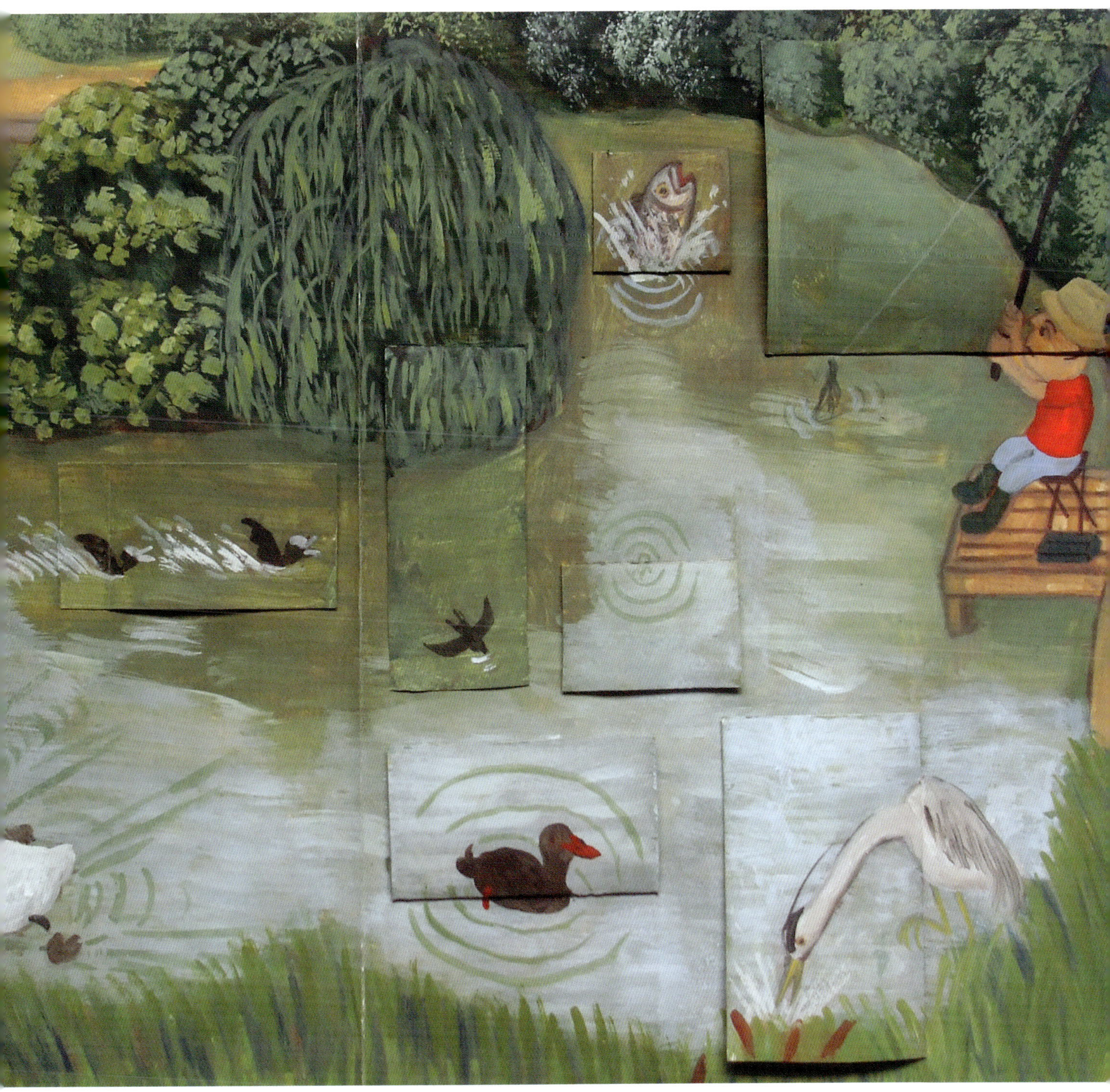

5.

STREATHAM'S ARTISTIC HERITAGE

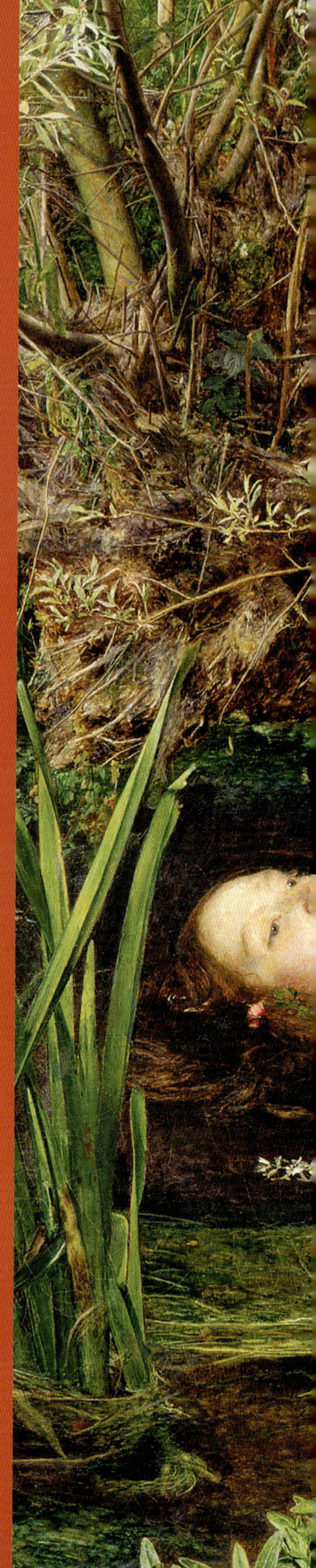

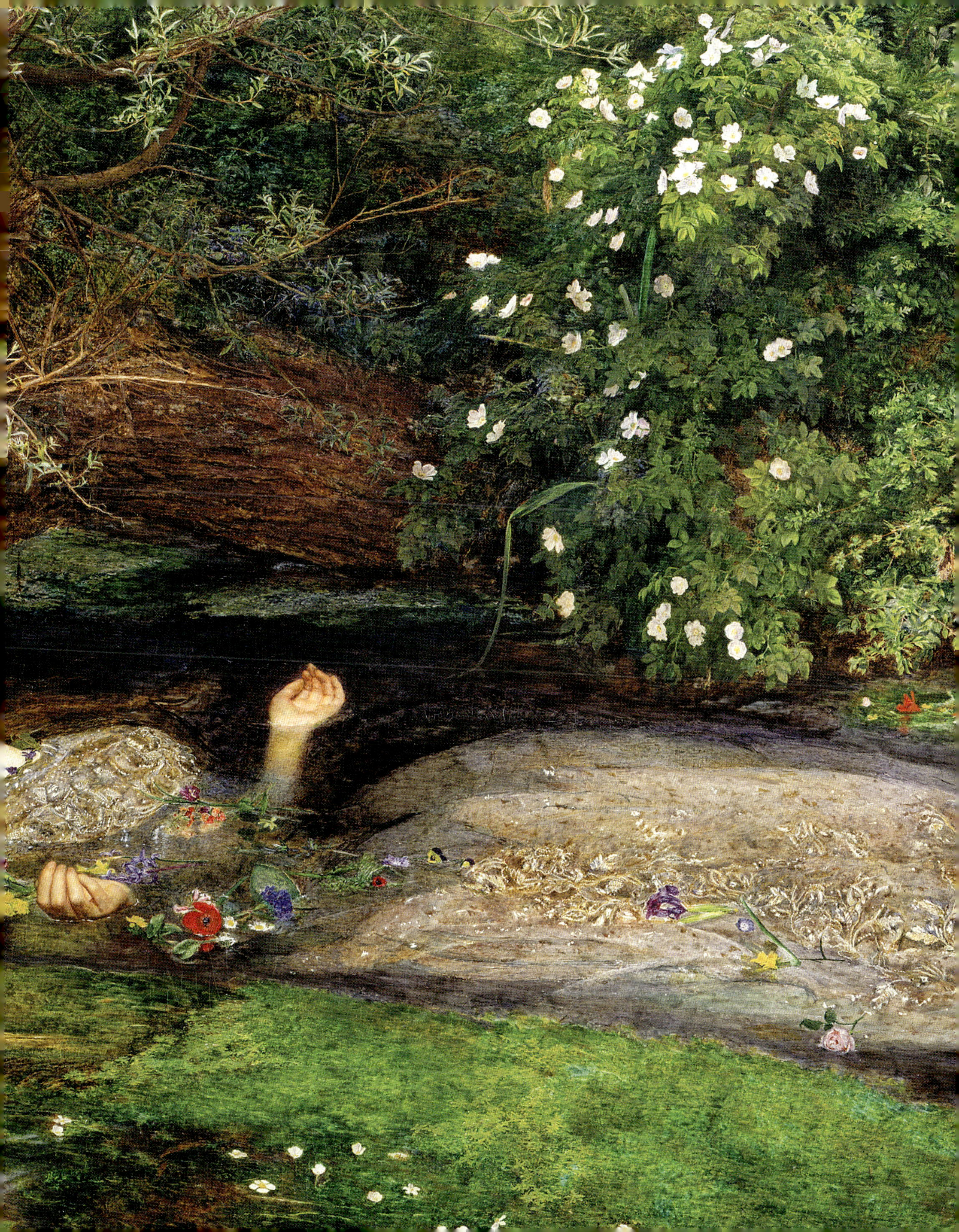

'An artist should be part of his community, should work for it, with it, and be used by it'

Benjamin Britten (1913–1976), composer

Streatham's artistic heritage has been neglected. How many people know that Streatham has important connections to three of London's key artistic institutions – the Tate and National Galleries as well as the Royal College of Art? And who knows that Vincent van Gogh, one of the giants of art, once set foot in this neighbourhood? Unlike its more famous neighbour Dulwich, Streatham does not have an art gallery or a long established college to bear witness to such heritage.

The story of art in Dulwich starts in the seventeenth century with the college and art collection founded by the wealthy Shakespearean actor Edward Alleyn. In Streatham it started a century later with the cultured and privileged Thrale family. They were affluent members of London society and passionate about the arts; but while Alleyn pursued a philanthropic mission which he succeeded in translating into a lasting institution, the Thrales' agenda was more personal and their circle of admirers and followers has vanished with them. Streatham residents only have a few relics in St Leonard's church.

At home with the Thrales

Why should we be concerned about this eighteenth-century family based on an estate called Streatham Park, when no building survives and their estate on the south side of Tooting Common is now so unrecognisable?

There are two main reasons why the Thrales loom large in the history of Streatham: first Mrs Thrale kept a diary which chronicles in great detail life in a wealthy Georgian household. It is corroborated by other Georgian diaries mentioning Streatham Park, for instance those of Fanny Burney (1752–1840) and Mrs Elizabeth Montagu (1718–1800). The second reason is that both seat and family were closely connected to one of the eighteenth-century's major literary heroes: Dr Samuel Johnson (1709–1784), of dictionary fame, whose witticisms such as 'when you are tired of London, you are tired of life' resonate in our ears to this very day.

Marriage-a-la-Mode?

The eighteenth-century artist William Hogarth painted a cruel satire of the marriage of convenience between a rich merchant and an impoverished member of the aristocracy in his famous 'Marriage a la Mode' (1743–45), six canvases which were also disseminated through engravings. The paintings, now in the National Gallery, chart the married life of the son of a bankrupt Earl with the daughter of a rich City merchant. Hogarth is extremely clever at visualising the social gap which exists between the couple, and leads us through to a tragic end: husband and wife living separate and dissolute lives which end when he is killed in a duel and she commits suicide.

Previous pages: Detail of 'Ophelia', painted in 1851–2 by John Everett Millais, one of the founder members of the Pre-Raphaelite Brotherhood of painters. It depicts a scene from Shakespeare's play *Hamlet*: at the news of the murder of her father by Hamlet, Ophelia, mad with grief, drowns herself. The work was one of the sixty seven works of art given by Streatham resident Henry Tate to the state – to accompany the gift of the Tate Gallery building on Millbank. *© Tate, London 2017.*

Right: Joshua Reynolds, 'Mrs Thrale and her Daughter', 1777. When the time came to sell this painting, Fanny Burney recorded: 'To Mrs Thrale's intense disappointment her own portrait went cheaply, causing her to complain that it was worth twice the price *'even as a History-Piece'*. *The Beaverbrook Art Gallery, Canada* .

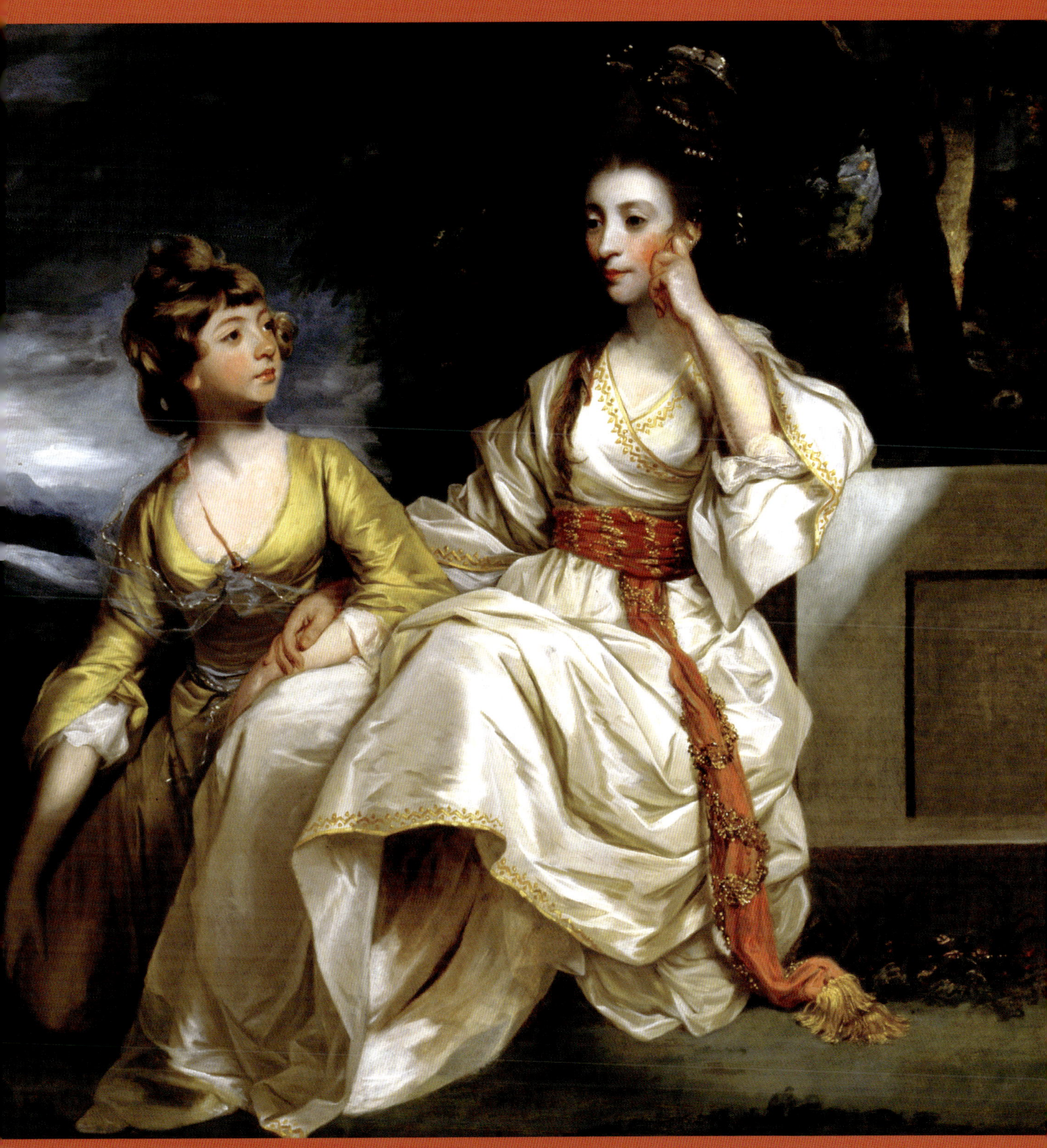

There was no such drama at Streatham Park but the Thrale wedding was carefully and successfully orchestrated by the uncle of the future Mrs Thrale, the Reverend Thelwall Salusbury. Hester Lynch Salusbury duly married Henry Thrale on 11 October 1763: she was barely 20 and he was an attractive and well educated 35 year-old. In this real-life scenario Mr Thrale is the rich merchant while Mrs Thrale comes from a Welsh aristocratic family fallen on hard times. There were tensions throughout the marriage (as the historian Mary Hyde chronicled in some detail, see bibliography) but they were kept in check. Mrs Thrale, writing a few years after Mr Thrale's death should have the last word:

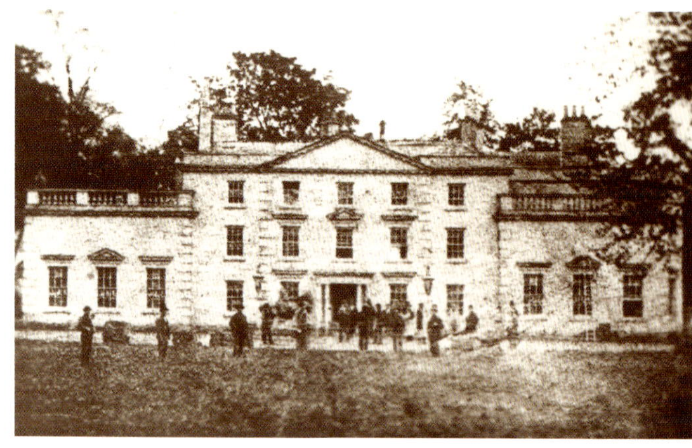

Photograph of Streatham Park, built by the Thrale family in the eighteenth century. This picture was taken in 1863 just prior to demolition. *Lambeth Archives.*

> Why do the people say I never loved my first husband? – tis a very unjust conjecture. … Ours was a match of mere Prudence; and common good Liking, without the smallest Pretensions to passion on either Side: I knew no more of him than any other Gentleman who came to the House, nor did he ever profess other Attachment to me, than such as Esteem of my Character, & Convenience from my Fortune produced … yet God who gave us to each other, knows I did love him dearly; & what honour I can ever do to his Memory shall be done, for he was very generous to me. (*Thraliana*, 1787)

MONSIEUR, HEAD OF THE STREATHAM THRALE FAMILY
Henry Thrale (1728?–1781) – painted by Joshua Reynolds in 1777 when the sitter was 49.
OCCUPATION Brewer and Member of Parliament for Southwark (1765–80).
HOW THEY MET Henry first met his future wife when he visited the Salusbury family seat in Wales. The visit was arranged by her uncle while Hester's father was abroad. They married on 11 October 1763.
GOOD TIMES Inherited his father's Southwark brewery in 1758 and finally won a seat in Parliament in 1765.
BAD TIMES Lost his Southwark parliamentary seat in 1780.
LEGACY By 1850, long after the death of Mr Thrale, his brewery, renamed Barclay Perkins then Anchor brewery, had become one of London's famous sights: 'The establishment in Park Street is now the largest of its kind in the world'.

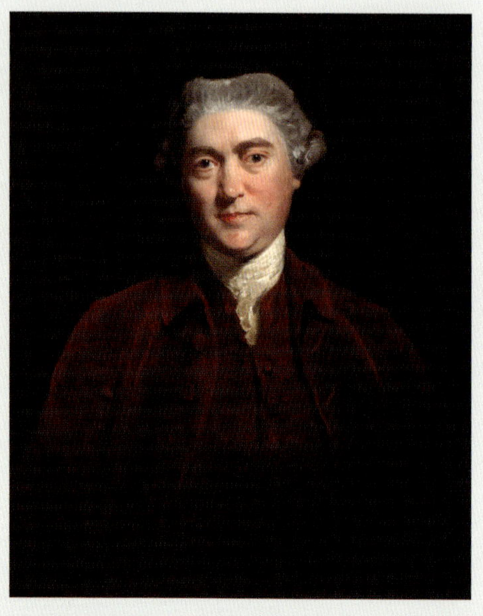

Joshua Reynolds, 'Henry Thrale', 1777. Henry Thrale inherited Streatham Park and his Southwark brewery from his father. As a result Mr and Mrs Thrale spent their time between Streatham and the large townhouse next to the brewery (close to Tate Modern). *© 10 2003JM-7, Houghton Library, Harvard University.*

MADAME, HIS WIFE (see p. 107 for portrait)
Mrs Hester Lynch Thrale (1741–1821), née Lynch Salusbury, later Lynch Piozzi was painted by Joshua Reynolds in 1777 with her daughter Hester (1764–1857) – Mrs Thrale was 36 and her daughter, nicknamed 'Queeney' by Dr Johnson, was 13.
OCCUPATION Developed an influential literary/social salon at her Streatham home.
GOOD TIMES Meeting Dr Johnson in 1765 and her life-long friend Fanny Burney around 1780.
BAD TIMES In 1776 the Thrales lost their only son, Henry, aged ten. At that point Mrs Thrale had given birth to ten children in thirteen years of marriage but only three were still alive. Two more children followed but only one of them survived childhood. In 1783 when Hester married Gabriel Piozzi (1740-1809), the household music teacher, she was ostracized by most of her friends.
LEGACY Her diary *Thraliana* was only published in 1942, but it was the basis of her book *The Anecdotes of the Late Samuel Johnson*, published in 1786.

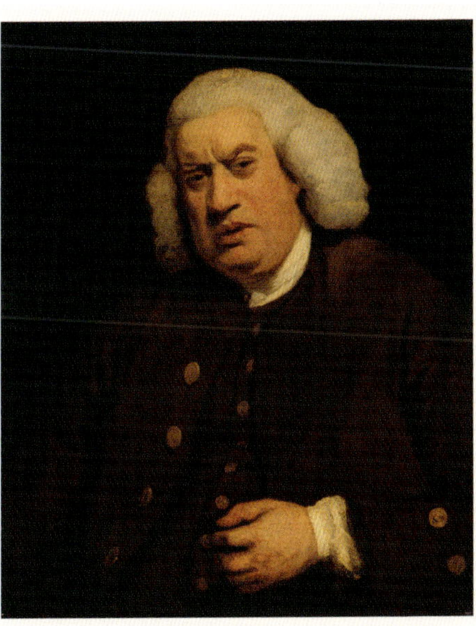

Joshua Reynolds, 'Dr Samuel Johnson', around 1772. Dr Johnson was the key member of the Thrales' circle of friends. He was described with realism by Fanny Burney in a letter to Mr Crisp (around 1779): 'He has naturally a noble figure: tall, stout, grand and authoritative; but he stoops horribly … his vast body is in constant agitation, see-sawing backwards and forwards: his feet are never a moment quiet; and his whole person looked often as if it were going to roll itself, quite voluntarily, from his chair to the floor'. *© Tate, London 2017.*

DR JOHNSON
The man who arguably put the Thrale household on London's social and cultural map was Dr Samuel Johnson (1709–1784) – his painting by Joshua Reynolds was begun in 1772 when the sitter was 63.
ADDRESS Numerous residences in London including 'Dr Johnson's House' in Gough Square off Fleet Street (1748–1759) which is now open to the public. Johnson's biographer, James Boswell (1740–1795), noted that 'invitations to their house [the Thrales] were more and more frequent, till at last he became one of the family, and an apartment was appropriated to him, both in their house at Southwark and in their villa at Streatham'.
OCCUPATION Man of Letters.
HOW THEY MET Dr Johnson was introduced to the Thrales by Arthur Murphy on 9 January 1765.
GOOD TIMES Johnson's creation of 'The Club' (for conversation and dining) around 1763, with his friends the painter Joshua Reynolds, the Irish statesman and philosopher Edmund Burke, the actor David Garrick and the author Oliver Goldsmith. All of them future 'Streatham Worthies' (see overleaf).
BAD TIMES The death of Mrs Johnson in March 1752; Hester Thrale's second marriage to the Italian singer Gabriel Mario Piozzi (1741–1809) in 1783. Johnson, appalled, exclaimed: 'You are ignominiously married!'
LEGACY *A Dictionary of the English Language* – published in 1755, Britain's most famous dictionary (150 years before the publication of the *Oxford English Dictionary*). His *Lives of the Most Eminent English Poets* is also regarded as a major contribution to literary criticism.

Streatham Park

It was Ralph Thrale, father of Henry, who purchased the land from the Lord of the Manor – the fourth Duke of Bedford. In 1730 he built a simple but comfortable house on the 109 acre property: Streatham Park (also known as Streatham Place). Ralph Thrale was a brewer of relatively humble origins. A nephew of Edmund Halsey, the owner of the Southwark brewery, he was a determined and hardworking employee who was able to purchase the brewery upon the death of his uncle Edmund.

Life at Streatham Park may be divided into three periods: in the first period when the Thrales were newly married, Mrs Thrale was quite isolated and had for sole company her mother and husband. This was followed by a period of great sociability, which is partially illustrated by the paintings of the 'Streatham Worthies'. Lastly, when Mrs Thrale remarried two years after the death of her husband, the new couple, Mr and Mrs Piozzi, travelled extensively (1790–95) before settling back at Streatham Park where they resumed a life of sociability. This ended with the death of Gabriel Piozzi in 1809 when it became clear that life Streatham-style was financially unsustainable: Hester Piozzi sold the brewery, moved out of Streatham Park and rented out the property. Shortly before her death in Bristol in 1821, Hester wrote to Fanny d'Arblay (née Burney): 'You would not know poor Streatham Park, I have been forced to dismantle and forsake it'.

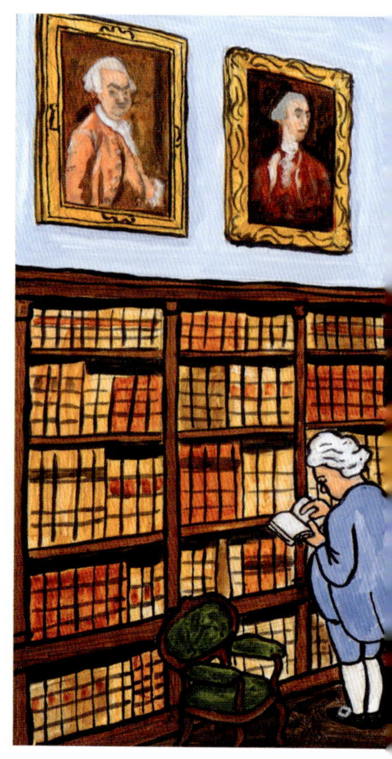

The key to the drawing above is overleaf. Each portrait is numbered 1 to 13, running from left to right. © Jiro Osuga.

Nothing survives of the Streatham Park mansion (see p. 108). Painter Jiro Osuga has visualized the appearance of 'the Streatham Worthies' in the Thrales' library at Streatham Park in the 1780s. These lively drawings aim to be as accurate as possible, relying on two principal visual sources: the reconstruction prepared by Mark Hallett (see bibliography) and the vivid record of people and furniture found in the drawing of one of the Thrales' daughters, young Cecilia (born 1777), which is housed in Manchester's Rylands Library. *© Jiro Osuga.*

'The Streatham Worthies'

Between 1772 and 1781, the Thrales commissioned the painter Sir Joshua Reynolds (1723–1792) to produce portraits of some of the circle of friends who were regularly entertained at Streatham Park, thirteen of them, which would adorn the walls of the new Library – an extension to Streatham Park which was finished in 1781. Mrs Thrale recorded the hanging plan in her diary, enabling art historian Mark Hallett to produce a diagram on which the reconstruction in this book is based. The writer and socialite Fanny Burney (1752–1840) coined the phrase 'Streatham Worthies'.

Historian Mark Girouard points out that 'the country house library was at its apogee' in the late eighteenth and early nineteenth centuries, adding 'it was also a comfortable, relaxed and sympathetic living room'. This was where Mrs Thrale held a splendid party in July 1790 to celebrate her wedding anniversary to Piozzi: 'Seventy People eat at our Expence, Thirty six of which dined at an immensely long Table in the Library —The Plate so fine too, the China so showy, all so magnificent, and at the Time of Dinner Horns Clarin &c w[hi]ch afterwards performed upon the Water in our new Boat that makes such a beautiful, such an elegant Figure'.

Perhaps the most remarkable feature about the 'Worthies' was its contemporaneity and how closely it reflected the life of its owners – real, tangible proofs of lives lived in a wealthy Streatham household. Of course there were more 'worthies' than those recorded in paint. David Thrale's most useful website on his ancestors *Thrale.com* adds further names to this list.

Although Mrs rather than Mr Thrale went down in history as the genial host at Streatham Park, this myth should be debunked a little. She was no doubt a charming hostess who was adored by Dr Johnson, the group's lynchpin; but it is clear from looking at human connections that Mr Thrale was in fact at the group's origin – Sandys and Lyttelton were his friends, as was Arthur Murphy who introduced Dr Johnson to the household. Then Dr Johnson introduced the others.

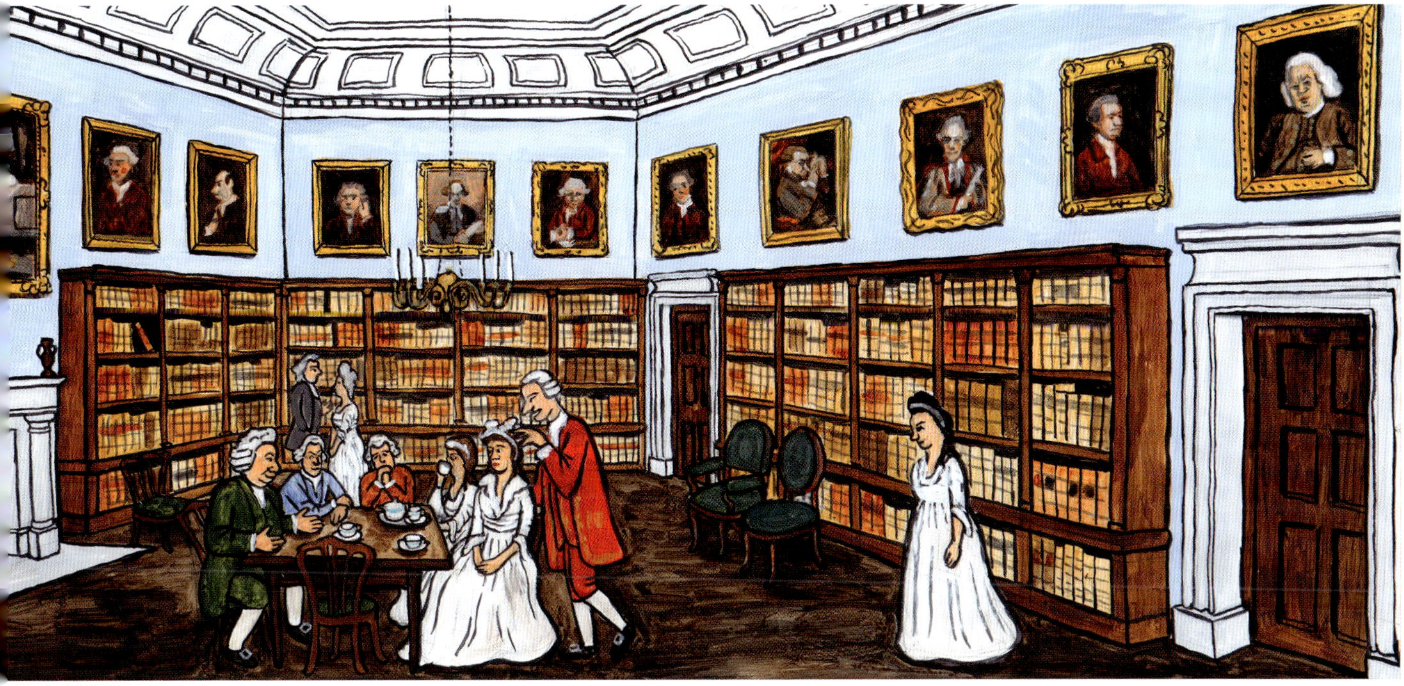

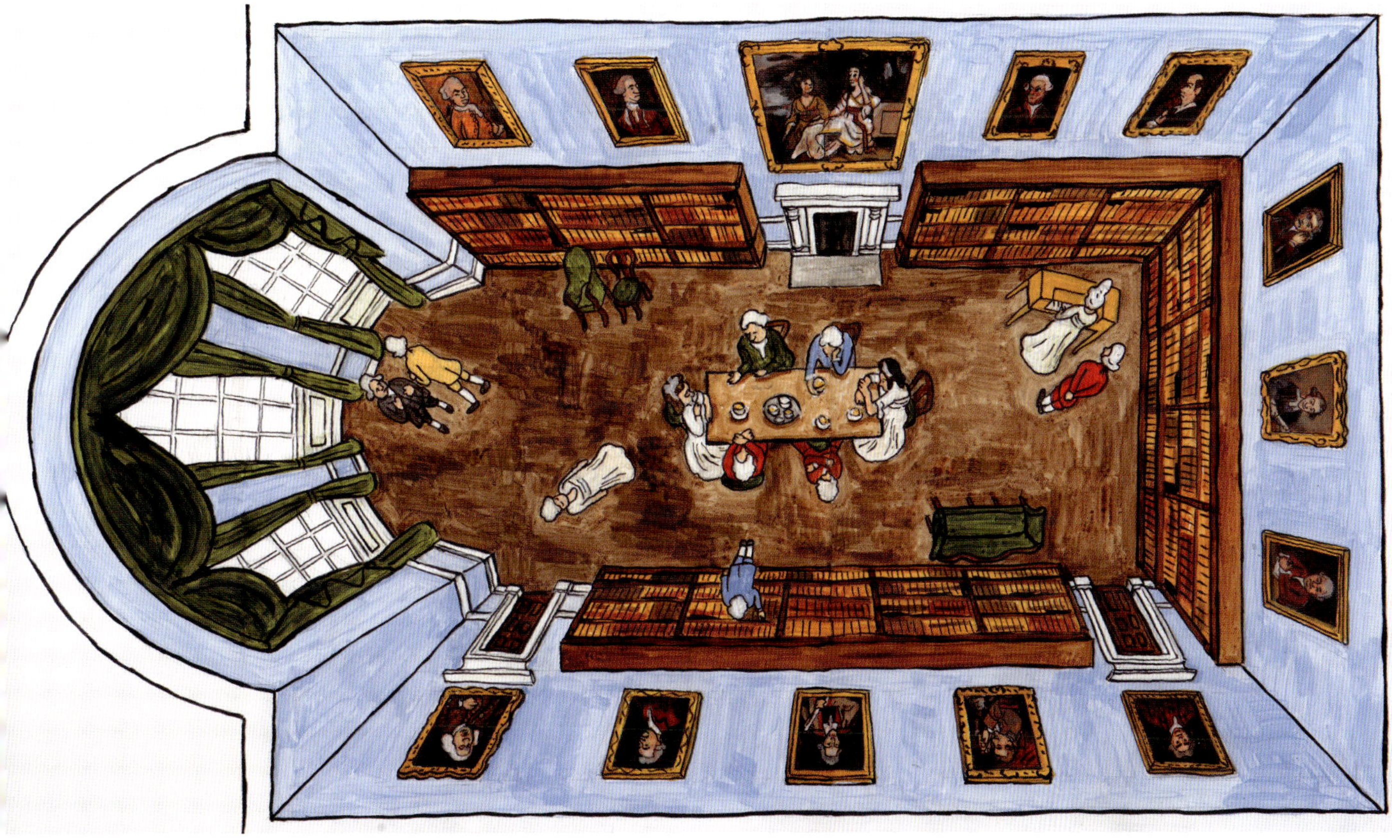

The 'identity cards' of the Streatham Worthies have been arranged according to Mrs Thrale's proposed hang of the portraits in the library, see reconstruction on the previous page, paintings numbered from left to right. Numbers 3 (Mrs Thrale), 9 (Mr Thrale) and 13 (Dr Johnson) are illustrated on the previous pages.

1. Edwin SANDYS (1726–1797), 2nd Baron Sandys, painted in 1773, aged 47.
OCCUPATION Member of Parliament for Droitwich (1747-54), then Bossiney (1754-61), and finally Westminster (1762-70).
HOW THEY MET Sandys was at Oxford University with Henry Thrale.
GOOD TIMES Being a devoted Member of Parliament?
BAD TIMES He had no issue, so his title became extinct at his death.

2. William Henry LYTTELTON (1724–1808), painted in 1772, aged 40.
OCCUPATION Governor of South Carolina (1755–60), then Jamaica (1761–65), envoy to Lisbon (1766–71); Lord of the Treasury (1777–82). Also Member of Parliament for Bewdley (1748–55 and 1774–90).
HOW THEY MET Lyttelton met Henry Thrale in Oxford and they went on the Grand Tour together.
GOOD TIMES Made Baron Westcote (in 1776, Irish peerage), later made 1st Baron Lyttleton of Frankley (in 1794, peerage of Great Britain).
BAD TIMES In 1760 his ship to Carolina was taken by the French and escorted to Nantes, as a result of unofficial hostilities between France and England.
LEGACY He wrote prophetically about the American colonies in 1765: 'I do not see how the mother country can hope for the future that her laws will be obeyed in such distant dominions'.

3. Mrs THRALE see p. 109.

4. Arthur MURPHY (1727–1805), portrait begun in 1773 when he was 46. He had a pseudonym: Charles Ranger.
OCCUPATION Irish barrister, actor and writer – he was a prolific playwright who also wrote poetry, essays, biographies and edited magazines.
HOW THEY MET Henry Thrale's oldest and dearest friend. Murphy met Dr Johnson in 1754 and introduced him to the Thrales in 1765.
BAD TIMES He was deeply affected by the death of his mother in 1761.
GOOD TIMES In the 1790s he received two legacies and was made commissioner of bankrupts – a post he had held before which stemmed perennial money difficulties for a while.
LEGACY He wrote the lives of his contemporaries: Henry Fielding, David Garrick and Dr Johnson – his best known works.

5. Oliver GOLDSMITH (1728–1774), painted in 1772, but what survives is a studio copy of an earlier painting exhibited at the Royal Academy in 1770 when Goldsmith was 42.
OCCUPATION Irish novelist/playwright/poet.
HOW THEY MET Founding member of 'The Club' set up by Dr Johnson and Joshua Reynolds in 1764.
GOOD TIMES Being introduced to his benefactor Sir George Savile, thanks to 'Club' member Edmund Burke. Savile arranged a job for poverty-stricken Goldsmith at Thornhill Grammar School in Yorkshire.
BAD TIMES Perennially in debt (he was addicted to gambling).
LEGACY Author of famous classics: *The Vicar of Wakefield* (1766), *The Deserted Village* (1770) and the play *She Stoops to Conquer* (1771).

6. Sir Joshua REYNOLDS (1723–1792), self-portrait dating from 1775 when Reynolds was 52.
OCCUPATION Portrait painter and first president of the Royal Academy.
HOW THEY MET Via Dr Johnson: Reynolds was a founder member (with Johnson) of 'The Club': members met in Gerrard Street, later in Sackville Street.
GOOD TIMES 1787: Reynolds painted the portrait of Lord Heathfield, who successfully defended Gibraltar (1779–1783) and had become a national hero. The canvas is in the National Gallery.
BAD TIMES 1789: Reynolds lost sight in his left eye. This soon forced him into retirement.
LEGACY Vast compendium of portrait paintings including 'The Streatham Worthies' – many of them quite breathtaking. He is the recipient of a blue plaque in Leicester Square.

7. Robert CHAMBERS (1737–1803), painted in 1773 when he was 36.
OCCUPATION Called to the bar in 1761, Vinerian Professor of English Law at the University of Oxford in 1766. Appointed judge in Calcutta and left England in 1774. He was eventually confirmed chief justice in 1791 and did not return to England until 1799.
HOW THEY MET Via Dr Johnson whom he knew from the mid 1750s: Chambers was a member

of 'The Club'.
GOOD TIMES Chambers had a reputation for integrity and was knighted in June 1777.
BAD TIMES His health was said to have suffered from his years in India and in 1802 he planned to retire to the South of France. But he fell ill in Paris and died there in May 1803.

8. David GARRICK
(1717–1779), copy of a painting sent to the Royal Academy in 1776 when Garrick was 59.
OCCUPATION Actor, playwright and theatre manager.
HOW THEY MET He was a pupil of Dr Johnson (at the school Johnson set up in Edial near Litchfield, which only lasted one year), later his friend and member of 'The Club'.
GOOD TIMES October 1741 when he appeared in Shakespeare's *Richard III* being noticed for his talent by both audience and theatrical profession. His reputation then went from strength to strength.
BAD TIMES 1756: the harsh judgement published by Theophilus Cibber: '… His [Garrick's] over-fondness for extravagant attitudes, frequently affected starts, convulsive twitchings, jerkings of the body, sprawling of the fingers, flapping the breast and pockets …'
LEGACY In Garrick's capable hands the Drury Lane Theatre which he ran between 1747 and 1776, became one of Europe's leading playhouses.

9. Mr THRALE See p. 108.

10. Giuseppe BARETTI
(1719–1789), painted in 1773 when he was 54. In England he was also known as Joseph Baretti.
OCCUPATION Italian literary critic and writer who was appointed Secretary for Foreign Correspondence at the Royal Academy in 1781.
HOW THEY MET Via Dr Johnson, though Baretti was not a member of 'The Club'.
BAD TIMES Baretti was charged with murder in 1769 when he wounded a man with a fruit knife, who later died in hospital.
GOOD TIMES He was cleared of murder and, overwhelmed by the support of his friends, wrote: 'those I had about me did their part so well that they have made me an Englishman forever'.
LEGACY His book *The Italian Library* describes the lives of eminent Italians. He was apparently the first to record Galileo's famous phrase 'nevertheless it [the earth] moves'.

11. Charles BURNEY
(1726–1814), painted in 1781 when he was 55.
OCCUPATION Composer, musician and English music historian. Father of Fanny Burney.
HOW THEY MET He was a friend of Edmund Burke.
GOOD TIMES In 1769 the University of Oxford granted him with the degrees of Bachelor and Doctor of Music.
BAD TIMES A few years after marrying his second wife in 1767, the couple decided to merge the two families – Charles' six children and his wife Elizabeth's three from a previous marriage – leading to tension and general unhappiness.
LEGACY His magnus opus was *A General History of Music* published between 1776 and 1789.

12. Edmund BURKE
(1729–1797), painted in 1774 when he was 45.
OCCUPATION Irish statesman, author, philosopher. He was an MP for Wendover (1765–74), Bristol (1774–80), Malton (1780–94).
HOW THEY MET Burke was a founder member of 'The Club'. He met Dr Johnson in the late 1760s.
GOOD TIMES He published *Reflections on the Revolution in France* in 1790. It became an instant best-seller both in England and in France.
BAD TIMES His interpretation of the French Revolution in *Reflections* led to the rupture of his long-standing friendship with the politician Charles James Fox in 1791.
LEGACY Now often regarded as 'the father of British modern conservatism', he seems to have had a knack for predicting major events: for instance the impeachment of Warren Hastings (for his conduct in India), Catholic emancipation and the American Revolution. Recipient of a blue plaque at 37 Gerrard Street where he lived between 1787 and 1790.

13. Dr JOHNSON
See p. 109.

Hester sold most of the portraits in 1816 by which time all of the sitters, bar Hester herself and her daughter, were dead. Fanny Burney noted that prices were dictated by 'the celebrity of the subjects' resulting in the following 'league table' starting with the most expensive: Dr Johnson, then Burke, Burney, Garrick, Goldsmith and Reynolds. To her great annoyance, Mrs Thrale's own portrait sold cheaply.

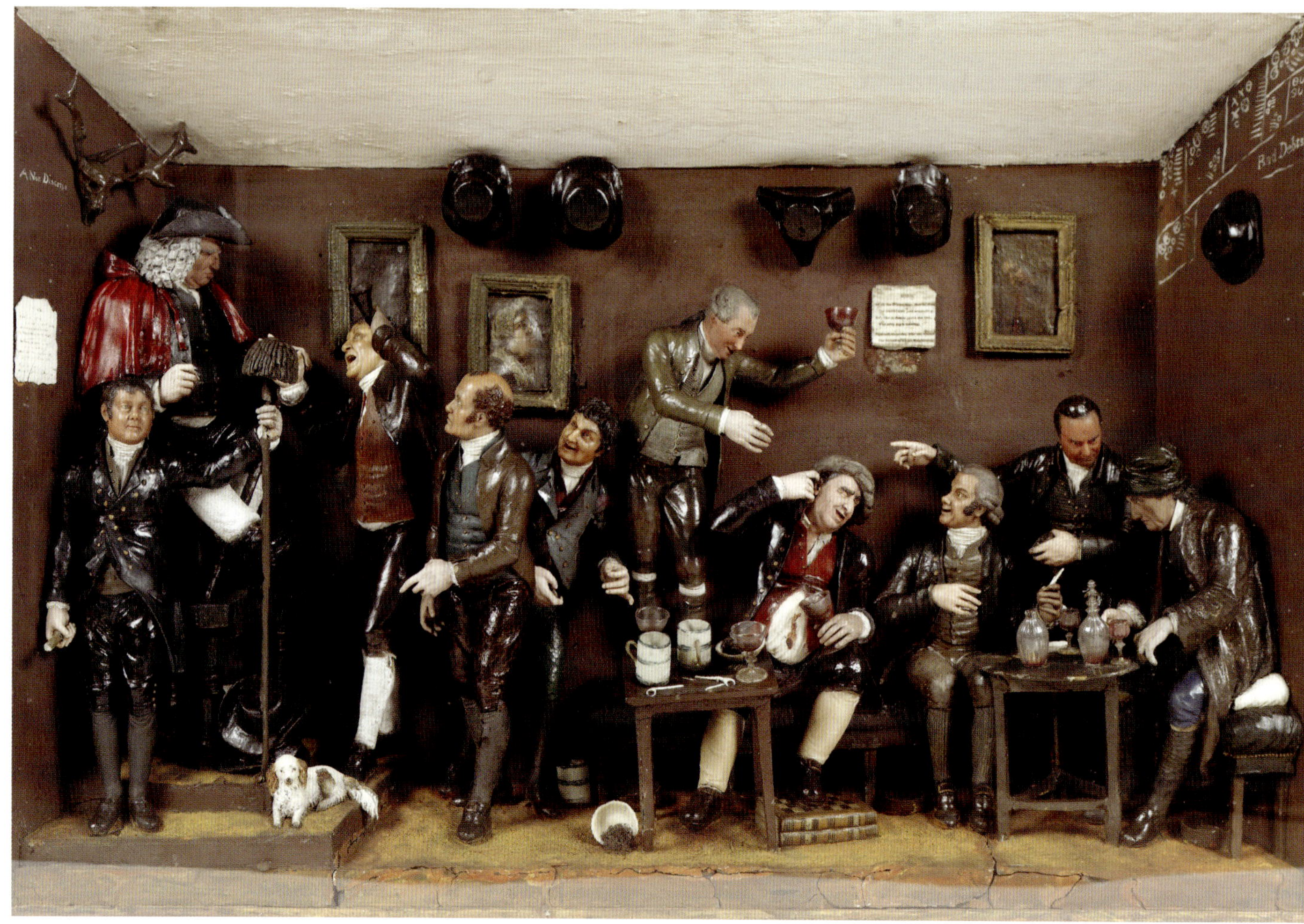

This wax model made by Samuel Percy around 1790, is a vivid evocation of the literary club set up by society painter Joshua Reynolds and Dr Samuel Johnson in 1764. 'The Club', as it was known, was inspired by the meetings the painter had held at his home in Leicester Square and also by an earlier club set up by Dr Johnson in Ivy Lane near Ludgate. Dining and conversation were the key activities and meetings were held at the Turk's Tavern in Gerrard Street, Soho, shown here. After 1783 The Club moved to Dover Street. Many of the 'Streatham Worthies' would also be members of this highly influential club. In the chair on the far left is Dr Johnson, wearing a red cape and turned towards Joshua Reynolds who is using his ear trumpet while the sculptor Joseph Nollekens (1737–1823) is clearly recognisable on the far right. Straight ahead, the politician Charles James Fox (1749–1806) is seated on the bench, holding a glass of wine. *Museum of London.*

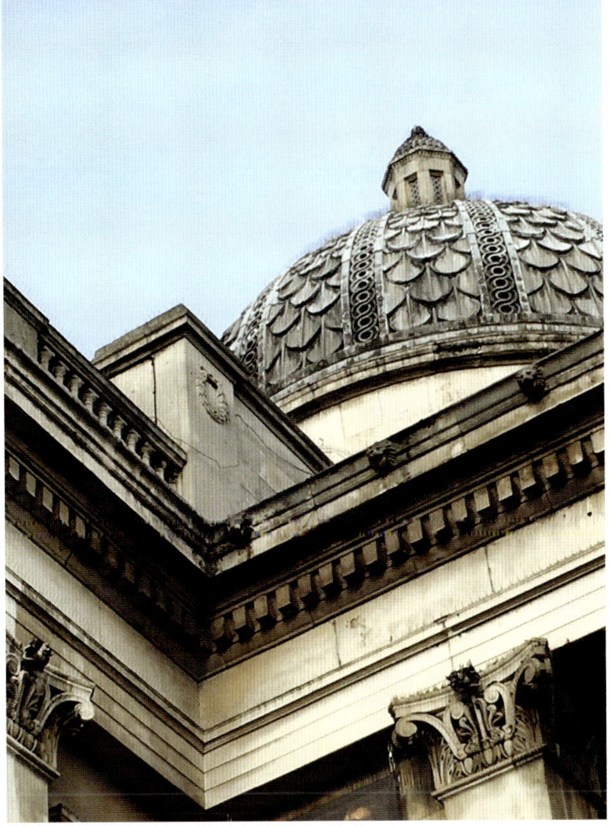

Some people may know that the National Gallery was designed by William Wilkins in 1834 and that it opened its doors to the public in 1838. But few will have heard of the man who actually built the National Gallery: John Malcott III who lived and died in Streatham.

Below: This early view of the newly completed National Gallery (1838) was engraved by W Wallis after a drawing by T H Shepherd. The view includes a fountain where Nelson column now stands – a plan which was obviously not carried out. *London Metropolitan Archives, City of London.*

The National Gallery and Streatham

There is a real connection between the National Gallery and Streatham which has been noted by the Streatham Society but not sufficiently emphasised.

The link to the National Gallery is well hidden: underneath the Streatham Hill Theatre. Local historian Graham Gower tells us (in his Heritage Trail [of the] Streatham Hill Triangle) that 'Streatham House, the home of John Malcott from 1838–1848, the builder of the National Gallery in London, previously occupied the site'. This was John Malcott III (c. 1777–1851), a noteworthy stonemason from a family of stonemasons originally connected to the eighteenth-century architect Sir Robert Taylor. Malcott III joined the family firm based in Newgate Street in the City in 1809. Rupert Gunnis' *Dictionary of British Sculptors* has fleshed out the main biographical details of the various members of the Malcott family, including the *Gentleman's Magazine*'s favourable press on Malcott III – 'an ingenious young artist'. Malcott succeeded his forebears as mason to the College of Physicians. The firm was particularly busy in the 1820s when it landed several major contracts: at Stationer's Hall, in Lombard Street for bankers Glyn Mills & Co, in Lincoln's Inn for the Insolvent Debtors' Court and at the General Post Office from 1826. This success may have influenced the decision to appoint Malcott principal mason at the National Gallery (the current building opened in 1838) . At his death in 1851, he left houses in Newgate Street and Streatham Hill.

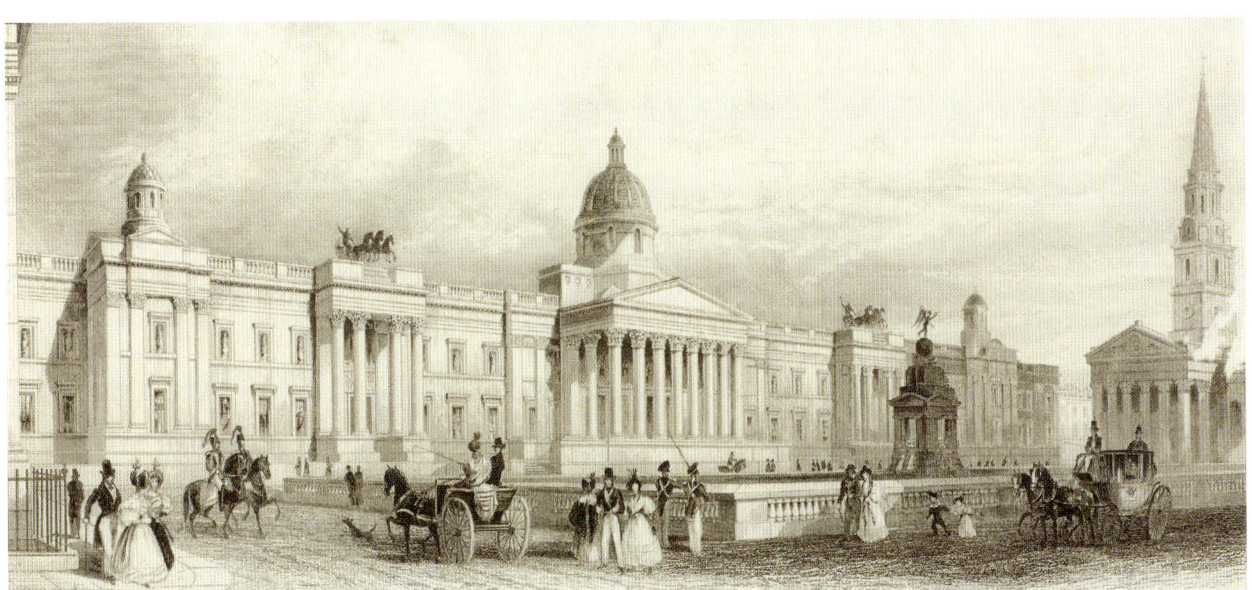

Merchant patronage: William Leaf and Henry Tate

The Streatham Society has researched in some detail the interesting history of Park Hill, a large estate overlooking Streatham Common: almost at the junction of Streatham Common North (the road) and Leigham Court Road. We will focus on just two of the many past occupants of this estate: William Leaf and Henry Tate.

William Leaf (1791–1874)

Graham Gower believes that the site was probably occupied in the Middle Ages but there is no documentary evidence until 1716 when it was leased to a City merchant, Christopher Garraway – a grocer. The property which has survived, with its park and mansion house, was created when another City merchant, William Leaf, purchased the land in 1829 and built himself a large and smart mansion, Park Hill, a project he placed in the hands of one of the best architects of his day, John B. Papworth (1775–1847).

Papworth trained as an architect in the office of John Plaw, later taking Plaw's nephew, Samuel Benwell, as his first pupil. Papworth had also been apprenticed to the builder Thomas Wapshott. Then as now art and architecture had close links to the Royal Academy, so 'architect' Papworth, a gifted draughtsman, was a regular exhibitor there – equally at home drawing architectural or figurative subjects, designing a garden or drawing on his experience as a town planner. His versatility earned him the nickname of 'Buonarotti' (sic) – as in Michelangelo [di Lodovico Buonarroti Simoni]. Papworth also designed another mansion in Streatham, Leigham Court House, formerly on the site of the ABCD estate (northern end); it was demolished in 1908.

It is generally accepted that the house was built by 1835 but constantly improved and developed throughout the time the Leaf family was based there until they sold it in the mid-1870s. Papworth died in 1847 and architectural work after that date has remained unattributed, including the lodge at the main entrance gates which bears Leaf's motto, monogram and the date 1870, but is a replacement of Papworth's original lodge which is known to have burnt down.

William Leaf's insurance records with Royal and Sun Alliance have survived at London Metropolitan Archives: his house was first insured in May 1832, so was probably habitable by that date. The £15,000 valuation of his property is made up of £9,000 for the house and adjoining offices, £2500 for household goods (including books and plate), £1200 for china and glass, £200 for pictures and prints, £100 for musical instruments, and £1000 for coachhouse, stables, cowhouse and piggery, the porter's lodge being valued at £500. When the policy was updated in 1834 the overall figure jumped up to £20,500 – the most noticeable increase being £7000 for household goods, £300 for musical instruments and £500 for Pictures and Prints.

One of the insurance figures which was increased, related to William Leaf's collection of 'pictures and prints'. After Leaf's death his 'very extensive and valuable' collection was sold at Christie's in May 1875. It was principally made up of watercolours but also including other media, over 500 works in all 'many of which were bought direct from the Artists',

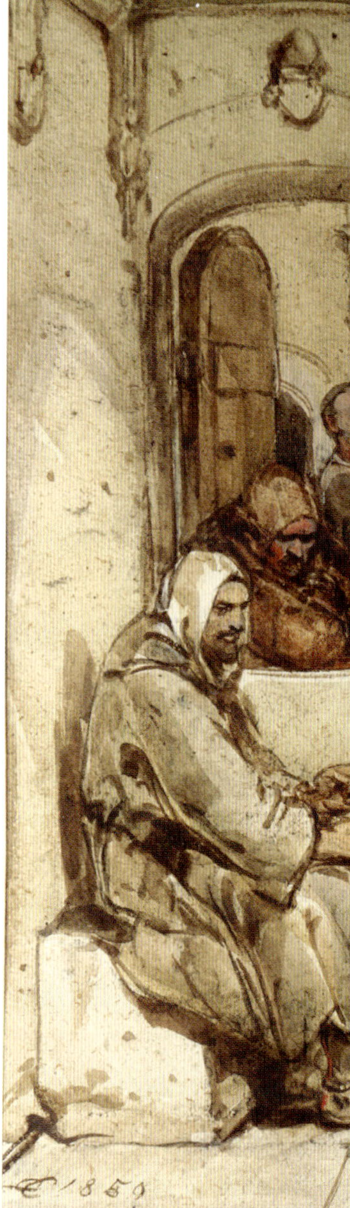

Above: 'Ancient Monastic Life' by George Cattermole, not dated. This watercolour is unlikely to have been in William Leaf's collection but its theme echoes one of the Cattermole's works known to have been in Park Hill – 'The Monk' which was in Christie's sale of May 1875. *© Tate, London 2017.*

Photographic portrait of the City merchant William Leaf (1791–1874). *Photo: Daphne & Richard Marchant (The Streatham Society).*

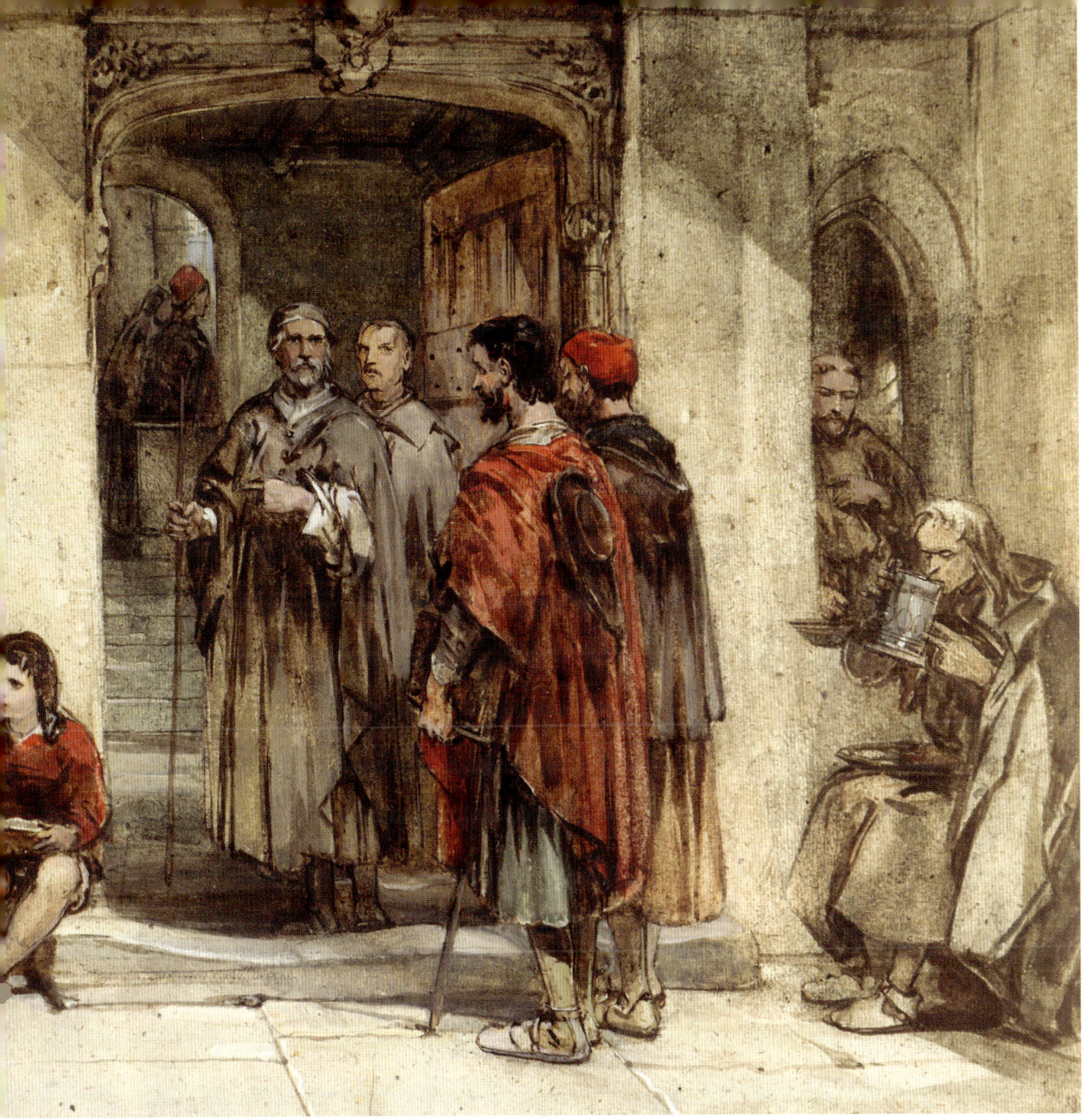

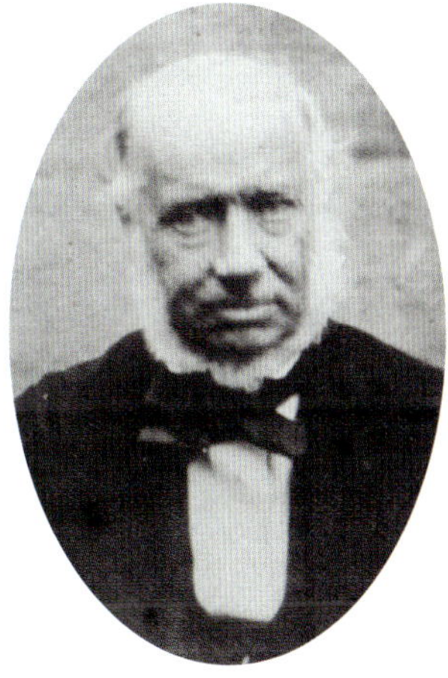

the collection being 'formed during the last 50 years by that well-known Connoisseur, William Leaf'. The auction catalogue may be consulted at the British Library, so we know that the majority of works dealt with landscape subjects (here and abroad) and also which artists were particularly well represented in this collection:

G(eorge) Cattermole with 52 works
T Hart with 27 works
W(illiam) Callow with 24 works
C Bentley with 18 works
W(illiam) Hunt with 13 works
S(amuel) Prout with 11 works
D(avid) Cox with 10 works
David Roberts* with 10 works
JMW Turner* with 9 works
C(larkson) Stanfield* with 8 works

*Royal Academicians (RA)

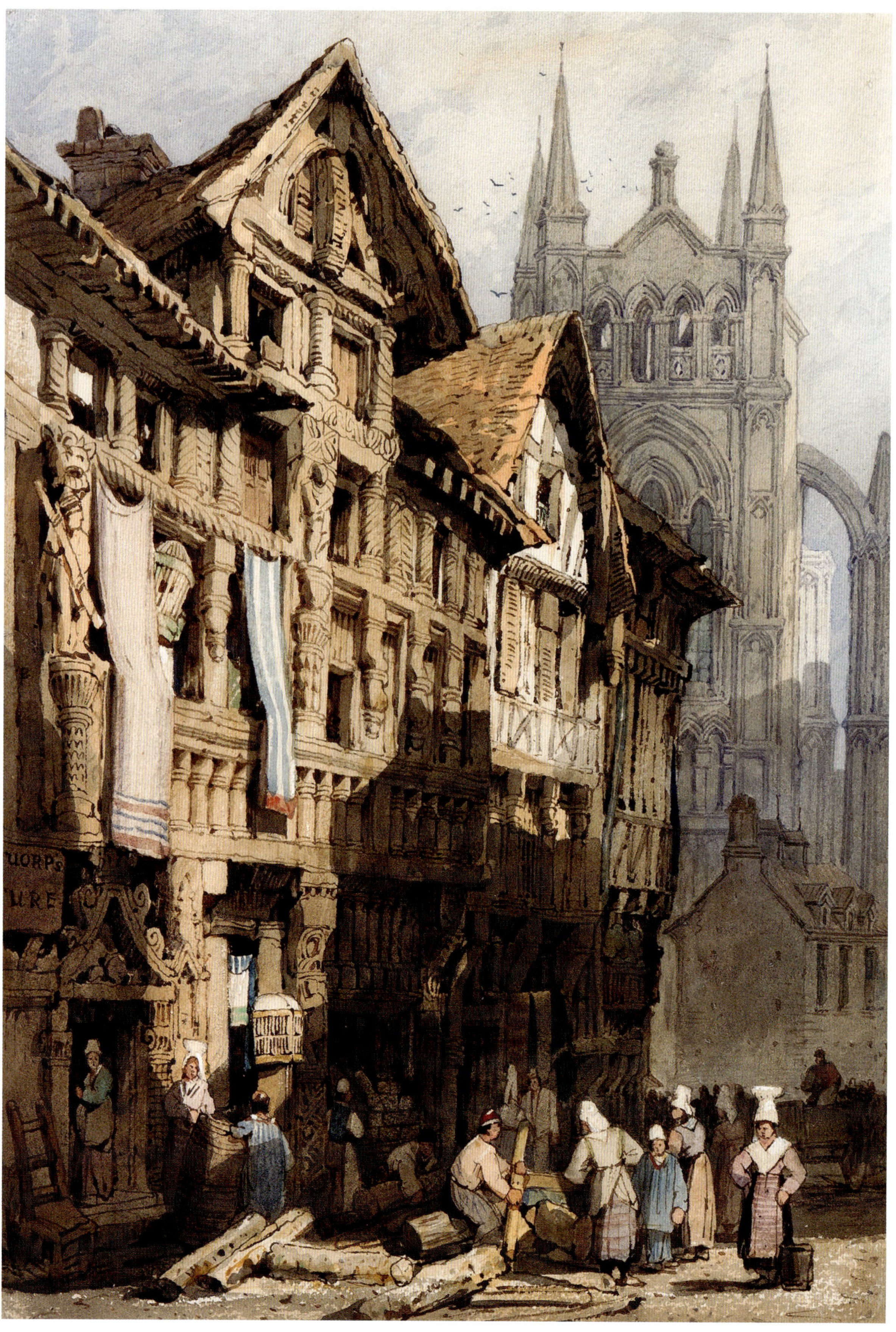

'Cathedral Town, Northern France' by Samuel Prout, around 1835. The art dealer Abbott & Holder stocks works by Samuel Prout, and recently sold this watercolour. It is a good example of what Graham Reynolds described as one of the 'avid seekers-out of crumbling medieval ruins and quaint recesses of old towns' which so appealed to his contemporaries.
Photo: Abbott & Holder.

But William Leaf must have strived to have a representative cross-section of artists because his collection featured well over 100 different names.

According to Christie's catalogue, William Leaf would have started collecting in the 1820s at a time when there was considerable activity in the world of watercolours following the birth in the early years of the nineteenth century of two societies specifically dealing with watercolours: the 'Old' Watercolour Society as it would later be known in 1804 and the New Society of Painters in Miniature and Watercolours in 1807.

In 1821, the MP and art collector Walter Fawkes of Farnley Hall exhibited his large collection of watercolours to the public: he was an early supporter of J M W Turner (1775–1851) and William Leaf's nine watercolours by this artist pale into comparison when considering Fawkes' 60 works by Turner. However, the two men belonged to different generations and Leaf's collection focused on 'travelling artists' who, in the words of art historian Graham Reynolds, 'encouraged the British middle classes to travel abroad … of these topographers, avid seekers-out of crumbling medieval ruins and quaint recesses of old towns, Samuel Prout was the most esteemed' (*A Concise History of Watercolours*).

Two of the artists represented in Leaf's collection, David Cox Junior (1809–1885) and William Bennett (1811–1871), actually lived in Streatham – Cox at 82 New Park Road and Bennett at Bleak Hall Villa in the same road. Would Leaf have purchased the works directly from these artists? We may never know. Other artists in his collection, David Cox Senior (1783–1859) and Samuel Prout (1783–1852) spent time in – and left their mark on – neighbouring Dulwich (see *The Dulwich Notebook*). John Ruskin, the famous art critic and another collector of watercolours (in particular Turner) also lived around the corner in Herne Hill.

An early map of the Park Hill estate

The 1852 map in the collection of Lambeth Archives is reasonably detailed, and it shows the general layout of the Leaf estate. Though we cannot always identify all features shown

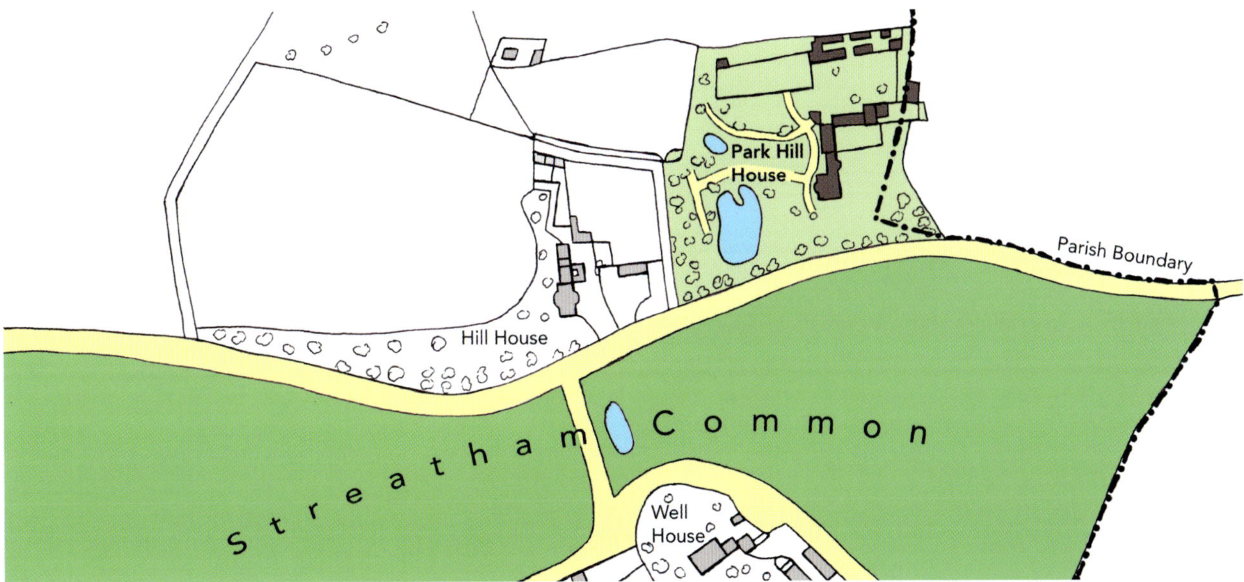

Drawing based on a detail from a parish map of Streatham dated 1852. At that date the property was in the hands of William Leaf. The following garden features are known to have been designed, but perhaps not always built, by his architect Papworth – a conservatory (visible on north side of the house), a greenhouse, melon ground, kitchen garden (the large rectangle at the top), gate piers, ice house, aviary, garden seat, orange tree house and farmyard.

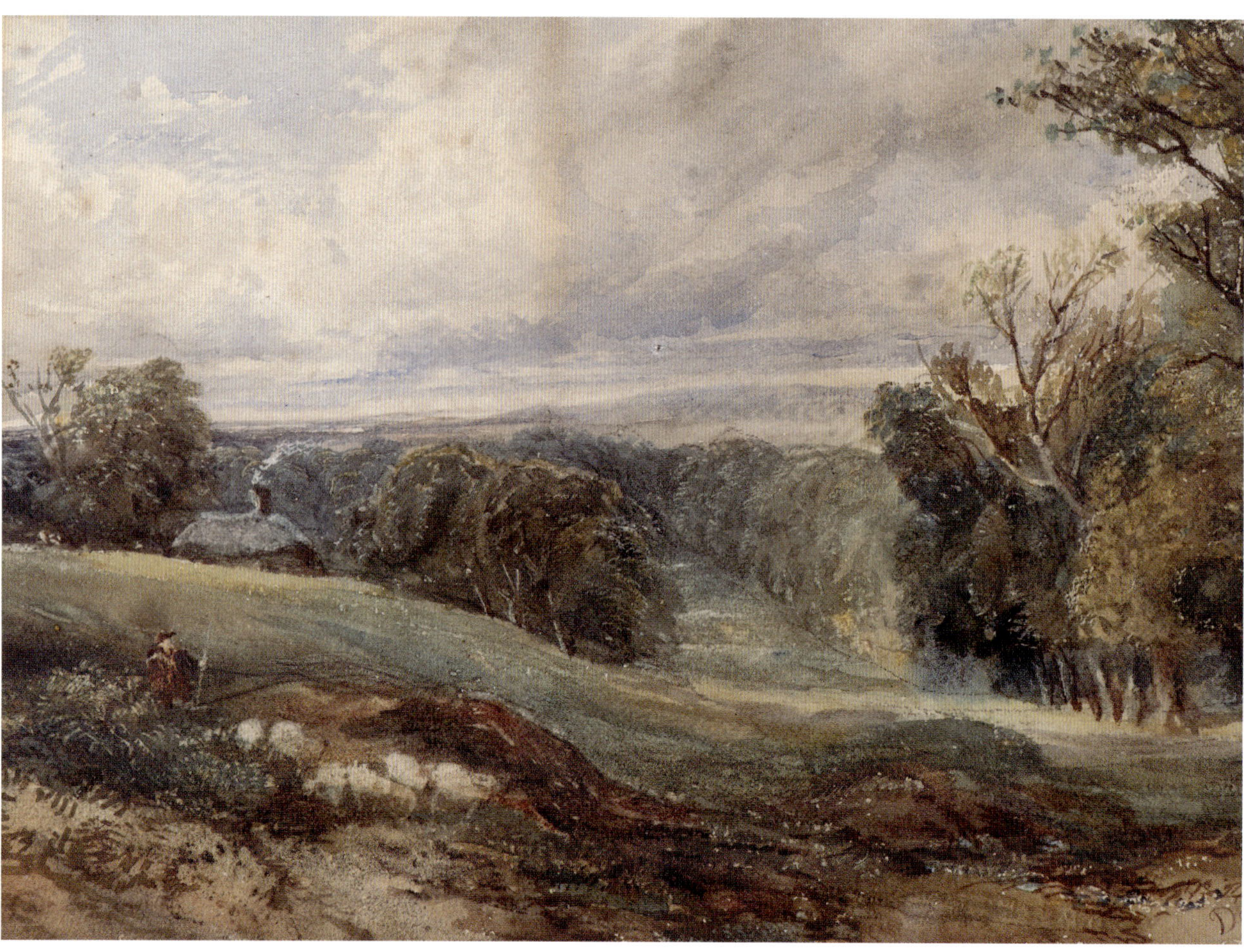

in Papworth's designs (in the collection of the Royal Institute of British Architects), the map shows the walled kitchen garden at the top, a large lake on the site of the present one, but shaped differently, and a smaller round one above (no longer there); it also shows paths around the property and trees, particularly along the south and west fences. It does not show the Lodge in its present position.

The folly and grotto which have survived to this day belong to a later era and to the next occupant: Henry Tate.

Above: This watercolour by David Cox Junior probably dates from the middle of the nineteenth century. The view is from Hill House, looking south towards the first Wells House with Wimbledon in the far distance. The cottage on the left hand side is from Park Hill farm. The landscape is utterly rural, complete with its shepherd and flock of sheep in the left foreground. *Gower collection.*

Right: This striking document celebrates Henry Tate's 80th birthday on 11 March 1899. It was commissioned by members of his close family who all signed the watercolour drawing – Children, Grandchildren and Great Grandchildren. The picture sets out to record all of Tate's philanthropic achievements – anticlockwise from top right: the Honorary Freedom of the City of Liverpool (1891), Tate Library in Liverpool (1892), Tate Library Manchester College in Oxford (1893), the Liverpool Hahneman Hospital and Homeopathic Dispensary (1887), the Tate Public Library in Streatham (1891), the Tate Library in South Lambeth (1883), the National Gallery of British Art (1897), the Tate Central Library in Brixton (1893) and the Tate Institute in Silvertown (1887). The document includes lovely vignettes of Park Hill (reproduced overleaf) and the Tate Gallery (bottom) as well as a portrait of Henry Tate. *© Tate, London 2017.*

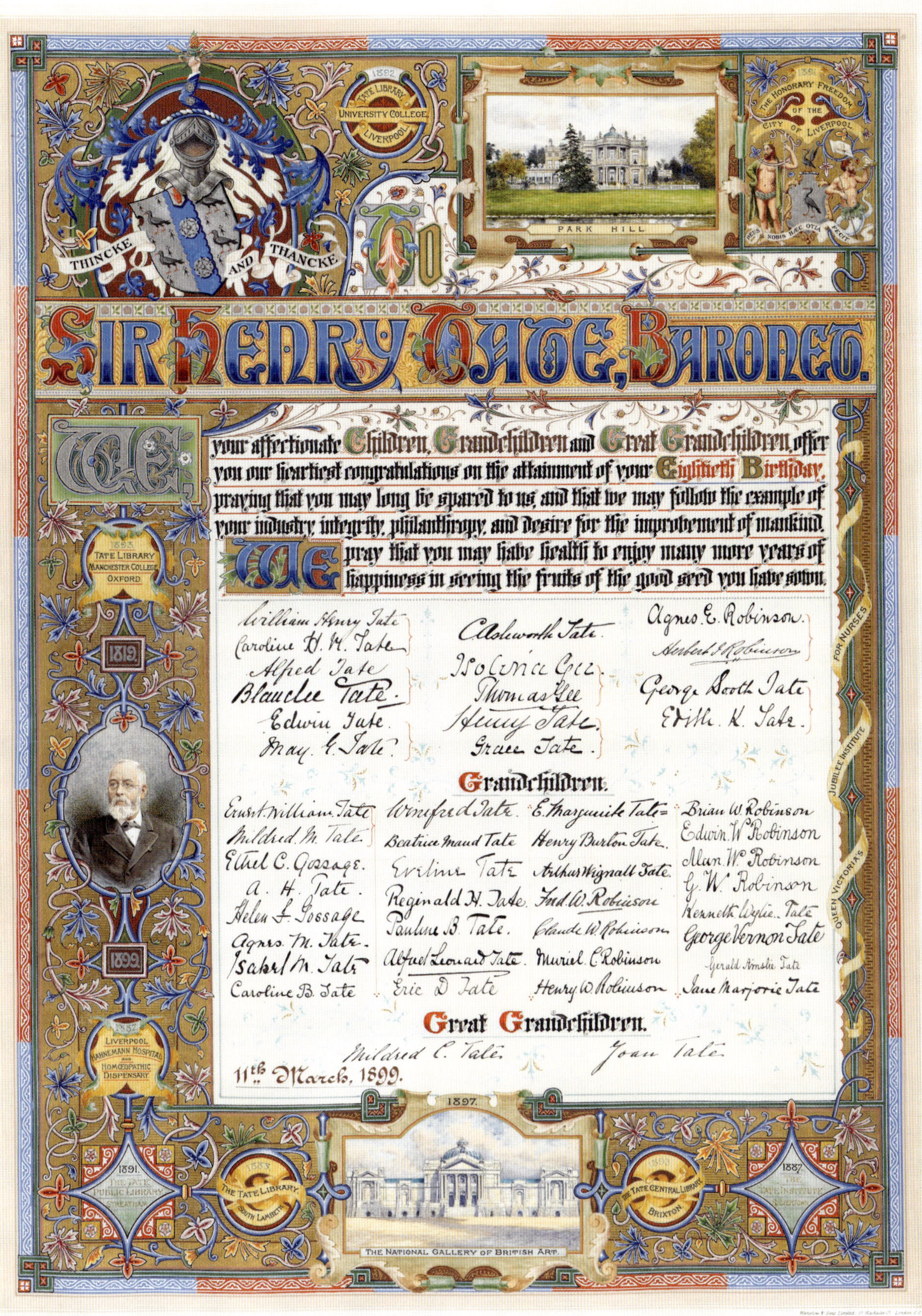

THINCKE AND THANCKE
1882
TATE LIBRARY
UNIVERSITY COLLEGE
LIVERPOOL
PARK HILL
1891
THE HONORARY FREEDOM OF THE CITY OF LIVERPOOL
DEUS NOBIS HÆC OTIA FECIT
To
SIR HENRY TATE, BARONET.
We your affectionate Children, Grandchildren and Great Grandchildren, offer you our heartiest congratulations on the attainment of your Eightieth Birthday, praying that you may long be spared to us, and that we may follow the example of your industry, integrity, philanthropy, and desire for the improvement of mankind.
We pray that you may have health to enjoy many more years of happiness in seeing the fruits of the good seed you have sown.
1893
TATE LIBRARY
MANCHESTER COLLEGE
OXFORD
1819
1899
1887
LIVERPOOL
HAHNEMANN HOSPITAL
AND
HOMŒOPATHIC
DISPENSARY
William Henry Tate
Caroline H. M. Tate
Alfred Tate
Blanche Tate
Edwin Tate
May E. Tate
C. Holeworth Tate
Isolinda Gee
Thomas Gee
Henry Tate
Grace Tate
Agnes E. Robinson
Herbert S. Robinson
George Booth Tate
Edith K. Tate
Grandchildren.
Ernest William Tate
Mildred M. Tate
Ethel C. Gossage
A. H. Tate
Helen F. Gossage
Agnes M. Tate
Isabel M. Tate
Caroline B. Tate
Winifred Tate
Beatrice Maud Tate
Eveline Tate
Reginald H. Tate
Pauline B. Tate
Alfred Leonard Tate
Eric D. Tate
E. Marguerite Tate
Henry Burton Tate
Arthur Wignall Tate
Fred. W. Robinson
Claude W. Robinson
Muriel C. Robinson
Henry W. Robinson
Brian W. Robinson
Edwin W. Robinson
Alan W. Robinson
G. W. Robinson
Kenneth Wylie Tate
George Vernon Tate
Gerald Ainslie Tate
Jane Marjorie Tate
Great Grandchildren.
Mildred C. Tate
Joan Tate
11th March, 1899.
QUEEN VICTORIA'S JUBILEE INSTITUTE FOR NURSES
1897.
THE NATIONAL GALLERY OF BRITISH ART.
1891.
THE TATE PUBLIC LIBRARY STREATHAM
THE TATE LIBRARY
SOUTH LAMBETH
THE TATE CENTRAL LIBRARY
BRIXTON
1887.

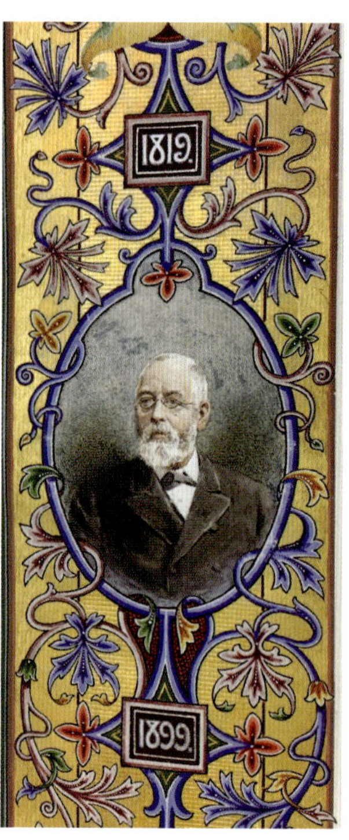

Henry Tate (1819–1899)

Most people will be aware of the connection between Henry Tate and this country's sugar industry – the familiar Tate & Lyle was formed in 1921 by merging the sugar empire of Henry Tate & Sons with that of Abram Lyle & Sons. Both companies had started outside London (Liverpool for Tate and Scotland for Lyle) and both moved to the East End of London. Messrs Tate and Lyle were bitter rivals and they never met: the merger took place long after they had died.

Henry Tate from Chorley in Lancashire was a born entrepreneur and despite his humble beginnings – a grocer shop in Liverpool's Old Haymarket – but he was soon running six shops and a wholesale business. In 1859 he entered the sugar trade, in partnership with one of the smallest firms in Liverpool. Two years later he sold his six shops to concentrate on sugar. In 1878 he established a new refinery in London at Silvertown and subsequently decided to focus his energies on the London operation, relocating his home and family to Streatham. Tate married twice – first to Jane Wignall of Aughton in Lancashire (they had ten children though one of them died in infancy) and after the death of Jane, to Jane Amy Fanny, the daughter of Charles Hislop of Brixton Hill, a connection which may have influenced the choice of Streatham as his residence.

Details from document on previous page.
Left: Portrait of Henry Tate.
Below: view of Park Hill from the park.

Right: The gallery and billiard room of Henry Tate at Park Hill: one of thirty five photographs of the house and gardens taken in 1887. There is no trace of Ophelia, which Tate only acquired in 1892. But some of the paintings can be identified. The most prominent, ahead, is J W Waterhouse's 'St Eulalia' (1885) and the largest (bottom right) is another Waterhouse painting, 'Consulting the Oracle' (1884). The two paintings above the latter are G H Boughton's 1882 'Weeding the pavement' (right) and John Linnell's 1865 'Reapers' (left). The top-lit room meant that the walls yielded maximum hanging space as they were not interrupted by windows. *© Tate, London 2017.*

Henry Tate's Collecting

'Ophelia' is one of the Tate Gallery's most popular paintings and has been one of their best-selling postcards for many years (see pp. 104–105). It is so famous that in August 2014, when Tate Britain's touring show on the Pre-Raphaelites returned home after two years,

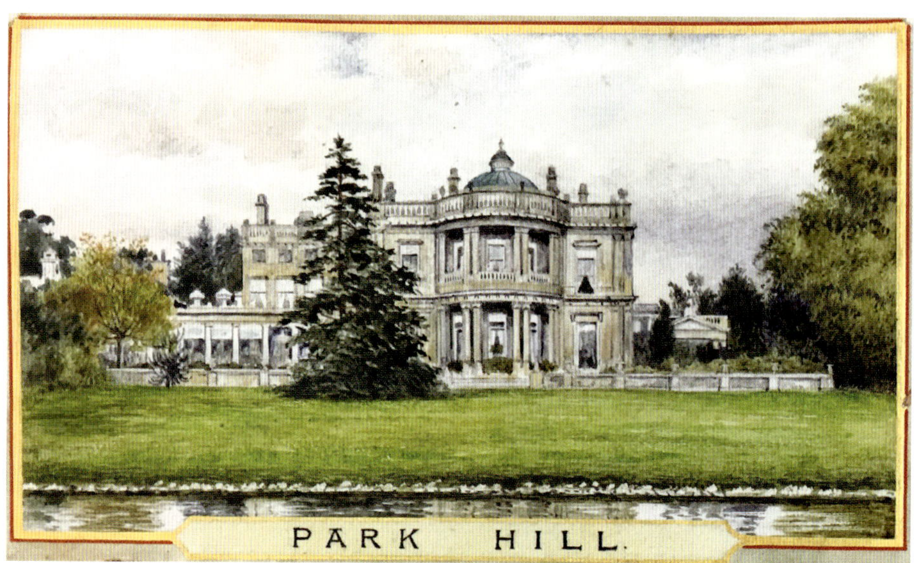

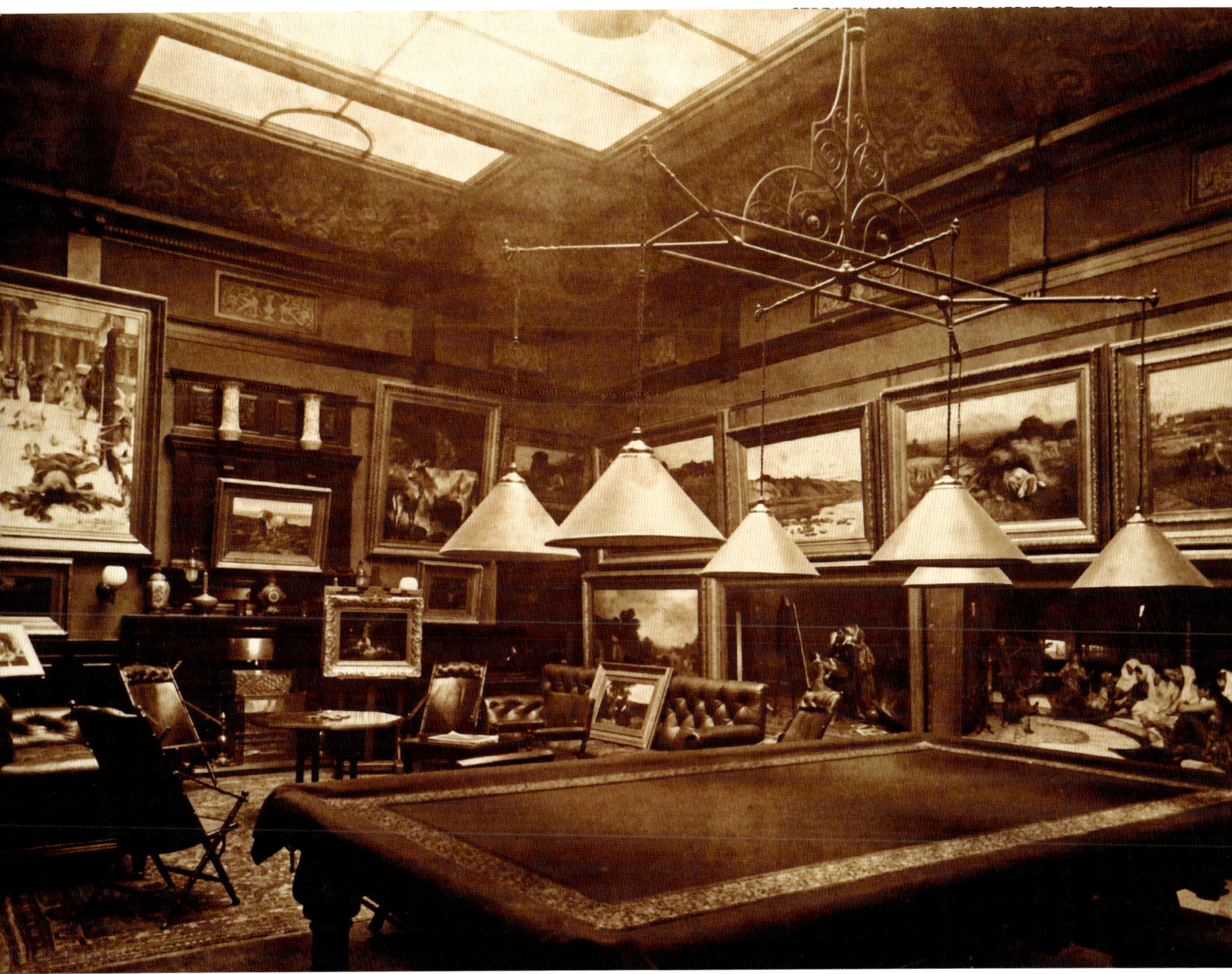

'Ophelia' was the hook on which the press release was issued: 'Tate Britain welcomes home Ophelia'. The painting was shown at the National Gallery of Art in Washington, The Pushkin State Museum of Fine Arts in Moscow; the Mori Art Center in Tokyo; and the Palazzo Chiablese in Turin, altogether attracting 1.1 million visitors. But between 1892 and 1897, away from the limelight and prior to being donated to the Tate Gallery, 'Ophelia' hung in Henry Tate's grand villa at Park Hill.

'Ophelia' is one of seven works in Tate's collection by the painter John Everett Millais (1829–1896). Although Henry Tate is generally thought of as a collector of Pre-Raphaelite works, Millais is the only artist he collected from the seven-member Brotherhood. William Waterhouse (1849–1917), who was later regarded as affiliated to the group is represented by three paintings in Tate's collection including the much-loved 'Lady of Shalott' (overleaf). The famous art critic John Ruskin (1819–1900), a passionate defender of contemporary art had hoped that the Pre-Raphaelites might 'lay in our land the foundations of a school of art nobler than has been seen for three hundred years' (letter to *The Times*, 30 May 1851).

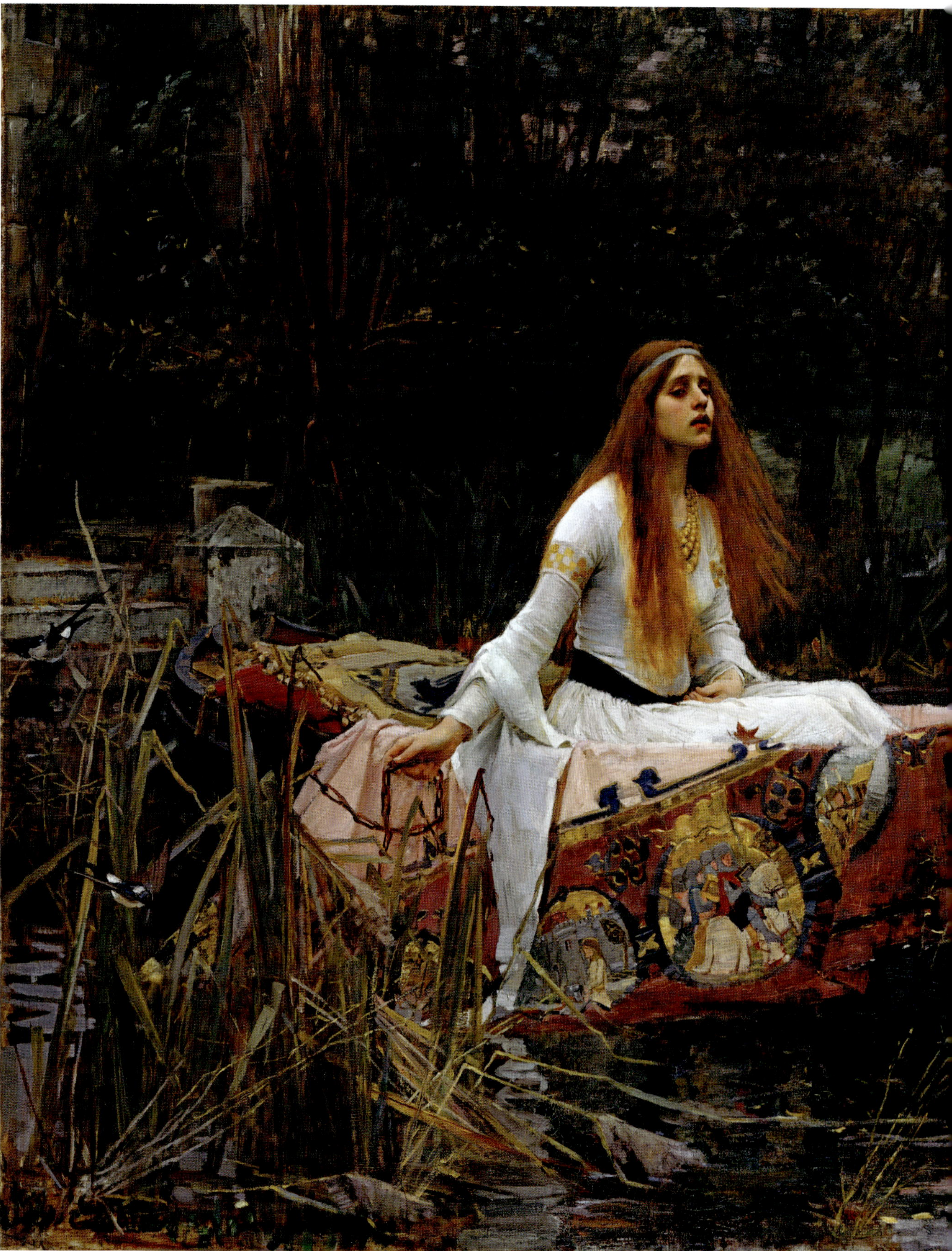

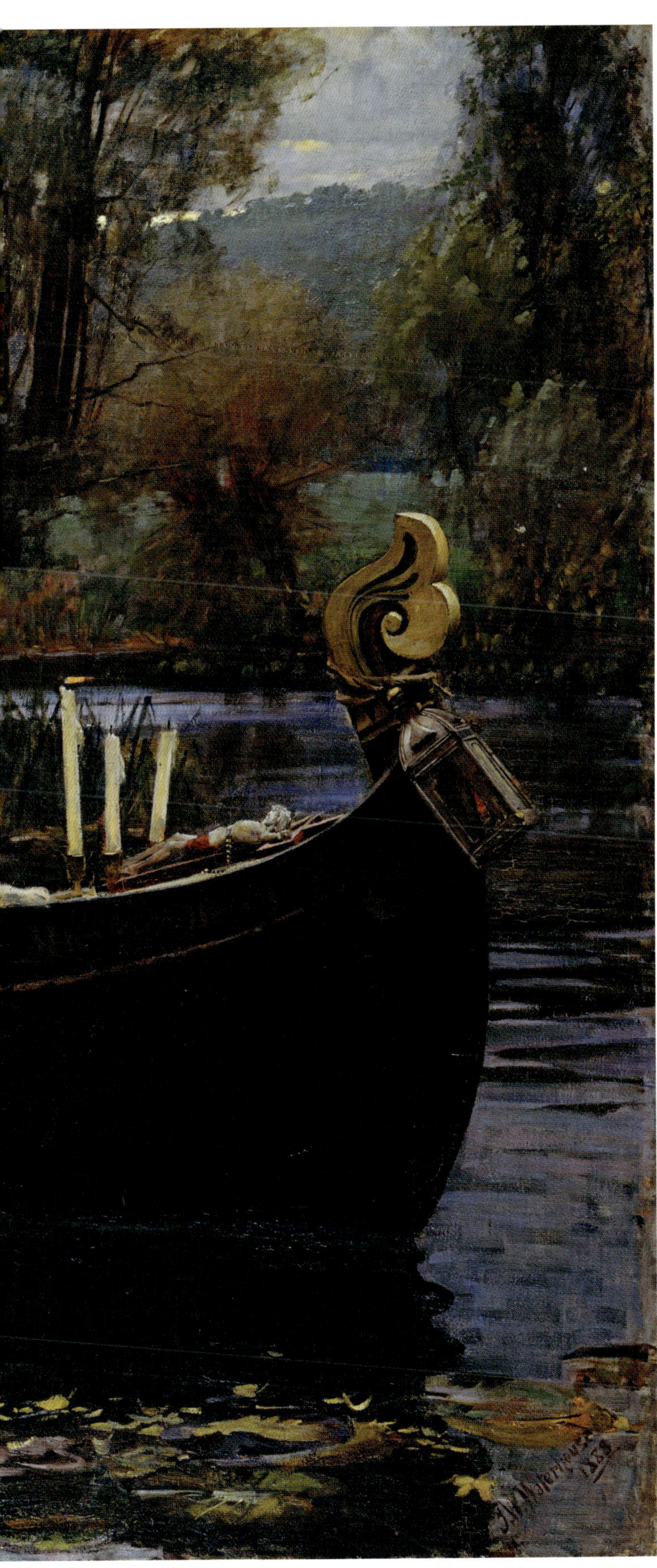

William Waterhouse, 'The Lady of Shalott', 1888. The painter was an avid admirer of the poet Alfred Tennyson: he owned a copy of his *Collected Works* whose blank pages were filled with sketches of ideas for paintings. This melancholic work is based on Tennyson's eponymous 1832 poem, homing in on the lines:

> 'The broad stream bore her far away,
> The Lady of Shalott.'

The cursed Lady Shalott (the story does not say why) could only look at reality through a mirror. She defied that rule when she encountered the beautiful Lancelot. She met her fate head on by leaving her island to float down the river to Camelot, the famous Arthurian site. She was dead before reaching it. *© Tate, London 2017.*

The Tate Gallery in Streatham

The idea of the Tate Gallery, a new gallery for British art, was not envisaged from the start. When Henry Tate conceived the idea of donating his collection to the State, the first port of call had been the National Gallery (established in 1824): their representation of British paintings was 'haphazard and uneven' remarked John Rothenstein, director of the Tate Gallery between 1938 and 1964, adding 'the collection of British art in national possession was in fact scattered, miscellaneous and difficult to see'. But the National Gallery was unwilling to take the whole gift, against Tate's wishes. There was incessant arguing over a number of years until Tate, exasperated, discreetly suggested he would be prepared to pay for a new gallery: the future Tate Gallery. It was *The Times* newspaper which had first voiced the idea that 'the time has come for the creation of a great British Gallery' on 13 March 1889. And when Tate's concrete offer followed, it was warmly welcomed by this newspaper.

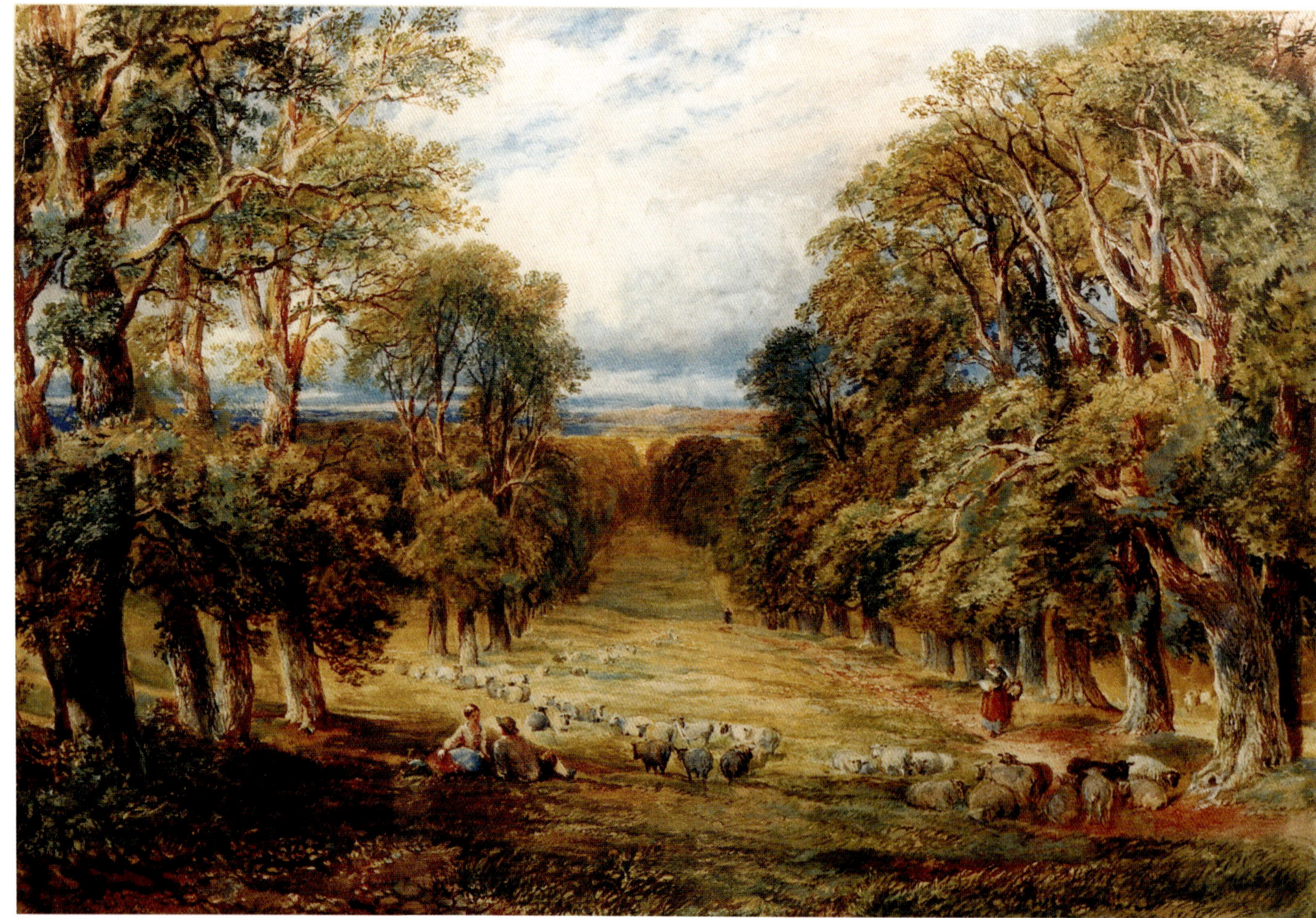

Finding a site led to more arguments, twists and turns and even dead ends, but eventually the site of the Millbank Penitentiary was suggested and despite the odd misgiving – 'It is on the Thames, at a dirty spot', negotiations resumed and were successful: the future Tate Gallery, designed by Sidney R J Smith was opened on 21 July 1897 by the Prince of Wales. Henry Tate, who hated public speaking, made a speech in which he promised to finance an extension if it was found to be needed: this was opened on 28 November 1899 – adding nine rooms to the original eight galleries, making 'the Tate the largest art gallery in London'.

It is not too difficult to see how successful merchants settling in the suburbs and commuting to London for work were not only pioneering middle-class-living in Streatham but also developing a substantial artistic heritage both in terms of architecture and art collections. The Thrales, the Leafs and the Tates set a pattern in Streatham which existed elsewhere but which was particularly outstanding in this part of South London. However Henry Tate, more than most, understood the limitations of purely private ownership and was keen to entrust the future of his collection within a public-funded institution. His legacy has survived but not that of the Thrales or the Leafs.

Van Gogh: South London wanderings

> Things are going well for me here, I have a wonderful home and it's a great pleasure for me to observe London and the English way of life and the English themselves, and I also have nature and art and poetry, and if that isn't enough, what is?
>
> *Vincent van Gogh writing to his brother Theo, January 1874*

Vincent van Gogh (1853–1890), the Dutch post-Impressionist painter famous for cutting his ear off, for failing to sell his work (only one work sold in his life time), for committing suicide at the young age of 37 and for securing record prices for his work in the twenty-first century, that Vincent lived in South London between 1873 and 1875. He was twenty two when he wrote a 'Streatham' letter to his brother Theo which survives. It contained a drawing of Streatham Common which is missing:

> London, April 1875
>
> My dear Theo,
> I'm sending you herewith a small drawing. I made it last Sunday,
> the morning a daughter (13 years old) of my landlady died.
> It's a view of Streatham Common, a large, grass-covered area with
> oak trees and broom.
> It had rained in the night, and the ground was soggy here and there
> and the young spring grass fresh and green.
> As you see, it's scribbled on the title page of the 'Poésies d'Edmond Roche'.
> [passage dealing with poetry]
> Warm regards, and I wish you the best. Adieu
>
> Vincent

Van Gogh's visit to Streatham Common is recorded in 1875, twelve years after David Cox Junior painted 'The Avenue' which ran between Park Hill and the High Road – the ancestor of the Streatham Common North Road. Van Gogh would almost certainly have known and indeed walked up or down this grand avenue. *Photo: Lambeth Archives © Abbott and Holder.*

The 'landlady's daughter' who had died was Elizabeth Parker (see below).

Other letters written during the London period indicate that he was exploring South London, enjoying its landscape and cultural landmarks.
On 20 July 1873 he wrote:

> English art didn't appeal to me much at first, one has to get used to it. There are some good painters here, though, including Millais, who made 'The Huguenot', Ophelia, &c., engravings of which you probably know, they're very beautiful. Then Boughton, of whom you know the 'Puritans going to church' in our Galerie photographique. I've seen very beautiful things by him.

Both painters, Millais and Boughton, were represented in Henry Tate's collection at Streatham. Van Gogh adds:

> Things are going well for me here. I go walking a lot. Here where I live it's a quiet, convivial, nice-looking neighbourhood, in this I've really been fortunate.

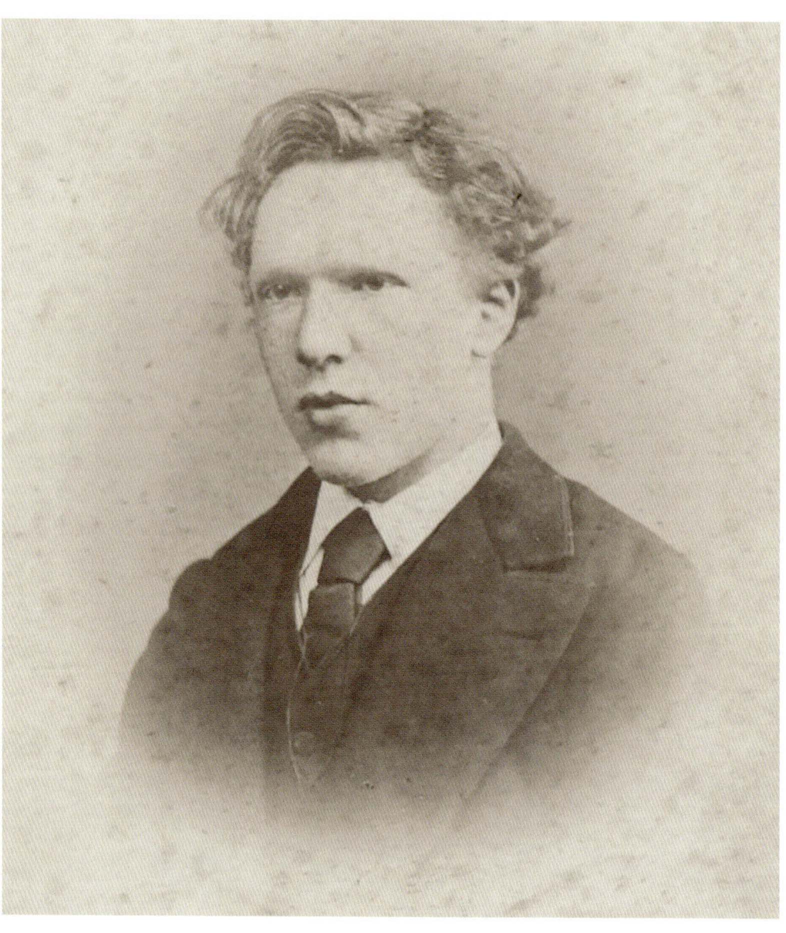

Portrait of Vincent van Gogh by Jacobus Marinus Wilhelmus de Louw (1823–1907).
The photograph was taken in January 1873, the year he started residing in South London; Van Gogh was nineteen.
Van Gogh Museum.
Photo: Wikimedia Commons.

On 4 August 1873 Van Gogh signed himself in as 'VWvanGogh the Hague' in the Dulwich Picture Gallery's visitor's book (Documentation Dulwich Picture Gallery). The visit is testified by a letter he wrote three days later:

> I had a nice day last Monday. The first Monday in Aug. is a holiday here. I went with one of the Germans to Dulwich, an hour and a half outside L.[ondon], to see the museum there, and afterwards we walked to a village about an hour further on. The countryside here is so beautiful; many people who have their business in L.[ondon] live in some village or other outside L.[ondon] and come to the city every day by train.

However, Van Gogh's London stay, which had started so well and seemed so promising – he had a good job with the art dealers Goupil & Co based in the Strand – ended up in tears. The future artist fell in love with Eugenie Loyer, the daughter of his Brixton landlady at 87 Hackford Road but she had secretly promised her hand to the previous tenant – a bitter pill to swallow and one which drove Van Gogh to move to a different address, staying with the Parker family at 395 Kennington Road (from mid-August 1874). His Streatham letter is particularly nostalgic – the sadness of a broken heart being compounded by the death of a teenager he knew well.

Cultural philanthropy spills onto the streets – William Dyce and Tate's buildings

One of Streatham' best known landmarks is the Dyce fountain which moved in 1933 from a site close to the church to the middle of Streatham Green, the patch of grass situated close to the junction of the High Road with Mitcham Lane, and 'a relic from the medieval village of Streatham' (Graham Gower).

The parishioners of St Leonard's wanted to express their gratitude to William Dyce (1806–1864), the churchwarden artist who had designed their chancel and made various contributions to parish life: they apparently raised the money to finance the building of a fountain which would commemorate their benefactor. They saved money on its design since this was prepared by William Dyce himself who produced two options to choose from.

This Scottish artist, born in Aberdeen, trained at the Royal Academy Schools and settled in Edinburgh after a trip to Rome. He was soon heading the School of Design there which subsequently led to his appointment as head of the newly formed School of Design in London – what would become the Royal College of Art. He ran the school between 1838 and 1843 and he remained a member of the council on his departure. His appointment came at the end of a period of consultation, including with the architect John Buonarotti Papworth, the designer of Park Hill, who was subsequently appointed part-time Director of the School.

The Dyce fountain was designed by the painter William Dyce and erected near St Leonard's church in 1862. In 1932, H W Bromhead described it as 'dirty and neglected'. It was moved to its current position in 1933 and restored in 2015. It became a Grade II listed building in 2005. Also see p. 76.

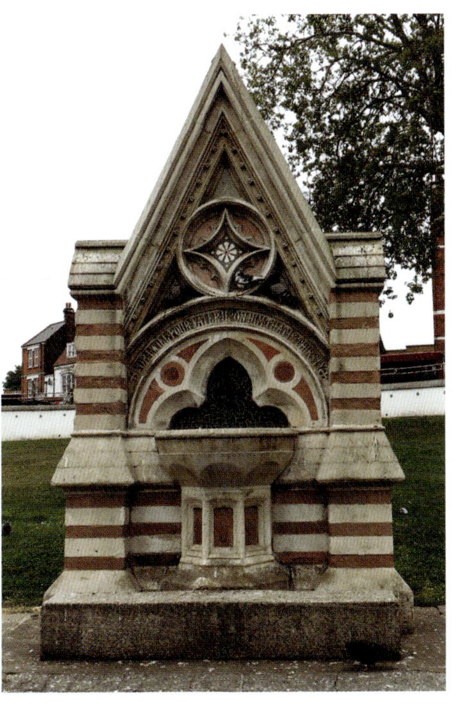

These were early days, as described by Christopher Frayling in his history of the Royal College of Art: 'at the beginning the School of Design could be nothing more than an experiment, for no one seems to have had any idea of what it was to teach' (the School started with twelve students only, the evening classes were more successful). Frayling adds that 'there was little consensus about the exact meaning of the term [design]'. Willliam Dyce, advising from Edinburgh, was encouraged to undertake a trip to similar schools in France and Germany. This research should have given him a head start but after being appointed Head of the School, his time there was a long and unhappy struggle. He nevertheless played a key role in the birth of this important institution and several of the contemporary artists discussed in this book either trained or taught at the Royal College of Art (Timothy Hyman, Jaime Gili and the co-author of this book – Jiro Osuga).

In 1856 Dyce moved with his family from 'The Oaks' in Norwood to a new building at the corner of Leigham Court Road and Streatham Hill (see p. 56 for his residence on the High Road). This house does not survive and St Leonard's church where he is buried was damaged by fire in 1975. The Memorial Brass to William Dyce, erected in 1865 at the expense of St Leonard's parishioners, was regarded as 'magnificent .... so fine in design' (Bromhead). It was damaged in the fire, dispatched to the Victoria & Albert Museum for assessment, judged beyond repair and disposed of by the Museum. Streatham insisted on remembering this adopted 'son' and there is a William Dyce Mews, a utilitarian car parking area near Streatham Green – which sadly does little to enhance Dyce's reputation, unlike Dyce's fountain, which is certainly a worthy reminder.

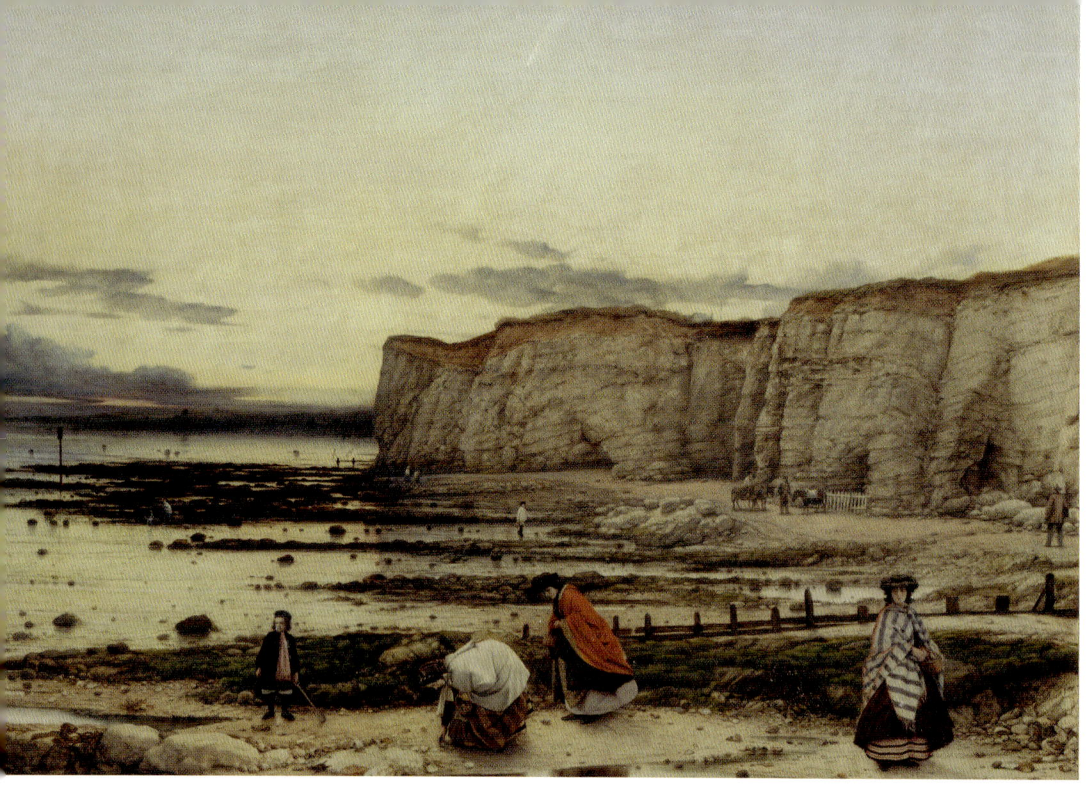

William Dyce, 'Pegwell Bay: A Recollection of October 5th 1858', oil on canvas, 63.5 x 88.9 cm, was exhibited at the Royal Academy in 1860. This composition started life as a watercolour made in 1858 when the whole family were on holiday near Ramsgate in Kent. Dyce produced this oil painting a little later. Often described as Dyce's finest painting, it was made in Streatham and the artist may have represented himself – see the far right figure. Some art historians have regarded the obvious interest in nature - including geology – as expressing religious doubt. *© Tate, London 2017.*

However, Henry Tate and his wife were astonishingly prolific philanthropists and their buildings still stand in Streatham and elsewhere (see p. 121 for Henry's overall legacy at the age of eighty). The Tate estate has miraculously survived at Park Hill, but Henry also left libraries in South Lambeth (1883), Streatham (Grade II opened in 1890), and Brixton (opened in 1893). Less often discussed is Mrs Tate's contribution to Streatham's built heritage: a School Hall, built in 1908 for Streatham High School for Girls (housed in an eighteenth century building on the High Road called 'The Shrubbery'). Women were traditionally associated with school life from the Victorian period onwards – so the choice of building is not surprising. This building still exists, almost opposite the Edwardian Royal Mail Sorting Office in Prentis Road, close to the High Road but in 1938 it was converted into the South London Synagogue.

Both the Streatham and South Lambeth libraries as well as the School Hall were designed by the Tates' favourite architect – Sidney R J Smith (1858–1913) who also designed the Tate Gallery at Millbank.

The painter William Dyce was commissioned to paint frescoes for the Queen's Robing Room in the Houses of Parliament in 1847. He chose the theme of Arthurian legends and presented its stories in the form of 'virtues'. From left to right: Courtesy, Religion and Hospitality. When the painter died nineteen years later, they were still unfinished and Charles West Cope (1811–1890) completed the task. *Photo: Palace of Westminster.*

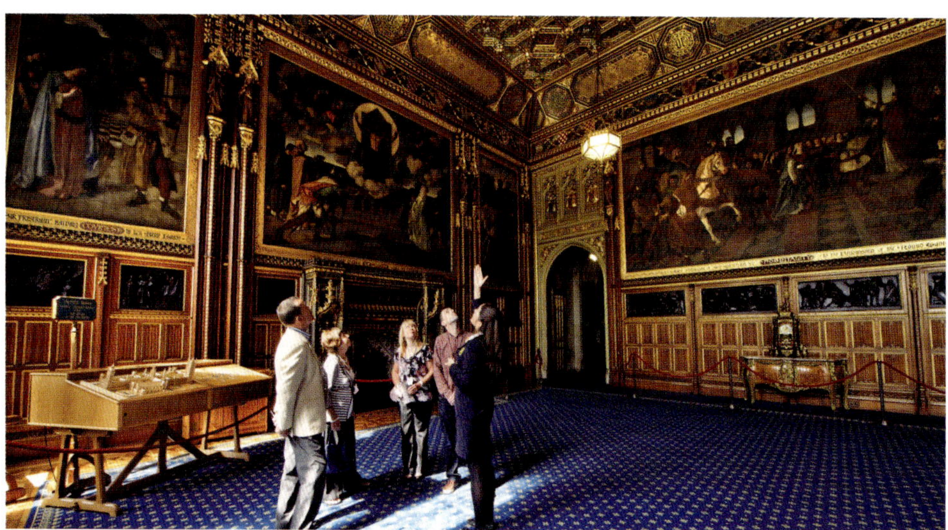

Women power – Suffragettes and Winifred Knights

In 2015 the Museum of London acquired a small group of Streatham suffragette material, further increasing the Museum's substantial Suffragette collection. This new acquisition consisted of items of clothing and printed ephemera linked to a Streatham resident, **Dorothy Louise Meihé** (1876–1969), born in West Norwood and who later lived at 34 Ambleside Avenue ('Limstburg', the house still exists) – scarf, sash, regalia, hat with band, belt, badges, photographs, brooch and rosettes. Dorothy, her mother, her sister and her aunt (Alice Ellen Wilson (1852–1930), a freelance magazine writer and inveterate traveller) were all involved in the Suffragette cause and were members of the Streatham branch of the Women's Social & Political Union (WSPU campaigned between 1903 and 1917). They did not have to worry about the reaction of the man of the family – Swiss born John Meihé, a Baltic timber merchant, had died as early as 1885 when the family lived in Brixton at 48 Gresham Road. His wife and children shared an estate of around £61,000.

This collection supplements another which entered the Museum's collection in the 1950s and which is linked to Suffragettes Leonora (mother), Helen (daughter) and Diana Tyson: they all received medallions in 1909 from the Streatham branch of the WSPU, in remembrance of the gruesome time they spent in Holloway Goal. Leonora Tyson (1883–1959) has been the subject of a useful pamphlet by Anne Ward (see bibliography).

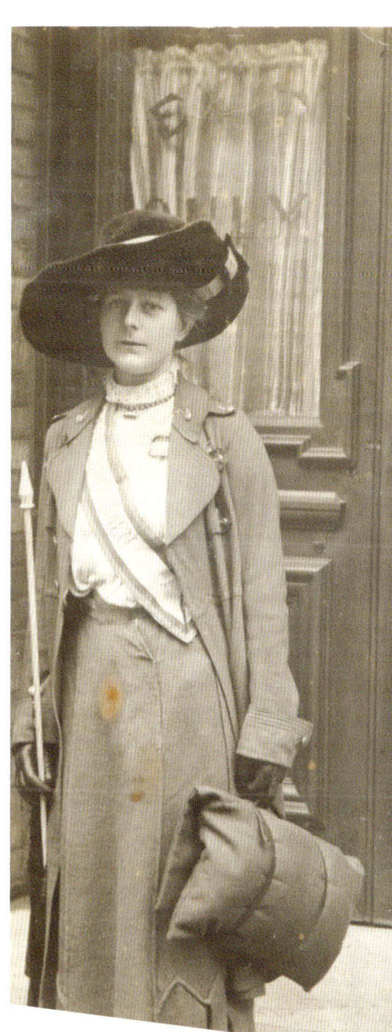

Portrait of Dorothy Meihé in full Suffragette regalia. The photograph is not dated but may have been taken on 17 June 1911, the greatest propaganda procession in which Dorothy and her sister Winnie took part. Dorothy would have been thirty five. *© Museum of London.*

'Votes for Women' brooch belonging to Dorothy Meihé, a Streatham Suffragette whose Suffragette memorabilia is now in the collection of the Museum of London. *© Museum of London.*

Arthur Frank Ebert, a relative of the Meihé sisters, recorded that they both attended art school, becoming competent amateur artists. Winnie, described as a miniature painter, exhibited one work at the Royal Academy in 1900 and two more the following year at the Society of Women Artists Exhibitors. Dorothy on the other hand was a member of the British Association for the Advancement of Science which probably led to the bequest of the 'Dorothy Louise Meihé Memorial Scholarship' for women medical students at the Royal Free Hospital School of Medicine (this was merged with gifts from others to become the 'Elizabeth Garrett Anderson Scholarships for Women'). The two sisters and their aunt supported Mrs Pankhurst and the Suffragette movement but as Ebert pointed out 'they were never arrested; they belonged to the rank and file, who served on committees, held gatherings in their home, attended demonstrations and public meetings .... The famous leaders in the limelight need hosts of followers in the background'.

The future painter **Winifred Knights** (1899–1947) was a mere child/teenager when the Suffragette movement was raging on the streets of London: by temperament she certainly was not the campaigning type but she still made feminist history in her own quiet way.

The Dulwich Picture Gallery's ground-breaking 2016 exhibition about this painter was a revelation: first it brought to public attention Knights's remarkable and barely known paintings and secondly, its curator, Sacha Llewellyn, charted in brilliant detail Winifred's life and early death in the accompanying catalogue. She was born and brought up in Streatham to parents who were from Brixton. The family lived briefly at 54 Hitherfield Road before moving to 22 Madeira Road in 1907. Both houses were destroyed in the last war – clearly marked as destroyed/beyond repair on the London County Council Bomb Damage maps.

Winifred would have been fifteen when in June 1914, the *Morning Post Newspaper* reported that three men were tried for attacking Suffragettes on Streatham Common: 'there was an effort on the part of the young men of Streatham to put the militants in the pond'. The judge did not impose any penalty on that occasion 'because the behaviour of these women had created a strong feeling of resentment and disgust' (information retrieved from the National Archives Suffragettes case studies).

While some of her neighbours were embracing the dangerous Suffragette cause, Winifred Knights, at the young age of sixteen, was admitted to the Slade School of Art – the first School of Art to accept women (from 1871). Her time there was marred by difficult events in 1917: she had a breakdown after witnessing several heavy air raids over Streatham. She was also travelling on a bus across London Bridge when the terrible Silvertown explosion of a West Ham munitions factory occurred: it was said the massive explosion could be heard from Streatham. These traumatic events led her to interrupt her studies and to escape to the country for a year.

On the surface her paintings bear no connection to Streatham at all. She pursued the career of a narrative painter, working on large scale decorative works that were scaled up from immaculate drawings – landscape and religion being her main sources of inspiration. However, the work was also extremely autobiographical – the artist peopled her pictures with friends, family members and herself too, thus representing a little piece of Streatham life.

She was an excellent student and the Slade put her forward for the prestigious British School in Rome in 1920. At the age of 21, she was the first woman ever to be admitted, despite encountering some unfair competition. The subject set by the organisers for the entry competition was a Biblical theme – the Deluge – no doubt influenced by the catastrophic Great War which was still fresh on everyone's mind. It must have resonated strongly with Winifred Knights, who only three years before, had been so traumatised by it. *The Liverpool Courier* described her painting as 'vigorous and essential'.

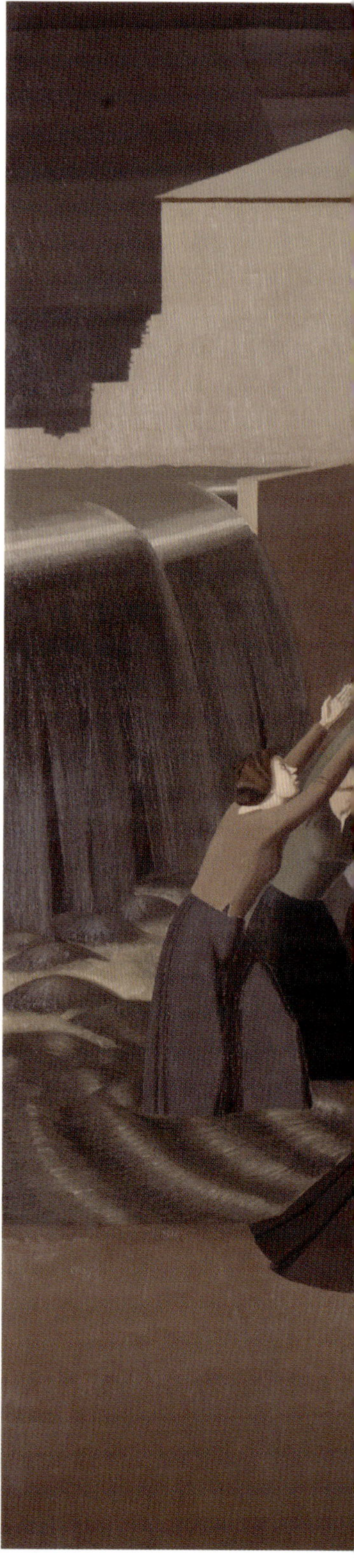

'The Deluge', oil on canvas by Winifred Knights, 1920. Strongly influenced by the Italian Renaissance and her contemporary, the painter Stanley Spencer (1891–1959), Winifred Knights discarded the classic depiction of Noah's Ark and cast friends and family in a mad scramble for safety, up a mountain. In effect Knights peopled her Deluge with Streatham residents and their friends, starting with the artist herself – shown twice but her portrait in the centre is the most compelling. Her mother Mabel is there, cradling David, the five-month old son she lost in 1915. Knights's boyfriend, the painter Arnold Mason is there too and the robed figure in the right foreground may well stand for the clergy of St Peter's Streatham – Knights stopped attending church after the death of her baby brother. *© Tate, London 2017.*

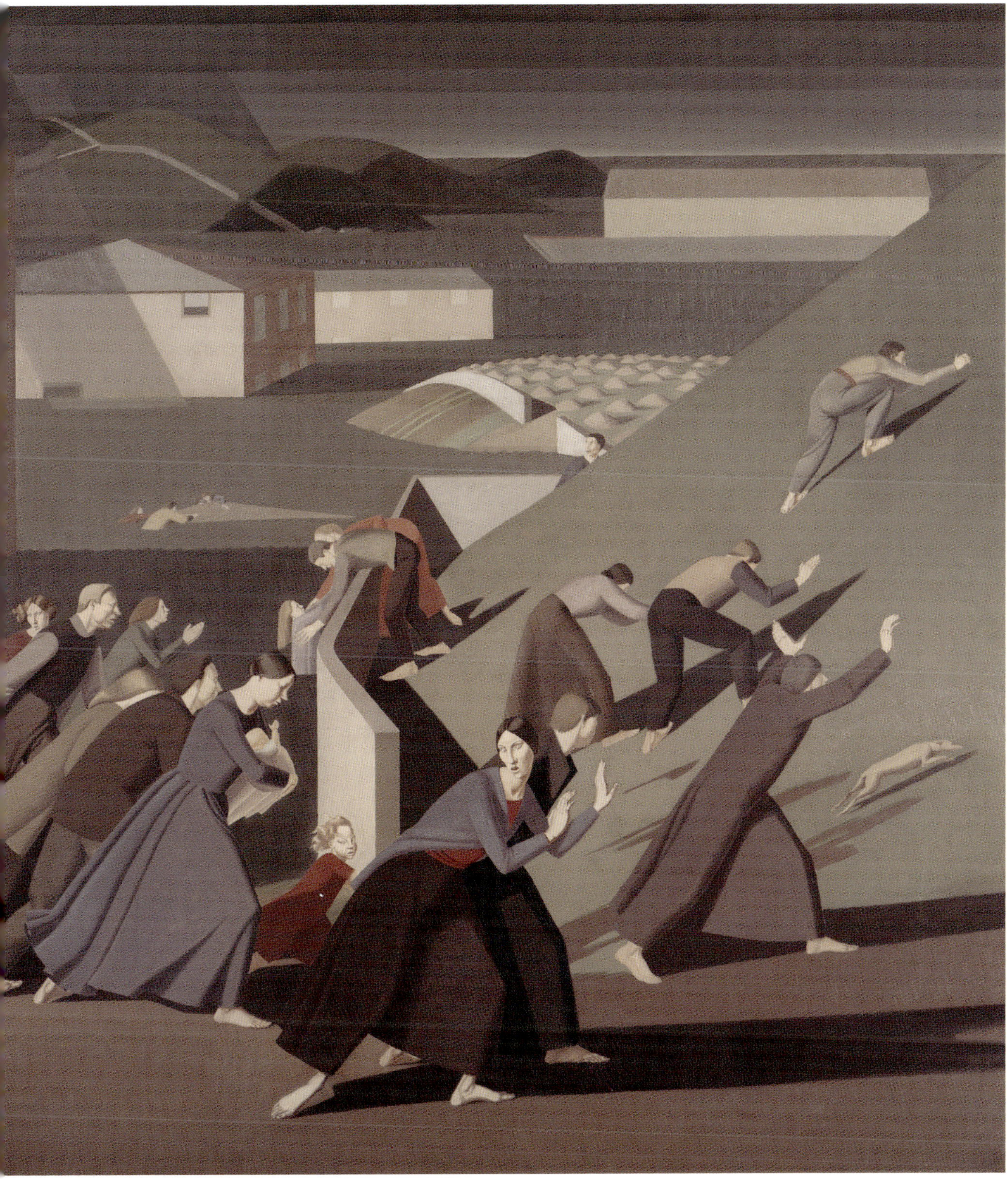

The Art Scene now

A chance encounter between photographer Nick MacRae and artists Gilbert & George established that the famous pair were regular visitors to Streatham: 'because it was on a direct bus route from their Liverpool Street home and studio'. This was reported in the *South London Press* on 30 October 2003, also adding that the two artists 'singled out the high road's Algerian cafes and fried chicken takeaways as their favourite Streatham spots'.

Streatham Festival

The single most effective way of encountering contemporary creative activity in Streatham now is through the annual Streatham Festival, held in July.

Residents will probably be surprised to hear that efforts to set up a Streatham festival started as early as the 1970s. This can be charted through John Brown's archive (see p. 23), with the first recognisable Festival held in May 1974. Based at St Leonard's church, it was led by an entirely musical committee chaired by Charles Barker, a member of the choir with Tom McLelland Young (organist and choirmaster) and Edward Bloomfield (Streatham Philharmonic Orchestra) as musical advisers. The festival aimed 'to provide a platform for local artists: musicians, painters, poets etc'. There were festivals in 1975 and 1976, followed by a twenty-two year gap, no doubt for the reason spelt out by the Rector Michael Hamilton-Sharp: 'some of the events were so poorly supported'.

Undaunted by earlier setbacks Lambeth Environmental Services published the programme for 'Streatham's first Festival of the Arts' in September 1994, crediting Sonia Morton from the South West London Arts Group as the principal organiser. The event, however, was really underpinned by St Leonard's Church and the Streatham Society; and as the latter was too busy in 1995 there was no festival that year. The event was re-launched in 1996 by the energetic John Cresswell, a Streatham Buddhist and the Secretary of the Streatham Society: 'The Streatham Society has been exploring the possibility of establishing a regular Festival of the Arts'. But this was the last festival until its millennial rebirth.

The challenge landed on the desk of Mel Larsen (née Jennings) in 2002 and she got things off to a really promising start. In the first Festival report Mel summarized the Festival's driving force: Streatham 'had some years of decline and is now 'on the up'. The Festival is part of this revitalisation'. Mel was also spurred on by the bleak findings of the *Evening Standard*. In their survey of least desirable postcodes in London, Streatham came at number three.

Mel is a born social entrepreneur who should be credited with starting many festivals in Streatham: the Festival, labelled 'Streatham Arts Festival' in 2002 – an inconsistency which illustrated where its heart lay – and its offshoot 'Yellow Bowl' (2003–2006); the highly successful Food Festival (started in 2009); the Little Big Peace Event (started in 2011); and lately, employed by BID (see p. 31) as the Director of the Streatham Business Awards, held at Hideaway (the award-winning jazz club near Streatham station). In its first year 'Yellow Bowl' featured Mel as an artist and in the accompanying pamphlet, she described her work as 'about patterns and connections' – a most apt definition for her own work as a community organiser! For Yellow Bowl artists' work was presented in various shops and restaurants in Streatham, a forerunner

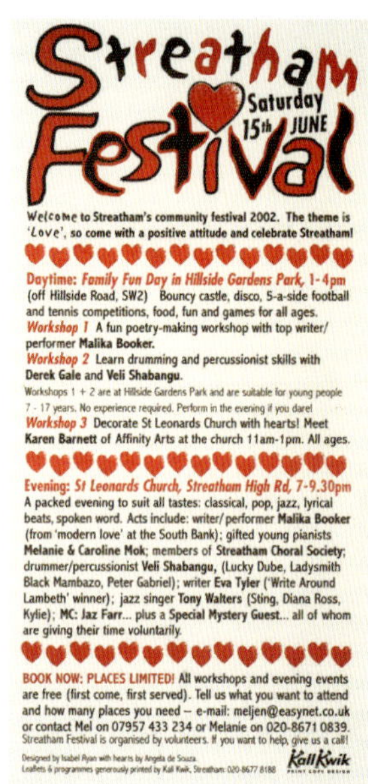

Streatham Festival's very first programme in 2002. *Courtesy of John W Brown, Local History Publications.*

Emma Condliffe, 'Absent', 2012, oil on canvas, 100 x 100 cm. This is one of three portrait paintings (out of a series of six) which Emma exhibited in 2014 in the window of the large Oxfam Shop at 24–26 Streatham High Road. This was the first year of Art23, the art project which Emma set up as part of the Streatham Festival. *© Emma Condliffe.*

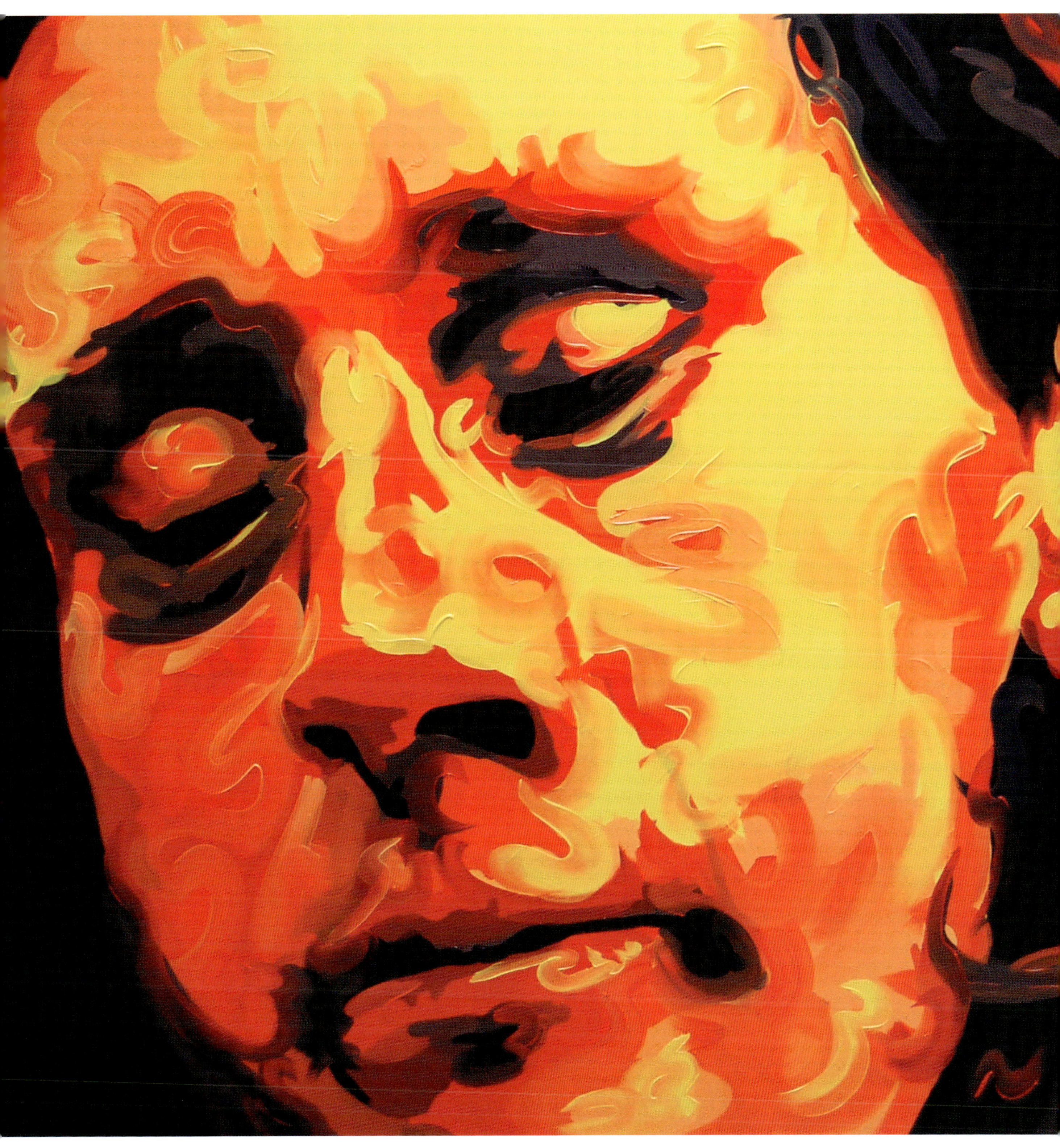

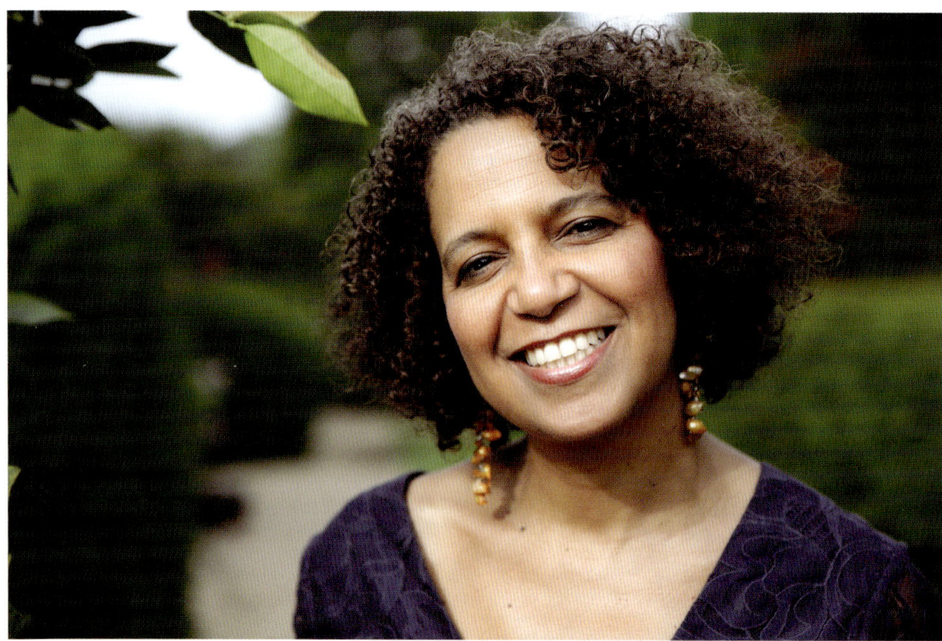

Mel Larsen photographed in 2016 by Andrea Sealey. Mel organised the very first Streatham Festival in the new millennium.

After moving to London in 2015, Istanbul-born Yaprak Akinci took part in Art23 in 2016. The 'frantic urban transformation' of her home city affected her deeply so she chose Streatham as her subject when she courageously offered to paint 'live' in the window of Oxfam Furniture shop at 24-26 Streatham High Road. *© Mireille Galinou.*

of Art23's more developed formula. Based on the idea that 'everyone is an artist', the scheme sought the involvement of professional artists as well as complete amateurs.

The first Festival was free and it was delivered with the help of two key organisations: the church of St Leonard with its broad-minded vicar Jeffry Wilcox, and the Town Centre headed by Leah Levane. They provided help, venues and (modest) funds, supplemented by contributions from Streatham businesses. At the time of writing the Festival has been going for fifteen years and inevitably, it has changed and developed over that period of time. While the main task of the Festival organiser is to track down and broker events, people and ideas, her personality (as well as the budget!) has affected the Festival's theme and contents throughout its history:

2002–2006 Mel Larsen firmly set the artistic tone. She collected a Lambeth civic award at the end of her time and likes to think 'the arts have put their heart into Streatham'.
2007–2010 Patricia Sauer (chair) with Anna Godsiff developed family events and dared to think bigger, also increasing the Festival's funds.
2011–2012 Chix Chandaria, a business woman, directed the Festival with ambition and drive.
2013 Helen Smith
2014 – now Janet Leatherland has headed the Festival at a time of great difficulty and disappearing budget. The Olympics Games 'community fund' had been a generous supporter until money ran out: the Festival was in danger of being cancelled. For now it continues to inspire.

It is noteworthy that the Festival in its twenty first century incarnation was initiated by a woman and has always been run by women (it is the same in Dulwich) – a clear illustration, if one was needed, of the rising status of women in society – in the footsteps of pioneering Victorian giants such as Octavia Hill (1838–1912) and Henrietta Barnett (1851–1936).

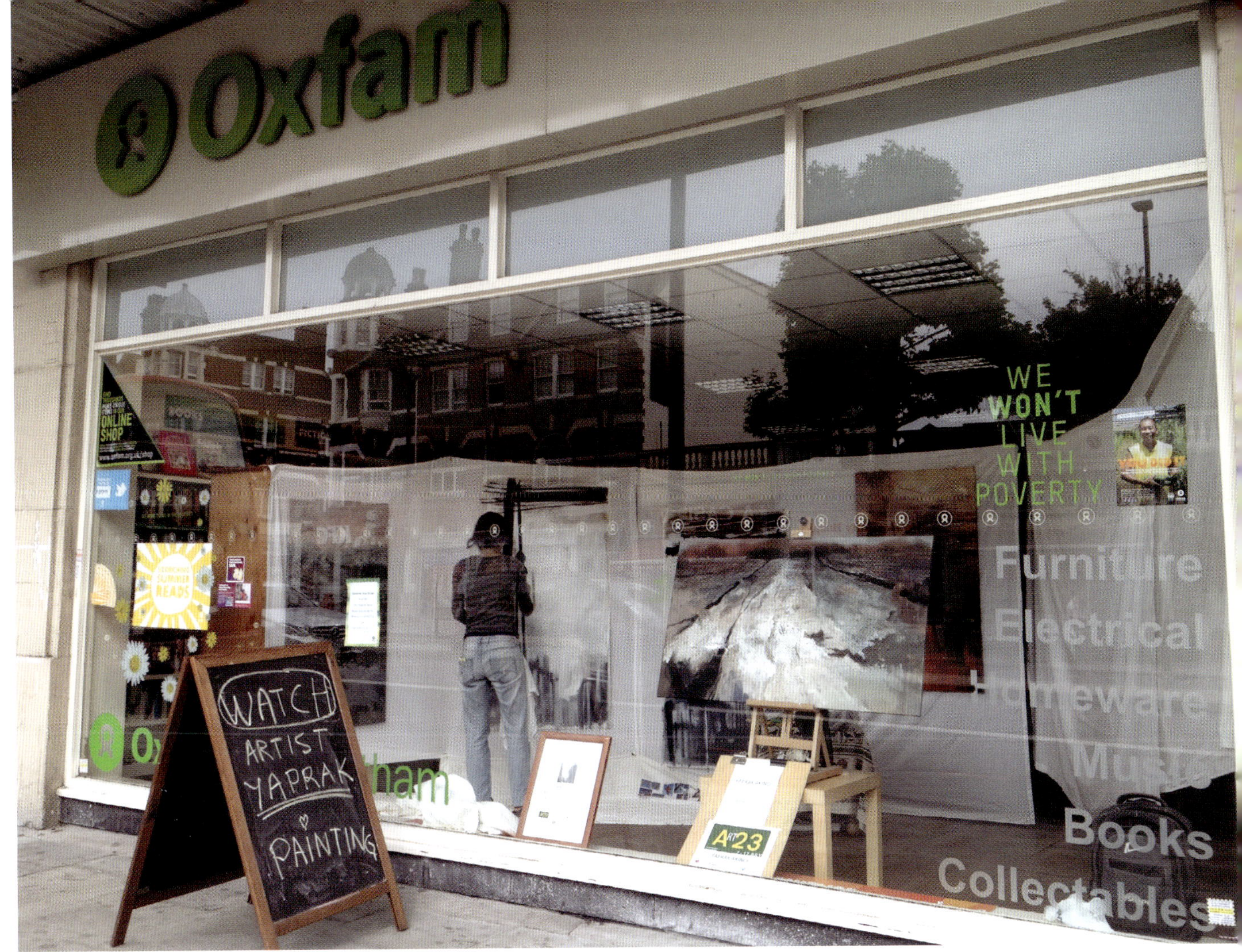

Art23

Art23, i.e. art along the A23 High Road which runs through Streatham, is now the main visual art component of the Streatham Festival. Unlike artists' Open House events in nearby Dulwich (started in 2005) and Sydenham (started in 2009), the classic formula of opening artists' studios to the public has not prevailed in Streatham. The organiser of Art23, the painter Emma Condliffe, based at ASC Studios on Streatham Hill, was frustrated by the gradual loss of appeal of the Open Studios scheme there: artists' participation was erratic and visitors dwindling. Her response was to take the art out to the main street – as pioneered by Mel Larsen in her 'Yellow Bowl' adventure (see above): there was life, shops and passing trade.

This interesting departure from open studios received added impetus because Emma had recently completed a series of large scale portraits (see p. 135) which needed a bigger environment than that offered by her studio to come together as paintings. That environment turned out to be the window of the large Oxfam furniture shop on Streatham High Road (above and also see Jiro Osuga's own version of this window in 2015 on p. 164). Oxfam was one of sixteen venues to take part in the first Art23 project (the shop closed in autumn 2016). In just three years the number of participating venues had jumped to over forty (2016). Jiro Osuga's contribution to the 2016 Art23 was also particularly memorable (see pp. 166 and 192–3).

Other networks

Artists living and working in Streatham do not necessarily see themselves as being part of a local network. In fact the labels 'local' or 'community artist' can be positively frowned: either because artists choose to work in isolation – this is largely the case with Jiro Osuga, while other artists connect to London-wide, national or even international networks and this applies to Jaime Gili.

Jaime Gili has two great loves: abstract art and modernist architecture. Born in Caracas (Venezuela) in 1972 to Catalan parents, he was brought up in a country with fabulous examples of modernist architecture. He was admitted to the Royal College of Art in London in 1996 and this temporary stay soon turned into a permanent one. When looking for a flat, he stumbled across Pullman Court and immediately fell in love with it because it reminded him so much of his native country. He has continued to be inspired by it to this day and organised a substantial event there in 2016 on the occasion of the estate's 80th anniversary – as part of the London wide Open House weekend. Six flats opened their doors to the public, ranging from a studio flat to two-bedroom flats. A historical exhibition by the main entrance introduced the context for this beloved landmark – the property of Tannen Group Ltd which is run with the help of a managing agent and a residents' association. Seventeen artists – part of Jaime's circle and not otherwise linked to Streatham – were also commissioned to respond to this group of buildings and the outcome of their work was 'Concrete', an exhibition which exhibited the artists' responses to the architecture. The only British artist was Bob and Roberta Smith – the (single) artist famous for his Letters to politicians, in particular his 2011 'Letter to Michael Gove'. He made the exhibition flag: 'Performance Participation Association'.

In the historical exhibition Pullman Court was in excellent company: Heathrow Terminal 1 (1950–69), Liverpool Metropolitan Cathedral (1960–67), Coutts Banks

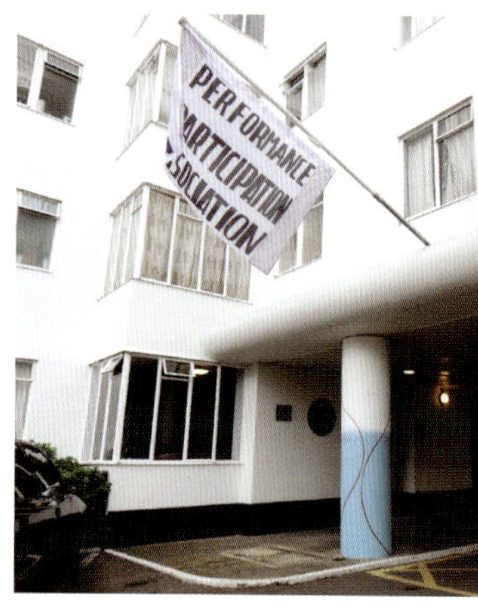

Top right and above: For the eightieth anniversary of Pullman Court (2016) Jaime Gili invited artists to respond to the building: a flag by Bob and Roberta Smith floats above Jaime's 'column intervention' at the main entrance, temporarily reinstating the shape (circular), size and colour of the original design. *© Mireille Galinou and © Jaime Gili.*

Bottom right: Jaime Gili: 'Diamante de las Semillitas' (Diamond Shards) is a permanent art installation at Barrio José Félix Ribas, sometimes described as a favela (= shanty town) or a neighbourhood of Caracas 2011. *Photo: © C G Rojas.*

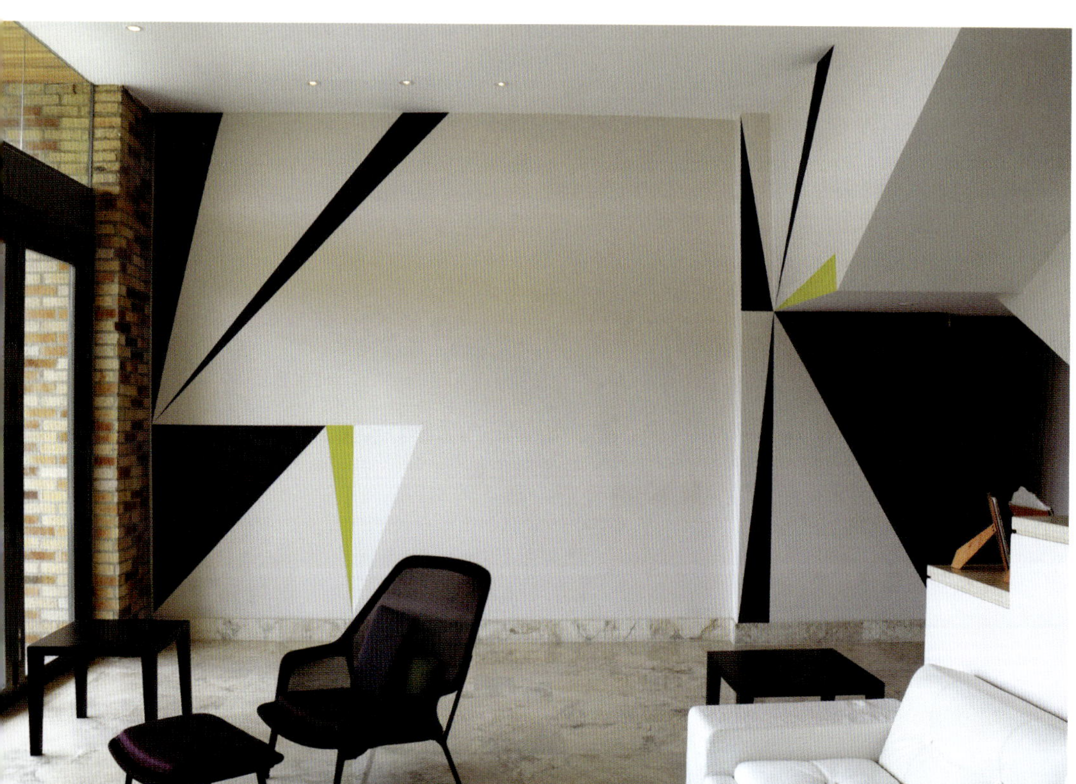

Below: Jaime Gili: one of a number of private commissions the artist received in Caracas, 2009. Jaime's own flat in Pullman Court has been painted with colourful abstract shapes (by an artist friend). Here this black and white scheme has an unusual and striking austerity. *Photo: Jaime Gili.*

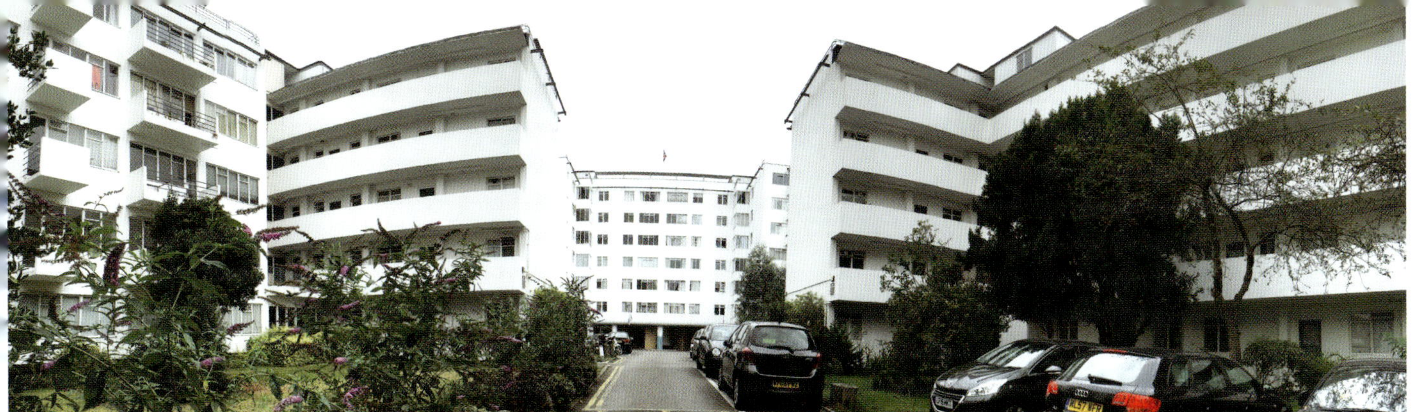

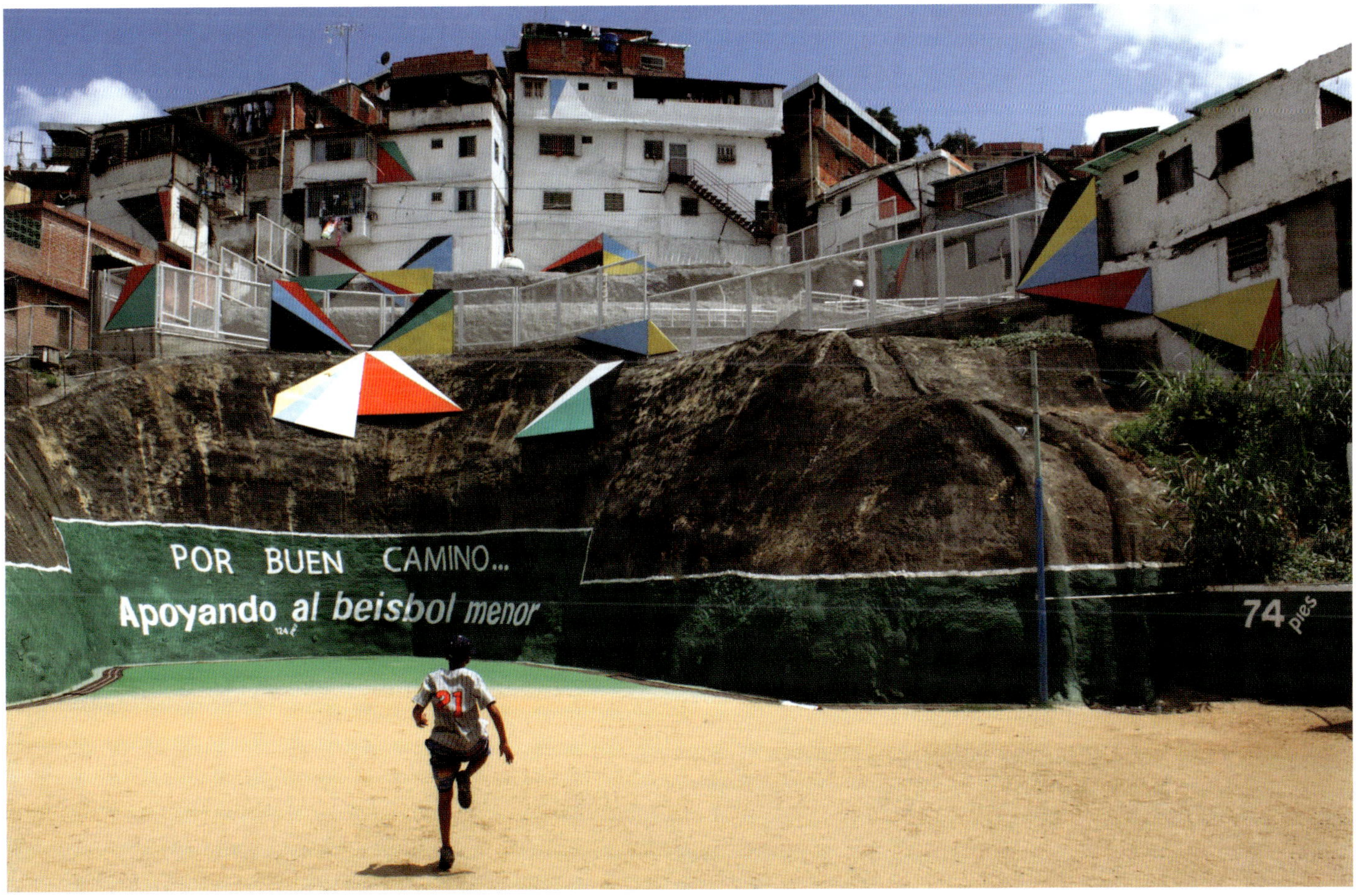

headquarters in The Strand (1969), the Regent's Park mosque (1970–77), all buildings designed by the architect Sir Frederick Ernest Gibberd (1908–1984) who built Pullman Court between 1933–36, a scheme contemporary with Sydenham's Park Court estate, but the latter sadly compromised by the addition of a top storey.

Jaime Gili feels he does not really belong anywhere – a Catalan in Venezuela, a Venezuelan in Spain or a Catalan Venezuelan in Britain. Much of his commissioned work comes from outside Britain. Although he has worked on a number of public art commissions in the UK, he dreams of being able to create a more permanent installation in his country of adoption.

Other groups

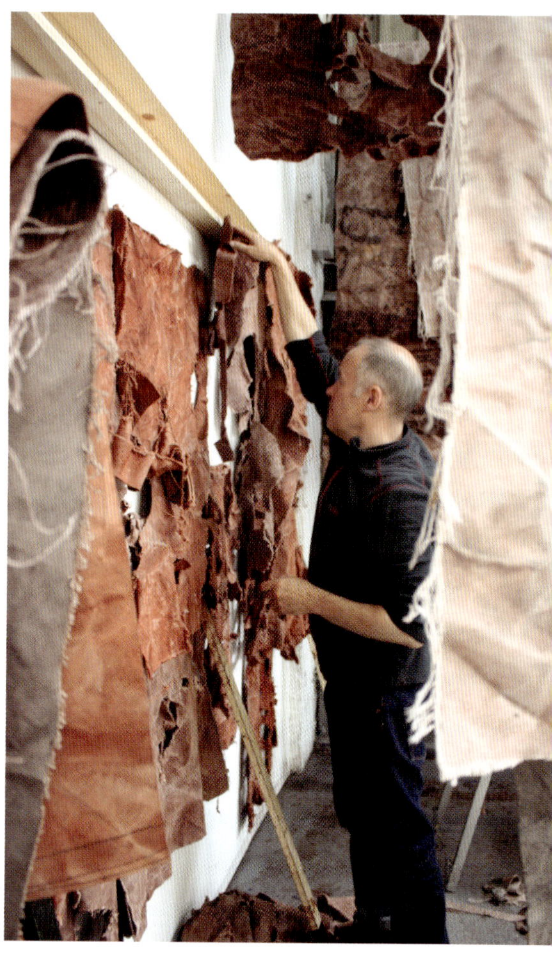

ASC Studios – for Artists' Studios Company – was mentioned earlier in connection with Emma Condliffe and Art23. However, this London-wide organisation is worth describing in its own right. Founded in 1993 by artists Peter Flack and Jonathan Coombes, they operate mostly in South London across nine different sites providing studio space for over 500 artists. The first studios to open were those at the Old Bus Garage in Camberwell New Road (the site has returned to use as a bus garage) and ASC went on to develop a further nineteen sites (Streatham Hill studios opened in 2006). ASC runs a gallery at their head office, situated in a Brutalist tower block on Thurlow Street, Walworth, just down from Marcus Harvey's 'Turps Art School'. They also promote (but not finance) a group of 'projects', one of which is at Streatham Hill variously described as 37C or DOLPH.

DOLPH, founded in 2014, is the brainchild of Paul Cole (b.1971) and Natasha Kahn (b. 1973), two artists based at ASC Studios in Streatham Hill. They curate exhibitions and organise talks in the gallery space which fronts the studios, and is devoid of a front window which makes reaching out to a local audience more difficult. Between November 2014 and 2016 they had fourteen shows – a remarkable track record given the fact they have no funding. Both artists are deeply curious about what makes artists do what they do: their aim is therefore to create conversations between artists. In May 2016 they persuaded Simon Callery (b. 1960) to be in residence and the work produced was both shown at the gallery and at St Leonard's church during the Streatham Festival. Despite the modest outreach of their activities, Tash thinks the project has a better chance to reach out to the world than to a local audience: 'with social media it is easier to get people interested in New York than in the local area. So we see ourselves as operating on a world stage'.

Above and right: Simon Callery at work in the Streatham Hill ASC Studios project space (above, © *DOLPH Studios*) during his DOLPH residency in 2016. This resulted in the work also being exhibited at St Leonard's church as part of the Streatham Festival. Revd Mandy Hodgson paid a moving tribute to this piece in one of her sermons, extracts from which we reproduce here.

The Streatham Vale artists on the other hand represent the enthusiastic amateur – all media and all levels. They form part of a nationwide membership organisation called the Society for All Artists or SAA which professes to be 'for everyone with a love of painting'. The website may claim that 'the SAA is the most influential and far reaching society of its kind anywhere in the world' – and they do indeed have over 45,000 members – but the Streatham outpost is rather modest. A group of around fifteen meet at the church of Immanuel and St Andrew on Streatham High Road (facing Streatham Common). Nevertheless, they organise workshops, competitions and have a life drawing session twice a year. Rather uniquely, they have secured the Council's permission to exhibit on the railings of the Rookery Garden and sell their work on Sundays in the summer and at Bank Holidays (also see p. 69).

The group started as early as 1973 – initially meeting at the Co-op Hall in Greyhound Lane, then moving to a back room in Streatham Baths before finally relocating, in 2011, to the church of Immanuel and St Andrew. It was set up by Anita Walker and Irene Pushong (with the help of others) to boost the ILEA classes they were enjoying at the Streatham and Tooting Institute. The newly formed group soon joined Lambeth Arts and Recreation Association and was the recipient of a small grant.

A STREATHAM SERMON ON ART

On 3 July 2016, St Thomas's feast day, the rector of St Leonard's church, Mandy Hodgson (the first woman to hold the office of Rector of Streatham), wrote her Sunday sermon in response to the Simon Callery exhibition housed in the church during the Streatham Festival. Here we reproduce extracts from her very moving sermon which started thus:

• **What do you make of the painting in the narthex? Do you like it? Does it frustrate you because you don't know what it is about? How long have you spent looking at it? Do you want to touch it? Have you read the text about it on the back of the postcard?**

• I have found that it has some interesting resonances with the feast of St Thomas. To start with there is something about those loops that I want to put my hand inside – a little like Thomas wanting to put his hand inside Christ's wounds. It provokes my curiosity. For me the colours also have resonances with the iconography of Mary and Jesus. In classical ikons both Mary and Jesus are usually portrayed in browns and blue to represent the mystery of the incarnation. The brown representing their humanity and earthiness and the blue the heavenly or divine dimension.

• This piece is a Streatham piece, it was made in the DOLPH studios on Streatham Hill. It is a landscape piece. The artist took a 50m length of canvas out into Streatham and found places with interesting textures and contours in Streatham. The canvas was then laid over those contours and textures and the artist marked them onto the canvas by cutting and piercing it … The colours are Streatham Colours, the red brown a reference to the bricks in the Leigham Court Estate, [close to] where the studio is. The blue the colour of the street furniture in Streatham.

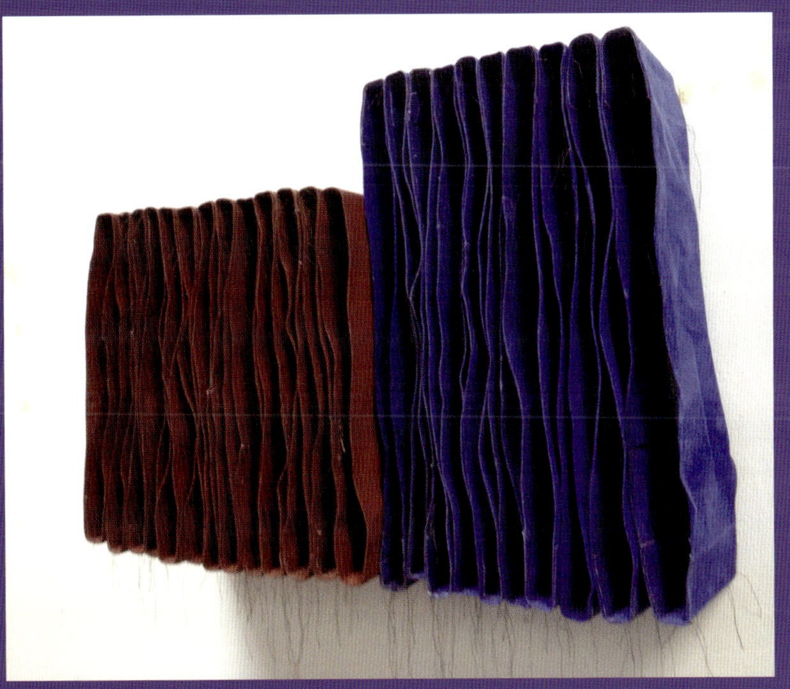

• This process of making and marking has a particular resonance for me now that the work is situated in the church. It reminds me of how the fabric of the church is marked by what has happened in it. You can see the scars and stains of the fire and read the development of the building over the centuries in the marks, textures and materials of the church.

They now meet monthly on a Wednesday – always in the morning. This tends to rule out the younger generation, who are generally at work or child minding at that time, but evenings would rule out the older generation. 'We are an aging group, many of us in our 70s', says Eileen Oldham, the treasurer and a member for around twenty years.

They take part in the Festival but not in Art23 which they feel is a step too far given their limited means and their existing commitments. The group performed a moving tribute to a member, Desmond Masters, when he died in September 2015; a gifted botanical artist, he left many of his paintings to the Streatham Vale artists. They were sold to members of the group and to the public, some of the best paintings in the form of greeting cards – a fitting and moving memento for those who knew him.

6.

MAKING ART IN STREATHAM NOW

Jiro Osuga

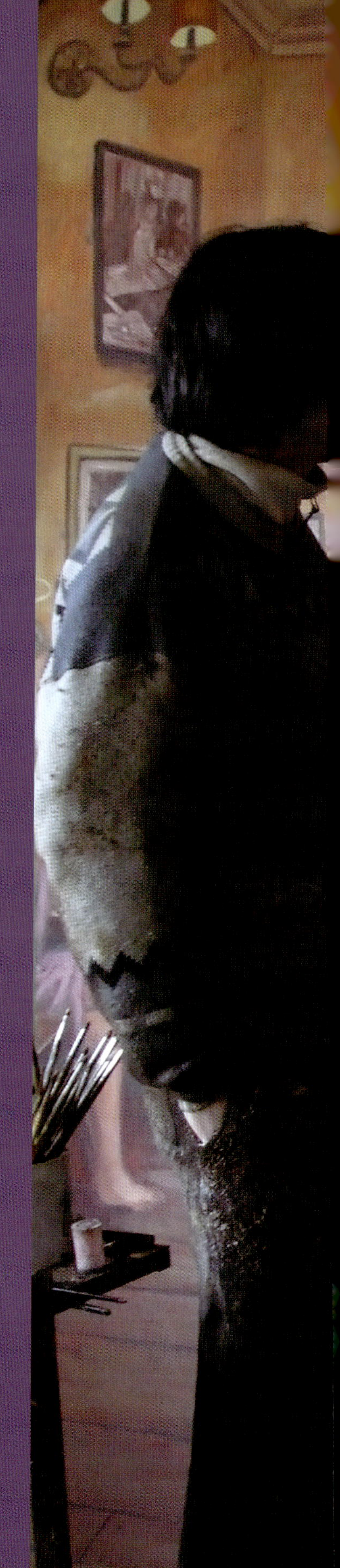

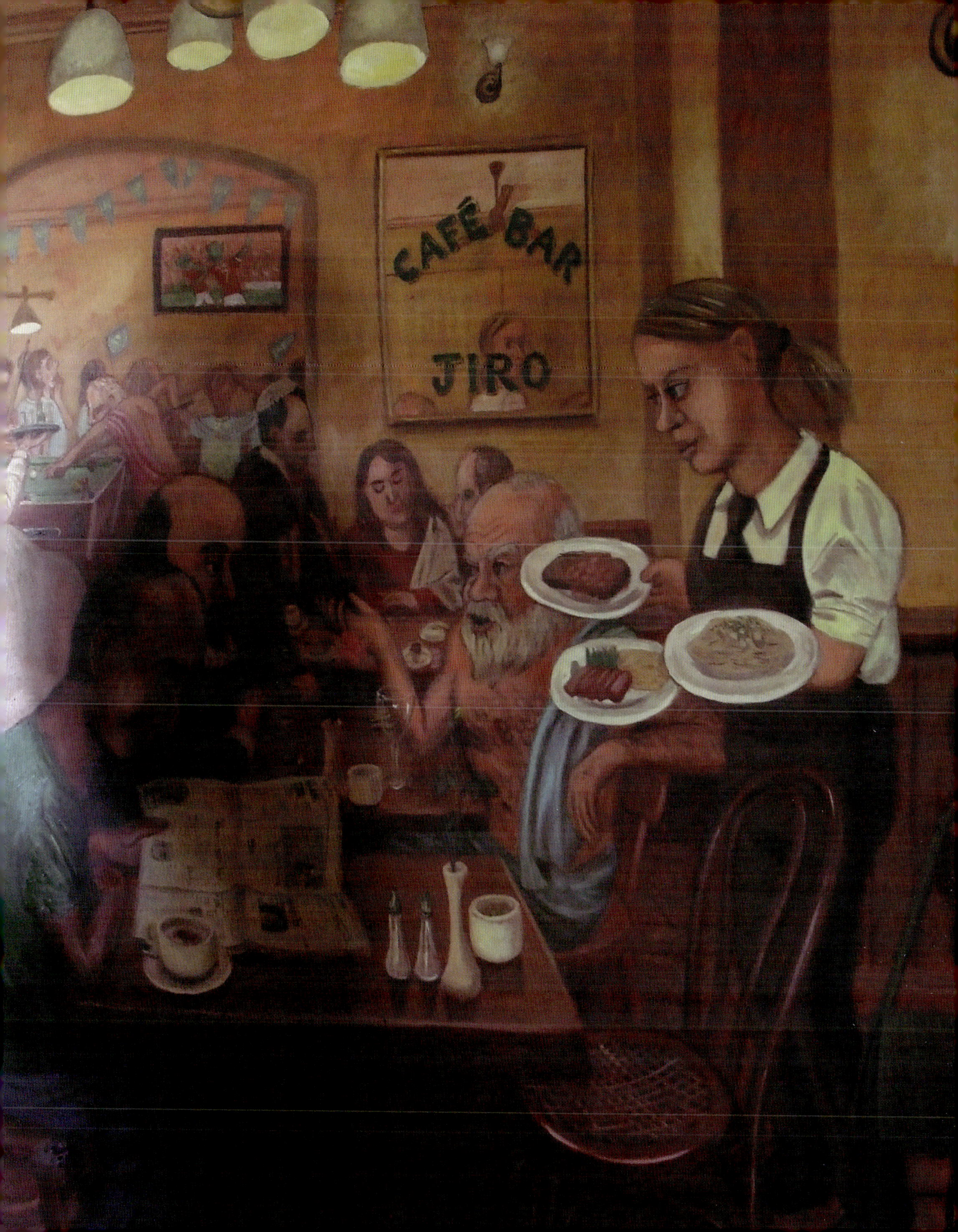
CAFÉ BAR
JIRO

A Day in the Life of a Painter

Some people imagine that artists have it easy – that we wine and dine till the small hours every night, get up when we please, and then don a smock and a beret to paint a vase of flowers or fishing boats in a state of blissful relaxation. Reality, in my experience is quite different. I generally keep regular hours. In the morning I get up early and go for a walk or a cycle-ride in and around Streatham. Back home I would then check the news and emails over breakfast, and after that work until lunchtime. Admittedly, my lunch break is probably much longer than that of an average office worker, but after lunch, I work solidly until about 7pm. In an emergency – for instance, if there is a deadline coming up, I would also work in the evenings. This is my routine for six days of the week. The seventh day is normally given over to domestic chores and excursions, though I would often ignore a dirty floor or the latest must-see exhibitions and work on the seventh day too.

Not that I am always so industrious. Painting isn't easy. On some days I really don't feel like it and procrastinate the hard slog in the studio by deploying classic displacement activities such as making endless cups of coffee or taking excessive care replying to an unimportant email. Even when I am in my studio I am not always hard at work – a far greater portion of my studio time is spent staring at a painting or day-dreaming than actually brushing paint on canvas. But such 'down-time' is important too. I believe it is these apparently wasted hours that endow paintings with a certain lived-in look which distinguish good paintings from the mechanical productions of a jobbing artist.

Previous pages:
Jiro Osuga in his studio standing in front of one of the canvases for 'Café Jiro', 2008.
Flowers Gallery.

Made in Streatham

An enormous number of paintings have been produced in my Streatham studio since I moved to SW16 fourteen years ago. The output varies in size and shape – ranging from tiny panel paintings to a huge room-sized installation. Subject matter ranges widely too – in fact you can point at almost any object at random, and more often than not, I would be able to find a painting featuring that object in my back catalogue. A suburban semi? Done it! A man holding Streatham Library in his arms? Done it! A cow jumping over the moon? Done it!

'Self-portrait in an Apotropaic Frame'

2003, mixed media, 49 x 32cm. Apotropaic means 'having power to avert evil influence or bad luck'. Apotropaic sculptures such as gargoyles and grotesque faces are often found on the walls of medieval churches. In this painting, I am ensconced in my Streatham Studio protected by a cordon of guardian grotesques made of air-drying clay. *Flowers Gallery.*

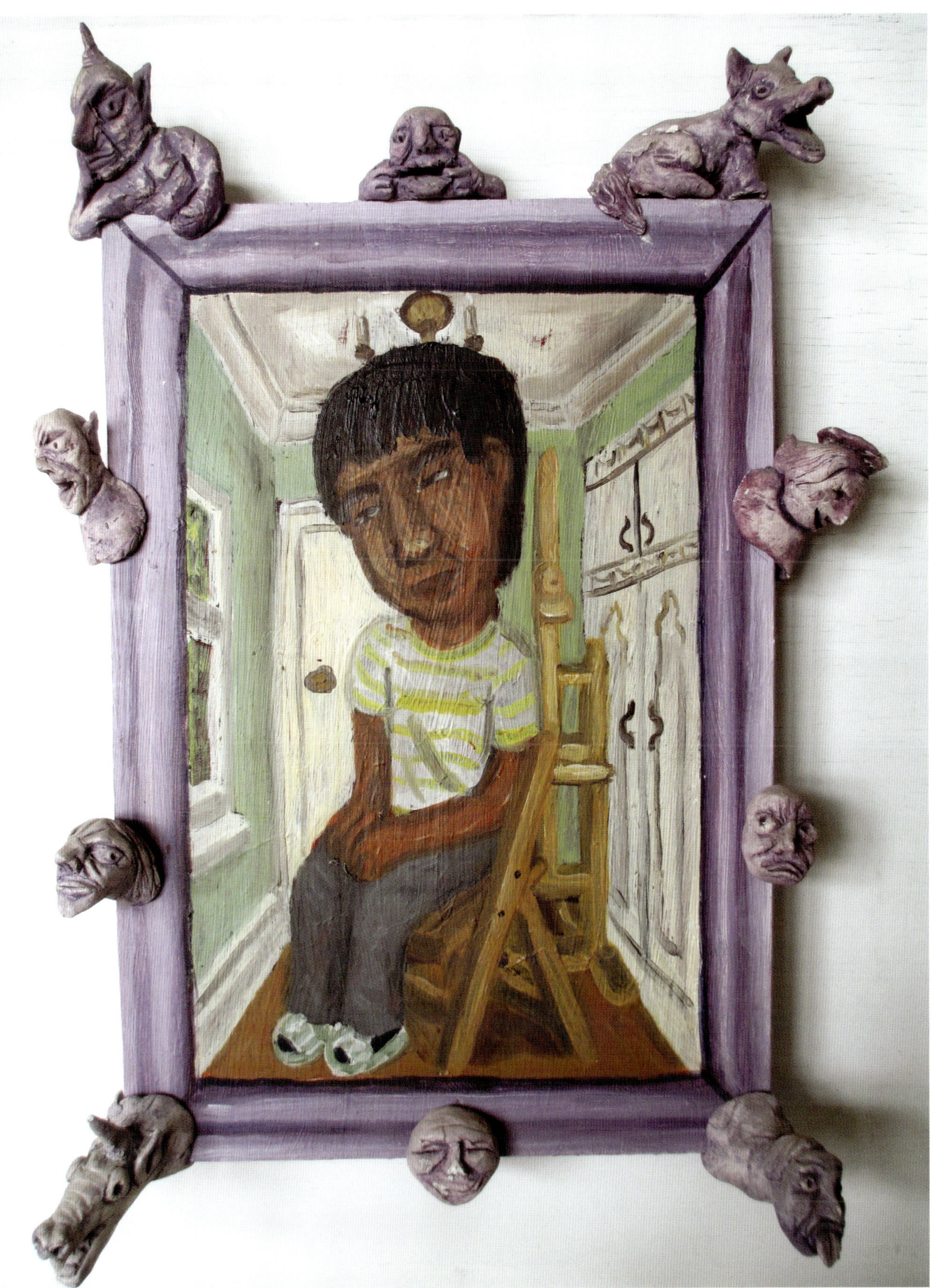

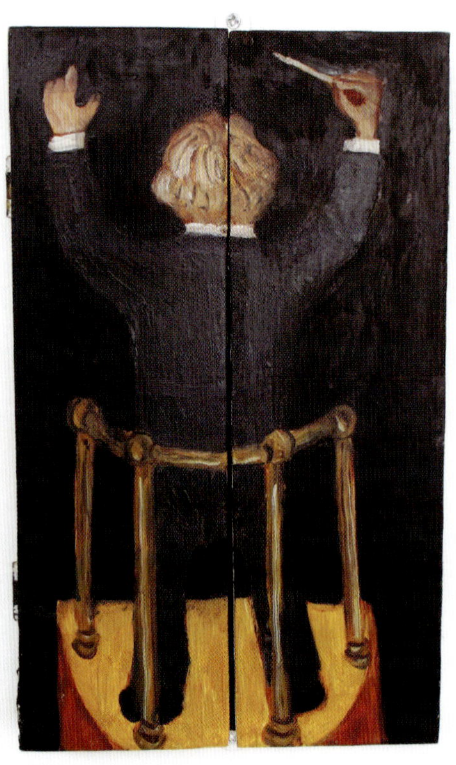

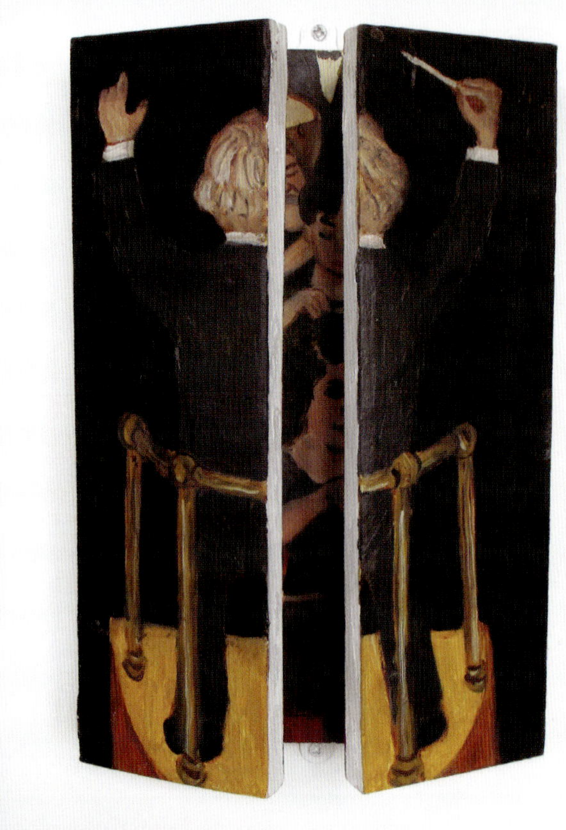

'Orchestra'

2016, oil on board, 30 x 38 cm. *Flowers Gallery.*

Hinged Paintings and Puppets

Pull open the hinged panels of one of these paintings, and a little story unfolds: an orchestra blasts out a symphony when a conductor swings his baton; a cork is yanked out of a bottle and wine pours out; a weight-lifter springs into action…

Over the last fifteen years I have made great many of these paintings, fascinated by the limitless possibilities this interactive format *opens* up – pun intended. The simple opening and closing action could be used to represent a multitude of different movements and concepts: up and down, push and pull, expansion and contraction, the inner and the outer, and of course, time (both linear and cyclical). These paintings could have anything from just one to four or more hinged panels in different proportions and configurations.

What I most like about my hinged paintings is that they are exactly the kind of thing we were taught not to do at art school – facile, gimmicky and silly. Precisely because they are so 'wrong', I feel uninhibited by all the niceties that govern 'good' art, and feel free to do what I damn well please, often coming up with some exhilarating results.

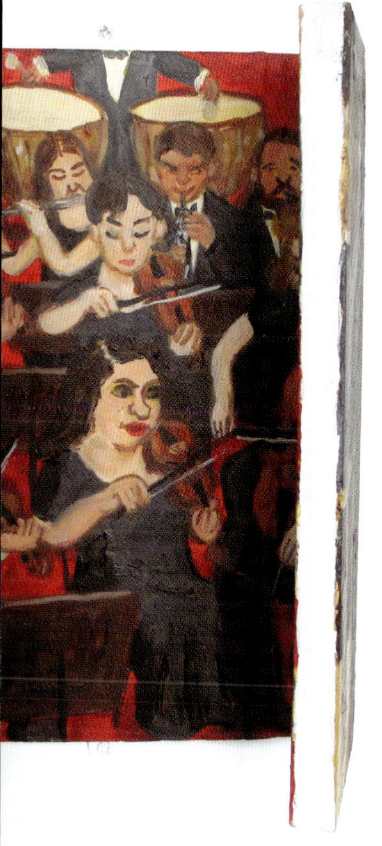

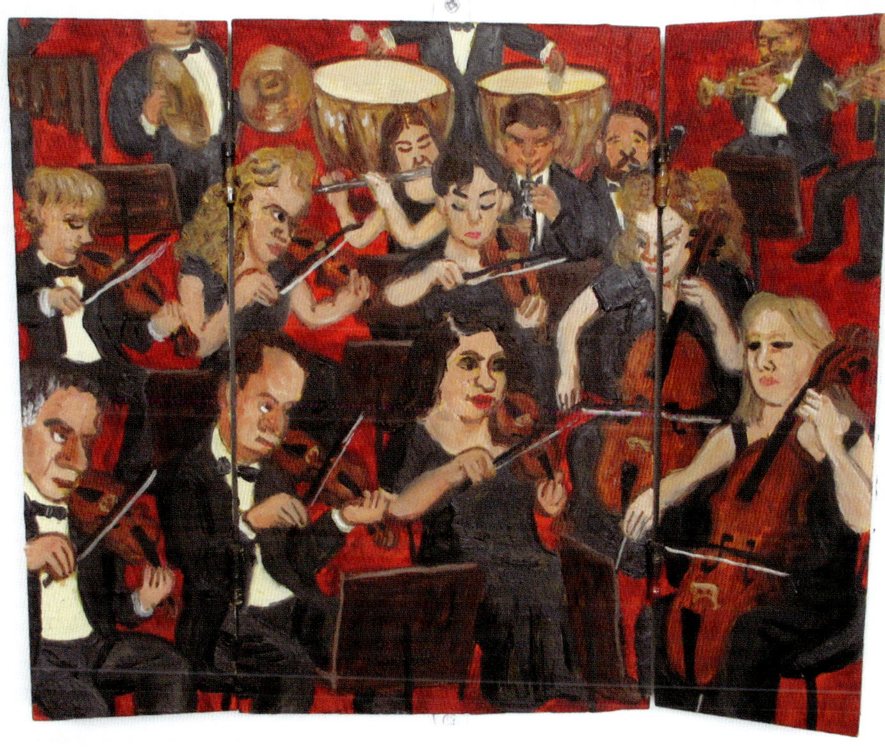

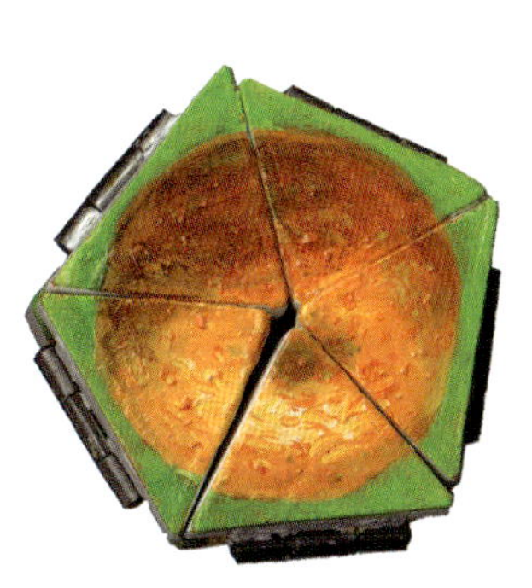

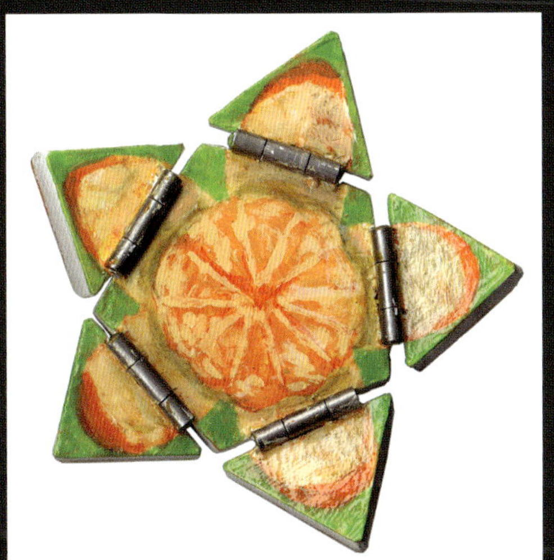

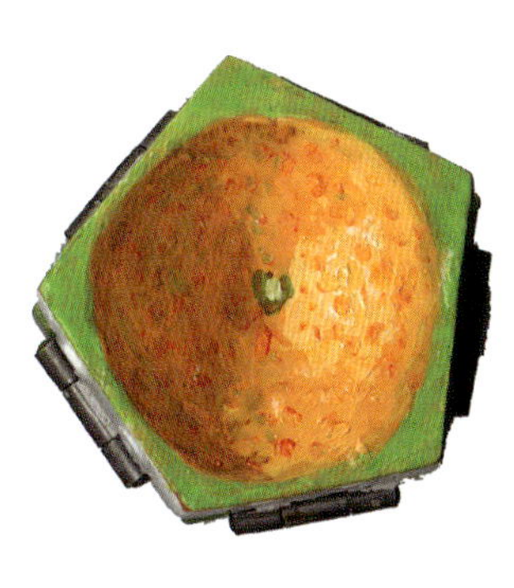

'Satsuma'

2013, acrylic on board, 13 x 13 cm,
Private collection. Photo: Flowers Gallery.

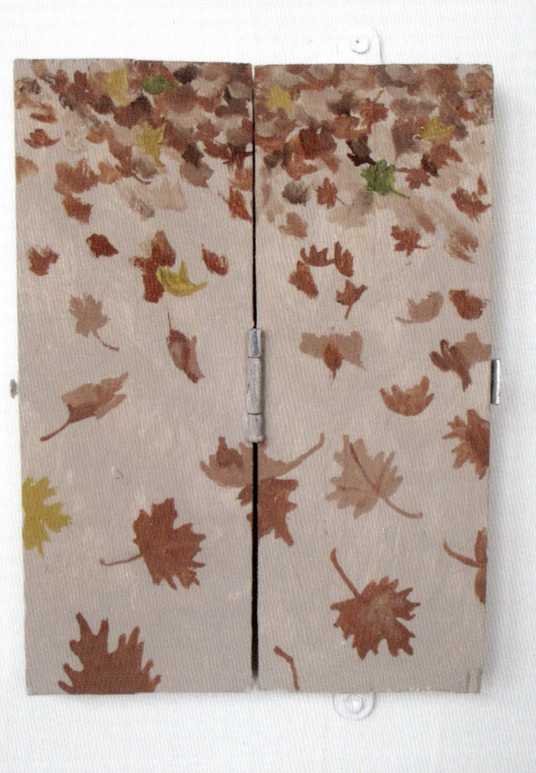

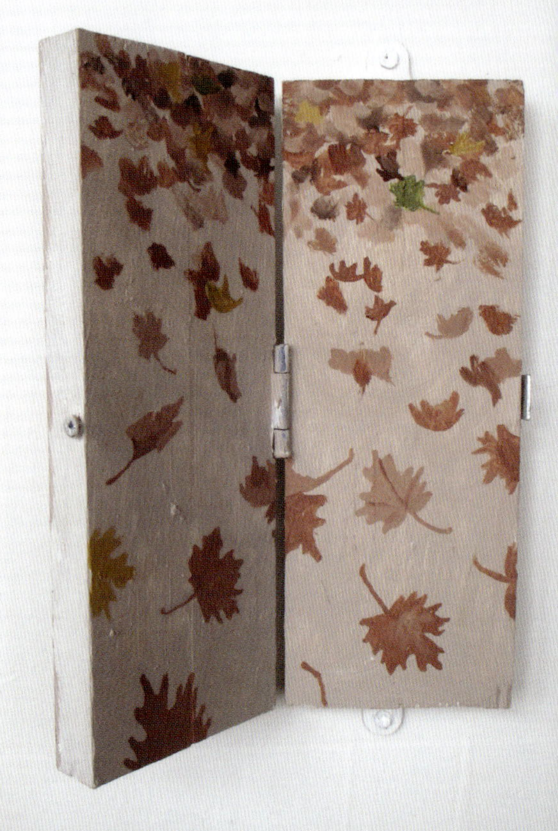

'Road Sweeper'
2013, oil on board, 23 x 17.5 cm.
Private collection.
Photo: Flowers Gallery.

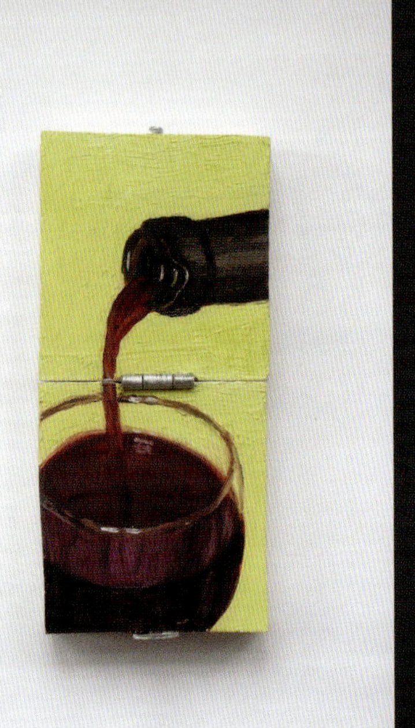

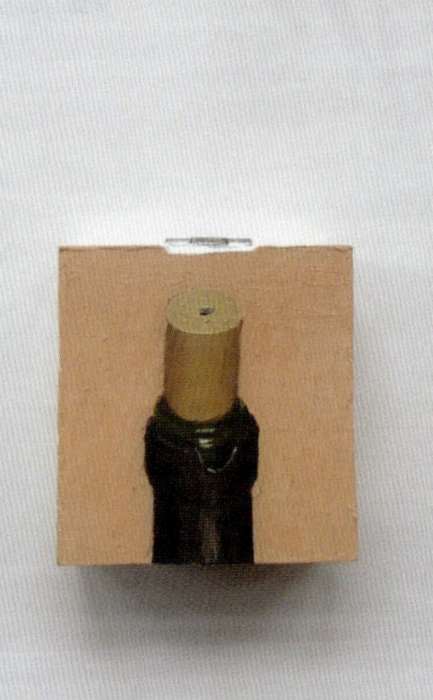

'Cork'
2013 oil on board, 12 x 6 cm,
Private collection.
Photo: Flowers Gallery.

'Red Wine'
2013, oil on board, 16 x 14 cm,
Private collection.
Photo: Flowers Gallery.

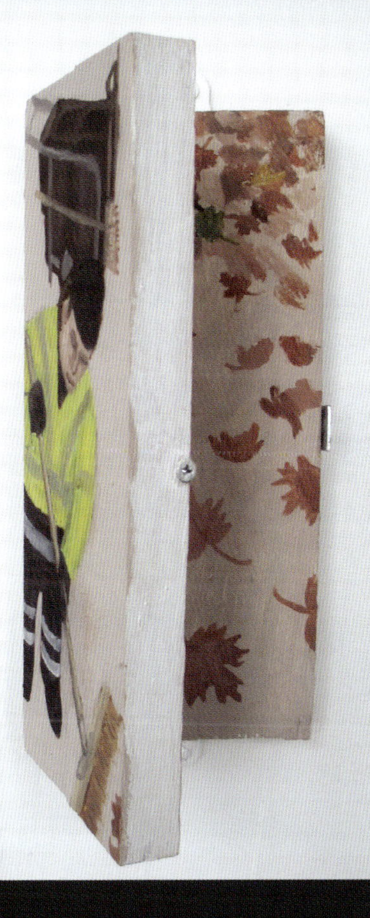

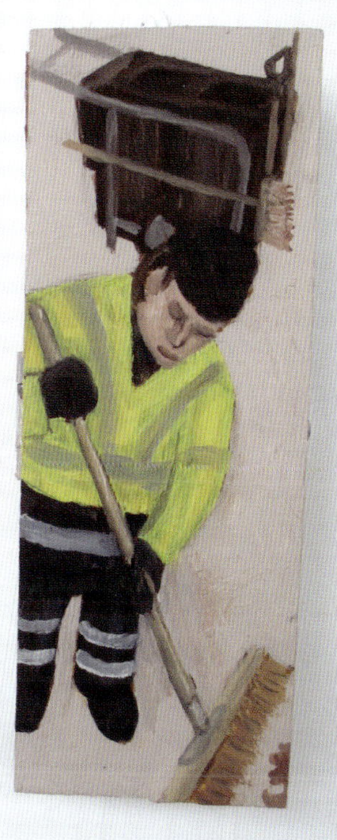

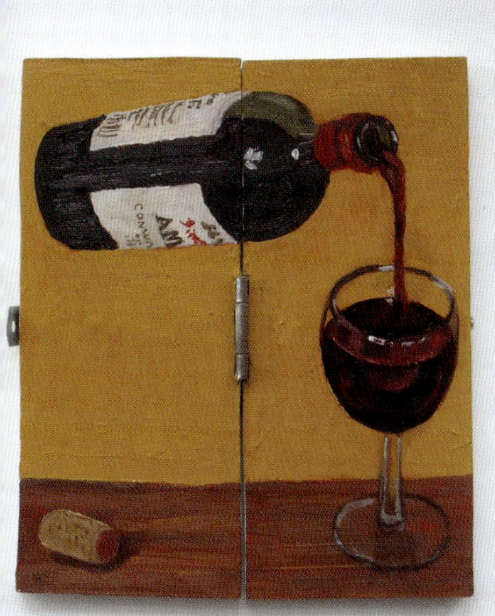

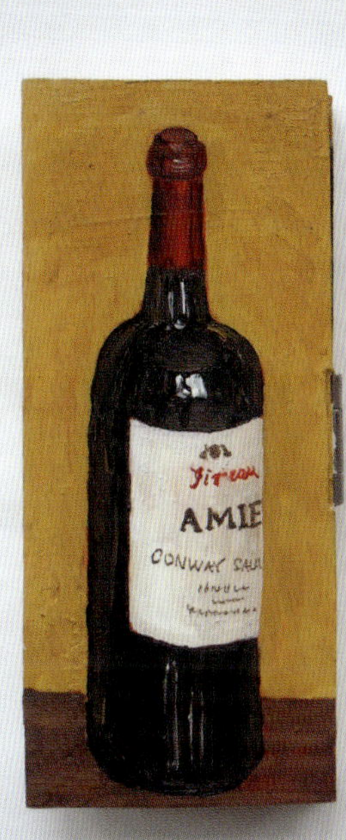
AMIE

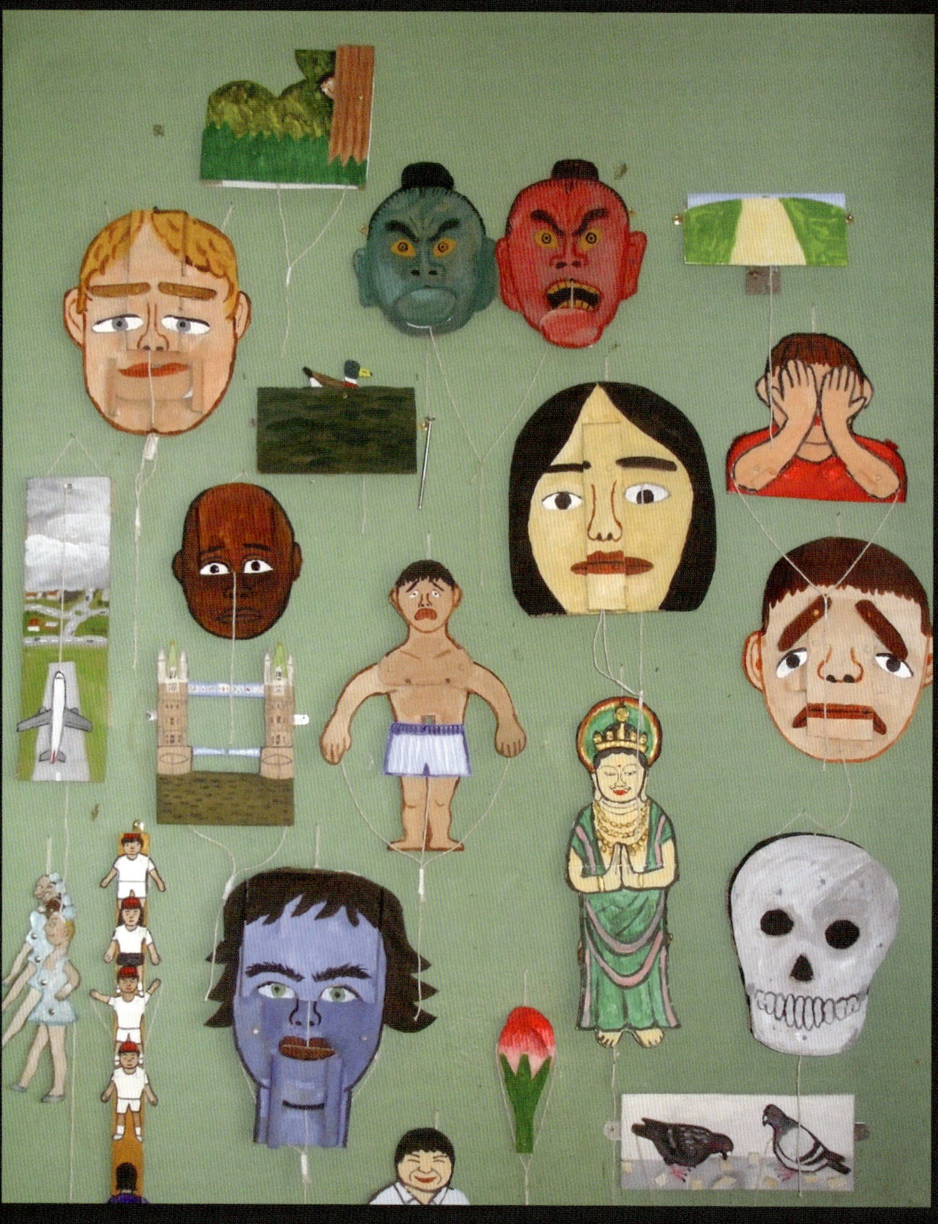

Some of my puppets in the studio, 2015.
Photo: ©Jiro Osuga.

I let myself go even more with my 'jumping jack' puppets. Quickly assembled from crude materials such as recycled cardboard boxes, these developed from simple figures with limbs that go up and down to quite complex contraptions involving weights and counter-weights. Making them are a useful tonic whenever I am stuck with my more heavy-weight paintings.

Tall Paintings

Another form I really like is the very tall and thin strip-like painting. The shape is surprisingly rich in possibilities – the elongated proportions naturally lending themselves to representations of sequences and layering. It also tests my compositional ingenuity in an effort to incorporate shapes you would think would not fit into such a confined space.

An artist friend once observed that horizontal paintings tended to signify the profane, upright paintings the sacred. The Chinese landscape tradition, in which landscape is imbued with spiritual values and is predominantly vertically oriented proves him right. It is noticeable that many of my tall paintings touches on cosmic concerns.

'Country Walk'

2016, oil on canvas,
100.5 x 11.5 cm,
Flowers Gallery.

'Cycling into the City'

2016, oil on canvas,
100.5 x 11.5 cm.
A representation of my routine cycle ride to Flowers Gallery in Shoreditch down Streatham High Road, through Brixton, Elephant and the City.
Flowers Gallery.

'London's Bridges'

2006, oil on canvas 191 x 45 cm.
All London bridges between Tower and Battersea bridges are depicted on a straightened-out River Thames on this tall canvas.
Private collection.
Photo: Flowers Gallery.

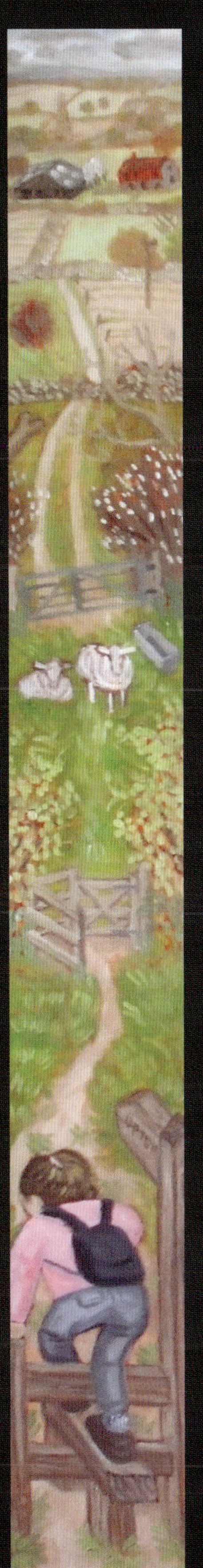

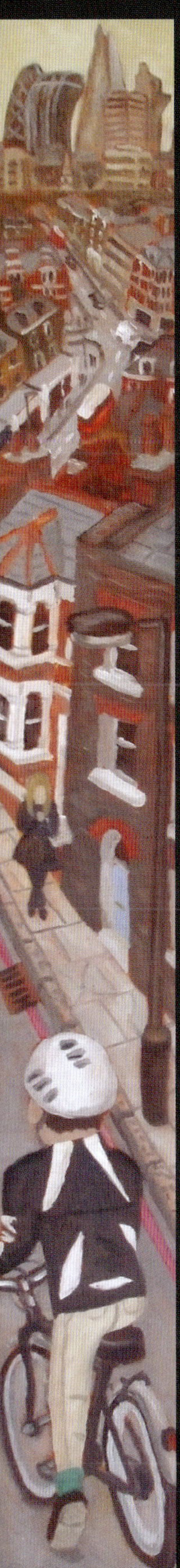

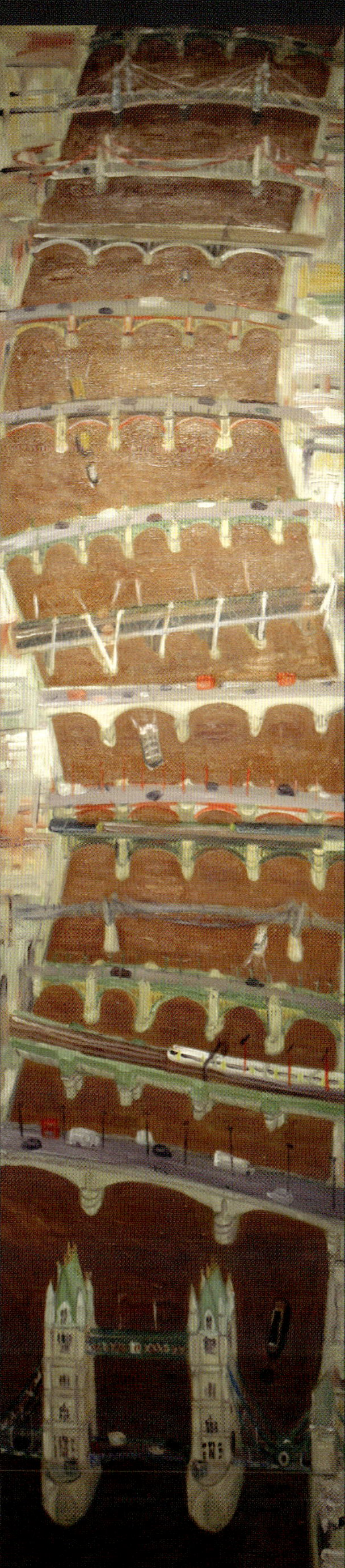

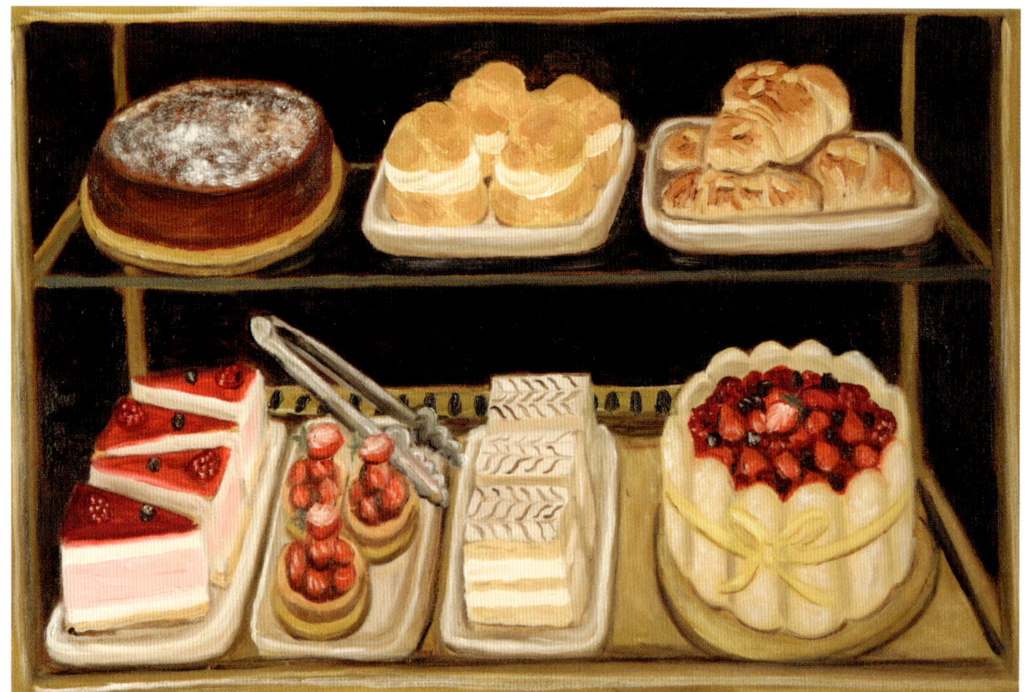

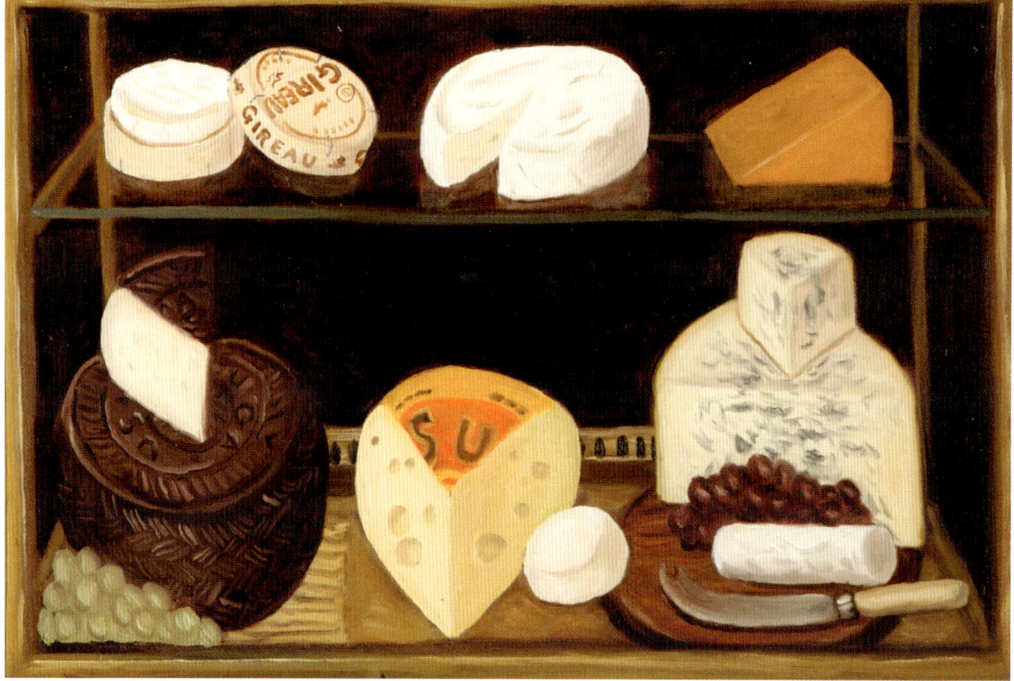

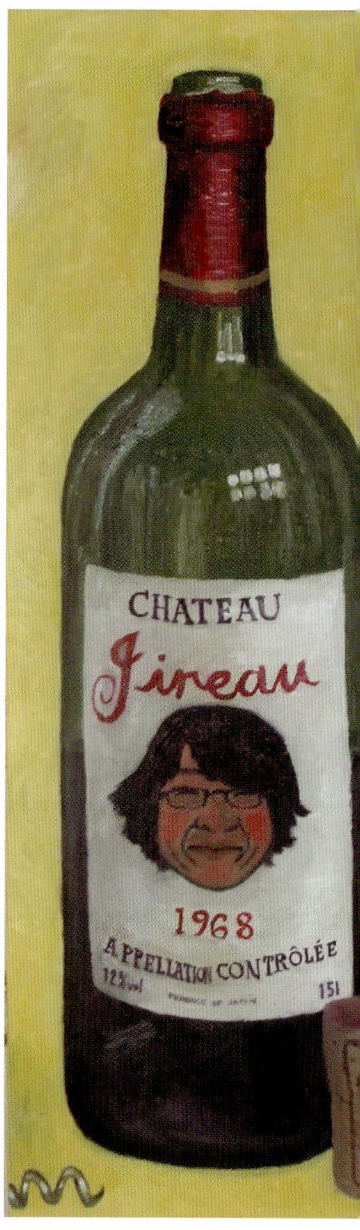

'Cakes'
2011, oil on canvas, 52 x 76cm,
Flowers Gallery.

'Cheeses'
2011, oil on canvas, 52 x 76cm,
Flowers Gallery.

'Chateau Jireau'
2014, oil on canvas, 100 x 35cm,
Flowers Gallery.

Food and Drink Paintings

Maybe because oil paint is basically pigments bound in vegetable oil, I find the medium has a luscious quality that lends itself to representation of food. Someone once said that painting in oils is like painting with margarine, and it's probably not a coincidence that many artists are also good cooks. I wouldn't count myself in that number, but I enjoy painting comestibles like cakes and cheeses, and over the years made many paintings set in the kitchen. Some of these are 'recipe' paintings, showing the successive stages of the preparation of food. Others take simple delight in the sensuous qualities of a slice of cake or a pot of steaming coffee.

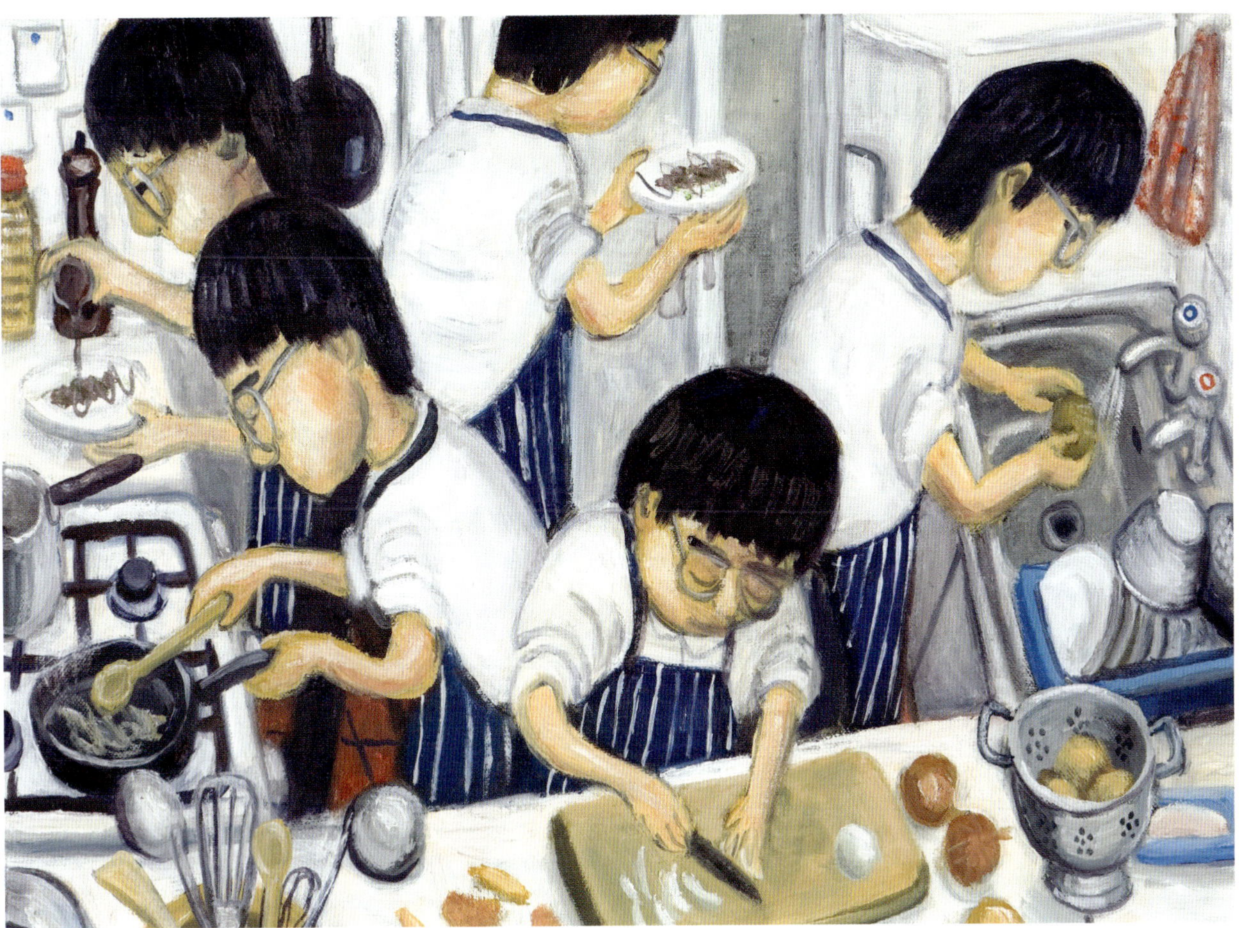

'Cooking'

2005, oil on canvas, 33 x 47cm,
Flowers Gallery.

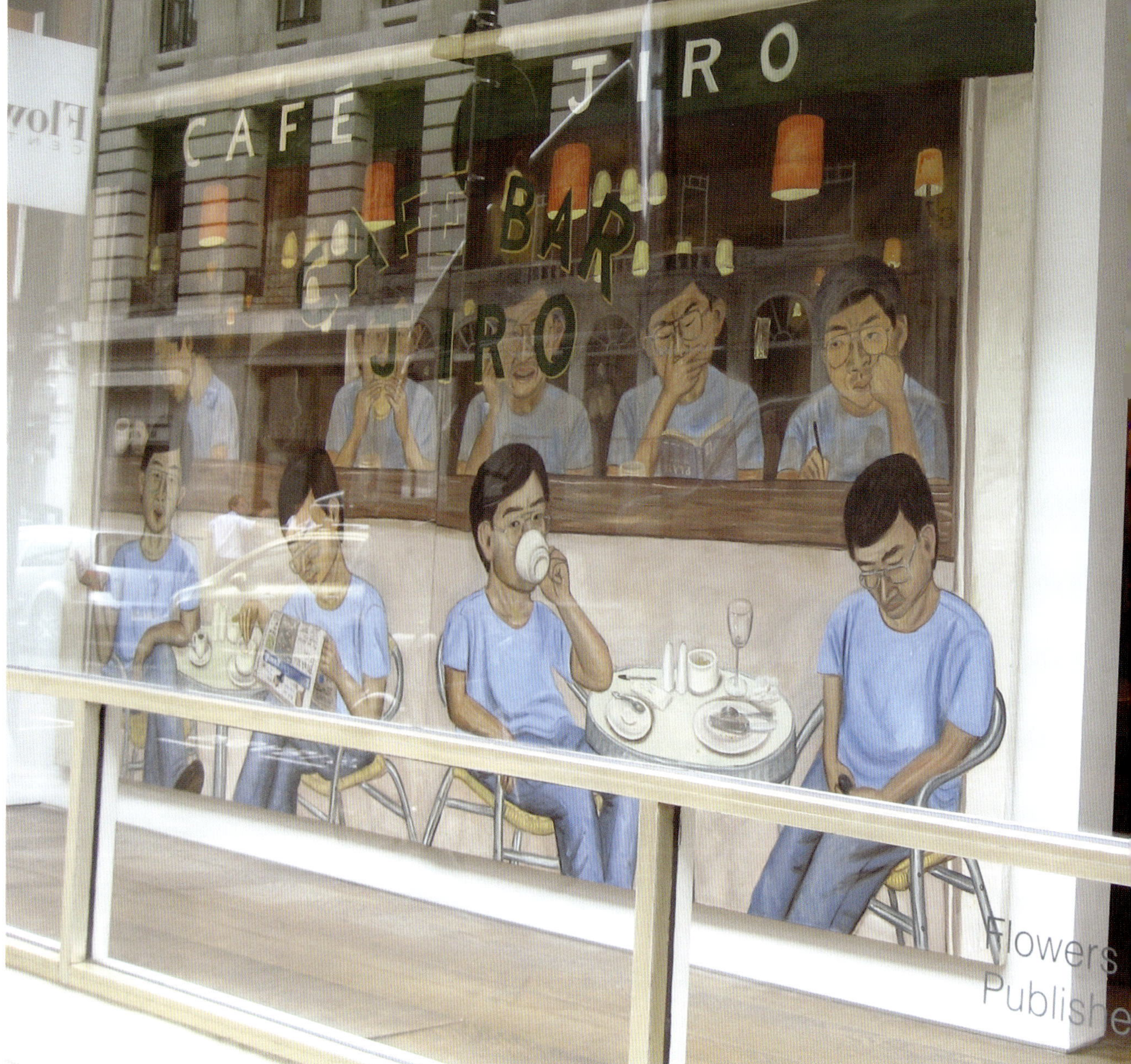

Café Jiro 2008/9

'Café Jiro' is an immersive painting/installation I made specifically for Flowers' Cork Street gallery. Over 3 metres tall and 30 metres long in total, it is the largest painting I have ever made.

Stepping into the gallery, the visitor enters another world – a fantasy café patronised by an unlikely clientele which include the likes of William Shakespeare and the Grim Reaper. The walls of the café are decorated with a queer collection of objects like the Rosetta Stone and a hunting trophy of a stuffed unicorn. A small office adjacent to the gallery space has been transformed into the café's kitchen, where apron-clad chefs have the faces of Flowers Gallery staff. The wall facing the street is painted on one side with a view looking into the café from outside, while the other side shows the view looking out towards cars and passer-bys in the street.

'Café Jiro' external view.

Photos: Mireille Galinou.

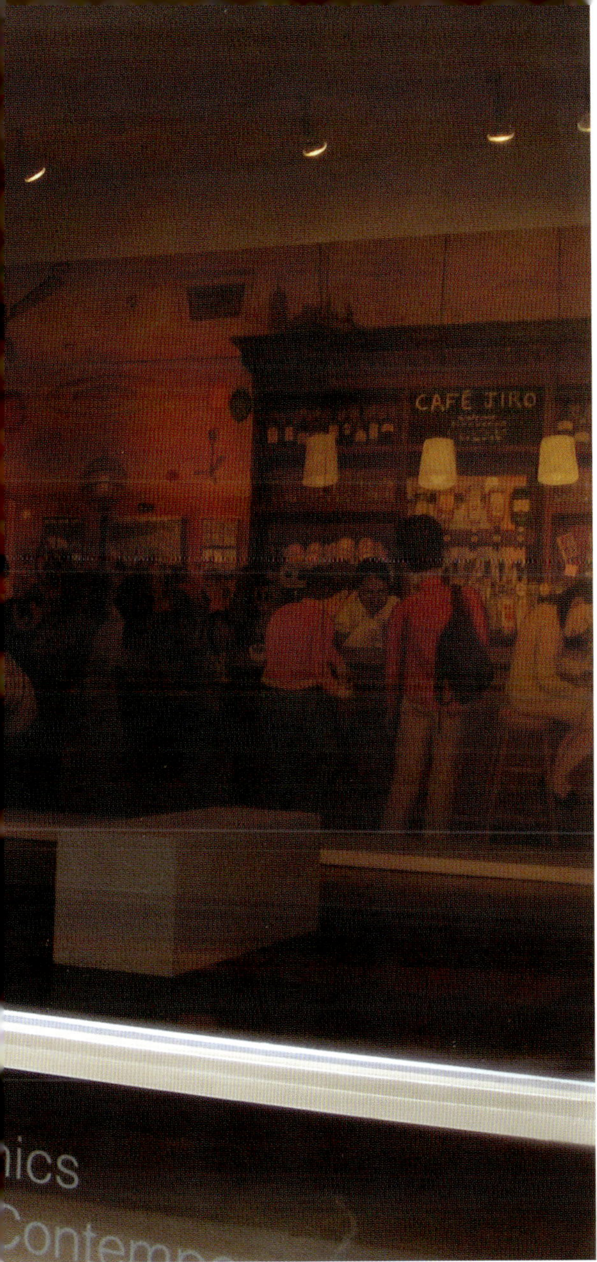

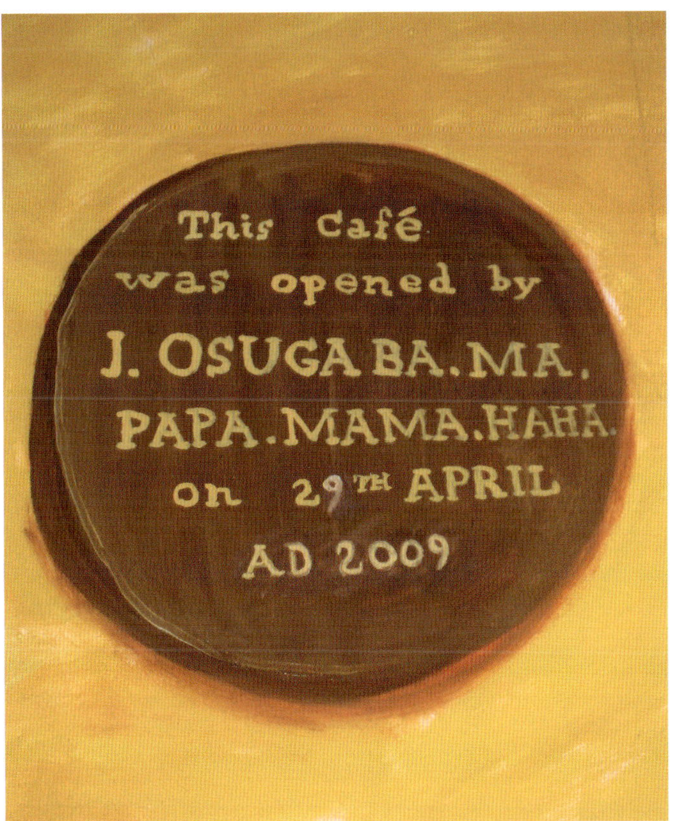

As well as being a lot of fun, 'Café Jiro' touches on a number of deeper issues. Walking into the installation could be interpreted as being equivalent to entering inside my head or a Platonic cave. The intermingling of disparate images in the café a visualisation of the nature of creativity, or a representation of an ideal society – open, pluralistic and creative.

Painting 'Café Jiro' in my small Streatham studio presented a formidable challenge. Only two of the huge ceiling high canvases would fit into the studio at any one time, and only if placed diagonally across the room. When finished, the canvases had to be removed from their stretchers, rolled up, and reassembled in the gallery as they were too big to go through the door. The project took eight months to complete. Sadly, after the end of the month-long exhibition, the rolled up canvases have languished for years in storage gathering dust.

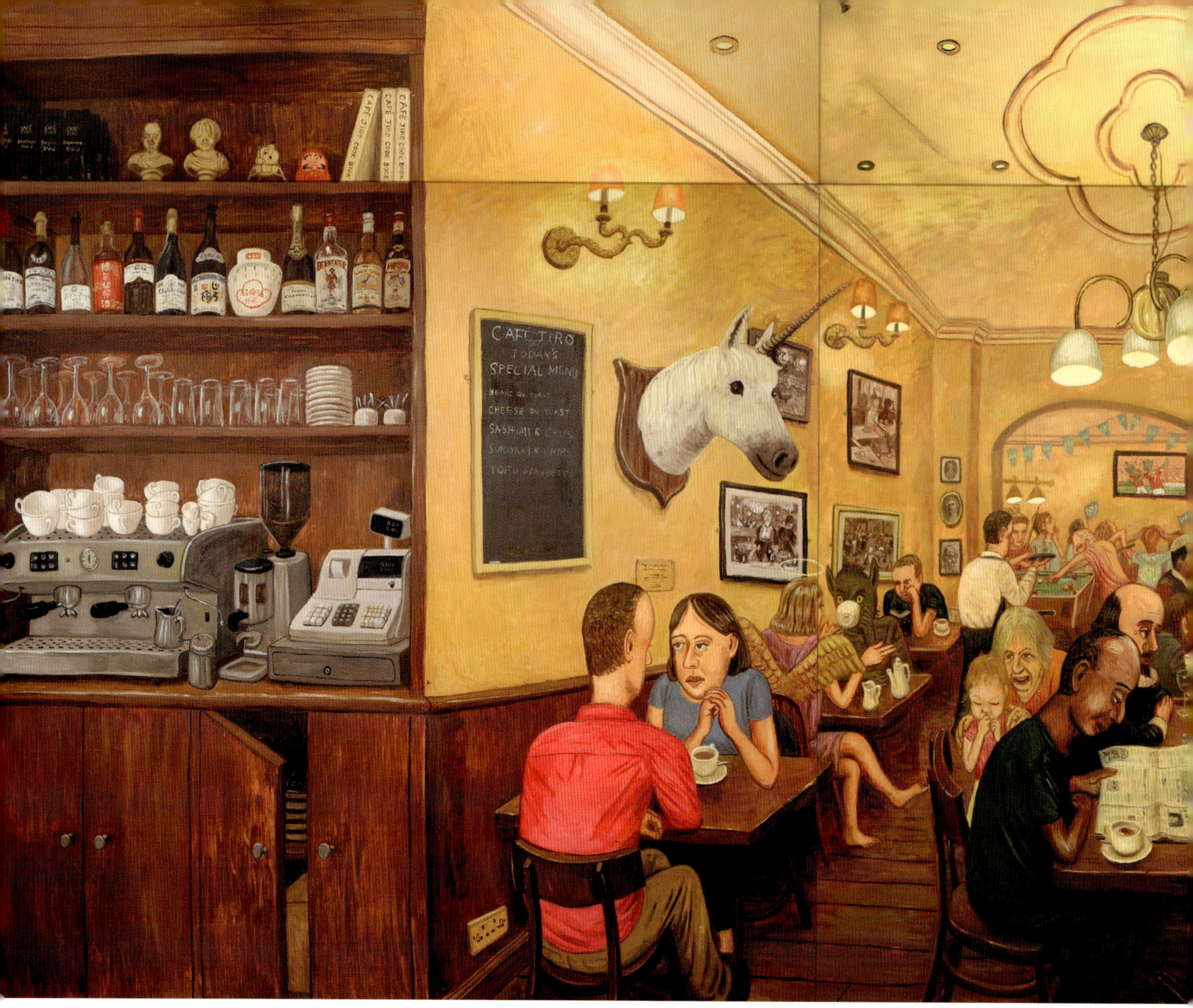

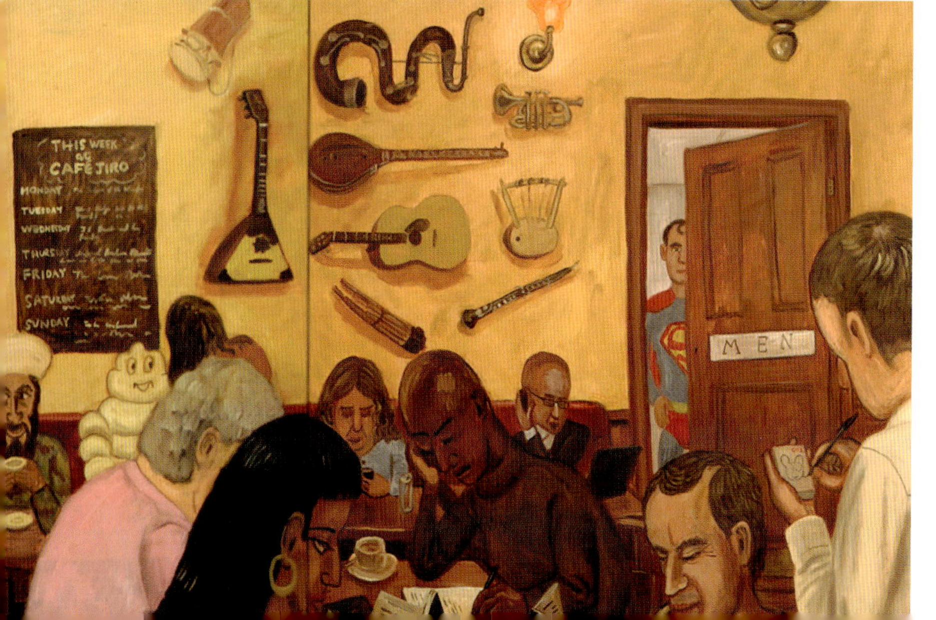

Above:

The long wall of 'Café Jiro'.

2008–9, oil on canvas. Flowers Gallery.

Left

Detail of 'Café Jiro'.

Right:

Installation view of 'Café Jiro' at the Flowers Gallery in Cork Street.

Photo: Mireille Galinou.

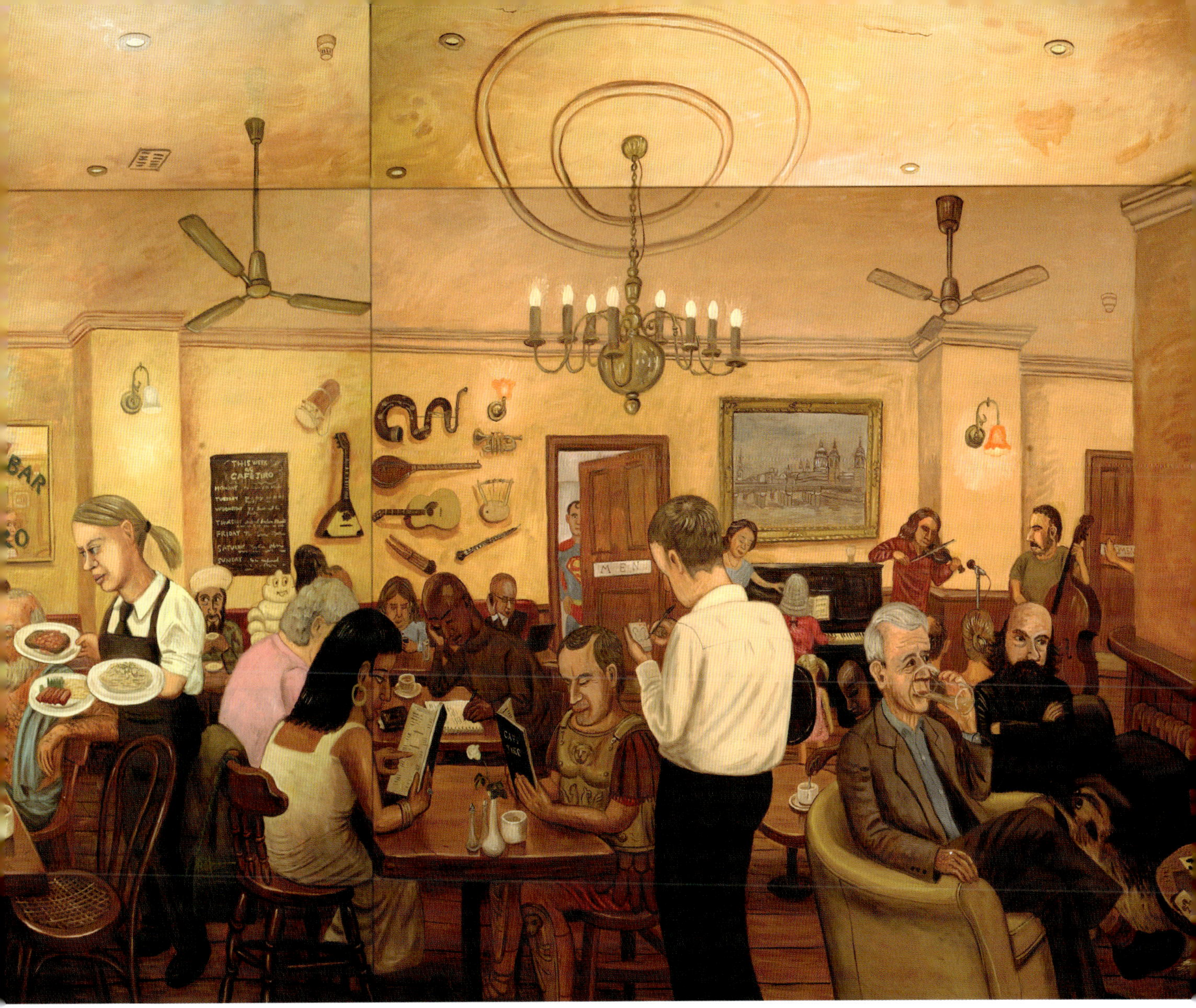

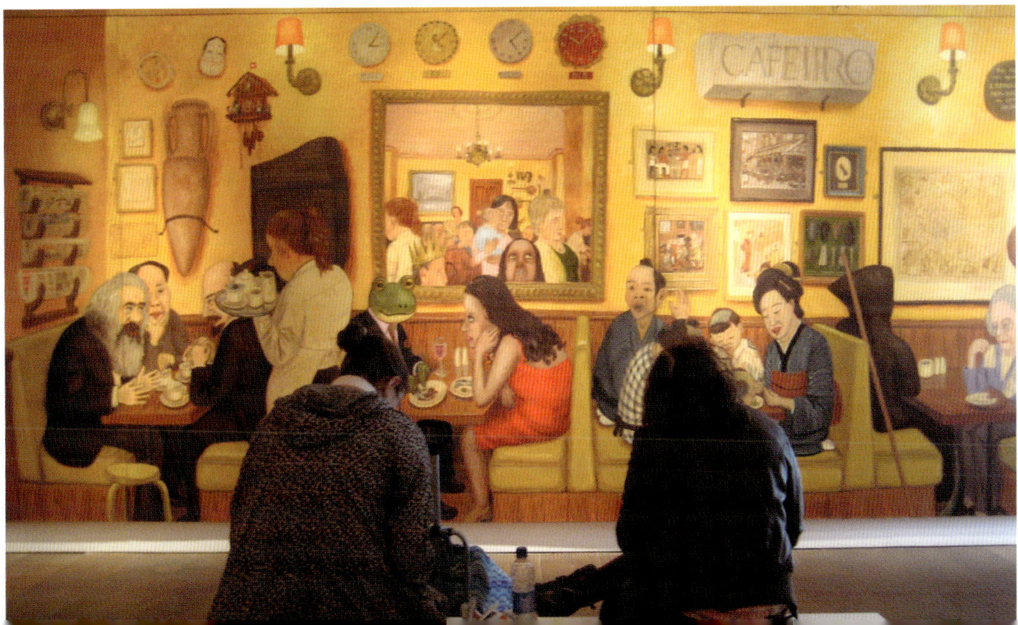

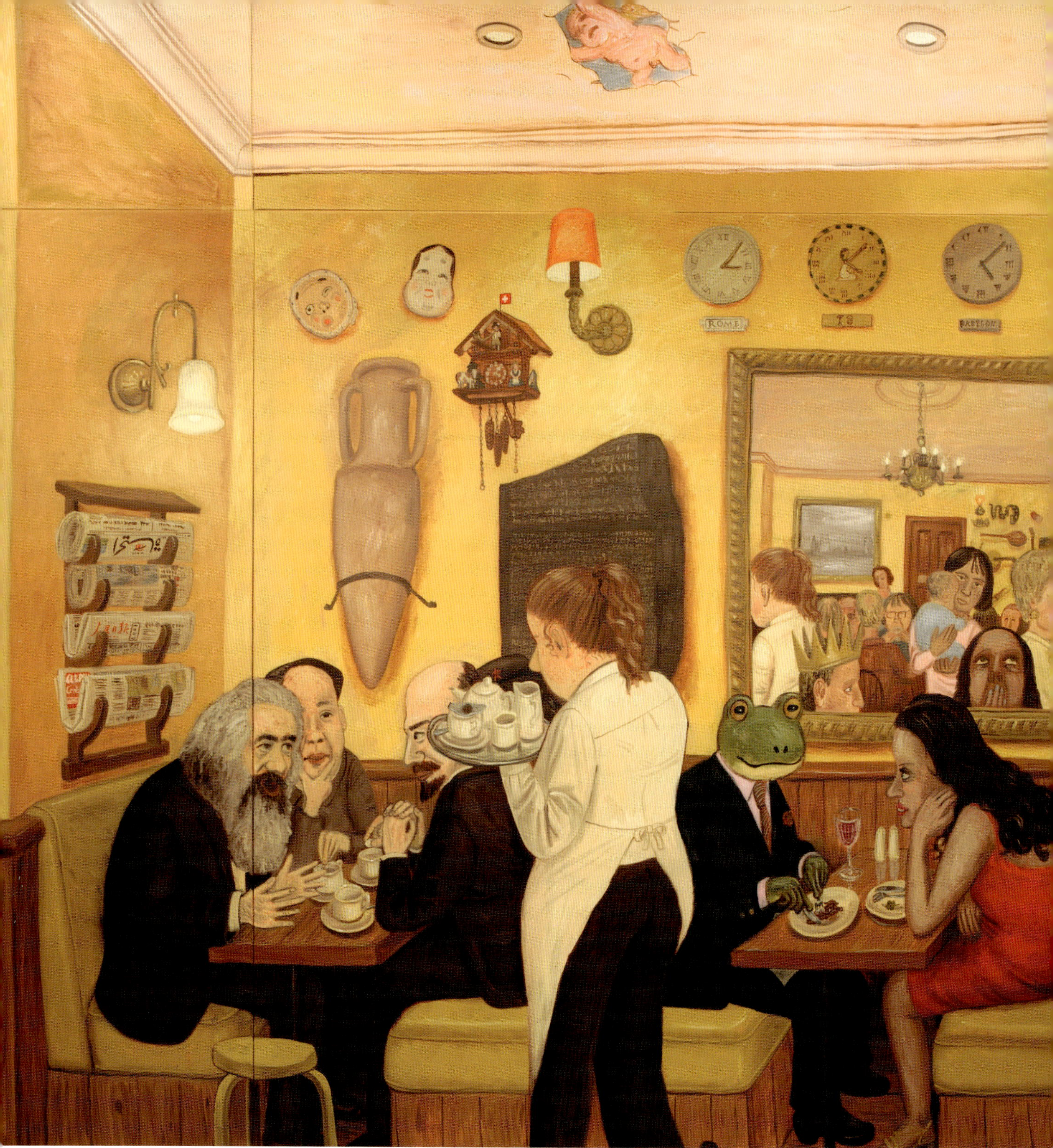

The shorter wall of 'Café Jiro' showing in the far left Karl Marx in discussion with Mao, Lenin and Che.

Flowers Gallery.

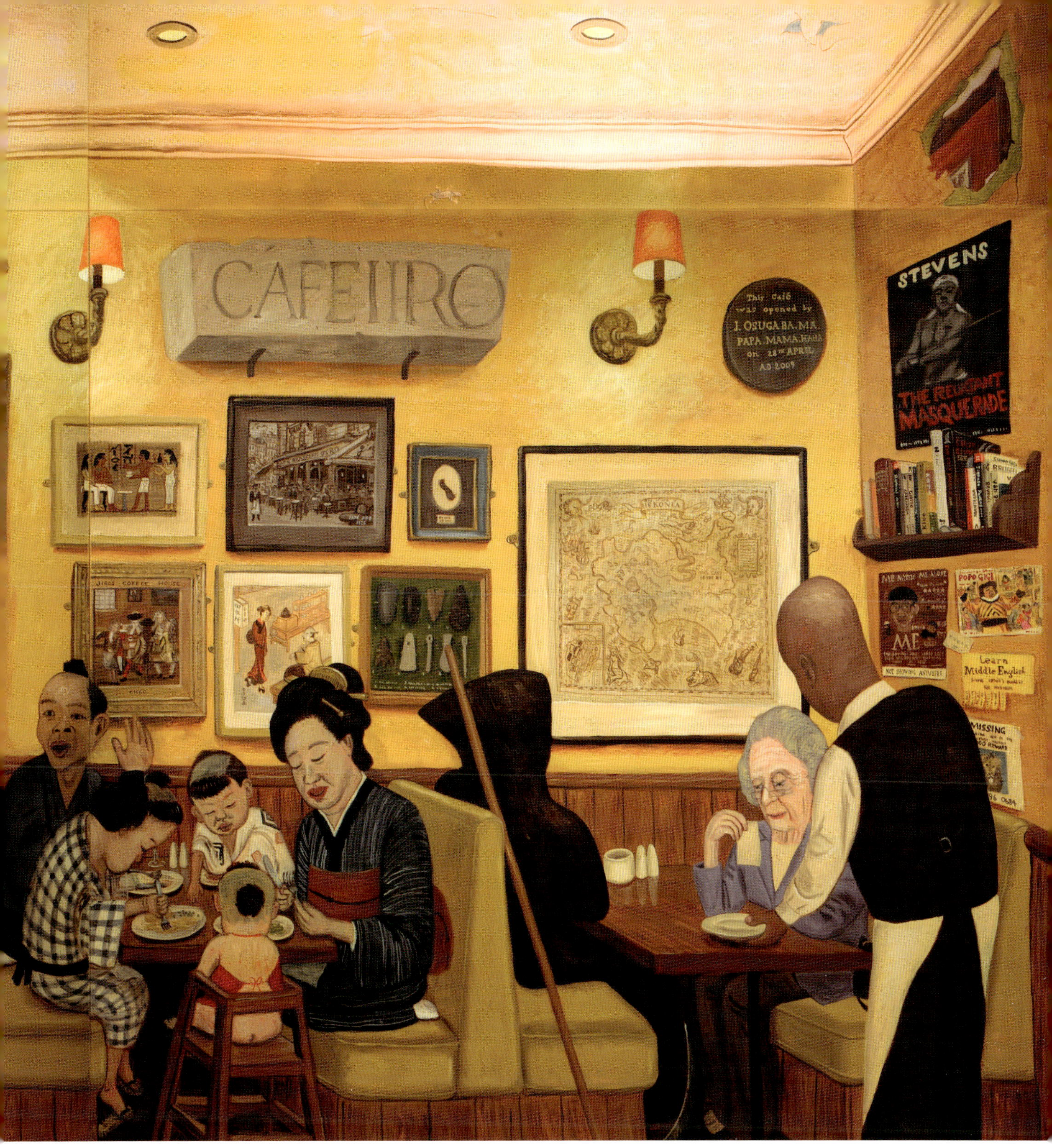
CAFE IIRO
This café was opened by J. OSUGA BA.MA. PAPA.MAMA.HAHA on 28th APRIL AD 2009
STEVENS
THE RELUCTANT MASQUERADE
ME
NOT SHOWING ANYWHERE
POPO GIGI
Learn Middle English
MISSING

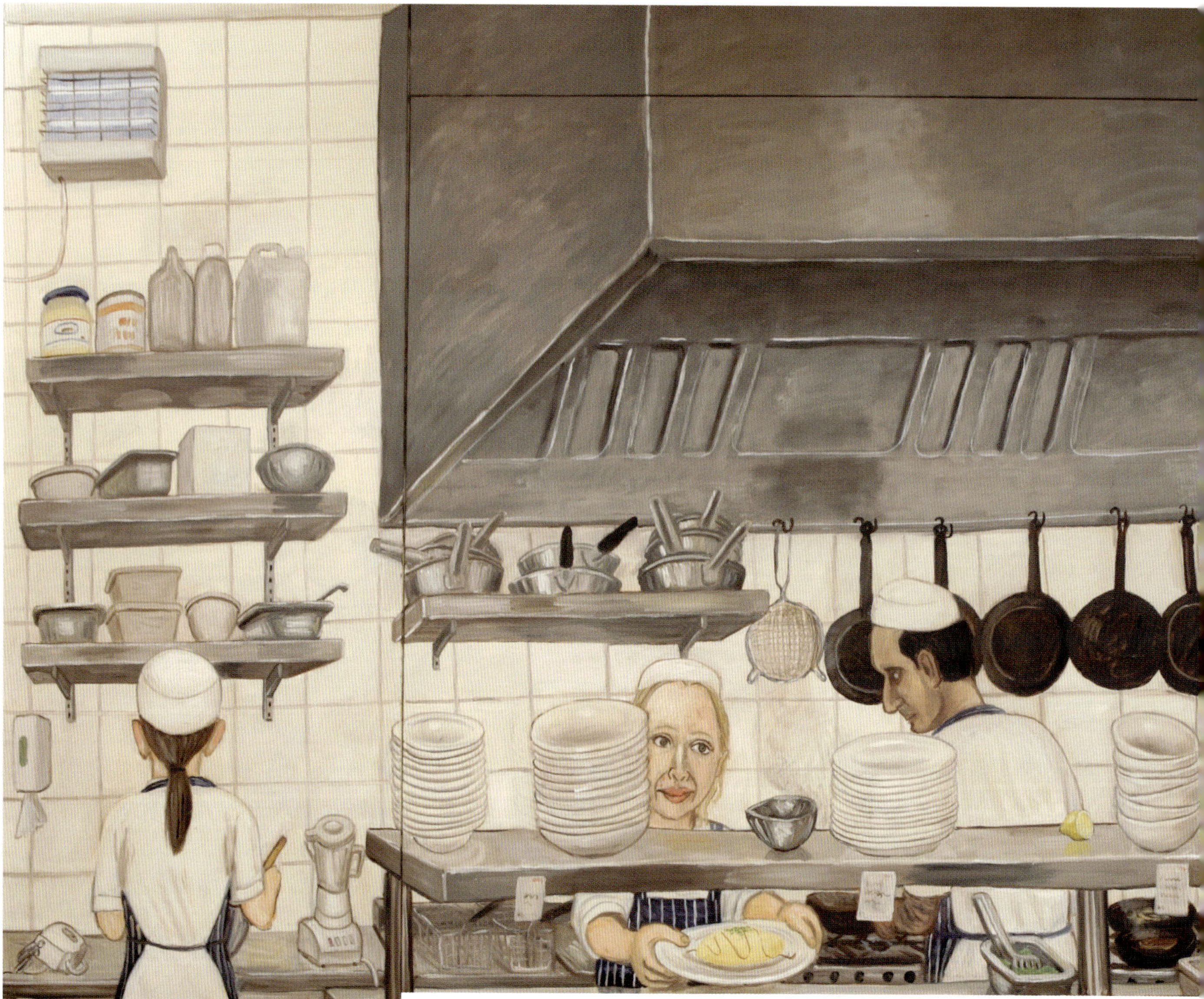

Above:
The kitchen of 'Café Jiro'.

Right:
'Café Jiro' details.

Flowers Gallery.

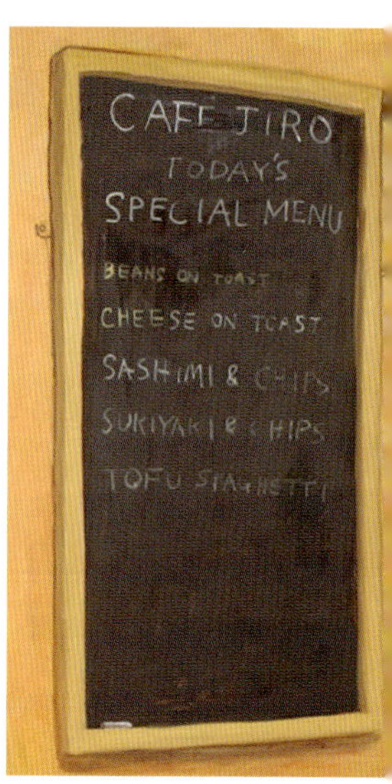

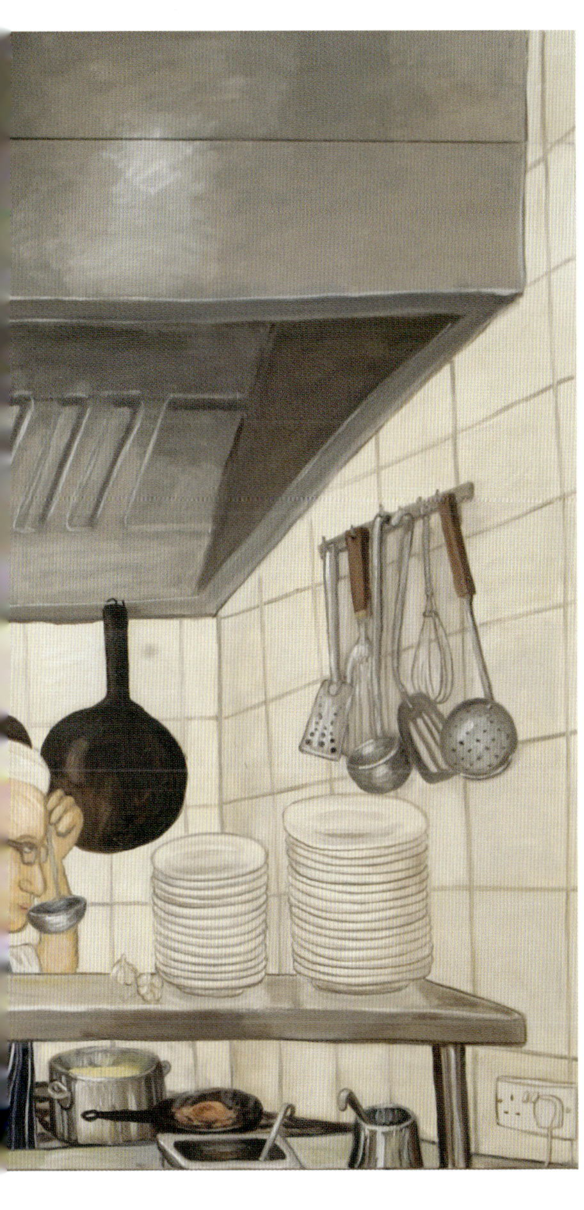

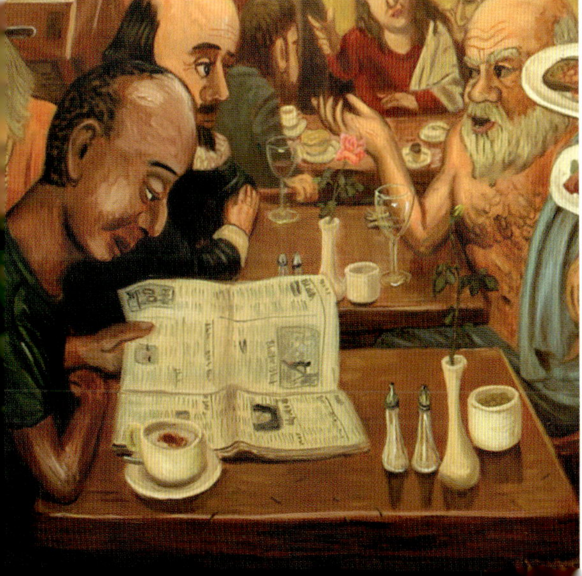

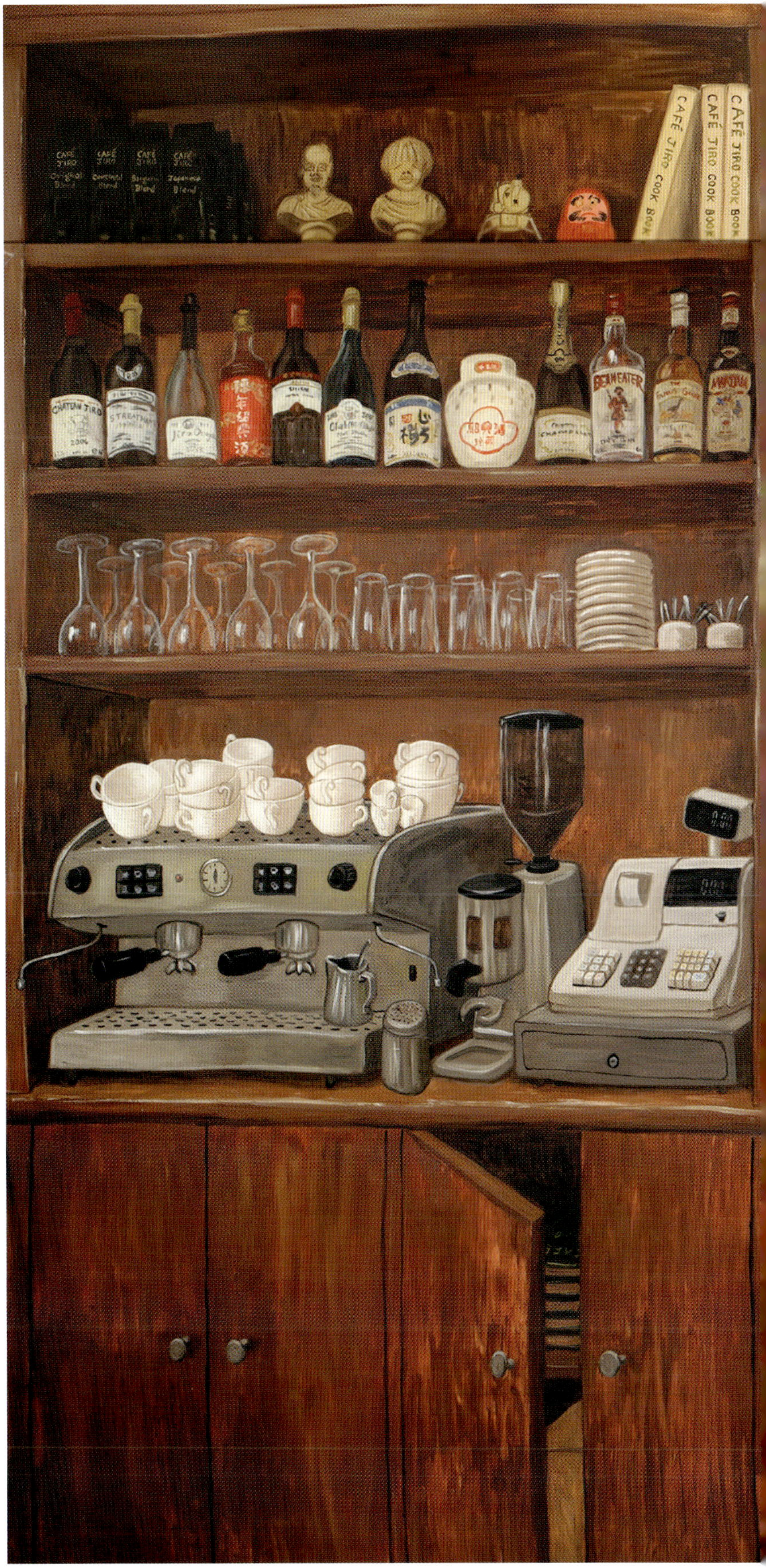

Planet Jiro.com 2012/13

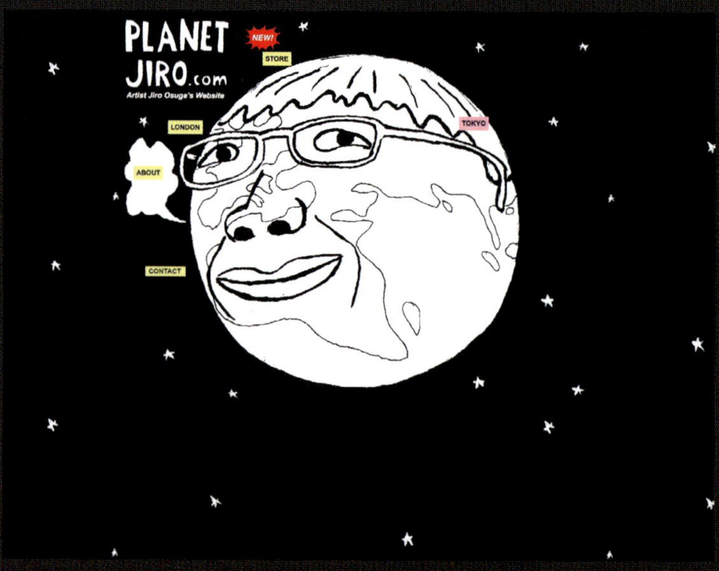

When the time came for me to embrace the digital revolution and create my own website, I was adamant that it should not look like a spool of toilet paper stacked with rectangles like most other websites. I wanted it to be built to my own specifications, and for it to feel more like a place – my very own planet – than a collection of electronic pages. It had long puzzled me how most people haven't woken up to the spatial qualities of the internet, continuing to perceive it as a kind of book, despite the fact that it is routinely referred to by spatial terms such as web, net, site and Cyberspace.

Planet Jiro.com is a complete world which you are invited to explore, navigating mostly visually rather than verbally. On the Home page, you are greeted by the full view of the planet, which bears my grinning face. There you have a choice of two cities to visit: London or Tokyo, representing the two loci of my life. Clicking the city of your choice transports you to an aerial view of each city, which in turn offers you a selection of places within them to visit: the park, the shops, the museum, the airport and so on, each containing paintings related by themes.

Let's say you choose to visit the cinema. Clicking the cinema button lands you outside its doors. Then a click on the door-handle takes you inside a multiplex, where you have a selection of films to choose from: a Western in screen 1, a horror movie in screen 4, a Biblical epic in screen 5. The "movies" on show in the auditoria aren't actually films, but slide-shows of my paintings arranged in such a way to create a simple narrative, and book-ended with title sequences and credits just like a movie.

Other parts of the website are designed along similar lines, making imaginative use of scrolling and links. You can scroll down an escalator to board a horizontally scrolling underground train which transports you to other parts of the city. There are streets lined with various shops, each containing a different collection of themed paintings. At the airport you can click on a destination on the departures board and 'fly' to a painting depicting Barcelona or Florence. Hidden here and there throughout the Planet there are simple animated effects that are triggered by the movement of the visitor's mouse. I am particularly proud of the security camera which swings its head when a mouse hovers nearby, and the ghosts who emerge when the mouse hovers over a graveyard.

All this sounds like great fun, but the website was most certainly no fun to make. I had to build it entirely on my own from scratch, as web designers proved prohibitively expensive and no template could accommodate my idiosyncratic ideas. Being a complete novice to coding, Planet Jiro took eight months of sometimes brain-busting, sometimes brain-shrinkingly dull effort to complete, during which time I could not paint at all.

'Planet Jiro'

Right: Screenshots of 'Planet Jiro' showing the visitor's progression from a global view of the planet, an aerial view of London, the exterior of the cinema and then its foyer. *© Jiro Osuga.*

Far right: Screenshots of the 'film' in Screen 1 in progress. Entitled 'Sukiyaki Western', this is a selection of my paintings with a cowboy theme. It is a Japanese 'Sukiyaki' (a classic Japanese beef dish) Western, just as 'Spaghetti Western' is Italian. *© Jiro Osuga.*

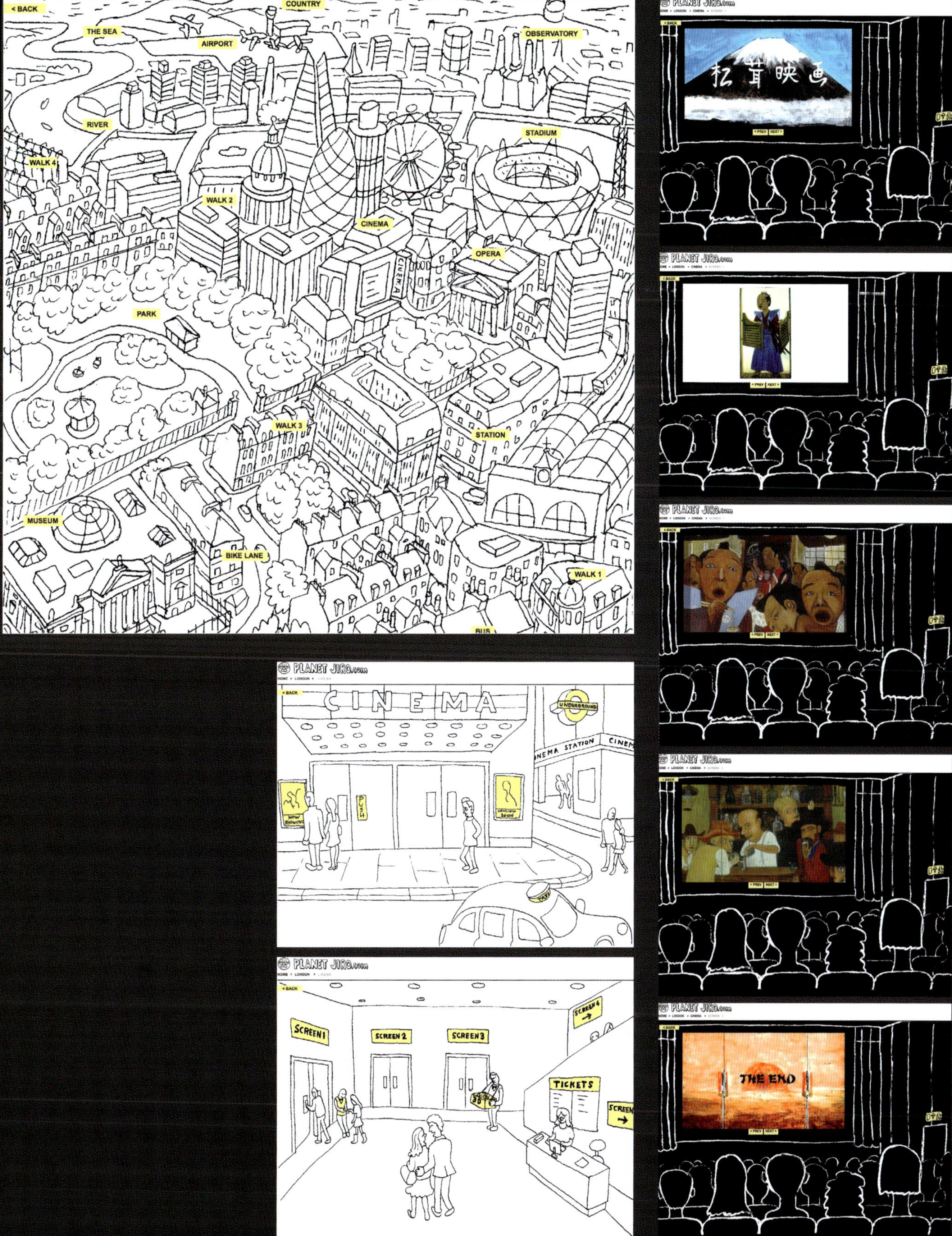

< BACK
COUNTRY
THE SEA
AIRPORT
OBSERVATORY
RIVER
STADIUM
WALK 4
WALK 2
CINEMA
OPERA
PARK
WALK 3
STATION
MUSEUM
BIKE LANE
WALK 1
PLANET JIRO.com
松茸映画
THE END
CINEMA
UNDERGROUND
CINEMA STATION
PUSH
NOW SHOWING
COMING SOON
TAXI
SCREEN 1
SCREEN 2
SCREEN 3
SCREEN 4
TICKETS

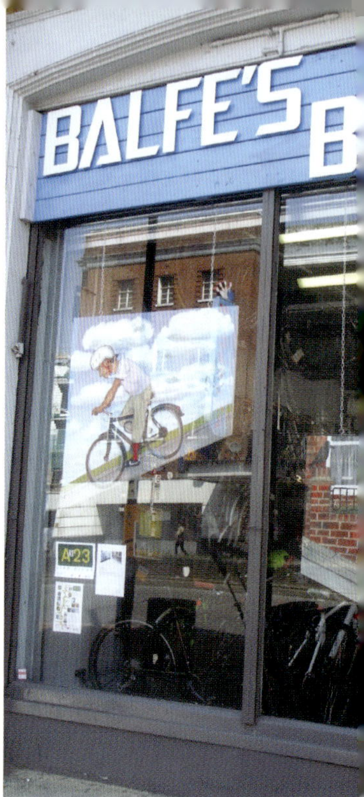

Made for Streatham

In recent years, I have exhibited a number of works in Streatham, most of which were specifically designed for particular Streatham locations. I first displayed my paintings in Streatham in 2011 when the local entrepreneur Chix Chandaria chose to use my paintings to decorate the walls of her pop-up wine bar in an empty shop near Streatham station. In 2013, a selection of my hinged paintings were exhibited in the same empty shop alongside the work of another Streatham artist, Karen D. Tregaskin, this time as part of the Streatham Festival for the first time.

'Uphill Downhill' at Balfe's Bikes, 87 Streatham Hill, 2014

My involvement with the Streatham Festival took to another level when I was asked to contribute to Art23 in 2014. Art23, the brainchild of the artist Emma Condliffe, is an art trail in which local artists display their work in shop windows across Streatham (see p. 137). In its first year in July 2014, I was allocated the window of Balfe's Bikes on Streatham Hill, for which I painted this pair of tailor-made canvases. 'Uphill Downhill' are double-sided paintings designed to be viewed both from the street as well as from inside the shop. When seen from the street, a man is free-wheeling his bicycle downhill, while a woman struggles uphill. Seen from inside the shop, the roles are reversed: the man has dismounted and pushes his bike up a steep slope, while the woman breezily cruises down. The scenery that form the backdrops were loosely based on local views.

Bicycling is a theme close to my heart. While I am not one of those lycra-wearing bike-nutters who shave their legs for aerodynamic reasons, the bicycle is my chief mode of transport, something I can't function without. I ride my trusty steed to get to anywhere within the M25.

'Lanterns' at Café Barcelona, 344 Streatham High Road, 2014

These lanterns were originally part of my Tokyo-themed show at Flowers Gallery in 2011. They normally illuminate my sitting room, but during Christmas 2014, they graced the window of Café Barcelona on Streatham High Road as part of 'Lights On Streatham!', a light-art project hosted by a number of venues across Streatham for Chistmas that year.

The twelve lanterns are based on decks of lanterns that adorn temples in Japan at festival time. Normally, they only bear the names of individual and business donors to the temple, but in my version, I have decorated them with images related to either light or rotundness. Hence there are lanterns painted to look like the Buddha's head (Buddha means 'The Enlightened One'), a goldfish bowl and the solar system.

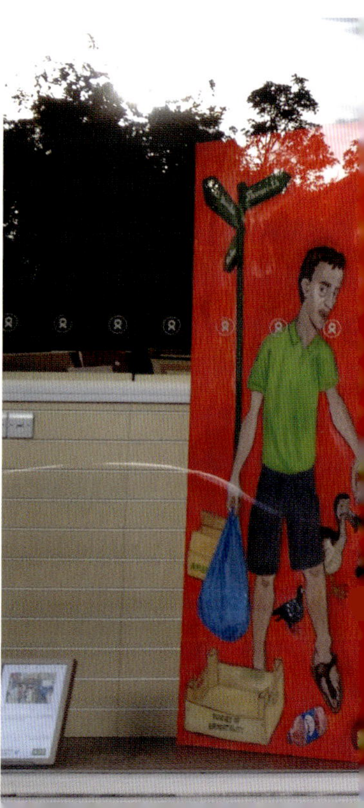

'Stall' at the Oxfam Furniture Shop, 24–26 Streatham High Road, 2015

This was my contribution to Art23 in 2015 when I was hosted by the Oxfam Furniture Shop on the High Road (the shop closed down in 2016). With this six-fold screen, I wanted to create the impression that a strange stall had suddenly started trading on the High Road. Any passer-by who cared to peruse the wares would have found bizarre items on sale there – including a flying carpet, Eden apples, Jack's beans and the Emperor's new clothes. The superstructure of the stall was modelled on ones in Brixton Market.

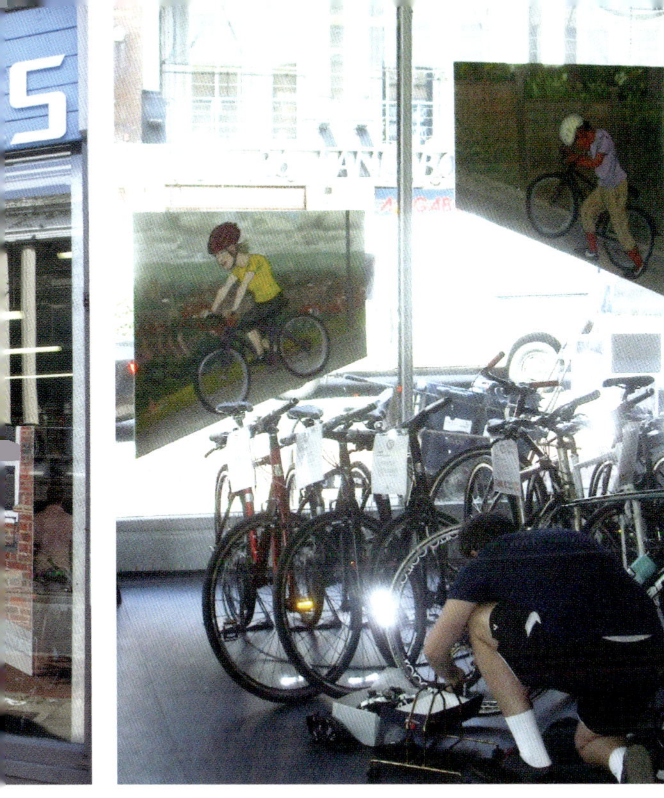

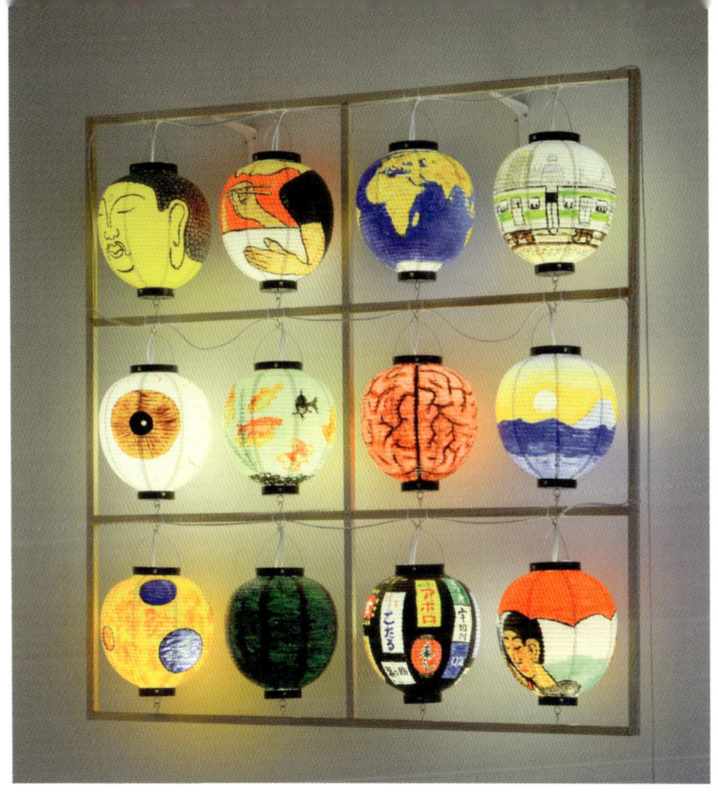

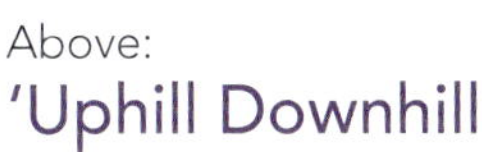

Above:

'Uphill Downhill'

Paintings in situ at Balfe's Bikes, seen from inside and outside the shop. See p. 79 and 95 for more images. *Flowers Gallery.*

'Lanterns'

2011, mixed media, 140 x 140 cm. *Flowers Gallery.*

'Stall'

2015, oil on canvas 190 x 444 cm. *Flowers Gallery.*

Photos: Mireille Galinou.

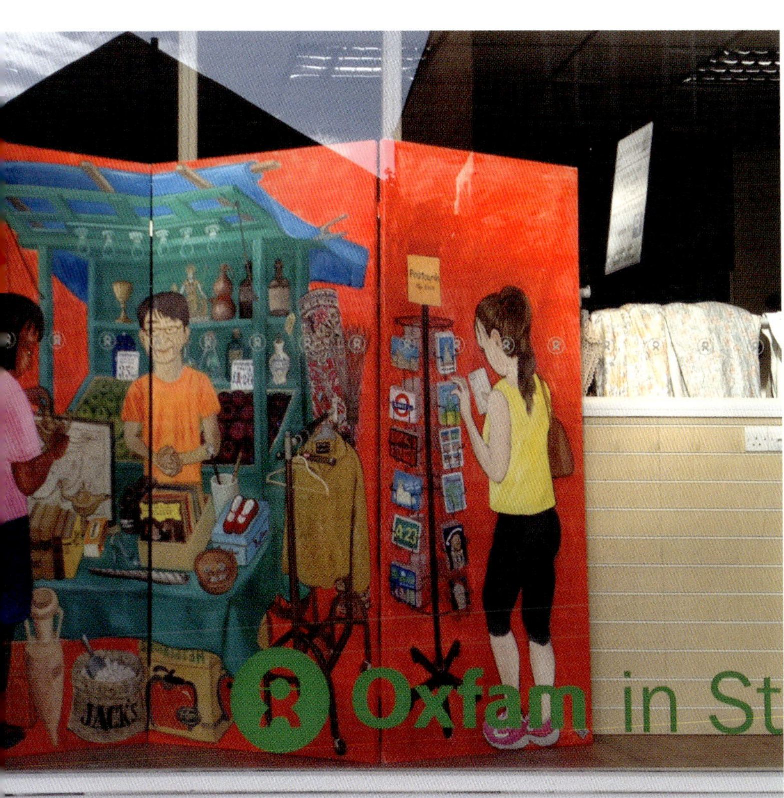

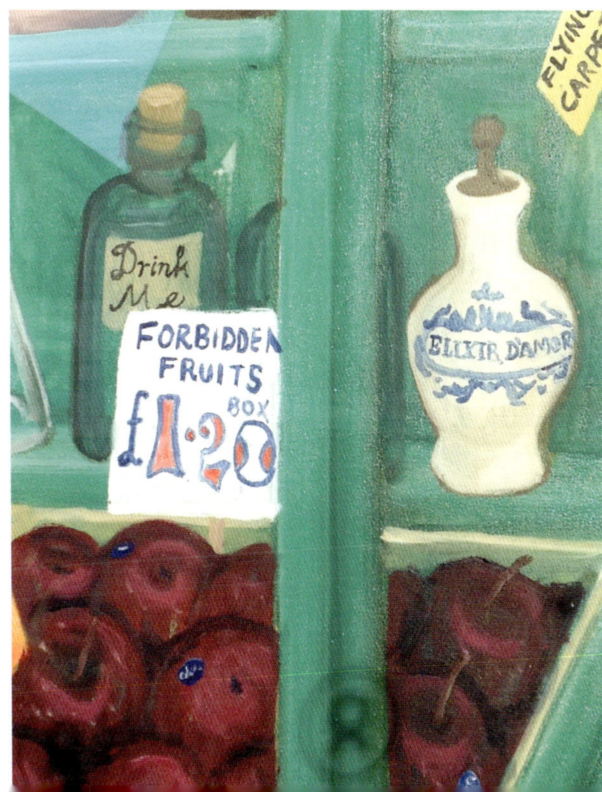

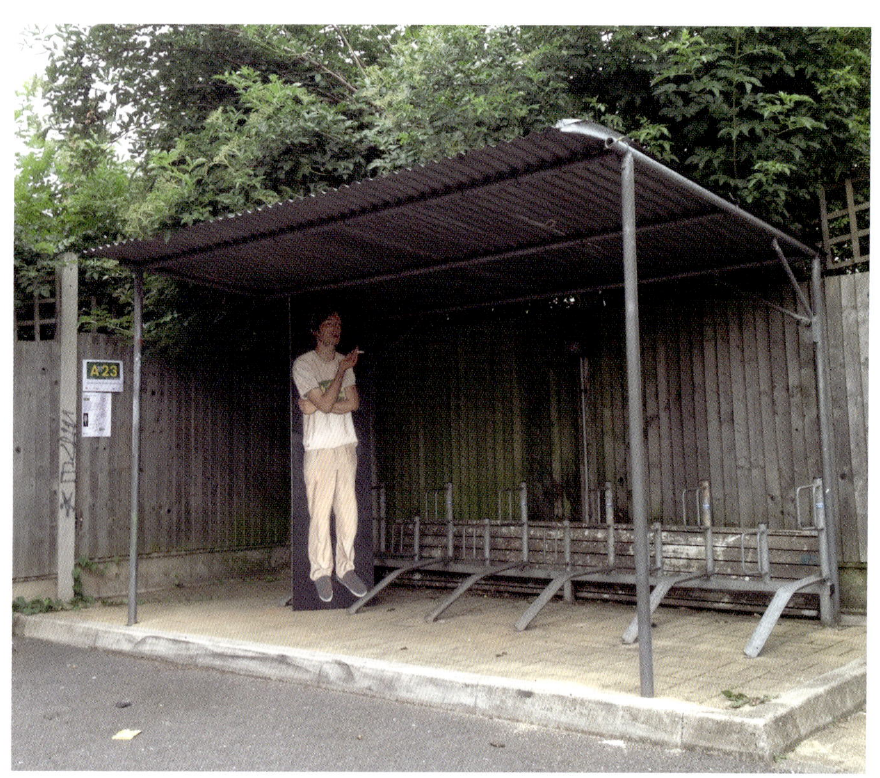
A23

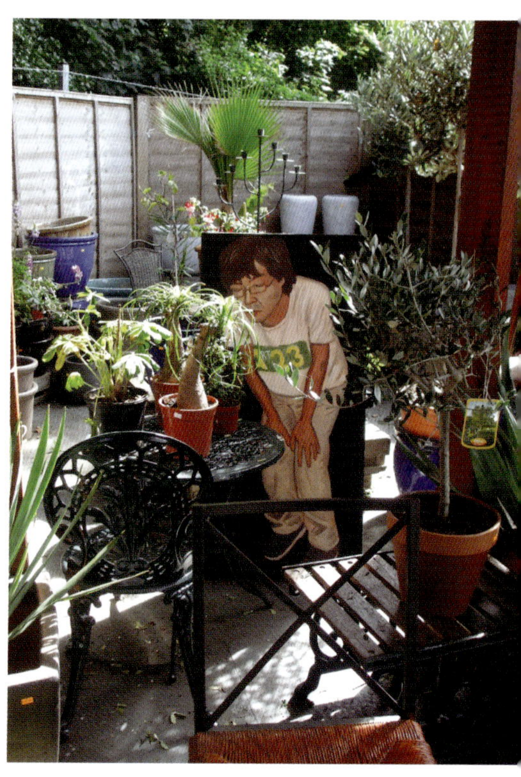
A23

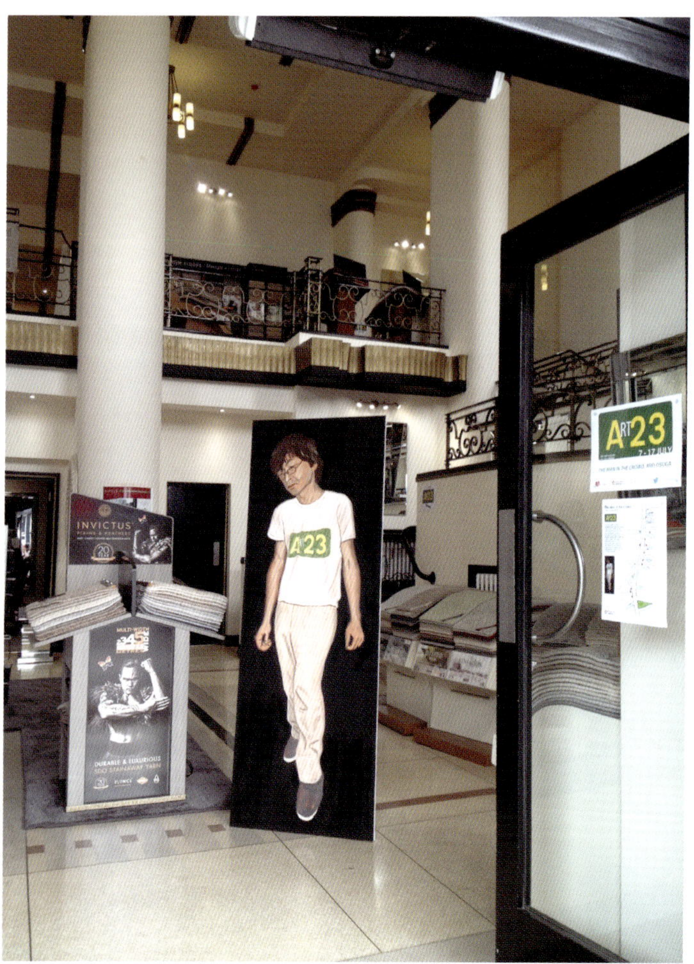
INVICTUS
A23
ART23
7–17 JULY

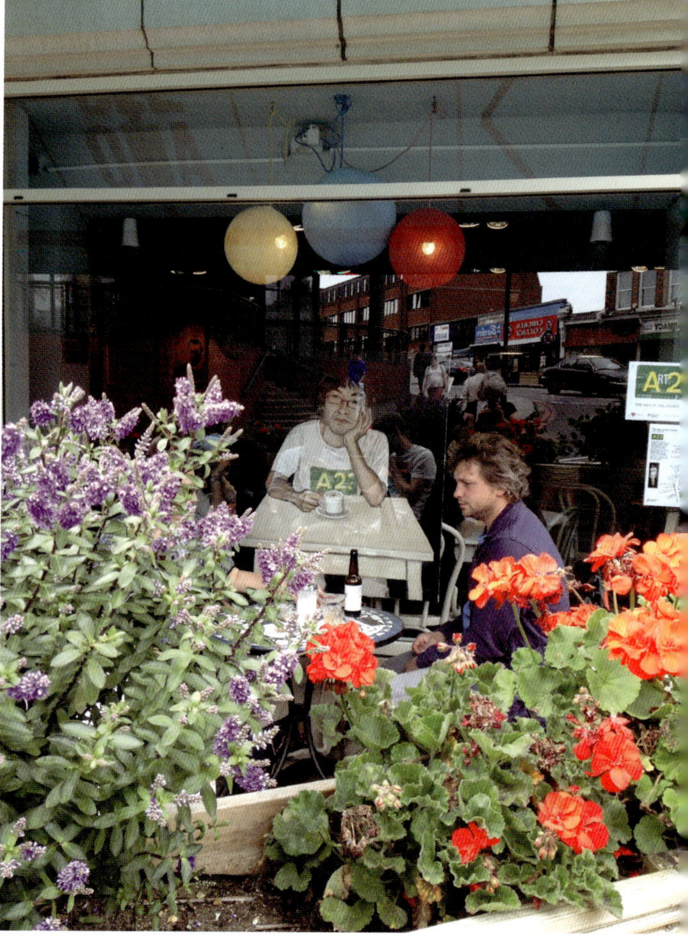
A23

'The Man of the Crowd', various venues around Streatham, 2016

My project for Art23 in 2016 was the most ambitious to date. The Man of the Crowd comprised of 14 self-portraits dotted around 11 different venues in Streatham – from cafés and the library to a pet shop and a bike shed. The idea was that Streathamites would stumble across the same mysterious stranger time and again as they went about their business in the neighbourhood. It was hoped they might wonder about his identity, and perhaps speculate about the ultimate unknowability of other people. The title was taken from a famous story by Edgar Allan Poe, in which a man follows a mysterious stranger around the nocturnal streets of London.

In practice, there weren't nearly enough self-portraits for people to really take notice, and although a couple of installations were quite striking, most were drowned out by the clutter of the High Road. The multiplicity of venues meant teething problems were also multiplied – and a project about the unknowability of the minds of others rather appropriately highlighted my own shortcomings when it came to adequately communicating my intentions with different shop-owners beforehand.

The complete series of paintings is reproduced on pp. 192–193.

Left:

'The Man of the Crowd'

Installation views around Streatham.
From top to bottom: the bike shed outside ASC Studios, 47C Streatham Hill;
Continental, 25 Leigham Court Road;
Picturehouse Interiors, 7 Streatham High Road;
Café Barcelona, 344 Streatham High Road (also see p. 8).
Photos: the authors.

7.

STREATHAM CONNECTIONS

Mireille Galinou and Jiro Osuga

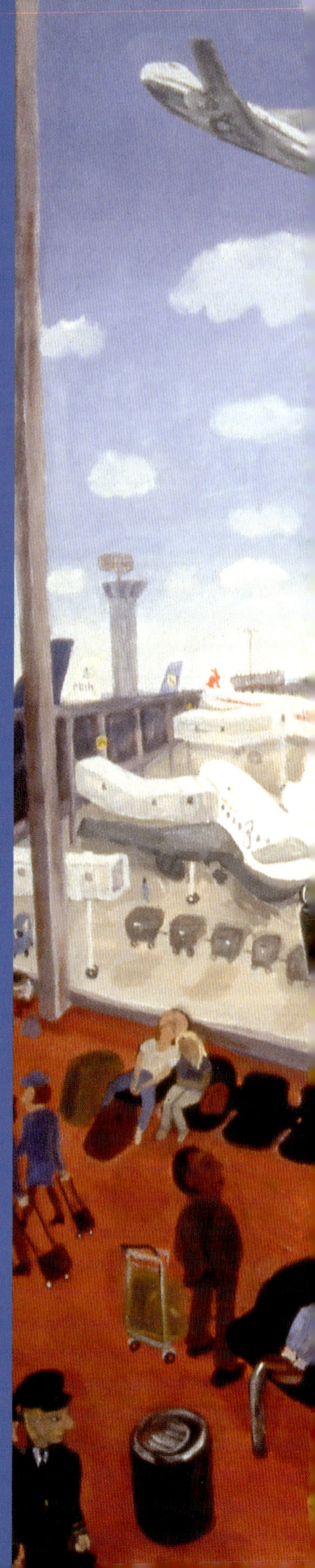

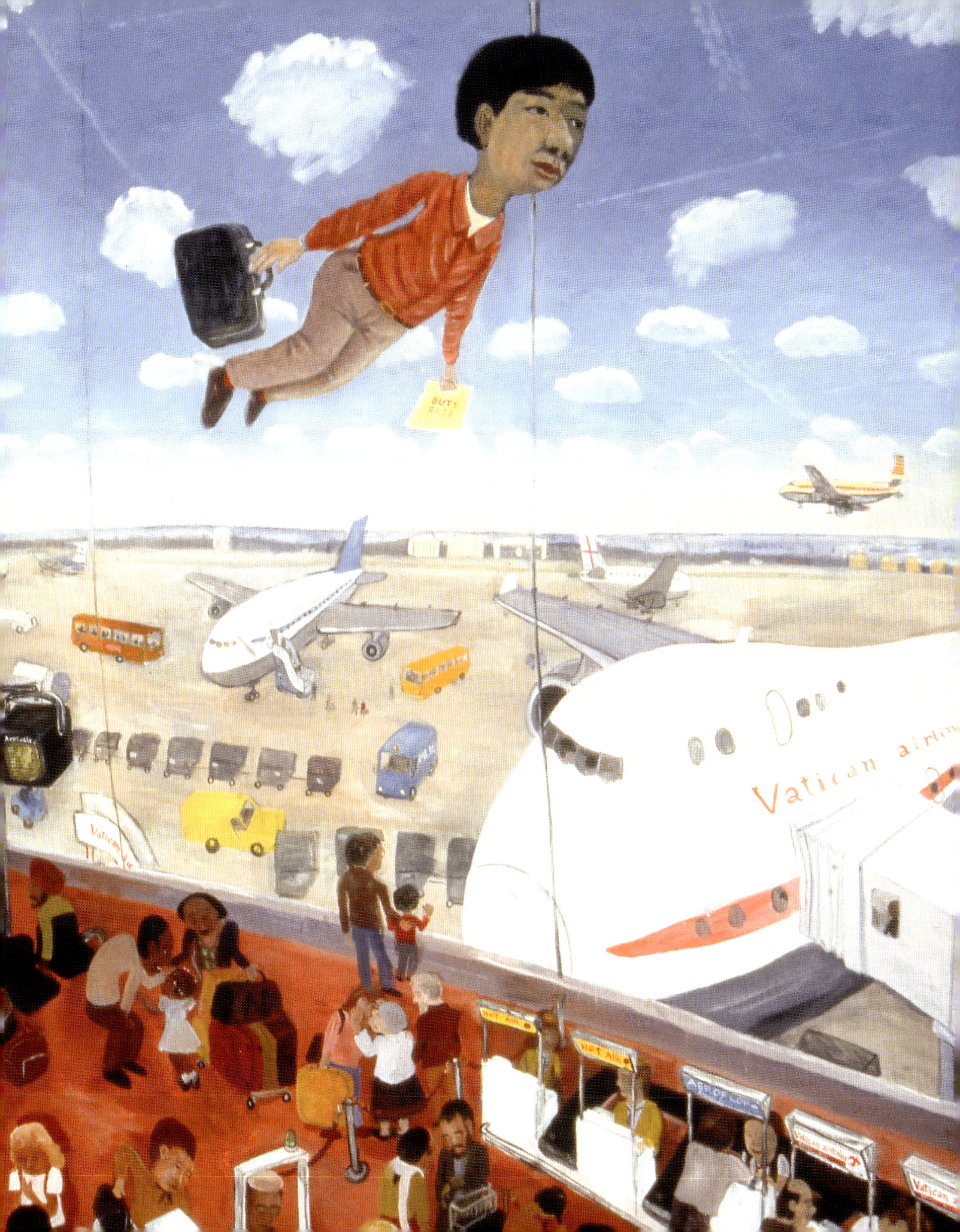
BUTT
HOT AIR
HOT AIR
AEROFLOP
Vatican airlines

A multi-cultural community

Mireille Galinou

'I don't think I will ever think of myself as English, or even British (there is a subtle distinction between the two), but I am quite comfortable being called a Londoner. My upbringing has been such that I probably do have streaks of Englishness (whatever that is) in my make-up, but then there is a substantial dollop of Japanese-ness too, along with other qualities that derive from God-knows-where which probably have nothing to do with any specific geographical location.' Jiro Osuga, 2016

Migration to Britain was encouraged after the Second World War when there was a serious labour shortage. Up until then immigrants had come mostly from Europe. But in 1948, the British Nationality Act created 'the citizen of the United Kingdom and Colonies' for people born or naturalized in either the UK or one of its colonies. For the first time large numbers of workers came from the Caribbean, India and Pakistan.

In his book *West Indian Migrants and the London Churches*, Clifford S Hill described the great Caribbean migration between 1955 and 1962 when 260,000 West Indians arrived and settled in Britain. 'This was the first large-scale entry of coloured people into Britain … The curtain came down with dramatic suddenness at midnight on 30 June 1962 when the Commonwealth Immigrants Act became law' (The Act, which limited the right of entry to the UK for Commonwealth citizens, was revised in 1968 and 1971).

The 1961 census for London, the accuracy of which Clifford Hill has questioned, recorded around 141,000 people from Caribbean countries (*London County Report of the 1961 census*). The London boroughs of Lambeth and Wandsworth had different boundaries prior to 1965 (most of Streatham came under Wandsworth) but according to Hill, Lambeth then had just over 10,000 West Indians and Wandsworth just under 5,500.

The experience of two Jamaican photographers in South London – Armet Francis and Neil Kenlock – is movingly chronicled in the book *Roots to Reckoning*. Armet came to Elephant & Castle at the age of ten (1955) and Neil to Brixton at the age of thirteen (1963): both to be greeted by parents who had left Jamaica a decade ago and whom they did not recognise. Armet describes the shock of coming 'into a frozen urban jungle, into some serious racism' He also recalls the shock of 'walking into a block of council flats. There were no trees, no gullies, no chickens, no goats, no black folks, but we weren't called black then'. In 1968 Neil Kenlock and his friends went to a disco in Streatham: they were turned away and told to come back the following week. They returned and were not allowed in for a second time. When the Black Panthers were leafleting Brixton shortly afterwards, Kenlock was at his most receptive and soon became their official photographer.

Previous pages: Jiro Osuga 'Flight', 1999, oil and acrylic on canvas, 166 x 183 cm. Jiro Osuga is fascinated by airports: once a year he flies to Japan to see his family. He has painted many airport pictures and devised an art installation based on airports which he has not yet been able to realise.
Private collection.
Photo: Flowers Gallery.

Right: Arthur Wint (1920–1992), Jamaican High Commissioner between July 1974 and March 1978, was photographed by Neil Kenlock when he visited Brixton in 1975. The Jamaican High Commission in London was founded in 1962 under the leadership of Sir Laurence Lindo. Wint, nicknamed the 'Gentle Giant', was the second Commissioner, having made his name in the 1948 Olympic Games held in London as the first Jamaican Olympic Gold medallist (400 m).
© Neil Kenlock.

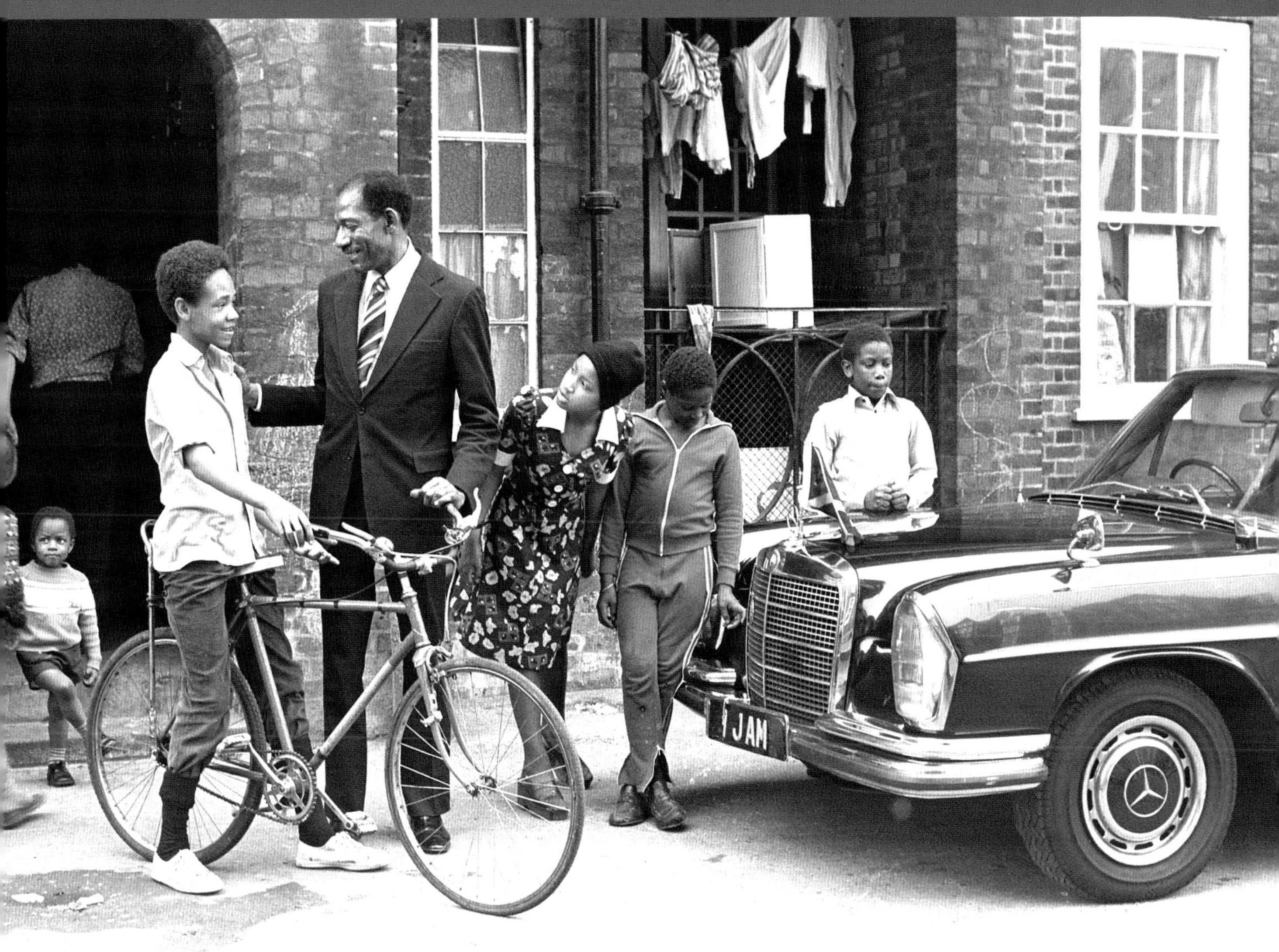
JAM

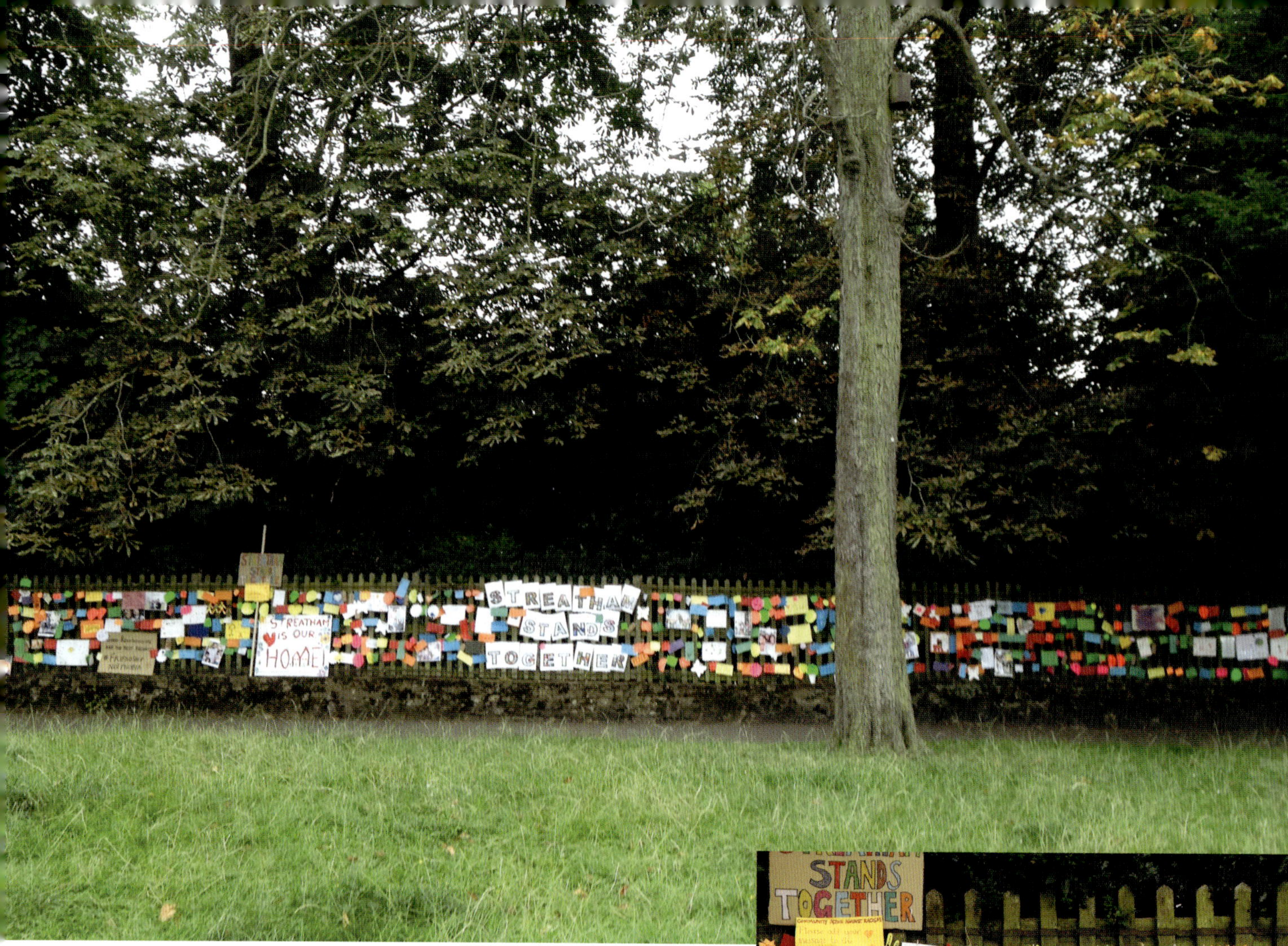

'Streatham Stands Together against Racism'

A touching community event, organised on 17 July 2016, drew Streatham residents and visitors to the Rookery railings on Streatham Common: the installation of a 'Love Board'. The Facebook campaign described it thus: 'Over the past weeks, we have seen an unprecedented rise in the number of people being racially abused and made to feel unsafe in our community. We want to come together to make a visible stand against racism in our community and to support anybody who may be feeling vulnerable.'

Love Board, Rookery railings, photographed in July 2016: general view and detail © *Mireille Galinou.*

Everyone was invited to come along and pin 'messages, artwork, photos, flowers – whatever you like' on the Love Board.

> 'The Love Board will stand plain for all to see, conveying unequivocally that Streatham Stands Together against racism'

This gesture was brought on by anti-racial outbursts following the announcement of Brexit on 24 June 2016. Within two days *The Independent* reported that over one hundred racial incidents had taken place. In Streatham, however, racially motivated crime is apparently extremely rare, according to local police though intolerance, like bullying, is most likely to go unrecorded. But this issue was not new. In 2014 Streatham MP Chuka Umunna had been 'targeted by racist online trolls' in a row with UKIP (*Evening Standard* 24 June 2014); another black MP, Diane Abbott, summarised the issues in blunt terms prior to attending the national Anti-Racist march organised by the United Nations on 21 March 2015:

> *'A wave of ugly immigrant-bashing racism is sweeping through Britain, led by UKIP, pandered to by the media and conceded to by many others. This demonstration is the start of the fight back. We have to gather everyone willing to stand up to racism.'* (*International Business Times*, 21 March 2015)

One neighbourhood, many people

It is easy to see, walking around Streatham, that it is a multi-cultural community. But what kind of multi-cultural community? A partial answer can be found in the latest census of 2011 in which Streatham is divided into four neighbourhoods: Streatham Hill at the top (north), St Leonard's below, flanked on the right by Streatham Wells (east) and underneath by Streatham South. The classification of the different areas by the Office of National Statistics makes interesting reading: Streatham Hill, St Leonard's and Streatham Wells are described as 'Prospering Metropolitan' while South Streatham is 'Multicultural Metropolitan: inner City'.

The map on p. 9 shows the different census areas in Streatham and the list below is a very brief summary of the enormous amount of data found in the 2011 census:

Population	Just under 60,000
Households	Around 24,000
Born in the British Isles	Just over 35,000
Born in Europe	Around 8,500
Born elsewhere	Just under 14,500
Ethnic group: White	Around 33,000
Ethnic group: Black	Around 13,500
Ethnic group: Asians	Just under 6,500
Age group 30–44	Around 17,000 (largest group)
Age group 45–59	Around 4,500 (next largest group)

These figures come to life a little when we examine some of the world's communities jostling, trading and breathing on the streets of Streatham. The ten largest groups are listed here (but there are many more countries represented). The figures seem small because they are only targeting those individuals who were born abroad:

Figures taken from the 2011 Census: 'Country of Birth (detailed) (quick stats)' across Streatham South, St Leonard's, Streatham Wells and Streatham Hill.

1. Poland	3,367
2. Jamaica	1,714 (and just over 2,200 if you include other Caribbean countries)
3. Portugal	936
4. Pakistan	842
5. Nigeria	834 (and just over 2,300 if you include other Central/ West African countries)
6. India	823
7. Ghana	781
8. Italy	749
9. Somalia	566
10. France	542

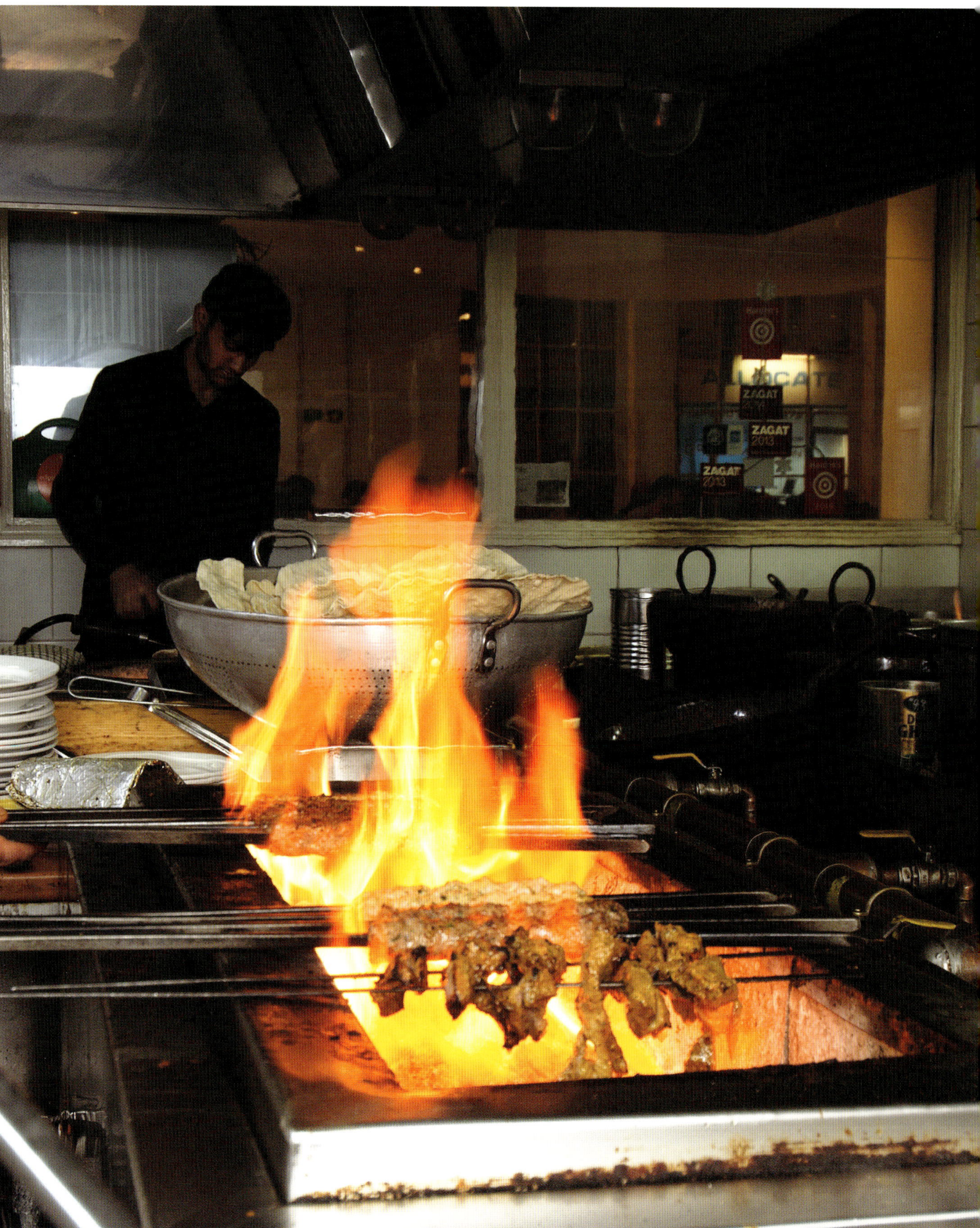
ZAGAT
2013
ZAGAT
2013
ZAGAT
2013

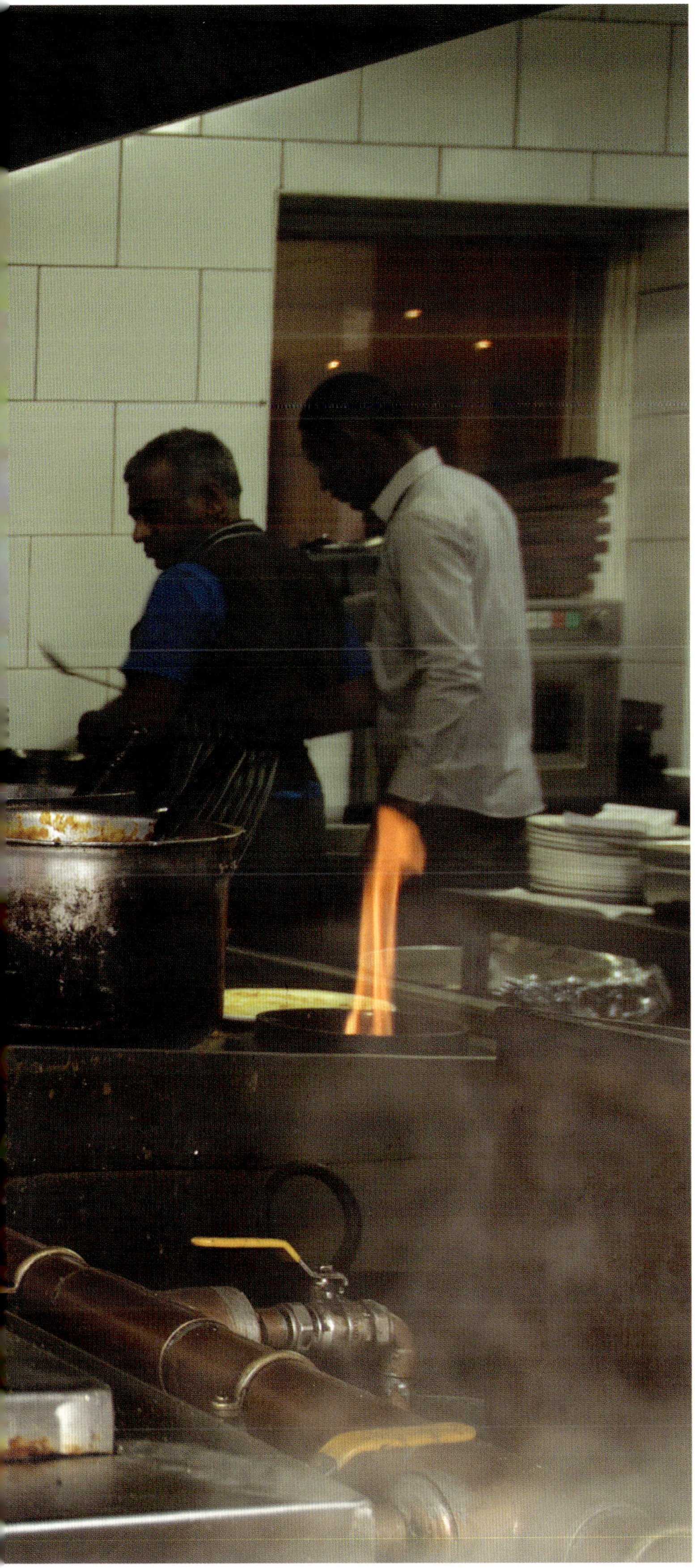

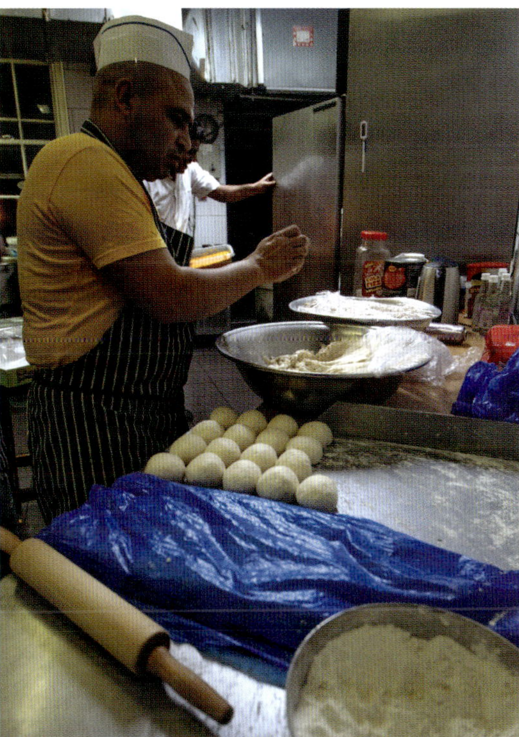

The owner of the **Lahore Kebab House** at 668 Streatham High Road, Assif Siddique, opened its doors in 2010, a full 38 years after the original Lahore Kebab House was set up off Commercial Road. But the link with the East End is strong – it was Assif's father, Muhammed, who started the East End restaurant and who took in his two sons, Imran and Assif, to help him run the operation. Now Imran owns the Whitechapel branch which caters predominantly for a white British clientele, while Assif in Streatham attracts a predominantly Asian clientele. We were delighted to be granted unlimited access to the busy kitchen, separated from the main dining area by a glass window. For the history of the building see p. 56.

These pages pay homage to a restaurant which served delicious food at very competitive prices. In February 2017 a visit from the Home Office had devastating results and led to the immediate closure of this excellent eating house. Many people miss it, including this author.

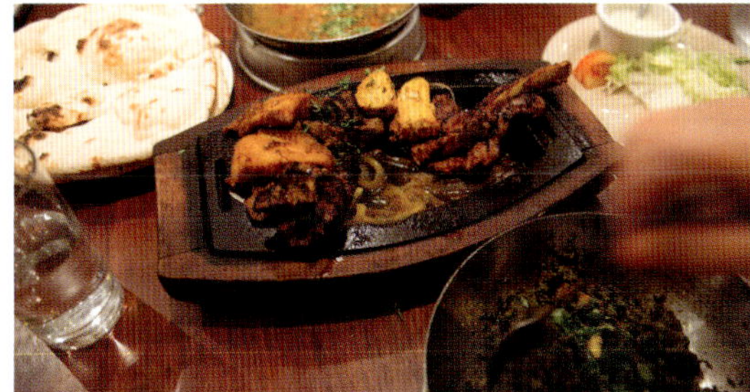

When **Bartek**, the Polish supermarket at 254 Streatham High Road opened in 2012, there were five Polish shops in Streatham. But Bartek has gathered such momentum that it now dominates the High Road. This is done through long opening hours seven days a week, excellent customer service, and variety and freshness of produce, all entirely sourced from Poland. The owner Glen runs a well-organised operation, ordering the produce online: it takes two days for it to arrive at Bartek's which has good storage facilities. Glen is particularly proud of the extensive range of organic products – from groceries to speciality meats such as duck and rabbit. The cakes are either home-made or sourced from one of Poland's best patisseries – Sowa. The store clearly attracts Eastern European shoppers but Glen is keen to cater for all communities and foods are labelled in Polish and English. He recommends for instance the excellent 'Grandad's ham' (=Szynka Dziadkowa).

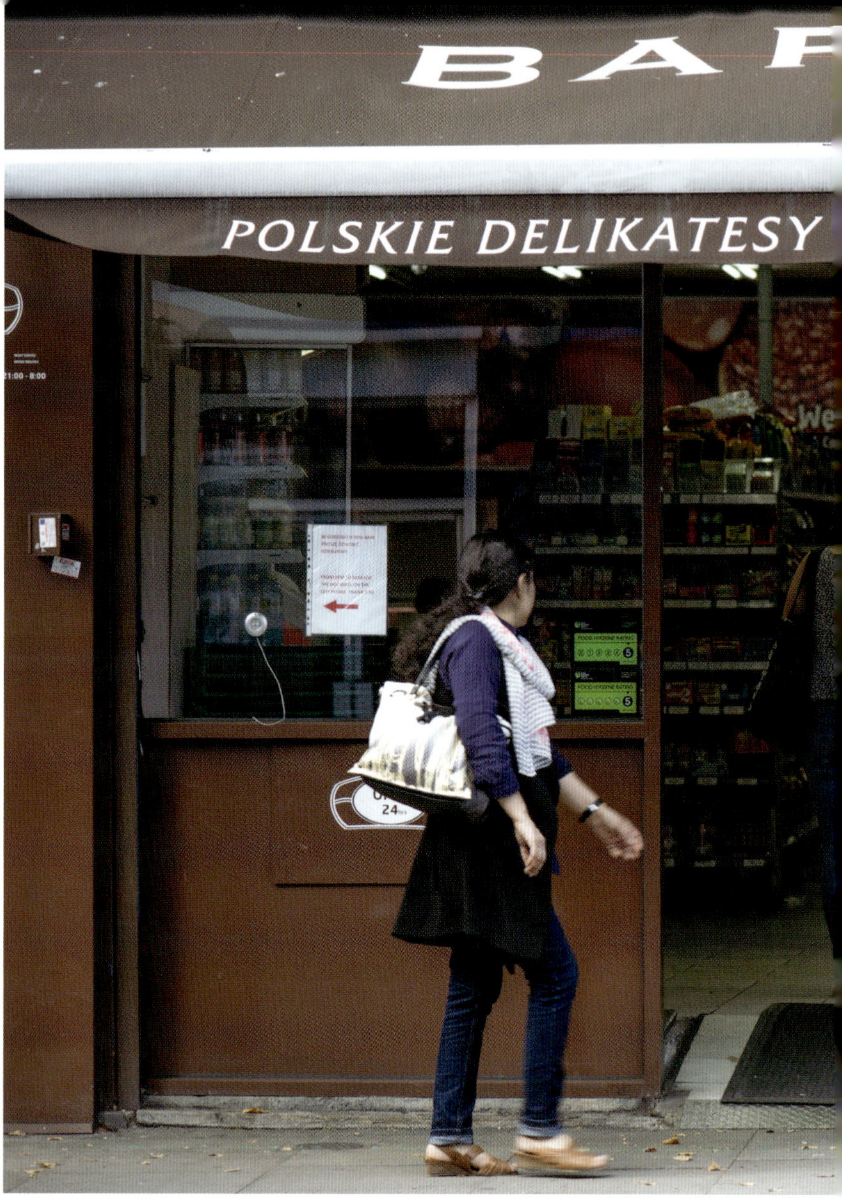

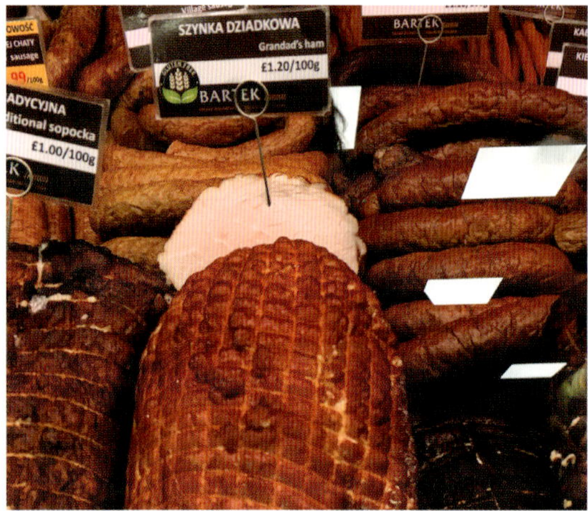

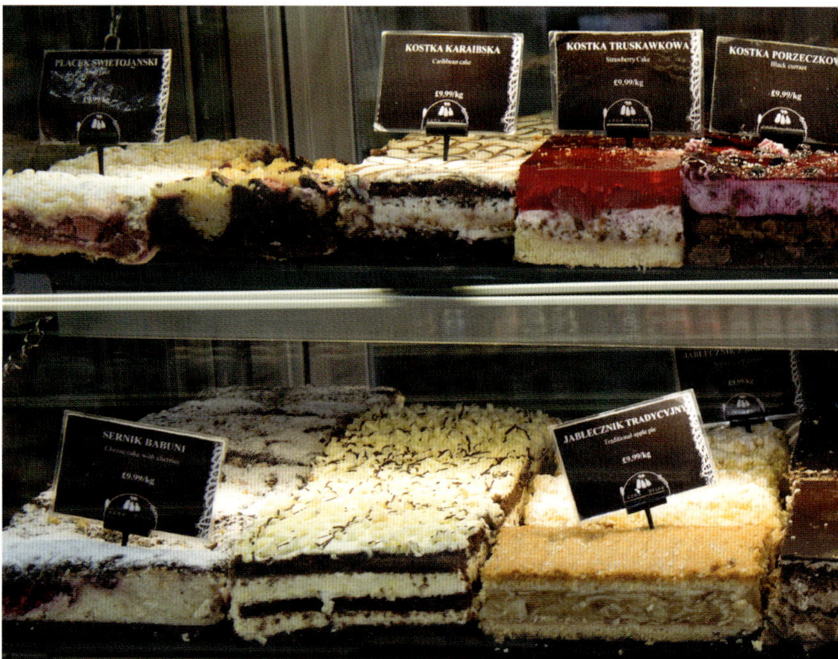

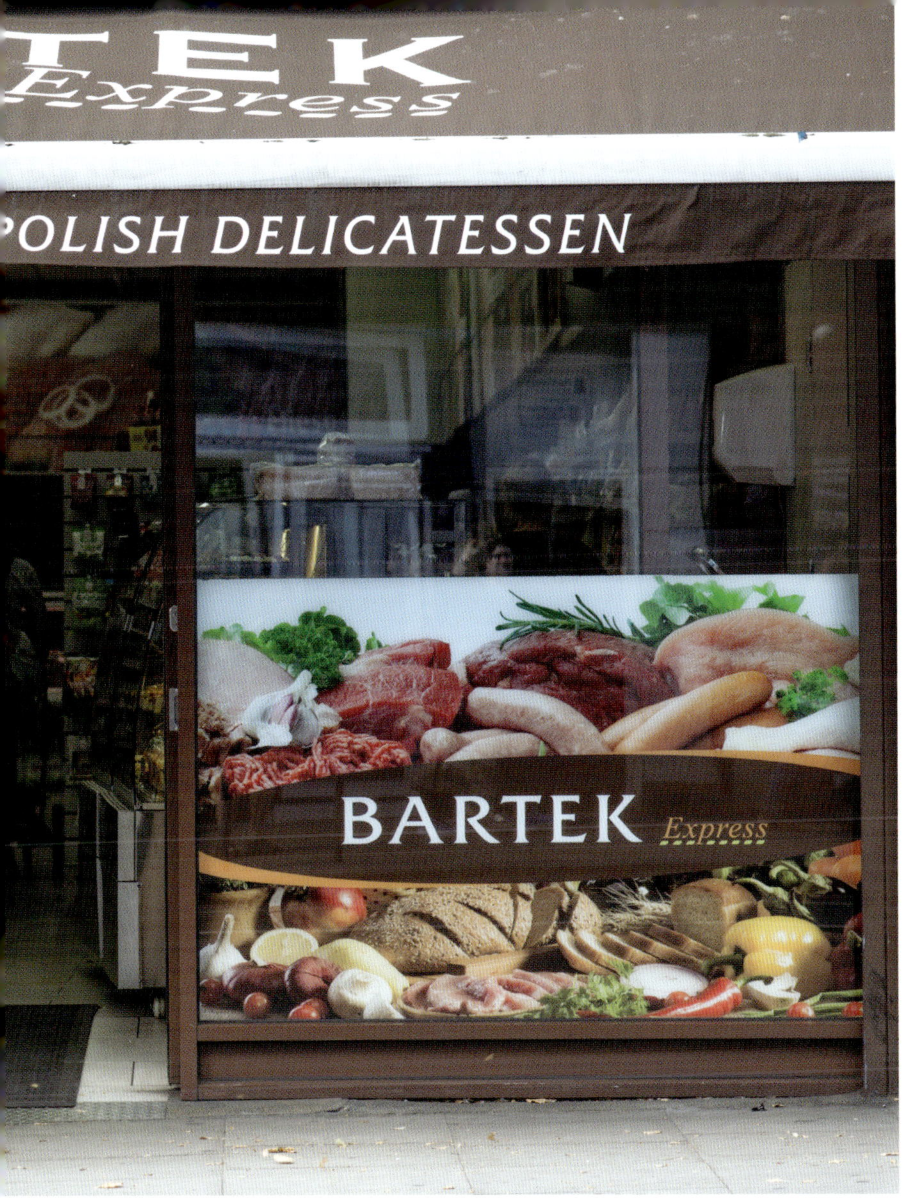

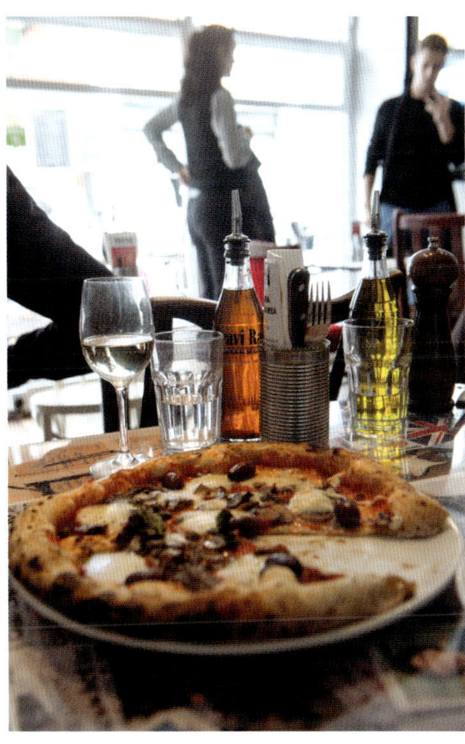

Bravi Ragazzi at 2A Sunnyhill Road may have tiny premises, but it did not stop this pizzeria from acquiring a reputation for best Neapolitan-style sourdough pizzas in Streatham.

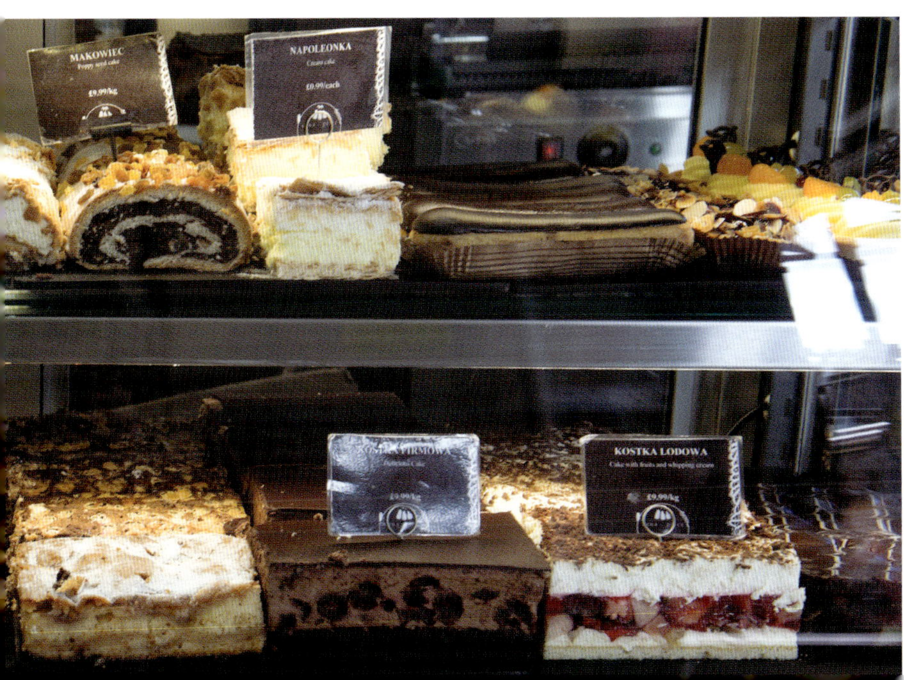

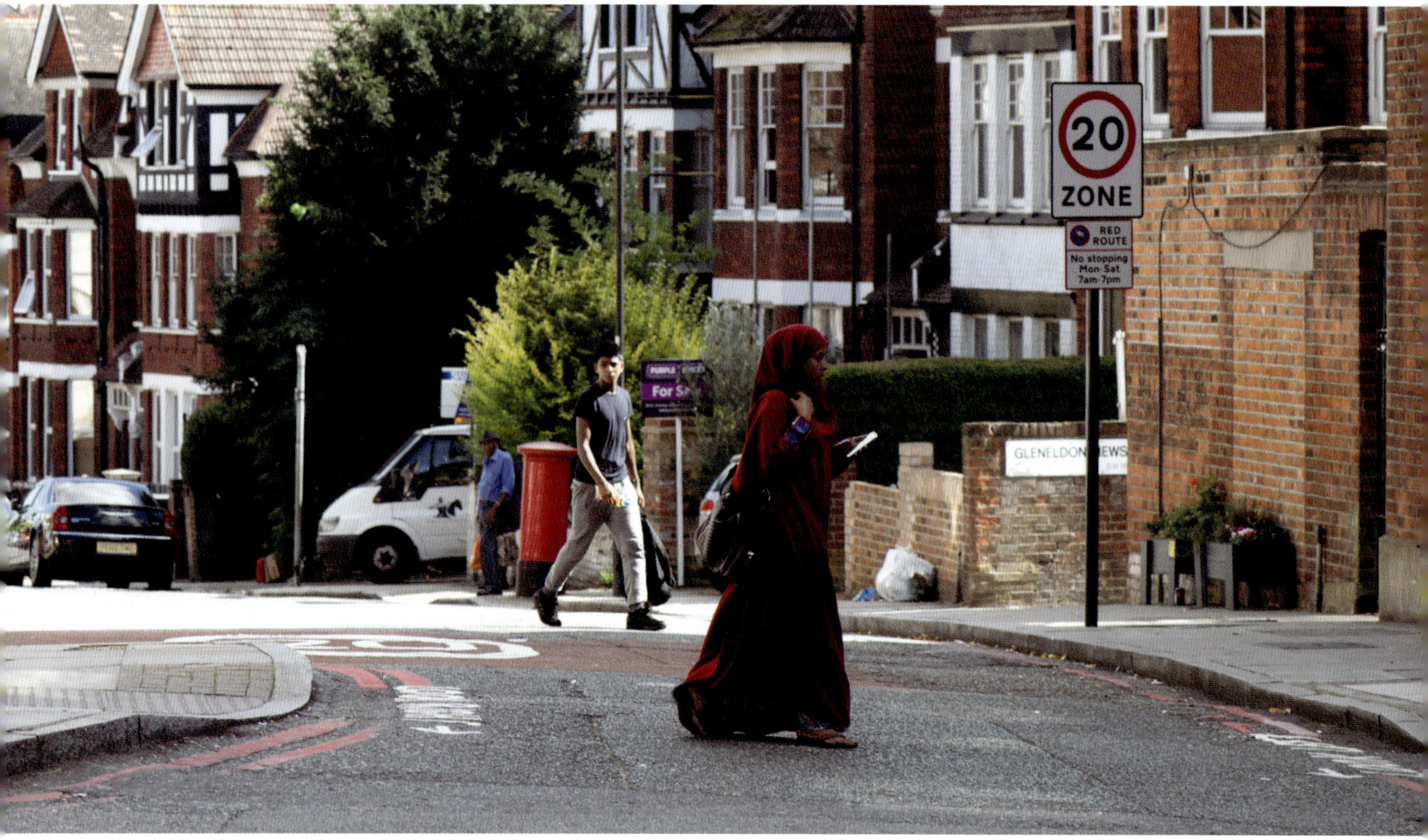

The all-important rule of modesty for Moslem women means that the hijab (head dress) and the chador (dress) are familiar sights on suburban London streets, particularly in Streatham.

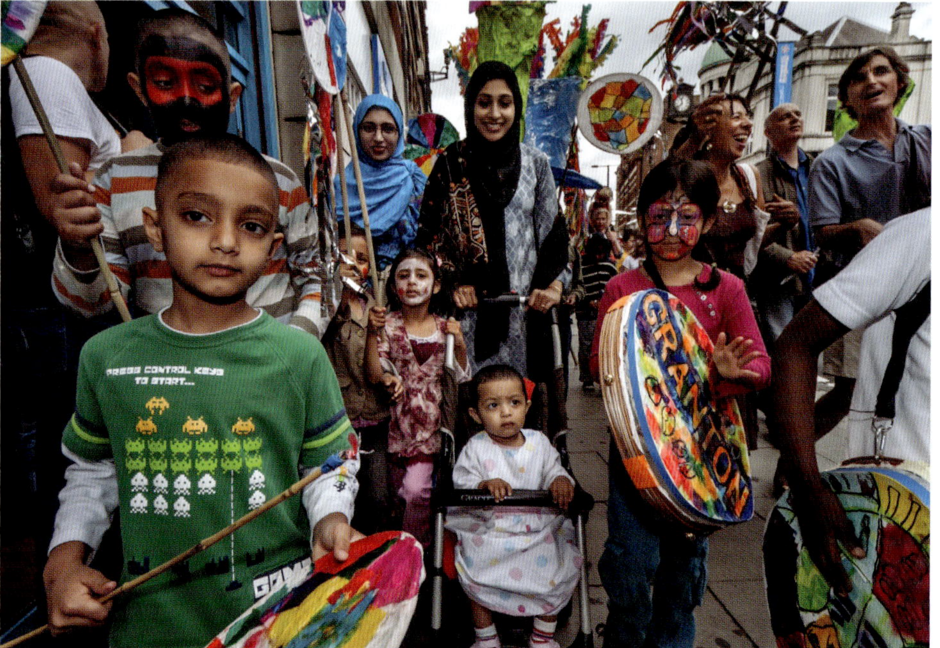

Peter Marshall photographed the Streatham Carnival parade along the High Road on 14 July 2007. This was part of the Streatham Festival.
© Peter Marshall
mylondondiary.co.uk

262 Streatham High Road houses an extraordinary array of smaller traders and organisations inside – a feature of many shops in the southern stretch of Streatham High Road. The left hand corner of the window is occupied by a phone accessories trader; opposite in the right hand corner of the window is a tailor. Further in, a Polish internet operation occupies the left hand side and next to it on the right there is a hairdressers. Signs on the wall indicate that the down staircase on one side of the 'shop' takes you to the 'Horn Africa Community Centre' or the **'Citizenship Test'**. Concerning the latter we have this testimony from Richard Woollard:

'After learning British facts beyond the knowledge of any native, and after all the form-filling and the supplying of expensively translated verifying documents, comes the final Official Ceremony. Held in the local registry office, it is a surprisingly moving and heartening occasion. The registrar seems slightly embarrassed at asking the candidates to pledge allegiance to the Queen and her successors, but each one stands proudly beside the official royal portrait to be photographed holding their citizenship certificate. A myriad of nationalities are represented, and behind each person there must be a fascinating story that leads to their hard-won presence here.'

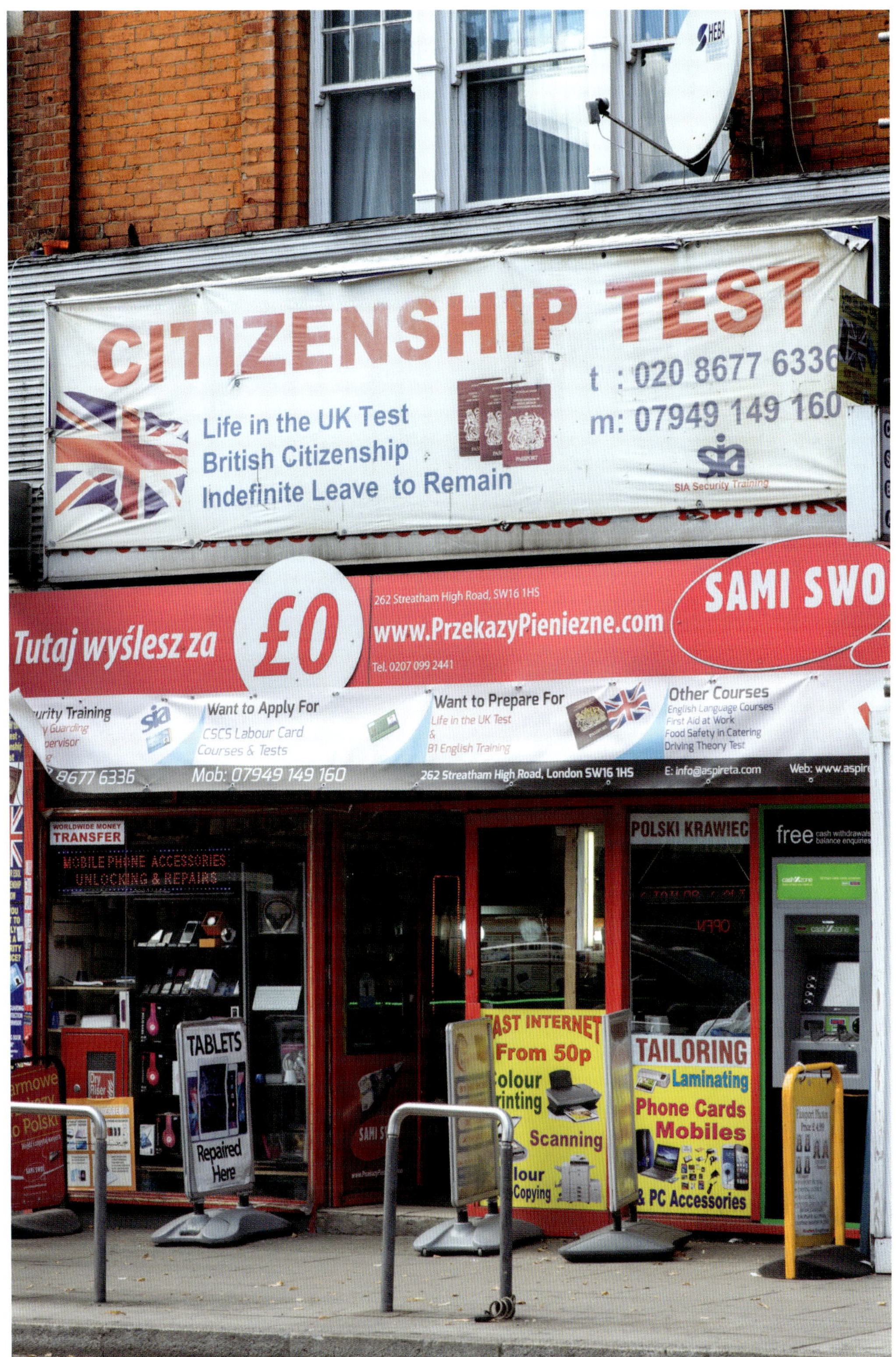

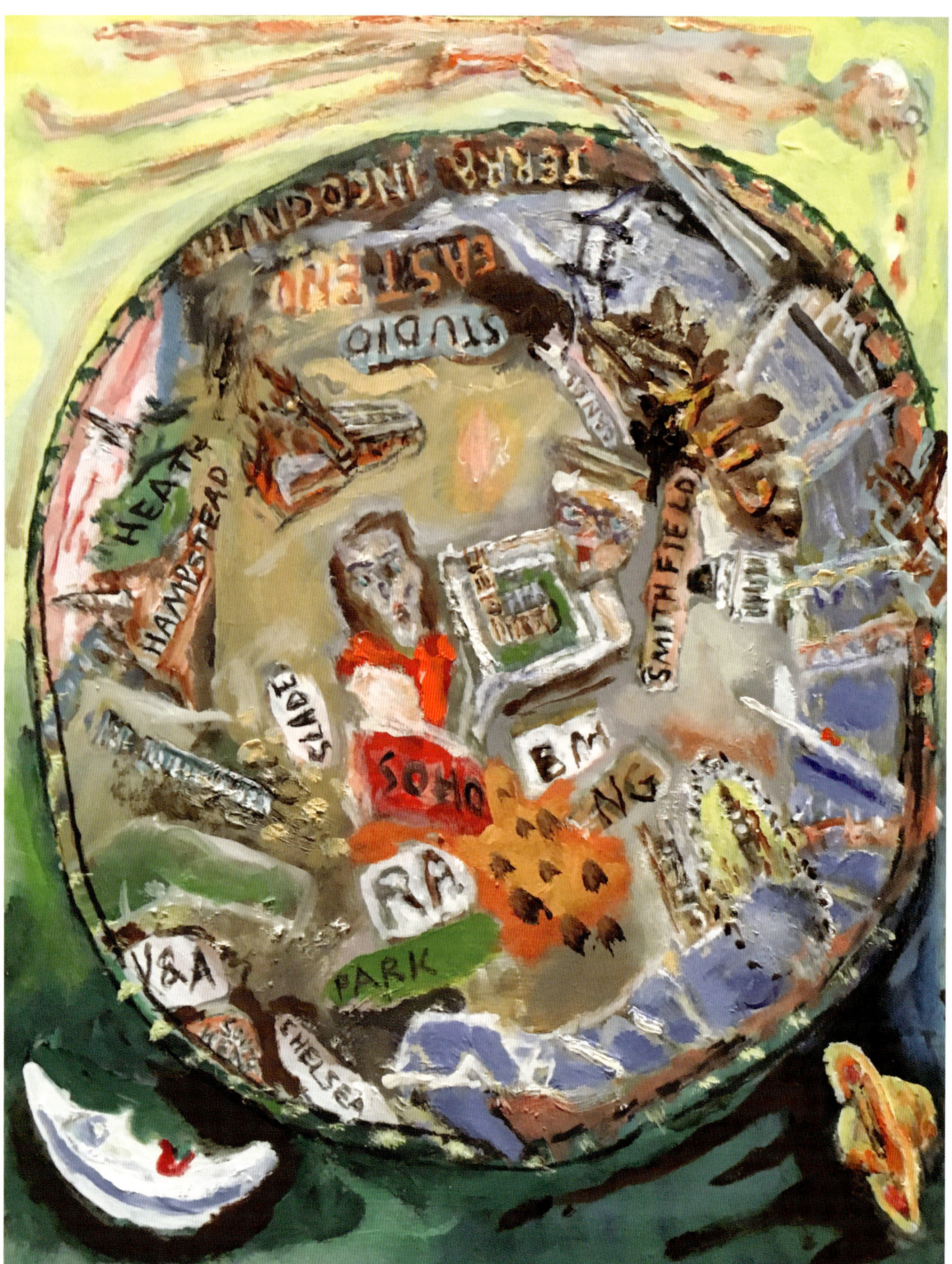
TERRA INCOGNITA
EAST END
STUDIO
HEATH
HAMPSTEAD
SMITHFIELD
SLADE
SOHO
BM
NG
RA
PARK
V&A
CHELSEA

Timothy Hyman, 'My London Cosmos', oil on wood, 38 x 30 cm exhibited at the Royal Academy in 2016. The Thames runs around two thirds of the edge of the painting, crossed by many bridges. In the centre is the double portrait of the artist Tim Hyman and his wife Judith on either side of Myddelton Square in Islington where they live. Westminster (bottom right) and the City (top right) are clearly depicted. The places which have particular meaning to the artist are named including 'terra incognita' in the south. From the top: 'Studio East End', [Regent's] Canal, Smithfield, Hampstead Heath, Slade [School of Art] where the artist trained, Soho, BM (British Museum), NG (National Gallery), RA (Royal Academy), V&A (Victoria and Albert Museum), (Hyde) Park and Chelsea. Jiro Osuga points out that many of his own London connections would be found in Tim Hyman's '*terra incognita*'.
© Timothy Hyman, private collection.

It is captivating to observe the presence of these communities on and around Streatham High Road. A 2007 project captured perfectly this lively cosmopolitan blend. The booklet *Streatham Stories* co-ordinated by Anna Godsiff, was published with a selection of well-presented interviews ranging from Dawn Trevors/Travers' Cat Rescue Mission at Hillside Road to Haneef Patel's coffee and cigarettes stall/shop at Streatham station via the energetic Abdul Ahmed/ Mohamed (14 Gleneagle Road) who set up the Somali Youth Education & Development Centre (registered with the Charity Commission in 2005). Like many of his Streatham compatriots he fled Somalia in 1989 when civil war threatened – he was 17. He arrived via Kenya and Hungary and landed in a West London 'detention centre' prior to being housed in Streatham Hill. He obtained a Greenwich University degree in economics and worked for a firm of immigration lawyers after graduating. For him, life in Streatham meant 'finding sanctuary', while Jane Skead – a local artist – summed up Streatham High Road as providing her with 'food from anywhere in the world in an instant'.

That is the visible part of a neighbourhood's activities but a multi-cultural community also has invisible roots. For every nation represented on the streets of Streatham, including Britain, innumerable connections are made from Streatham to the places people come from – another part of London, another part of Britain, a European country or the rest of the world: telephone calls, visits, emails, letters, plane and train journeys. Streatham on its own will have connections with the whole world – an extraordinary thought.

In this book we are also keen to explore the role artists play in making connections and in visualising the invisible. The painter Timothy Hyman (born 1946), a Royal Academician and Jiro Osuga's mentor, has captured his own invisible connections to London at large in the delightful 'My London Cosmos'.

We are all immigrants

In 1993 the Museum of London presented a ground breaking exhibition, 'The Peopling of London', accompanied by an eponymous publication. The curator, Nick Merriman, an expert on prehistory started his migration story from the very beginning, i.e. in prehistoric times: 'slowly spreading from their original homeland in Africa, early humans reached Southern Britain during the Ice Age'. When the climate warmed up around 15,000 years ago, the animal and vegetal world thrived again and Merriman concluded: 'From this time Britain has been continuously inhabited. It is possible to argue that, from these early immigrants to the refugees of today, everyone living in London is descended, however distantly, from people who have come from abroad'.

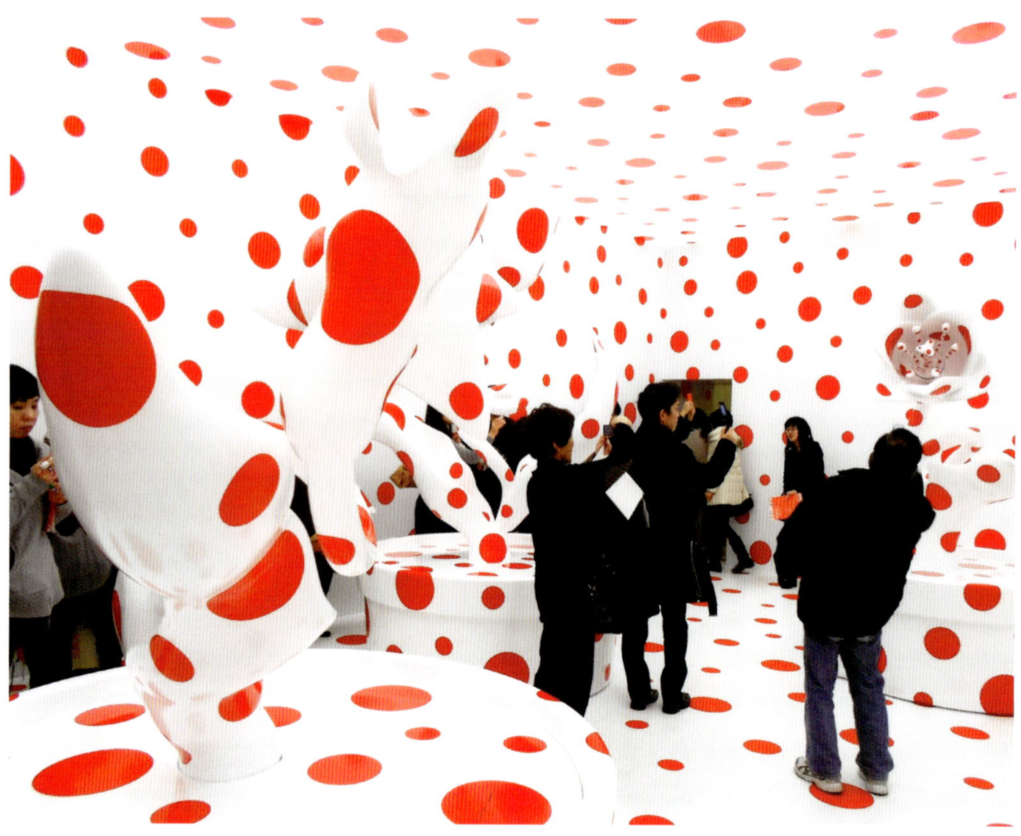

Left: Yoyoi Kusama, 'I pray with all my love for tulips' installation at her exhibition at the Osaka National Museum of International Art, 2012. Photo: Samuel Mark Thompson (Commons Wikipedia).

Japan in London Mireille Galinou

The Japanese connection is of particular interest since Streatham-based artist Jiro Osuga plays such a vital role in the making of this book. He is one of only nineteen Japanese people living in Streatham! The Borough of Lambeth as a whole had a modest 369 Japanese people in 2011, the largest concentration being around Oval tube station. Looking in South London for large groupings of Japanese people is unwise, as they greatly favour north of the river, in particular the boroughs of Barnet (2,870), Ealing (2,713), Westminster (1,866) and Kensington & Chelsea (1,140). Overall, there are just over 20,000 Japanese people living in London.

Since Jiro's contribution to London is in the world of art, it is worth considering this Anglo-Japanese context. In 2012 Londoners flocked to Tate Modern to visit his compatriot Yayoi Kusama's retrospective show. In her 80s and dubbed 'the princess of polka dots', she made a big impression on the art-loving public with her bold, colourful paintings and installations. Her life, too, fascinates: she made her name in New York in the 1960s, through controversy, and when she later returned to Tokyo, plagued by mental issues, she admitted herself to a psychiatric hospital in 1977: she has lived there ever since. Her art, abstract and seemingly timeless, suits the international scene and her imagery does not seek to interpret her immediate environment. In that sense, Jiro clearly operates on a different 'Planet' (see p. 162).

Right: Jiro Osuga, 'The World goes by', 2006, oil on canvas, 130.4 x 104.5 cm. Jiro's painting depicts the successive waves of inhabitants from the past and present to have walked the streets of suburban London. *Flowers Gallery.*

Far right: Yoshio Markino, 'Street scene in Fulham', watercolour reproduced in his book *A Japanese Artist in London* published in 1910.

Jiro and Yoshio – uncanny parallels

Jiro's life and times bear similarities to the adventures of another Japanese artist, born 100 years earlier and who also settled in London: Yoshio Markino (1869–1956).

> 'My life is as simple and unworthy as my pictures', Yoshio Markino in *A Japanese Artist in London*, 1910

When Jiro Osuga was asked to describe two main achievements in his life as an artist, he replied:

> 'I have achieved little of note', *Art and Cities Magazine*, Winter 2005

In 1893 Yoshio Markino suffered ferocious racial abuse when he emigrated to San Francisco from Tokyo. He was therefore very surprised by the mild-mannered reception he received in London when he arrived here in December 1897. In California, where 'it is a world-known fact that they hate Japanese', they threw 'stones and bricks at me' and occasionally spat, in real contrast to his English experience from the very start: 'Those English officers aboard the Channel boats had such gentle faces: they talked to me so kindly' (he came from Paris therefore crossed the Channel). He described his encounter with a London newspaper seller:

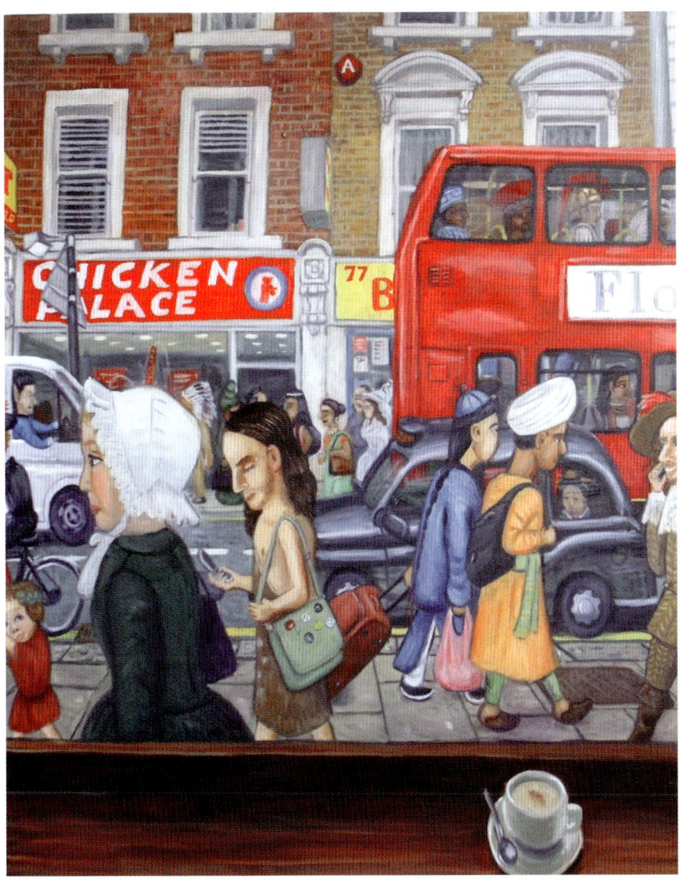

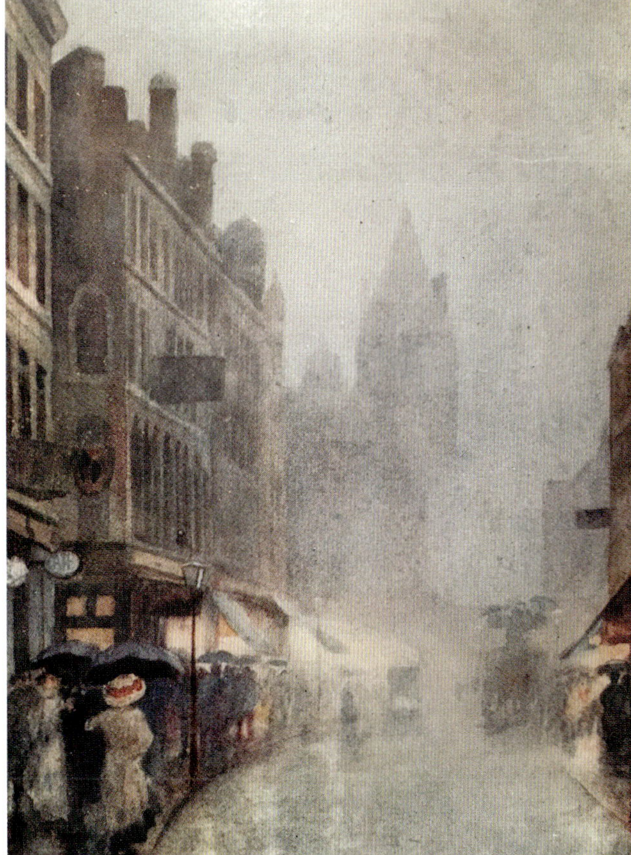

> I asked him if he has seen Japanese before. He said: 'No'. Then I asked him again if he was not curious of me? He said: 'No, sir. You see, sir, we 'ave our colonies all hover the world, sir – white men, yellow men, brown men and black men are forming parts of the British nation, so I am not curious of a Japanese gentleman at all.

It is uncanny to observe how the lives of Yoshio Markino and Jiro Osuga (born in 1869 and 1968), share a number of distinctive features. They both connect to the samurai class: Yoshio was 'a most spoiled child of the samurai and a boy king in his village once', and one of Jiro's grandparents came from a low-ranking samurai family. They both attended art schools in London. They both lived all over London, moving around to follow work or housing opportunities – but with an emphasis on South London. They both experienced the poverty of struggling artists. They both produced work stimulated by their immediate environment. They both found English people to champion their work: the art critic of the *Magazine of Art*, M H Spielmann for Yoshio; and Flowers Gallery for Jiro. And they are both represented in the collections of the Museum of London.

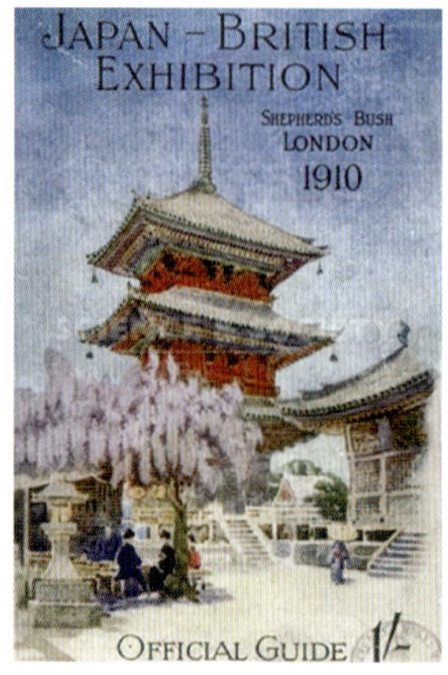

Front cover of the 'Official Guide' to the Japan-British exhibition held at the White City in Shepherds Bush, London, 1910
Photo: Commons Wikipedia.

Global connections

Both artists lived through a period of history when Japan was open to the world rather than isolationist. The samurai class had ruled Japan from 1185 to 1868. Although trade links with Europe started in the sixteenth century, they were of a strictly restricted nature. For two centuries only the Dutch could trade with Japan and exports focused primarily on lacquer work and ceramics. Japan started opening to the outside world from 1868, with the beginning of the Meiji period.

A year later, in 1869, Alfred, Duke of Edinburgh and Queen Victoria's son, was the first European prince to visit Japan and he had an audience with Emperor Meiji in Tokyo. The Japan Society of London was founded in 1891 and soon afterwards, in 1894, the Anglo-Japanese Treaty of Trade and Navigation was signed. In addition, a series of special exhibitions and events offered the London public a glimpse of the charm of little-known Japan, most notably: 'The Japanese Native Village', a replica of a Japanese village centre, on show at Humphrey's Hall in Knightsbridge between 1885 and 1887 (full description in *The Survey of London*, Vol. XXX), as well, of course, as the famous Gilbert and Sullivan operetta *The Mikado* which opened in London in 1885. Somewhat later 'The Japan-British exhibition' was staged at White City in 1910 .

Yoshio arrived in London, in December 1897. He witnessed and benefited from these positive cultural exchanges between Tokyo and London. His first job, at the Japanese naval office reflected the rapprochement of the two countries. In his autobiography, *A Japanese Artist in London*, he mentions the 1902 Anglo-Japanese Alliance. At that time he lived in Dulwich/Norwood borders, recording that he and his flatmate 'often had walk in Dulwich Village and Streatham'. A year later he was advising and producing drawings for a play *The Darlings of the Gods: a Drama of Japan* by David Belasco (1853–1931) and John Luther Long (1861–1927), the Americans who had produced, to great acclaim in New York and London, the play *Madame Butterfly – A tragedy of Japan* (Puccini saw it in London in the summer of 1900 and was inspired to write his famous opera). *The Darling of the Gods*, performed at Her Majesty's Theatre, dealt with the difficult outcome of a controversial ban in Japan of sword-wearing for samurai (introduced in 1876).

The Streatham-based painter Jiro Osuga, on the other hand, was born in 1968 at

Right, top: Yoshio Markino, 'Outside St George's Hospital', watercolour reproduced in his book *A Japanese Artist in London* published in 1910. At that time the hospital was sited at Hyde Park Corner (it closed in 1980 and was relocated to Tooting); the building is now a hotel.

Right: Yoshio Markino, Earl's Court Station, watercolour reproduced in his book *A Japanese Artist in London* published in 1910.

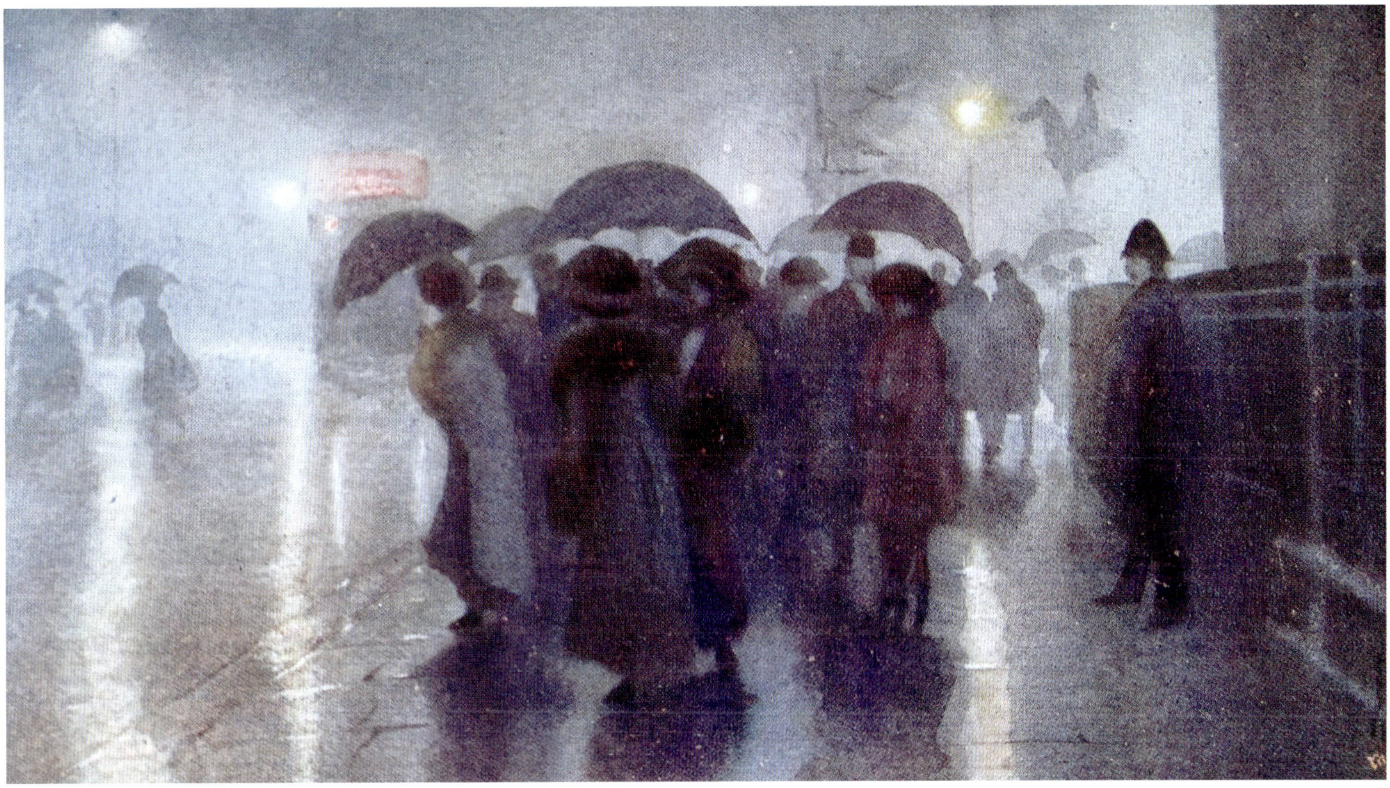

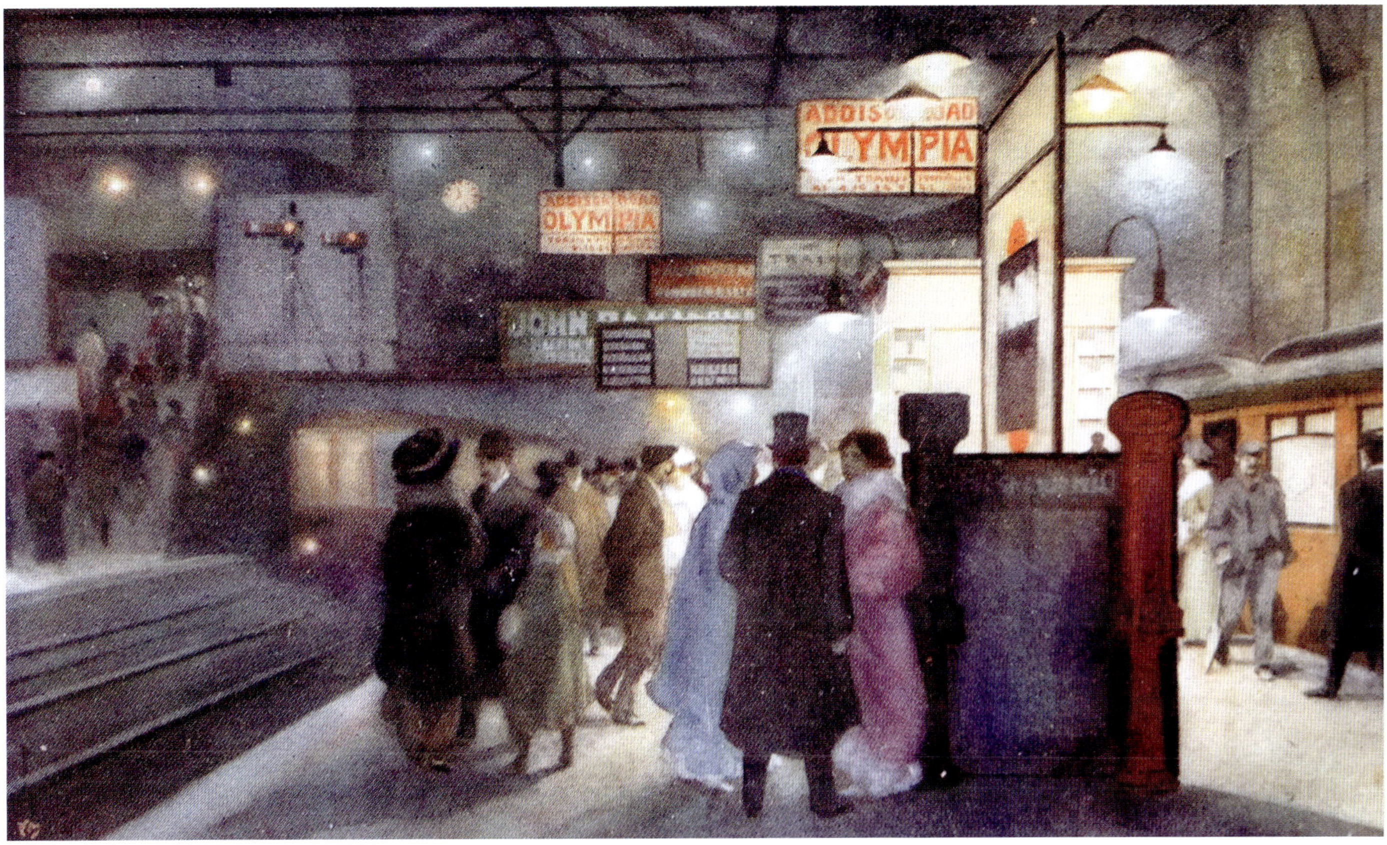

OLYMPIA
OLYMPIA
JOHN

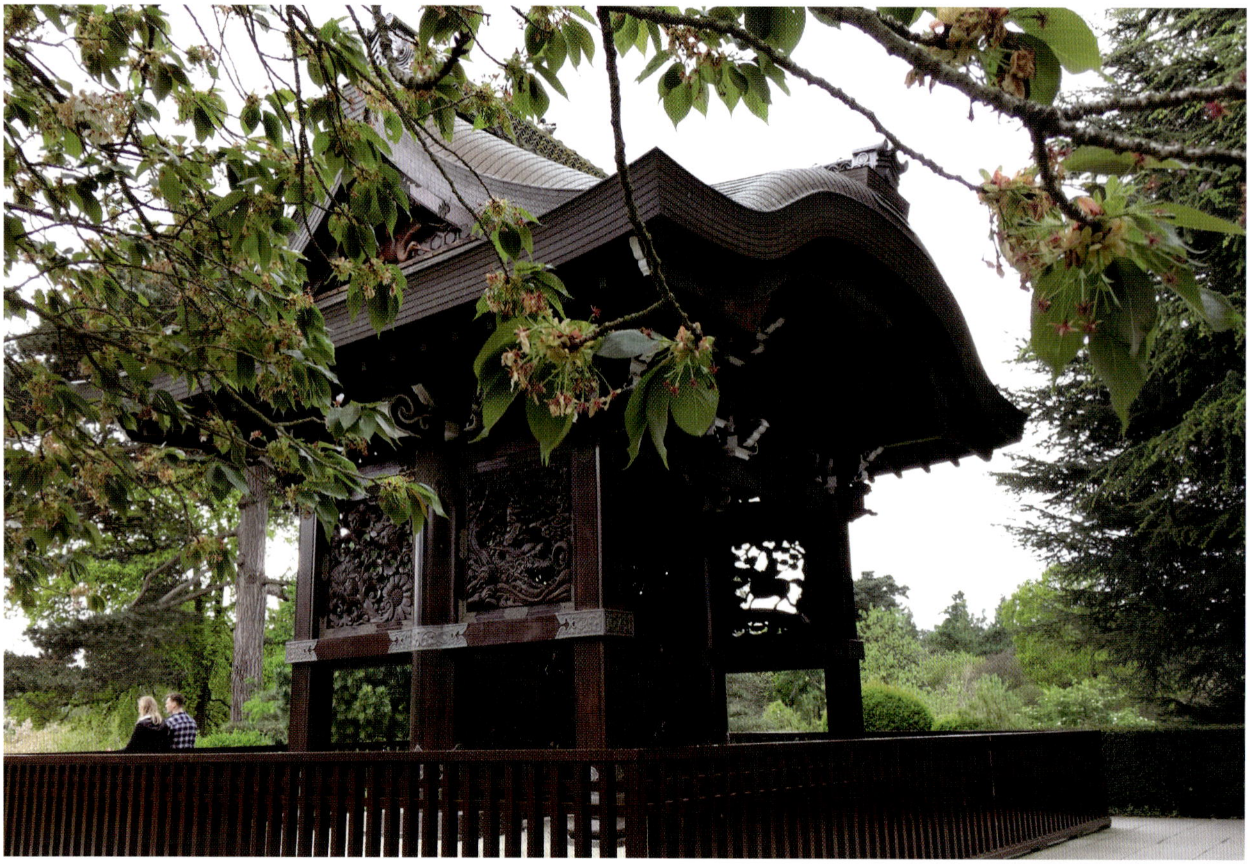

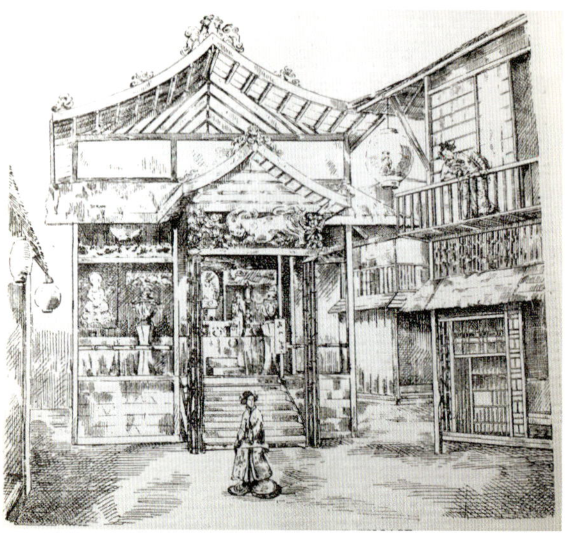

Above: This Japanese gate, re-erected in Kew Gardens in 1911, was created for the Japan-British exhibition of 1910.

Left: The Japanese village in Knightsbridge's Humphrey's Hall opened to the public on 10 January 1885. 'This sketch shows the Temple and the gentleman's house at the "Japanneries" at Humphrey's Hall' read the original caption. The altar of the Buddhist Temple is decorated with a shrine of Buddha. The village was an immediate success which was shattered four months later when hall and village burnt down. But the village was rebuilt and reopened at the end of that year; it flourished until 25 June 1887. *Photo from* The Building News, *23 January 1885, 121.*

a time when Japan and Britain had renewed normal relations after the dark days of the Second World War. Japan had not taken part in the 1948 Olympic Games held in London but the 1951 Peace Treaty of San Francisco had normalized relations between the two countries. Two years later the nineteen-year-old Crown Prince Akihito represented Japan at Elizabeth II's coronation and the British Council was established in Japan. In 1963 the University of Oxford introduced the study of Japanese in its Oriental Institute.

However, despite the similarity of circumstances between Jiro and Yoshio, the oeuvre of both artists is very different. They may well share London as a subject matter but they have contrasting ways of presenting it. Yoshio, fascinated by the London fog, produced many misty London scenes. He worked predominantly in watercolours, primarily as a magazine and book illustrator. Jiro on the other hand, works in oils, focusing on the human figure, and populating his paintings with fragments of the urban crowd – from the past and the present.

Japanese art

The two outstanding public collections of Japanese art in London are at the Victoria and Albert Museum and the British Museum. Both bear the names of their sponsors: the Toshiba Gallery at the V & A opened in 2015 (previous refurbishment: 1986) and the Mitsubishi Corporation Japanese Galleries at the British Museum opened in 2006 (previous incarnation: Konica-Minolta Gallery which opened in 1990). The V & A started collecting from the beginning, 1852, when it was called the Museum of Manufactures, then the South Kensington Museum – their collecting policy centered mostly on contemporary art, 'which attracted considerable criticism' remarked curator and historian Joe Earle. The historic material came later through the acquisition of experts' collections. The British Museum, formed in 1751, has a longer history with collections rich in very ancient artefacts.

However, Jiro's work bears no relationship either to 'traditional Japanese art' as embodied in the collections of the V & A and the British Museum or to 'contemporary Japanese art', which is thus described by London gallerist Yukiko Ito: 'There has not been enough opportunity here for Japanese artists, and so the general public tends to recognise only [Takashi] Murakami and [Yayoi] Kusama (*The Art Newspaper* 17 October 2014). Kusama was briefly discussed at the beginning of this section, while Takashi Murakami courts controversy by blurring the line between 'high' and 'low' art. This deliberately cursory look at contemporary Japanese art is intended to highlight Jiro's singular approach to painting his city of adoption.

Jiro Osuga – An appreciation

Jiro is a painter of place, people and ideas. His narrative style attracted the attention of the Japanese Embassy in 2011 and he was offered a show there. The project ran into difficulty when the Embassy insisted he removed all references to World War II in a painting which set out to illustrate 'cliché Japan' – all the things we instinctively associate with Japan, from Mount Fuji to geishas. Jiro's work is focused upon the world in which he lives: to ask him to change his perception of the world around him amounts to an attack on his integrity as an artist.

He is indefatigable about depicting the two worlds he knows best – London and Tokyo; they exist side by side. He respects their different traditions, finding ever more resourceful ways of representing them but with no attempt at integrating them. There is, however, one unifying factor: it is Jiro himself – at times presented as the odd one out in the series focusing on 'The Person Who …', drawing embarrassing attention to himself as he stumbles across various environments – a bar, a tube carriage, a concert, even a deserted church (see p. 196). Alternatively, he paints himself as a God-like figure – a calm, non-judgmental, detached but interested observer of human life (overleaf).

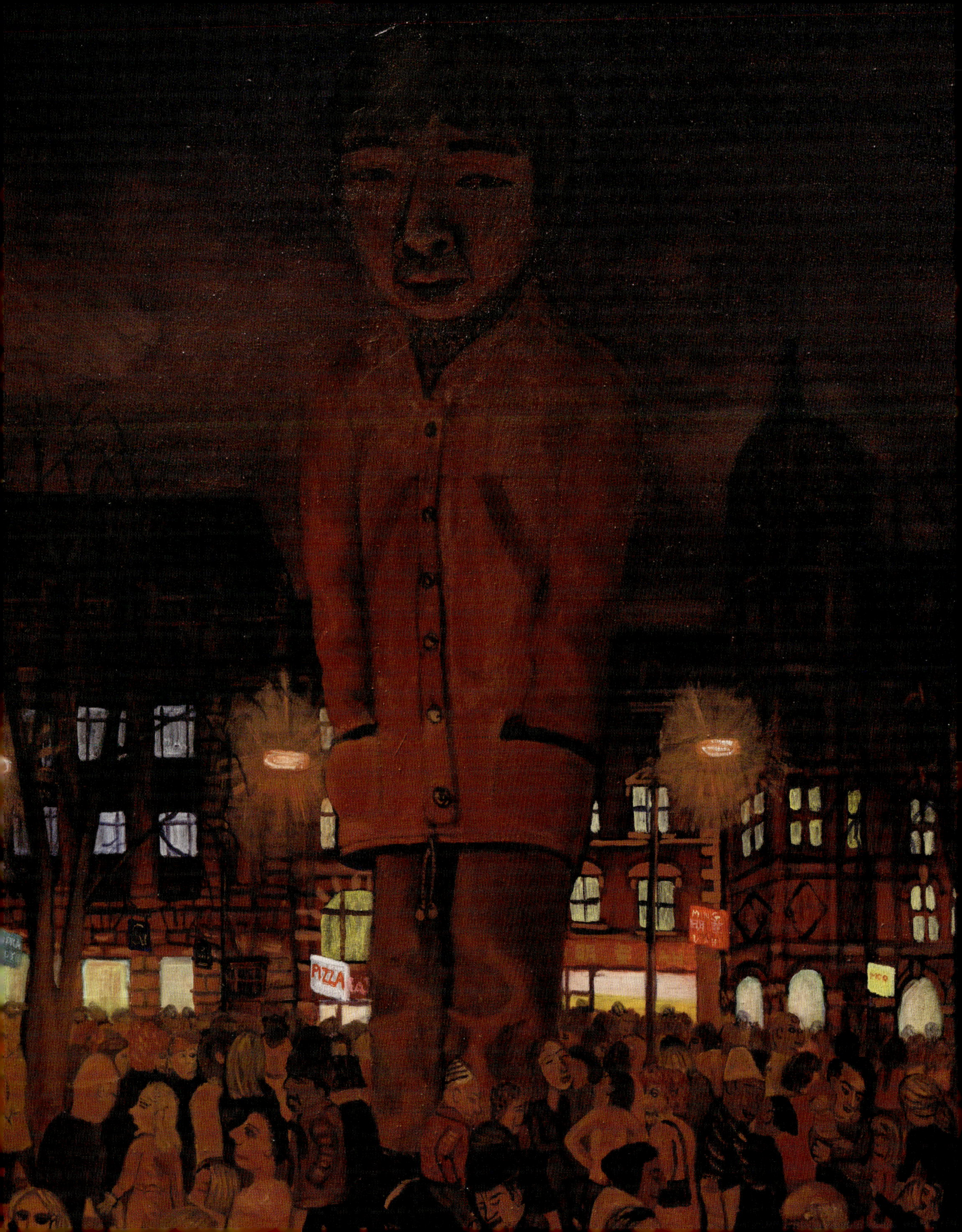
PIZZA

JIRO OSUGA: I AM AN IMMIGRANT

Mireille Galinou: You were four years old when your family moved from Tokyo to Lagos (1973), six when you first came to live in Bexleyheath, and eight years old when you and your family returned to Tokyo. What were the reasons for all this travelling?

Jiro Osuga: My father worked for Mitsui & Co., one of those big Japanese corporations with offices all over the world.

MG: Do you have any memories of London from that time?

JO: I remember quite a lot. This was the fabled hot summer of 1976. We rented a huge, somewhat decrepit bungalow whose overgrown garden backed onto Danson Park in Bexleyheath. There was a hole in the fence through which you could go straight into the park. The previous owner was a railway enthusiast, and there was a narrow gauge railway track complete with a trolley running through the garden.

School was idyllic compared to the hell that awaited me back in Japan the following year. I don't remember doing anything remotely academic – just colouring in drawings. Although my brother, myself and the owner's son of the local Tandoori restaurant were the only non-white pupils in the entire school, there was no serious racist abuse, and when you are young you pick up the language fast.

I once won the school painting prize, and the winning painting (a big nativity scene) was displayed in a shop window on Broadway in Bexleyheath.

MG: You were back again in London at the age of twelve. You did not know at that time that you would not return to live in Japan. Were you pleased to be back in London? What are your recollections from that time?

JO: I don't remember having any strong emotions about it. When you are a child you just take whatever is thrown at you without demur. It was four years since we were last in London – a very long time in the life of a twelve-year-old. My English language had vanished in the intervening years, but it came back quickly without much effort.

Our new home in Edgware was quite different from Bexleyheath. Part of Jewish north London, both our next-door neighbours were Jewish, as were many of the staff and pupils at the local comprehensive I attended, which also hosted a whole range of other ethnicities. In Japan I had been a struggling student, but in London, I discovered that I did quite well if I applied myself, and became a bit of a swot, I'm afraid.

During my early teens, before I got seriously into painting, I was obsessed with Romano-British archaeology. I used to travel to Roman sites in England on my own and compile reports illustrated with my own drawings.

My later teens were not fun. I increasingly isolated myself from people and the world – a big mistake, from which I still don't feel I have fully recovered.

MG: You went through the English schooling system. Does that make you a little bit English or at least a Londoner?

JO: I don't think I will ever think of myself as English, or even British (there is a subtle

Jiro Osuga, 'In Town at Night', 1999, oil on canvas, 94 x 73.5 cm. One of a small number of pictures where the artist depicts himself as a gentle giant looking down on the city. In the day-time versions Jiro positions himself behind buildings; but at night time he emerges to stand amongst the crowd. *Private collection. Photo: Flowers Gallery.*

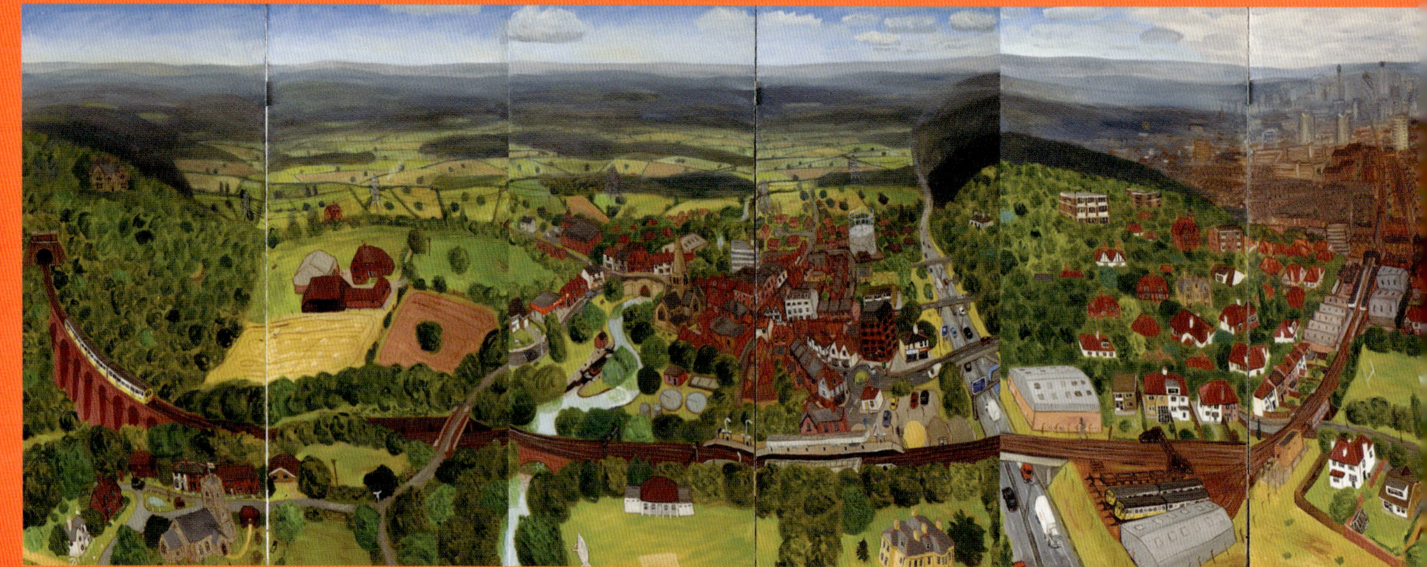

Jiro Osuga, 'The Great Train Journey', free standing screen, 2001, oil on canvas, 180 x 480 cm front (this page) and back (next page).
This six-fold screen is painted on both sides. One side shows a railway line snaking through the English countryside. Walk around to the other side and you suddenly find yourself in a wintry Japanese landscape. 'This unexpected shift represents the culture shock I experience each time I shuttle between Japan and the UK'. *Flowers Gallery.*

distinction between the two), but I am quite comfortable being called a Londoner. My upbringing has been such that I probably do have streaks of Englishness (whatever that is) in my make-up, but then there is a substantial dollop of Japanese-ness too, along with other qualities that derive from God-knows-where which probably have nothing to do with any specific geographical location. I favour the idea of multiple-identity, of drawing one's sense of oneself from a multiplicity of different sources. I think this is actually the case for most people in our modern interconnected world if you think about it, not just for people like me who grew up in a different country from that in which they were born. Mono-culturalism is a nineteenth-century romantic delusion.

MG: Do you have a British passport?

JO: No, but I will probably get one before I die. It makes no sense to be disenfranchised in a society in which you live and contribute.

MG: At the age of nineteen you decided to stay in London rather than return to Tokyo with your parents. It seems that you did this for the sake of your art studies (see p. 201)? Is that so?

JO: It just so happened that my father got his marching orders just as I was about to start my studies at Chelsea School of Art. It wasn't like I was made to stand on the edge of a precipice and choose between My Country and My Art. I simply drifted along the course that offered least resistance.

MG: Your first residence as an independent Londoner was in Streatham: Uplands Halls of Residence in Leigham Court Road, which was demolished to make way for Uplands Care Home. What do you remember from that time?

JO: Loneliness and desolation. Spacious and orderly, the Halls, run by the soon-to-be-abolished ILEA (The Inner London Education Authority), was quite civilised as these facilities go. The lady in charge was kindly, and I formed one lasting friendship there.

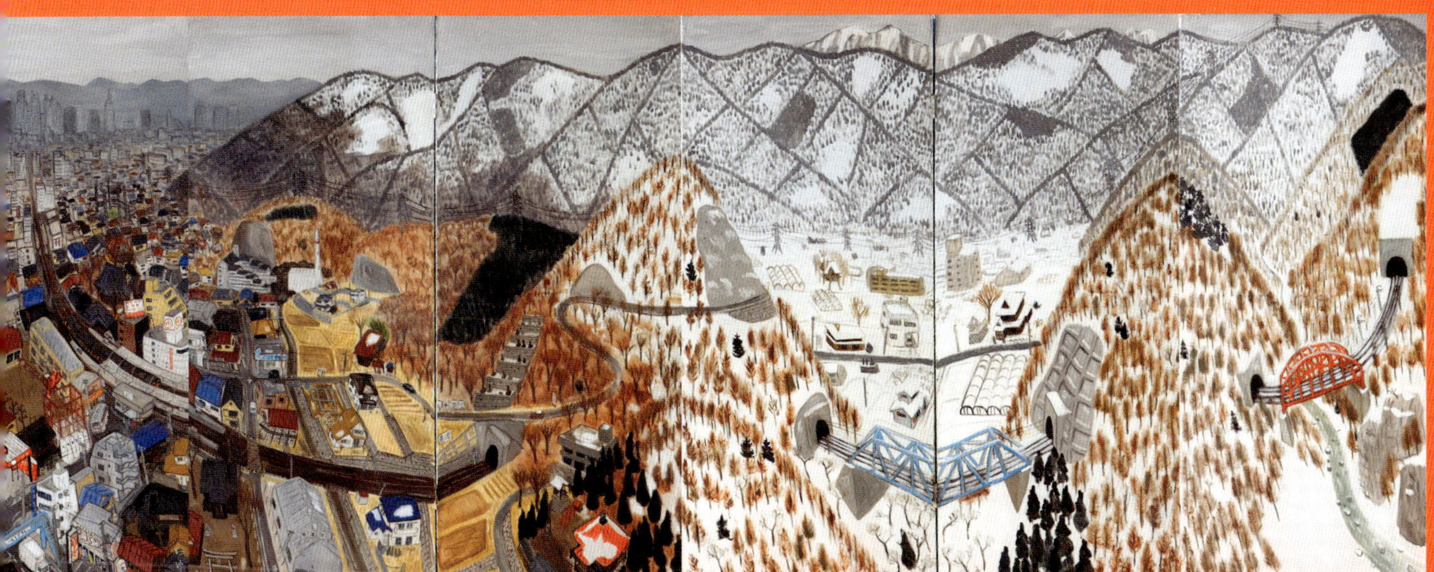

But on the whole I didn't make the most of my college years. Still deep in my isolationist cocoon, I chose to hide my difficulties behind my canvases. Strange to remember this now, but I didn't once set foot in the student union bar at Chelsea. Things improved a little bit at the Royal College of Art. I drank at the bar there about five times.

MG: You go to Tokyo every year at Christmas time and you spend a month there. You therefore switch from one culture to the other with ease and regularity. Do you feel a little schizophrenic or do you take the best of both worlds?

JO: It always feels strange for the first few days after landing in Tokyo, or in London after a stint in Japan. You see everything in double – each time you see a lamp post in Tokyo, for instance, you are reminded of the equivalent in London and vice versa. But that sensation fades with time. In the end human beings are much the same the world over. Punch them in the nose and they will all scream "ouch!" – albeit in different languages. Have anthropologists yet encountered a tribe, even in the remotest parts of the planet, where they smile and thank you when they are punched?

It is useful though to have a dual perspective on the world. You know with certainty that nationalistic bigots on both sides who claim the unique superiority of their own culture over others are just plain wrong.

MG: Streatham has rightly been labelled a multi-cultural neighbourhood. What sort of impact – if any – does that have on your life?

JO: The impact this has on me is that it has no impact. I can be myself walking the streets of Streatham without worrying about fitting in or modifying my behaviour in any way. In Streatham I'm just another foreign-born resident of far-eastern extraction. I feel much the same anywhere within London, but not so once I step outside the M25. On country walks in Sussex, I feel self-conscious when I meet other (invariably white) walkers on the footpath.

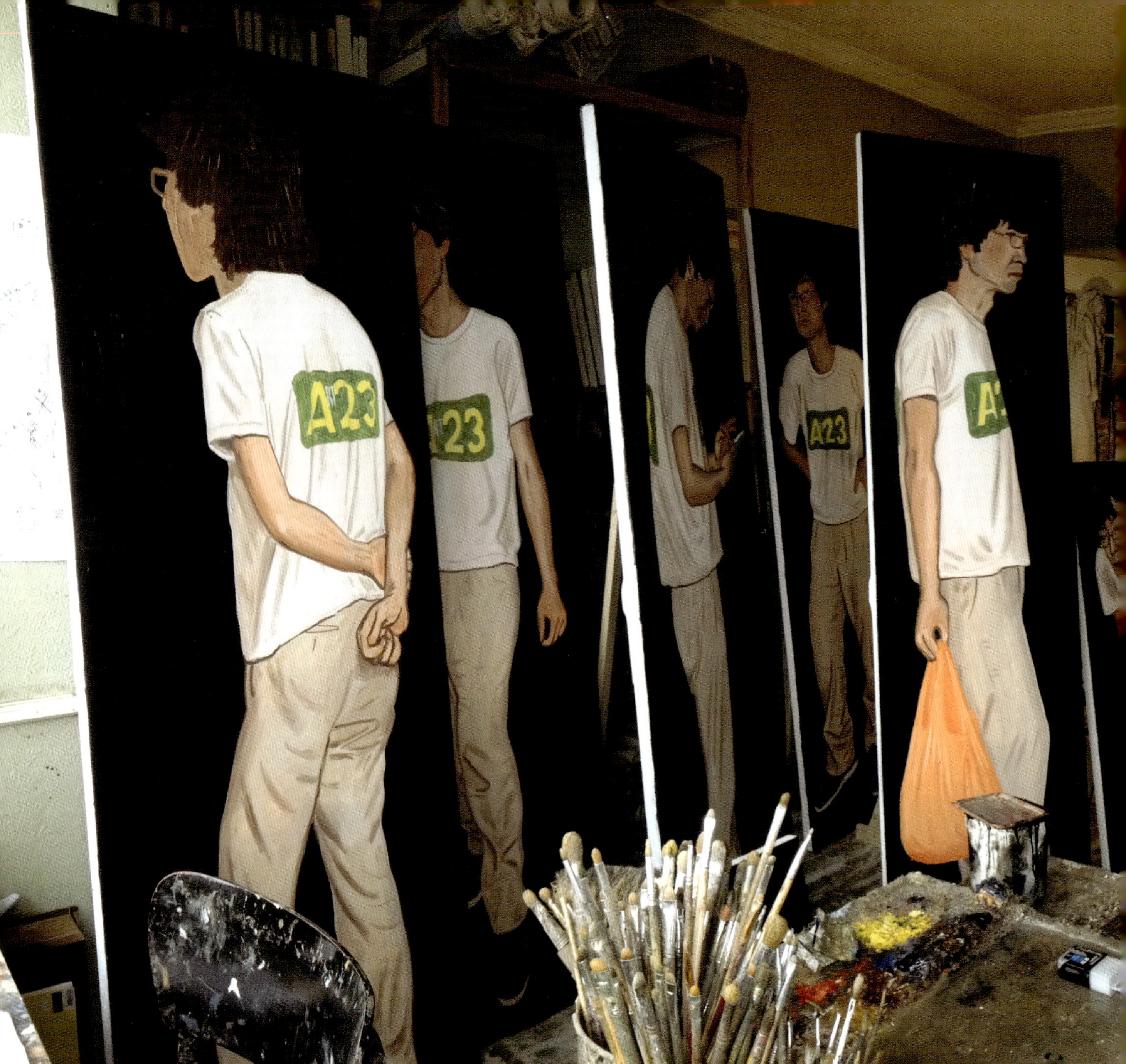

'The Man of the Crowd': Jiro Osuga's contribution to Art23 in the 2016 Streatham Festival. The artist painted fourteen full-size portraits which were placed in various shops such as Café Barcelona (see p xx) or institutions such as the Streatham Library.

MG: Your latest Streatham project is a series of life-size self-portraits which were scattered throughout various shops/institutions along the High Road in July 2016: the latest example in a large body of work dealing with you as the main subject for your pictures. Could this, at some level, represent a search for identity?

JO: 'The Man of the Crowd' could be read in several different ways, but it was primarily meant to be about the impossibility of ever penetrating the minds of other people, rather than a quest for personal identity. I could well have painted someone other than myself, but couldn't be bothered to look for a model who would pose for me.

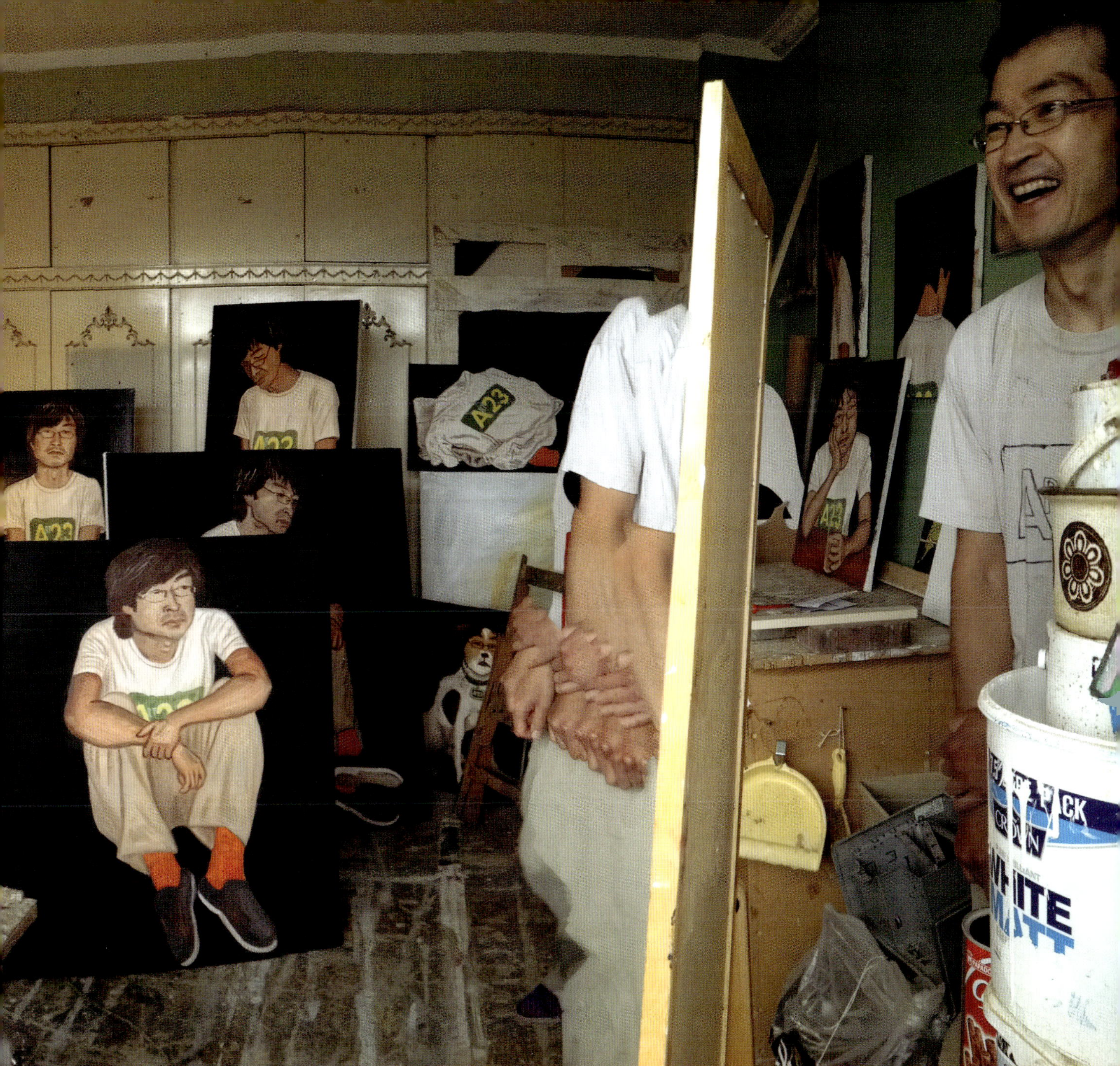

This photograph was taken in Jiro's studio and the artist is there too, on the right hand side, laughing. The blurred figure next to him also shows Jiro as he walked to the corner while the photograph was being taken. © *Mireille Galinou.* Also see pp. 166–167.

True, I do appear in my other paintings with such frequency that it's almost pathological. But again, I have always justified this on the grounds that I am trying to make paintings that are true to my personal experience, rather than in terms of a search for identity.

That said, from much of my work, you do get a sense of someone adrift in a bewildering world looking for something in which he might find peace and comfort. Perhaps this is a search for identity, if by identity we do not mean a politicised notion about belonging to this or that cultural group, but finding inner peace within oneself – finding oneself.

JIRO OSUGA: MY TOKYO

For many years I used to hate Japan. It largely stemmed from the horrendous few years I spent as a child there after my family's return from Africa and Britain. A foreigner in all but name and looks, I barely spoke the language and was unacquainted with Japanese customs. I struggled to fit in at school, and was mercilessly bullied. You expect cruelty from kids, but the teachers were no better, and the highly structured regime at school had no means of catering for failing pupils like me. Many years have passed since, but as a country's schools are a microcosm of its society at large, I think there were good reasons for my continued wariness of my country. I have never lived in Japan as an adult.

Over the last 25 years though, ever since my parents returned to live in Tokyo, leaving me stranded in London, I have been paying them a visit every Christmas, and in the process slowly re-acquainting myself with Japan. This involved a very conscious effort mediated by my work. On each visit, I would roam the city, sketchbook and pencil in hand, observing everything from manhole covers to the interior of train carriages with the fresh eyes of an outsider. Over the years I have compiled a huge visual dossier of all things Japanese, which I would then use to make paintings back in my London studio. Some of these are illustrated here.

To start with, it was the differences from my habitual environment in the UK that fascinated me – how even small things like the designs of street-side railings and bus shelters reflect a different sensibility and history. But in more recent years this has evolved into something approaching affection for certain aspects of Japanese culture. It might be the immaculately crafted confectionery stalls in department store food halls (this should top the must-see list of every tourist in Tokyo, not the Imperial Palace or Sensoji Temple), or the gleaming, punctual subway trains. I even enjoy looking at the tangle

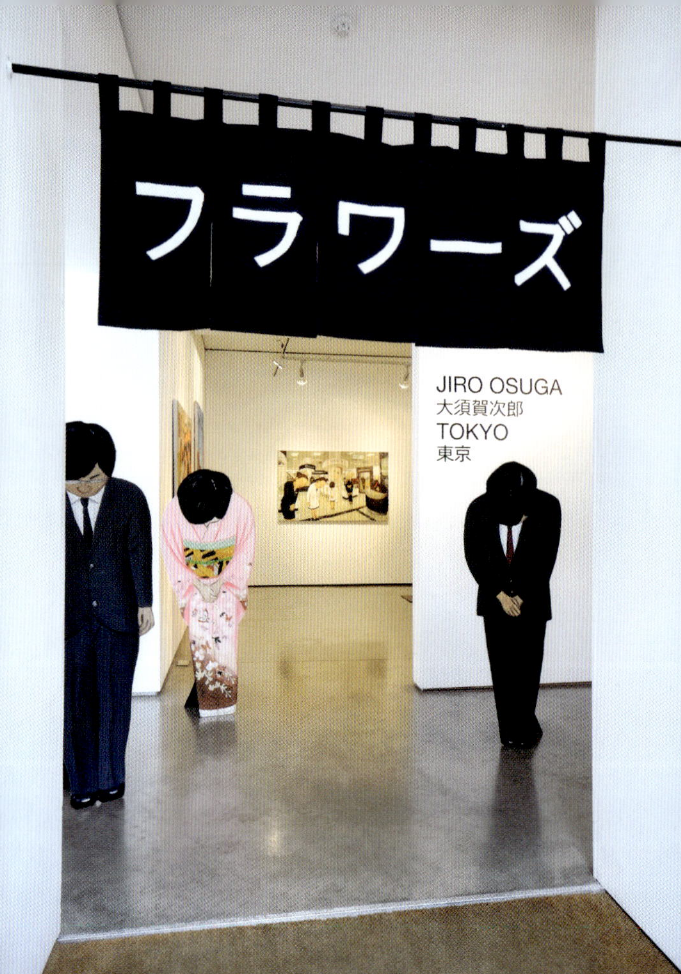

Above: Jiro Osuga's Tokyo exhibition, Flowers Gallery (Kingsland Road), London, March 2011. At the entrance of the exhibition, visitors passed under a traditional noren curtain and were greeted by life-sized bowing figures. The show also included a fortune-telling stall, a walk-over aerial view of Tokyo, and a corner where visitors could try on masks of Japanese characters. *Photo: Flowers Gallery*

Right: Jiro Osuga, 'Tokyo Street Scene', 2004, acrylic on canvas, 180 x 150 cm. This is a fairly typical back street in Tokyo. I love the intimate scale of the houses, and the fact that you are never more than a few feet away from the lives of its inhabitants. I also enjoy the way on a grey winter's day, the drab concrete of the streets brings out the colours of objects such as a postman's bright red scooter or a blue plastic bucket *Private collection.* *Photo: Flowers Gallery.*

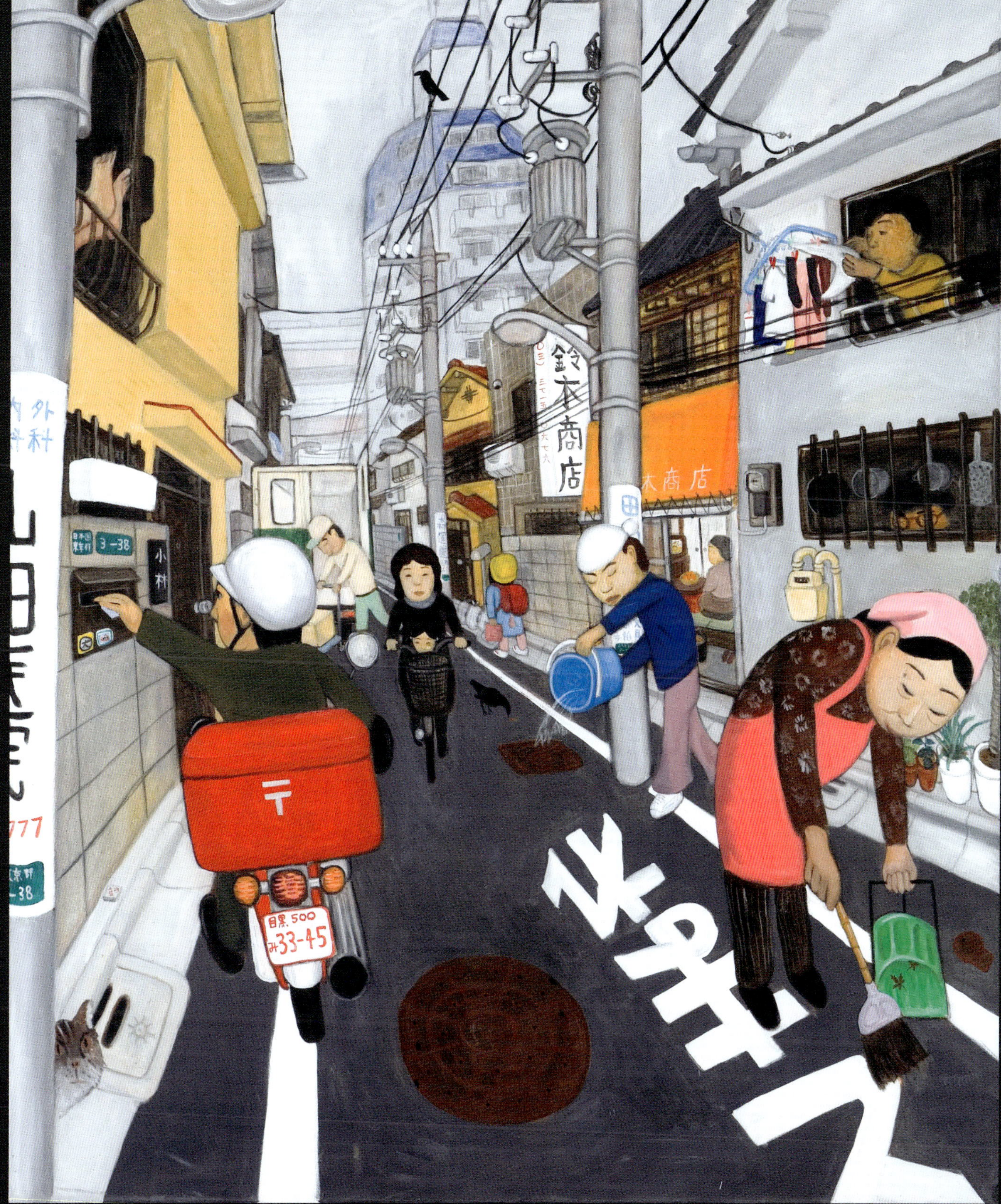

外科
鈴木商店
木商店
3-38
小村
目黒 500
み33-45

of overhead electricity cables that criss-cross above urban streets, which I used to consider an eyesore and a national disgrace. I now won't deny that they do some things better in Japan than in the West – the universal courtesy with which you are received in shops, or the cleanliness of the streets and public transport for a start.

In 2011 my Tokyo paintings were brought together in a show at Flowers Gallery which recreated a corner of the city in the Shoreditch gallery. The show for me represented a summation of my efforts to come to terms with my native culture.

Yet if truth be told, I remain detached from Japan. The insularity of Japanese society is such that anyone who spends a substantial amount of time outside it is forever excluded from it. I have no friends in Tokyo, and have never exhibited my work there. I remain an outsider looking in fascinated from the other side of a pane of glass. But then that is not dissimilar to the position I occupy in London. Here too, I am an observer – *An Anthropologist on Mars*, to use the title of a well-known book by neurologist Oliver Sacks.

Below: Jiro Osuga, 'The Person Who.... on the Tokyo Subway', 2000, oil on canvas, 200 x 147 cm. 'Everyone's staring at you! I have never quite faced such a reception on the Tokyo subway, but the painting does express something of the gulf that still exists between me and Japan. I am fascinated by Tokyo trains though. I love riding on the extreme front and rear carriages, where the train driver's cab is glazed, so that you get a driver's-eye-view of the tracks as the train hurtles into a station'. *© Jiro Osuga, private collection. Photo: Flowers Gallery.*

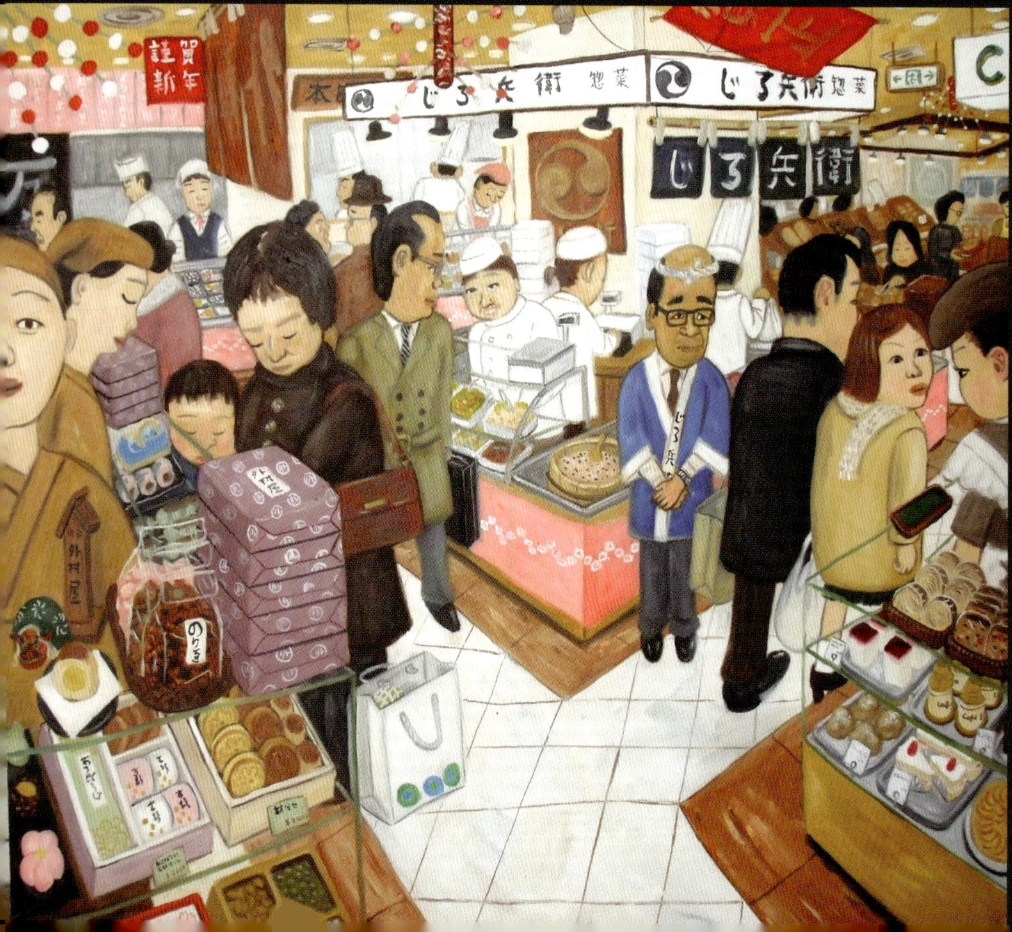

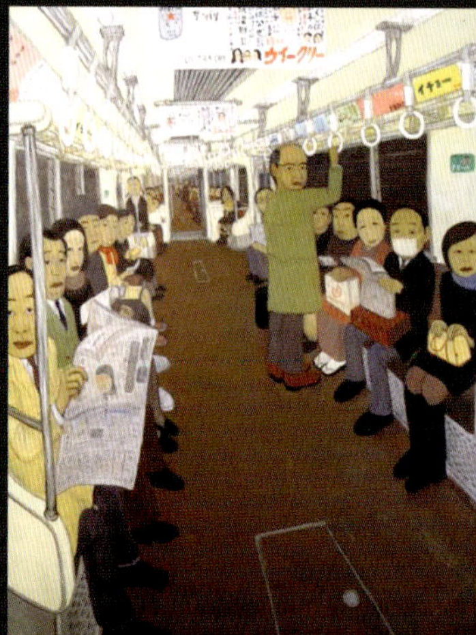

Left: Jiro Osuga, 'Depachika', 2009, oil on canvas, 130.5 x 149 cm. 'My attempt to capture something of the dazzling array of beautifully presented foodstuffs on offer in food halls that occupy the basements of Japanese department stores. "Depa" of Depachika is short for 'Department Store', and ' "chika" means subterranean'. *Private collection. Photo: Flowers Gallery.*

Right: Jiro Osuga, 'A Shopping Street', 2010, oil on canvas, 180 x 150 cm. *Flowers Gallery*

Below: Jiro Osuga, 'Tokyo Walk', 2013, oil on canvas, 73 x 80 cm. Tokyo backstreets, such as this one, are criss-crossed by a dense tangle of overhead electrical cables. *Private collection. Photo: Flowers Gallery.*

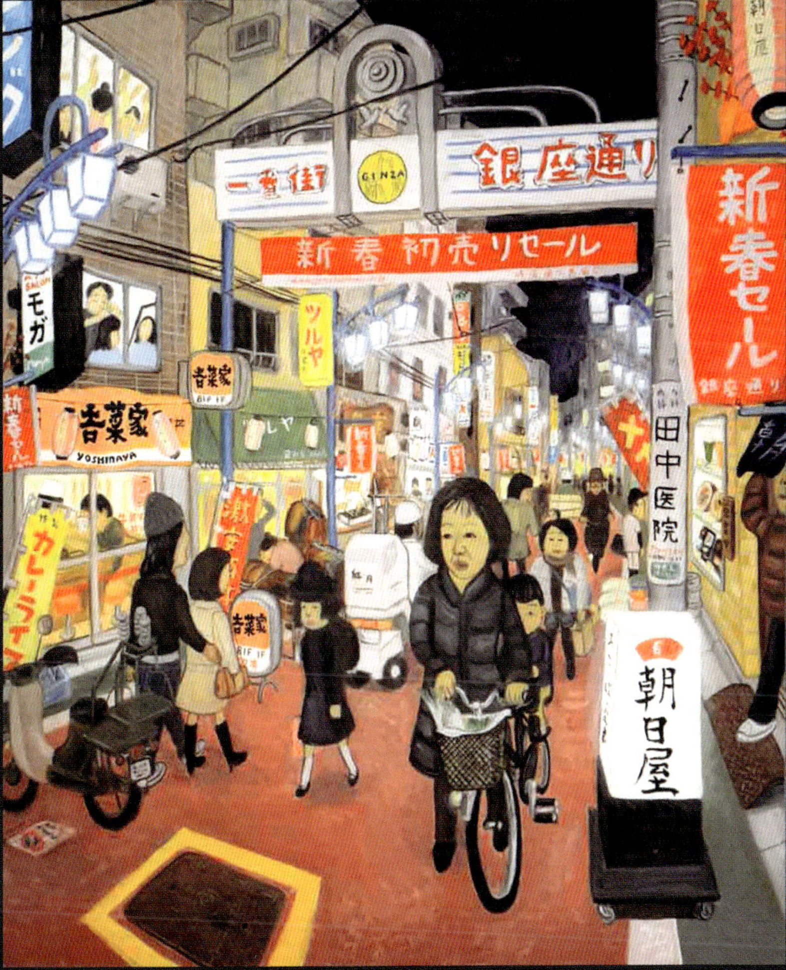

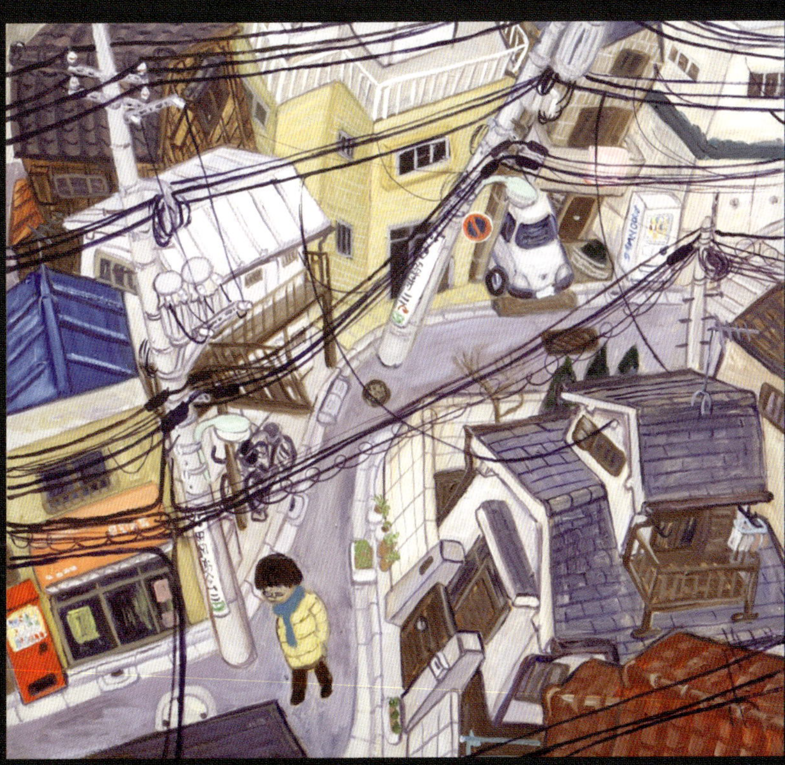

8.

JIRO OSUGA
A Chronology

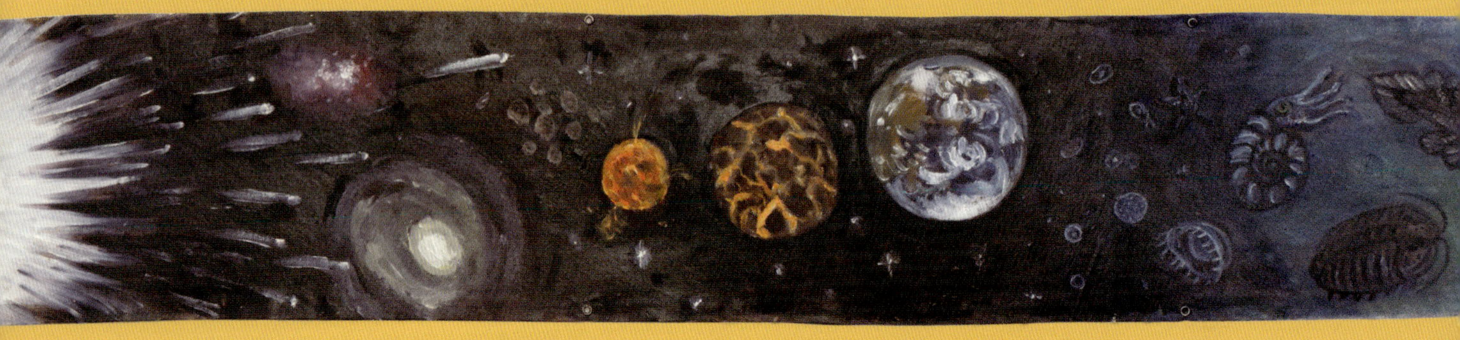

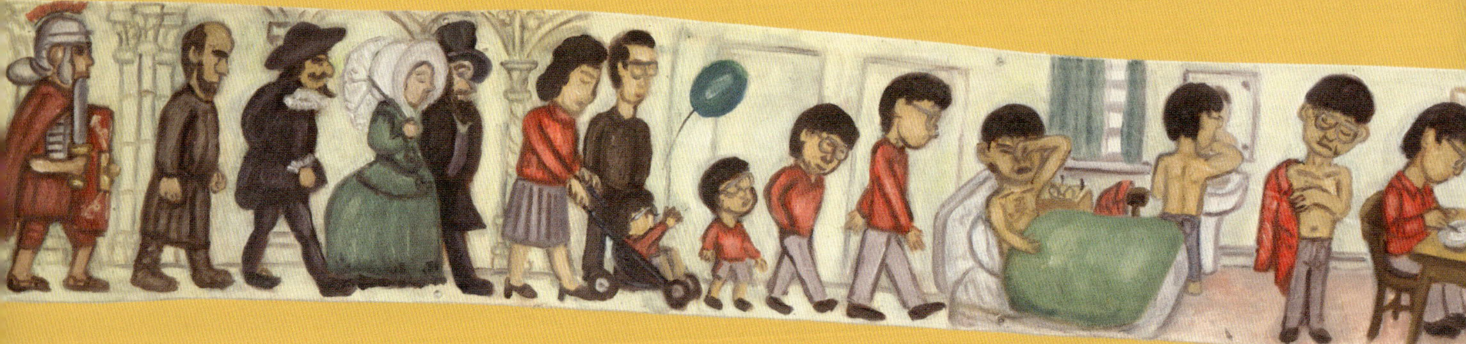

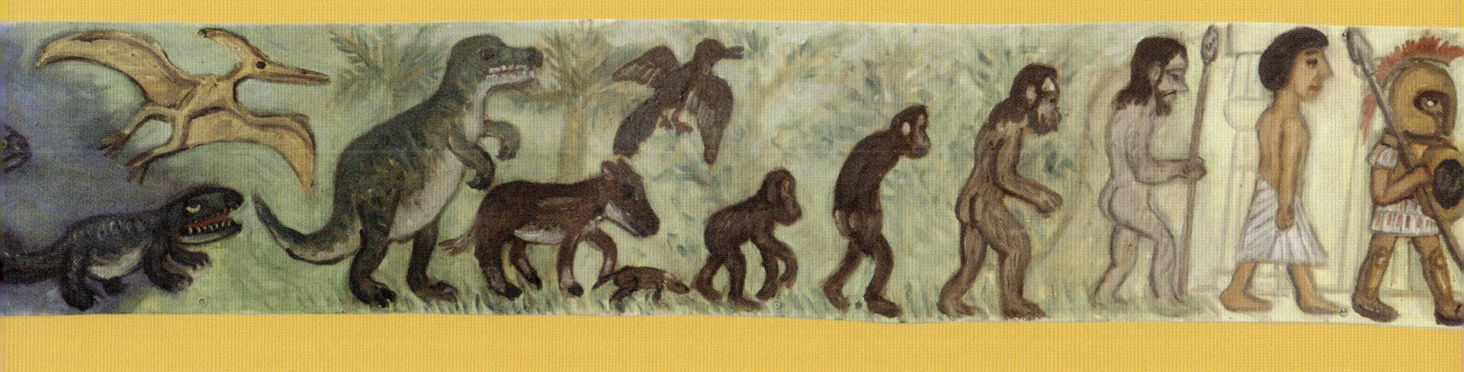

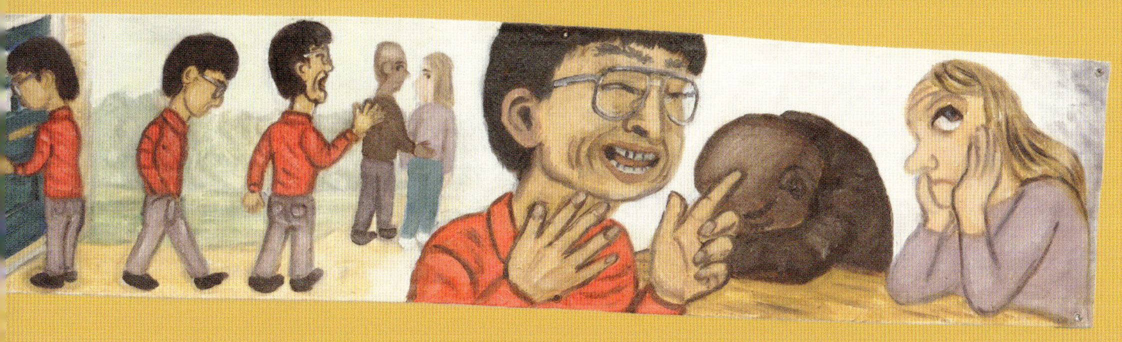

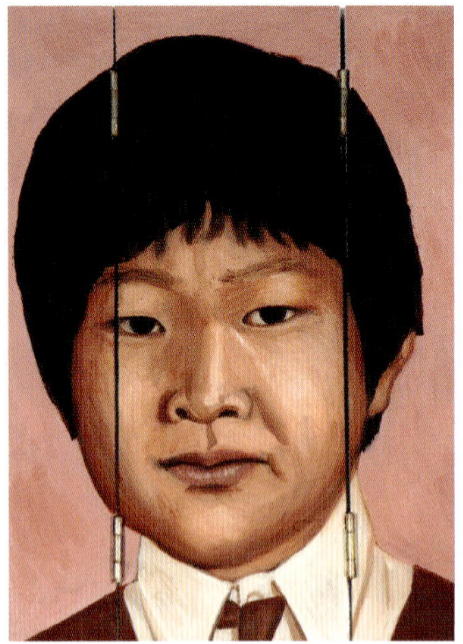

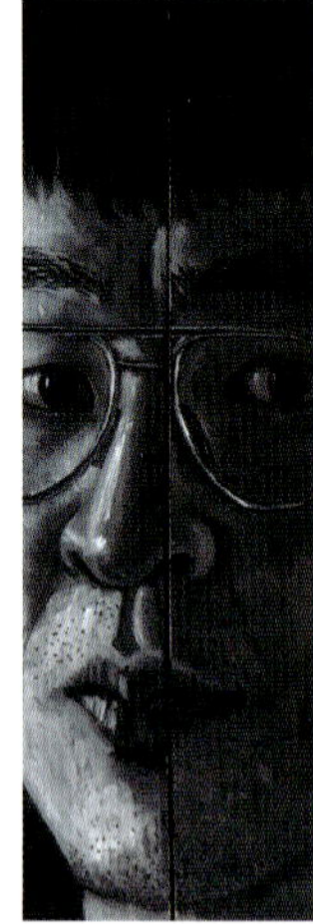

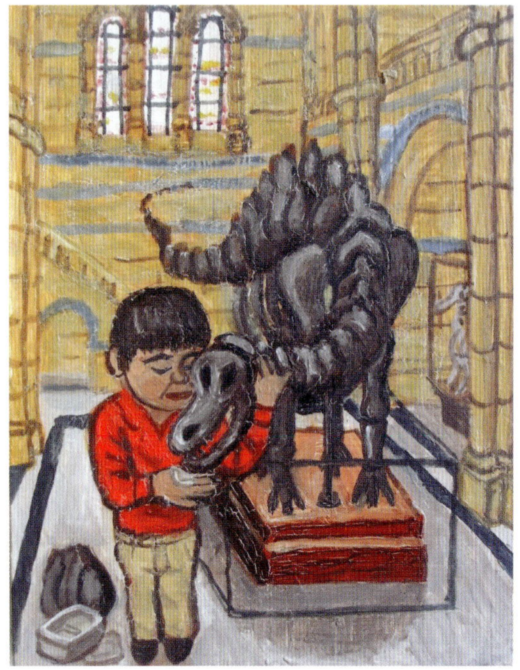

1968 Born in Tokyo, Japan, second of three children (two sons and one daughter), to Toshio and Yoshiko Osuga.

1973 Family moves to Lagos, Nigeria. A pupil at the American School in Lagos.

1975 Moves to London (Bexleyheath), attends the local primary school.

1977 Returns to Japan.

'On the whole I think it was a privilege to have had an international upbringing. You learn from the outset never to take cultural certainties for granted. But now and then, I do suffer from a kind of nostalgia for a sense of rootedness and continuity that I lack. Traditional culture has a beautiful built-in coherence. Those born into it have at least something to rebel against should they choose to go their own way. But trans-nationals like me lack any such footing, and anything we might concoct ourselves will always be a discordant assemblage of this and that element scrabbled together from disparate places.'

1980 Moves back to London with family. Lives in Edgware, north London, where he attends the local school.

'I think school is human rights abuse. For the most part the modern system remains true to its late nineteenth-century origins – a purveyor of standardised cannon fodder for the industrial state. Even the much vaunted claim that it teaches children how to get on with people fundamentally only amounts to inculcating respect for authority and the rule of the strong over the meek. I hated every minute of school and still well remember the gut-wrenching feeling as the end of the long summer break approached.'

1986 Attends Foundation Art Course at St Martin's School of Art in London. The course, though under-resourced, proves eye-opening.

1987 Family returns to Japan. Remains in the UK on his own. First lives in Streatham, at Uplands Halls of Residence on Leigham Court Road, now demolished. Thereafter

Previous pages:
'A Long Story', 2007, oil on canvas, 23 x 460 cm. This extremely long painting represents the entire history of the Universe from the artist's perspective. Starting with the Big Bang, it shows in succession the evolution of life, the entirety of human history and the artist's life story, concluding with Jiro boring his friends to death by regaling them with the story so far.
Flowers Gallery.

Top left: 'The Inner Child II', 2006, oil on board, 30 x 26 cm. The outer monochrome panels of this hinged painting showing an older Jiro open up to reveal the artist as a child in full colour inside. It was painted in memory of Jiro's school friend Ian Menzies who died tragically young, and was originally meant to be bequeathed to the school in Edgware where the two friends met.
Private collection.
Photo: Flowers Gallery.

Left: 'Dippy', 2016, oil on board, 22.5 x 18 cm. The setting of this painting is the Natural History Museum in South Kensington, a place redolent with childhood associations.
Photo: Flowers Gallery.

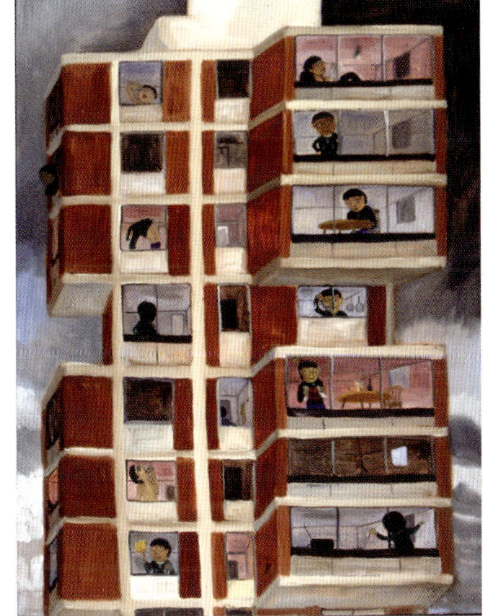

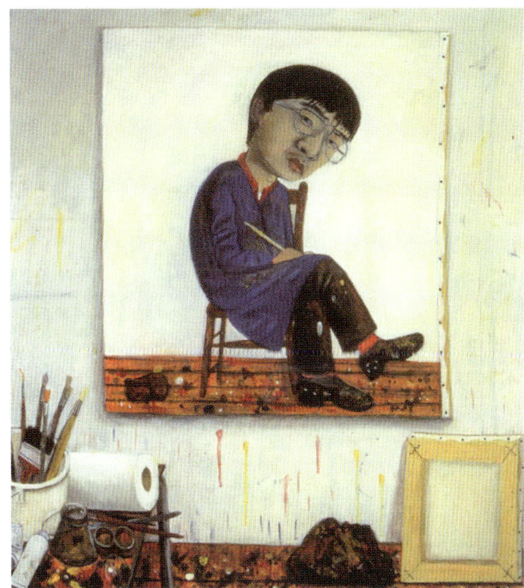

Right: 'Tower Block Dweller', 1998, oil on canvas, 131 x 100 cm. A freely imagined view of the tower block in Canada Estate, Rotherhithe, Jiro's home between 1995 and 1998. *© Jiro Osuga, Museum of London. Photo: Flowers Gallery.*

Far right: 'Portrait Painting', 1999, oil on canvas, 91.5 x 85 cm. *Private collection. Photo: Flowers Gallery.*

Below: Jiro Osuga on the cover of the last issue of *Art and Cities*, The London Arts Café Magazine, spring 2008. The oil on canvas, 'Twin Towns', 1997, illustrates the artist's allegiance to two cities: London (left) and Tokyo (right).

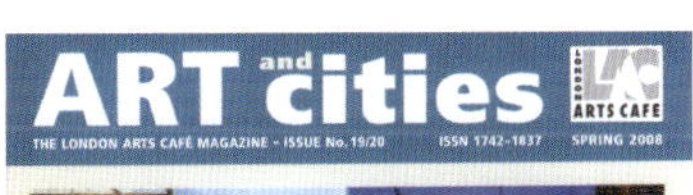

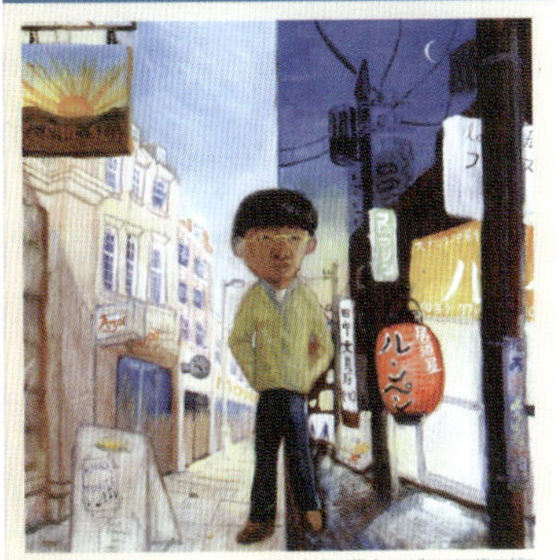

moves around different lodgings, mainly in south London, including Balham, Blackheath, Rotherhithe and Highbury.

1987–1990 Studies painting at Chelsea School of Art, London (BA course). Does not enjoy student life, and makes no friends.

1990–1992 Continues studies at the Royal College of Art, London, on the MA course. Meets two important teachers: Ken Kiff and Timothy Hyman. Also meets art dealer Matthew Flowers who would later represent him (Flowers East Gallery).

1992 Rents first studio after leaving college in Pixley Street, Limehouse, east London.

1992–1994 Studio at Lewisham Art House, near Goldsmiths College, south east London, where he becomes heavily involved with the running of the co-operative studios.

1994–1996 Studio at the Paragon Centre, near the Old Kent Road, London.

1995 First solo exhibition at Gallery M, Hackney, east London.

1996–2000 Studio at SANA, now Bussey Building, Peckham, south London.

'I am a contemporary of the YBA (Young British Artists) – but the whole phenomenon has passed me by with a comprehensiveness that is almost comical. Did all those wild parties and (supposed) creative ferment really go on in the self-same city that I live in? Cooped up in my studio and still making paintings, a medium long consigned to the dustbin of art history by the avant-garde, I blithely carried on doing my own thing, oblivious to the supposed re-birth of contemporary British art.'

1999 Solo show with Flowers Gallery, Santa Monica, California.

2000–2006 Active committee member of arts group, the London Arts Café.

2001 First solo exhibition at Flowers Gallery (Flowers East), London. Thereafter has solo shows with them every two years or so.

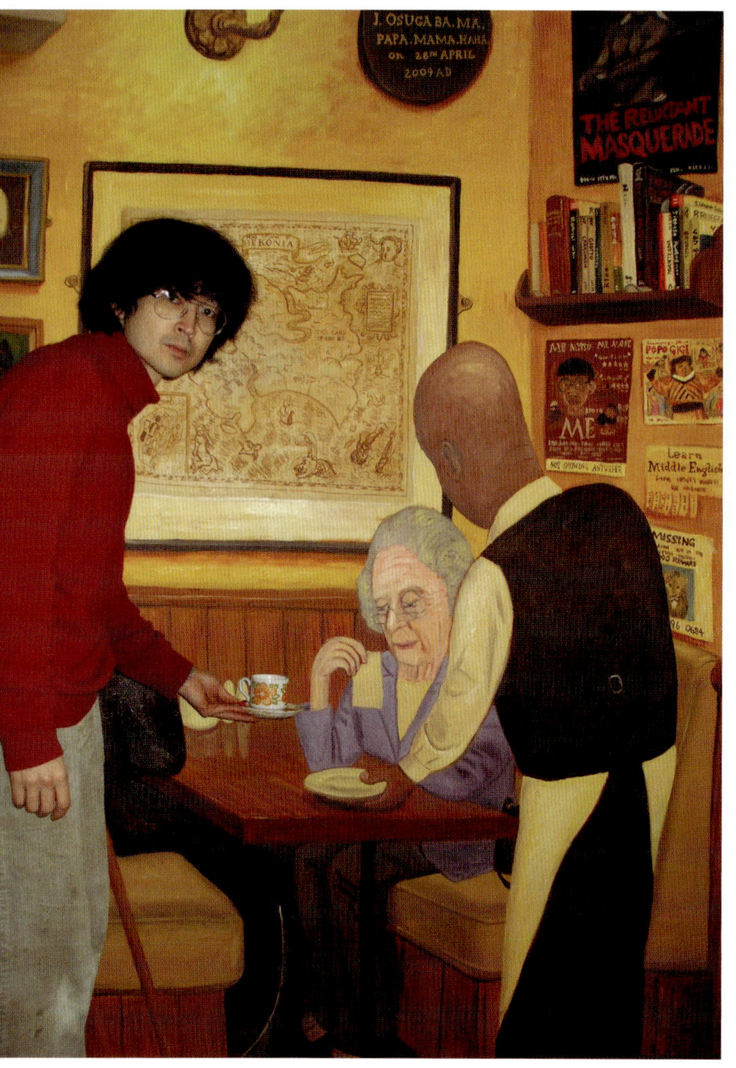

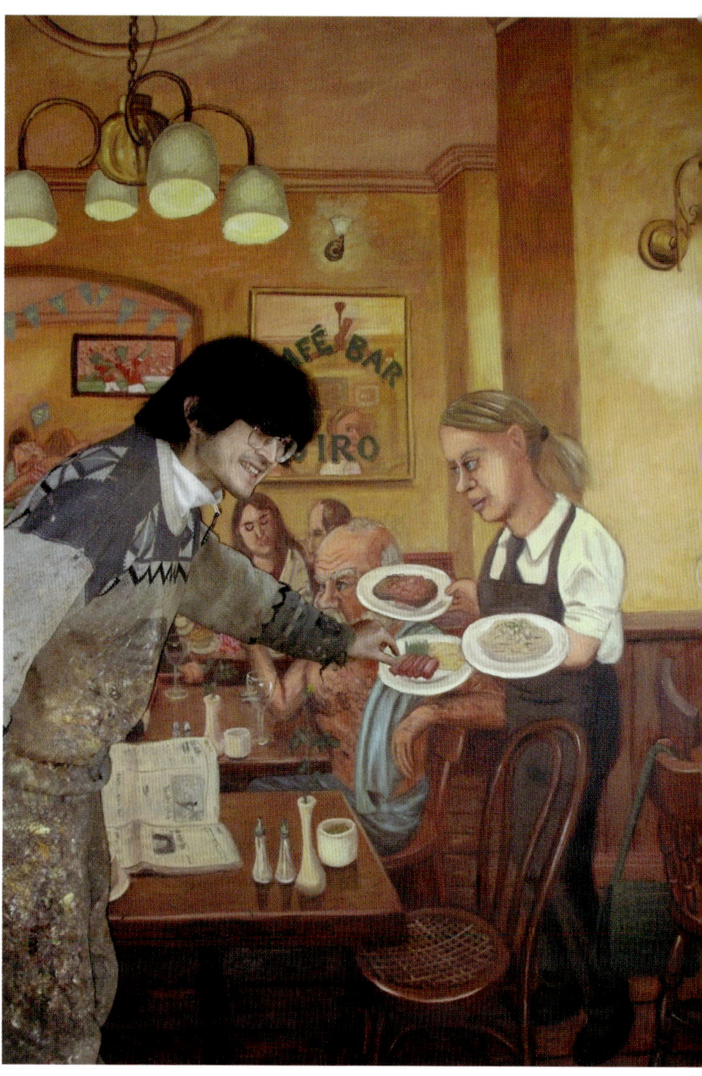

Jiro Osuga at lighter moments in his studio while working on 'Café Jiro' in 2008.
Photos: Jiro Osuga.

2003 Returns to live in Streatham (Woodbourne Avenue).

2009 Café Jiro exhibition at Flowers' Gallery (Cork Street), London, an ambitious immersive installation (see pp. 154ff).

2013, 2014, 2015, 2016 Participates in Streatham Festival (see pp. 164–167).

2015 Solo show at Flowers Gallery, New York.

2017 Publication of *The Streatham Sketchbook.*

'Painting hasn't got any easier with time and experience. I still have grave doubts about everything I do almost every day. But you often observe in the career trajectory of artists creative stagnation setting in the moment they lose the ability to be surprised and start endlessly repeating themselves. It is perhaps better to suffer self-doubt and pain than to be satiated and complacent. Long live doubt, uncertainty, pain and suffering!'

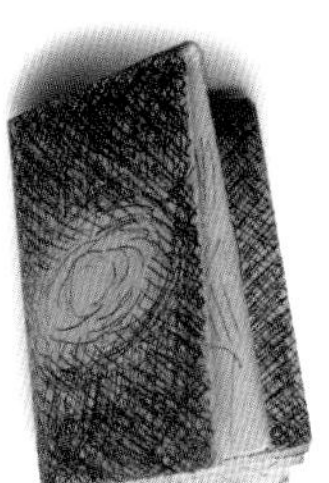

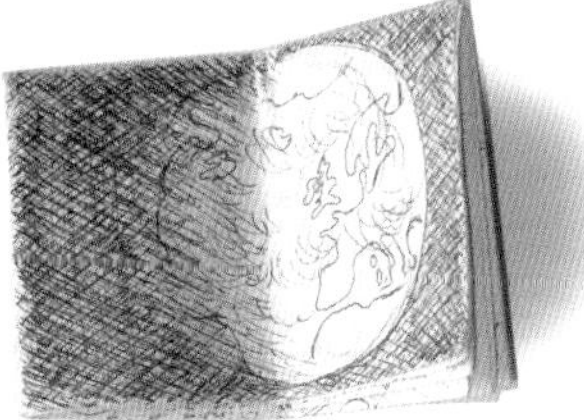

'Zoom', 2007, pen on paper, 29.7 x 21cm. One of a series of pen and ink drawings on folded paper, which unfold to tell a little anecdote. In this example, you zoom in as you unfold from the Milky Way Galaxy, the planet Earth and the British Isles, until you end up in the sitting room of Jiro's flat in Woodbourne Avenue. *Flowers Gallery.*

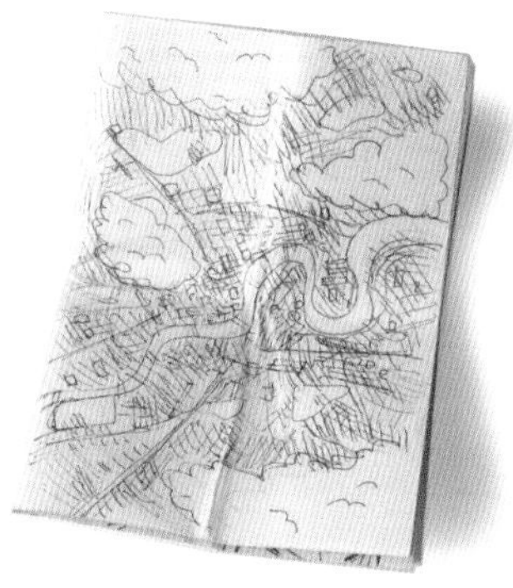

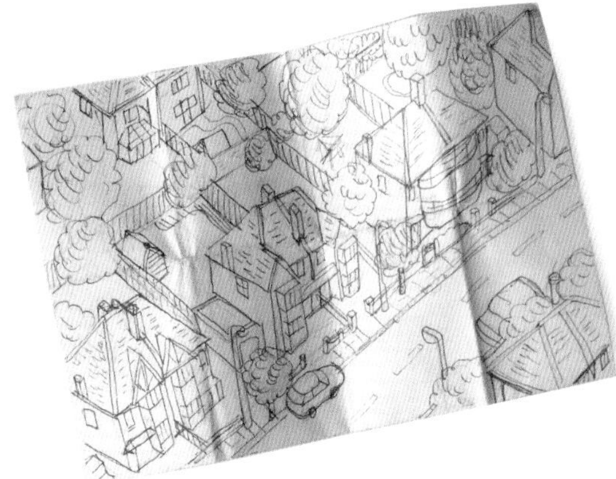

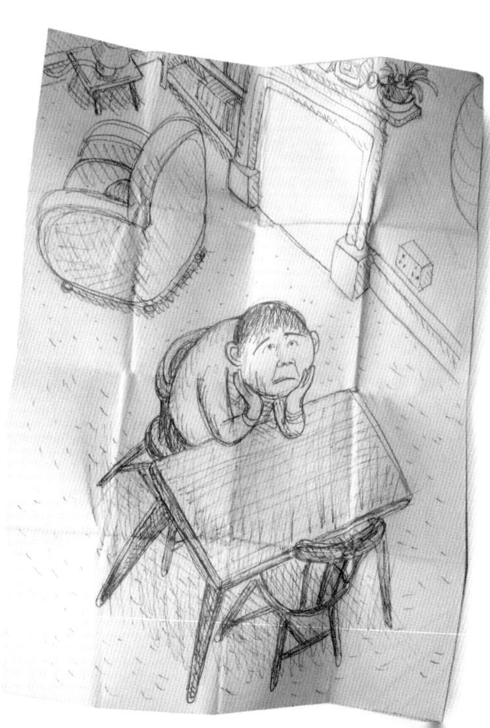

LIST OF SUBSCRIBERS

1. Anonymous
2. Matthew ASHBY
3. Philip ATTWOOD
4. Christopher BAUGH
5. Graham BAUGH
6. Ben BENNETT
7. Eva BOSCH
8. John W BROWN
9. Mark CAZALET
10. Paul CEELY
11. Chix CHANDARIA
12. Alberto CIRAVEGNA
13. Anne COUDRAIN
14. David CROOM
15. John and Valerie CUMMING
16. John DAVIDGE
17. Torla EVANS
18. Clare GALTON
19. Lesley GIBBS
20. Graham and Marion GOWER
21. The GURNEY family
22. Judy HARRIS
23. Mary Elizabeth HELLYER
24. Ed HOLLOWAY
25. Timothy HYMAN
26. Dave IVERMEE
27. Maggie JENNINGS
28. Andrew JONES
29. Michael KAUFFMANN
30. Mick KEATES
31. Veronica LAM
32. Mel LARSEN
33. Dominique LAUNAY
34. Zaun LEE
35. Vivienne LOREN
36. Peter MARSHALL
37. Susan MILES
38. Patrick and Marina MILMO
39. Juliet MOXLEY
40. John & Camilla NEWBEGIN
41. Peter NEWMARK
42. Antonio PARENTE
43. Matthew PEARCE
44. Rosey PRINCE
45. Oliver PROBYN
46. Edith RAMBURE LAMBERT
47. Cathy ROSS
48. Eva RUPPRECHT
49. Ian SESNAN
50. Jennie SMITH WILSON
51. Alan STEVENS
52. Robert SUMMER
53. Valerie TIPPETT
54. Michael & Eirlys TYNAN (TyFish Films)
55. Hazel WATSON
56. Dorene and Richard WERNER
57. Richard and Vicky WOOLLARD

ACKNOWLEDGEMENTS

Despite its light-hearted title *The Streatham Sketchbook* is a book of singular complexity which relies on the assistance of so many people that it will not be possible here to thank them all individually. Perhaps we should start with the illustrations, well over 250, many of them the excellent work of our resident photographer, Torla Evans (uncredited material throughout the book is Torla's), supplemented by other photographs – mostly through the kindness of other photographers (Peter Marshall, Roy Reed). The historical material comes mainly from London museums and collections – all of which are duly acknowledged in the captions. We should also thank Flowers Gallery for many of the images of Jiro Osuga's work.

The book oyfully relies on the expertise of local historians, in particular the Streatham Society. To John Brown, Graham Gower, Marion Gower and Judy Harris who have been so generous with their time, we owe an enormous debt. Also to the various organisations featured in the book, each for sharing their own expertise with us: Abbott and Holder (James McAusland), ASC Studios (Peter Flack and Julia Rees), Art23 (Emma Condliffe), Beep Studio (Peter Ayres and Ed Holloway), BID (Lee Alley and Louise Abbott), DOLPH (Tash Kahn), Neil French, the Friends of Streatham Common (Peter Newmark and Terka Acton), Heart Streatham (Lee Alley and Jane Wroe Wright), Timothy Hyman RA, Jaime Gili, Emelia Kenlock, Lambeth Archives (Jon Newman and Len Reilly), London Metropolitan Archives (Jeremy Smith and Elizabeth Scudder), the Museum of London (Beverley Cook and Dr Cathy Ross), the Streatham Festival (Mel Larsen), the Streatham Police Station (Alan D. Jeffrey), the Streatham Vale Artists (Eileen Oldham), Tate Gallery (Caroline Corbeau-Parsons), Richard Woollard.

We are also immensely grateful to the people who have granted permission to have their houses photographed, in particular the owners of Dixcot (the house designed by Voysey) and Sean Queenan (Leigham Court Road). And also to those shopkeepers who, in a collaborative spirit, were happy to operate around our photographer and her bulky photographic equipment, in particular Assif Siddique at the sadly missed Lahore Kebab House – collateral damage in a multi-cultural community (see pp. 174–175).

We also owe a huge debt to Flowers Gallery who represents Jiro Osuga and has been supportive of this project from the very start – Matthew Flowers and his team: the energetic Jessica Rutterford but also Astrid Helling, Juliette O'Leary, Dan Carroll, Benjamin Clarke and the gallery photographer Antonio Parente.

Those of you brave enough to purchase copies of *The Streatham Sketchbook* well ahead of publication, we salute you! A one-off subscription scheme – which is not the same as crowd funding – was not an entirely straightforward exercise but was able to create a small momentum of the utmost importance to a tiny publisher with no ready-made distribution network.

In this age of increasing copyright awareness we also approached people and institutions for permission to use and reproduce copyrighted written or visual material: to all those who said yes to material which was of vital importance to the book, we are thankful, in particular to The Duke of Bedford and the Trustees of The Bedford Estates for the map on p. 24, the Revd Mandy Hodgson for her 'artistic sermon' on p. 141, Colin Mabberley for the drawing by Grace Golden on p. 73 and John Pardoe Monnington for the painting by Winifred Knights on p. 133.

Last but not least, the authors owe an enormous debt to the publishing team – the editor Valerie Cumming, the photographer Torla Evans and the graphic designer Mick Keates. After *The Dulwich Notebook*, *The Streatham Sketchbook* brought us back together – a solid professional partnership. Stephen Conlin was also back in the fold: he drew the beautiful map at the beginning of the book; while, Jeremy Snell, the agent for our dedicated Italian printers L.E.G.O., ensured the smooth running of the final phase of production.

BIBLIOGRAPHY

http://www.ideal-homes.org.uk/ The Ideal Homes: a history of south-east London suburbs website was designed and produced by the University of Greenwich. Its content was prepared by a dedicated group of librarians, archivists and historians from the London boroughs of: Bexley, Bromley, Greenwich, Lambeth, Lewisham and Southwark with, increasingly, the input of members of the public with strong south-east London connections, from all around the world.

http://www.historyofparliamentonline.org/volume/1754-1790/member/sandys-hon-edwin-1726-97

http://www.historyofparliamentonline.org/volume/1754-1790/member/lyttelton-william-henry-1724-1808

http://www.historyofparliamentonline.org/volume/1754-1790/member/thrale-henry-1728-81

BARBER: *London A History in Maps* by Peter Barber, London Topographical Society, 2012

BLOICE: *From Silk Mill to Superstore – The Streatham Silk Mill 1820–1989* by Brian Bloice, 2002, The Streatham Society

BLOICE, GOWER & MARCHANT: *Park Hill Streatham* by Brian Bloice, Graham Gower and Daphne Marchant, 2004, The Streatham Society

BLOICE & MARCHANT: *Norwood Grove and the Rookery, Streatham Common* by Brian Bloice and Daphne Marchant, 2012, The Streatham Society

BROMHEAD: *The Heritage of St Leonard's Parish Church Streatham* by H W Bromhead and Mrs A Esdaile, 1932

BROWN: *St Leonard's Streatham* by John W Brown, 2015 – A guide to an ancient parish church that rose from the ashes after a fire in 1975, The Streatham Society

COLE: *Lived in London – Blue Plaques and the Stories Behind Them* by Emily Cole (ed.), 2009

CRESSWELL: *The Streatham Hill Theatre – the Story of a Suburban Theatre* by John Cresswell, 2000, The Streatham Society

FITZGERALD: *The Making of Modern Streatham* by Michael & Janet Fitzgerald, 2009

FRAYLING: *The Royal College of Art, One hundred & Fifty Years of Art & Design* by Christopher Frayling, 1987

GALINOU: *The Dulwich Notebook* by Mireille Galinou, 2015

GODSIFF: *Streatham Stories*, co-ordinated by Anna Godsiff, 2008 (copy at Lambeth Archives)

GOWER: *Streatham – Origins and Early History* by Graham Gower, 2008, The Streatham Society

GOWER 2008: *The High Road Streatham – An Architectural Appreciation* by Graham Gower, 2008, The Streatham Society

GOWER 2009: *Streatham Heights, Footpaths and Woods* by Graham Gower, 2009, The Streatham Society

GOWER M: *Guildersfield – The History of a Streatham Country House* by Marion Gower, 2012, The Streatham Society

HALLETT: Faces in a Library: Sir Joshua Reynolds's 'Streatham Worthies' by Mark Hallett, 2011. The content is also available online at: https://www.nationalgalleries.org/research/online-publications/sir-joshua-reynoldss-streatham-worthies

HARRIS: *A History of Lambeth's Horticultural Societies* by Judy Harris, 2003, The Streatham Society

HILL: *West Indian Migrants and the London Churches* by Clifford S Hill, 1963

HISTORIC ENGLAND: *Shopping Parades* by Kathryn A Morrison, 2016 (available online)

HYDE 1973: *The Impossible Friendship – Boswell and Mrs Thrale* by Mary Hyde, 1973

HYDE 1977: *The Thrales of Streatham Park* by Mary Hyde, 1977

INGLIS: *Played in London – Charting the Heritage of a City at Play* by Simon Inglis, 2014

LLEWELLYN: *Winifred Knights 1899–1947* by Sacha Llewellyn, Dulwich Picture Gallery, 2016

LOOBEY & BROWN: *The Twentieth Century – Streatham* by Patrick Loobey and John W Brown, 2000

MERRIMAN: *The Peopling of London* edited by Nick Merriman, Museum of London, 1993

MURDOCH: 'Talk of the Town' by Tessa Murdoch, *Country Life*, 3 November 1988 (this article is very informative about Samuel Percy's model of 'The Club' presented on p. 114)

OLD BAILEY online: *The Proceedings of the Old Bailey 1674–1913* at https://www.oldbaileyonline.org/

POINTON: *William Dyce RA 1806–64, A Critical Biography*, by Marcia Pointon, 1979

ROOTS TO RECKONING: *The photography of Armet Francis – Neil Kenlock – Charlie Phillips*. This book accompanied the eponymous exhibition held at and organised by the Museum of London, 2005

ROTHENSTEIN: *The Tate Gallery* by John Rothenstein, 1958

SEVERN: *The Halfpenny Rate: a brief history of Lambeth Libraries* by Ken Severn, 2006

THE THEATRES TRUST: http://www.theatrestrust.org.uk/

THRALE: David Thrale's useful website thrale.com for the history of the Thrale family of Streatham Park

VAN GOGH: His letters have been published in print form and online – a remarkable scholarly project carried out in collaboration with the Van Gogh Museum in Amsterdam. See http://vangoghletters.org/vg/

WARD: *No Stone Unturned – The Story of Leonora Tyson, A Streatham Suffragette* by Anne Ward, 2005

INDEX

Numbers in bold indicate a main entry.
Numbers in italics indicate a picture.

NB Entries about London (other than Streatham) have been grouped around North London, South London, East London, West London, the City; the West End (includes Westminster)

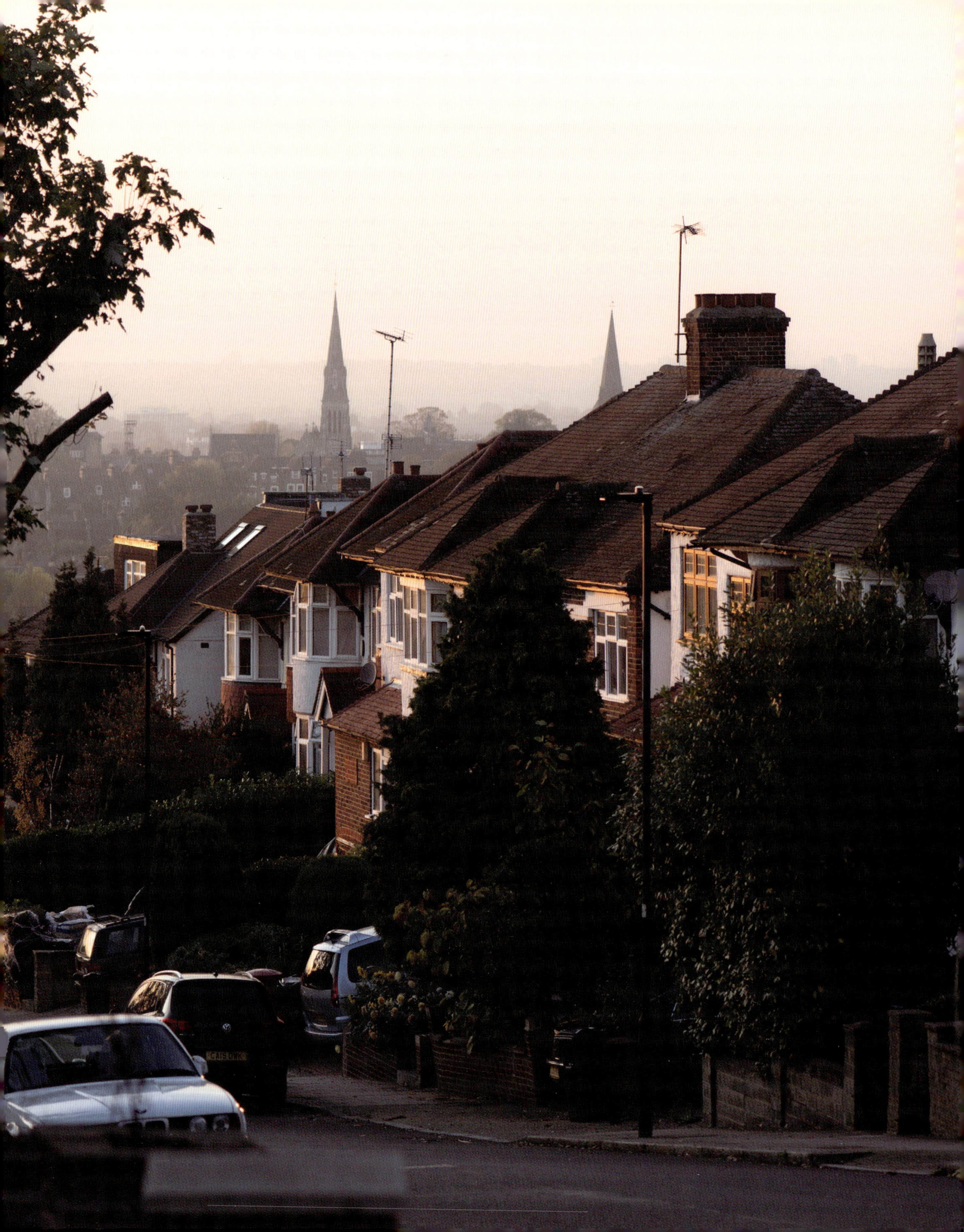